PREHISTORY AND PALEOENVIRONMENTS
IN THE CENTRAL NEGEV, ISRAEL
VOLUME I

Incorporated on May 11, 1966, the INSTITUTE FOR THE STUDY OF EARTH AND MAN is a graduate research center for the departments of Anthropology, Geological Sciences, and Statistics. The Institute was founded by William B. Heroy, its purposes being, as stated in the Bylaws, "...to encourage, foster, promote, and advance research and development and education in the field of the Anthropological and Geological Sciences and other related fields of scholarship within Southern Methodist University."

Communications should be addressed to:

The Institute for the Study of Earth and Man
111 N. L. Heroy Science Hall
Southern Methodist University
Dallas, Texas 75275

PREHISTORY AND PALEOENVIRONMENTS IN THE CENTRAL NEGEV, ISRAEL

VOLUME I

THE AVDAT/AQEV AREA, Part 1

Edited by
ANTHONY E. MARKS

Artifact Illustrations by
LUCILE ADDINGTON

INSTITUTE FOR THE STUDY OF EARTH AND MAN

Reports of Investigations: 2

SMU PRESS · DALLAS

Library of Congress Cataloging in Publication Data

Main entry under title:

Prehistory and paleoenvironments in the central Negev, Israel.

(Reports of investigations - Institute for the Study of Earth and Man; 2)

Bibliography: p.
CONTENTS: v. 1. the Avdat/Aqev area. pt. 1.
1. Man, Prehistoric—Israel—Negev—Addresses, essays, lectures.
2. Negev—Antiquities—Addresses, essays, lectures.
3. Geology—Israel—Negev—Addresses, essays, lectures.
I. Marks, Anthony E.
II. Series: ~~Dallas.~~ Southern Methodist University. Institute for the Study of Earth and Man.
Reports of investigations - Institute for the Study of Earth and Man; 2.
GN855.I75P7   933   75-40116
ISBN 0-87074-153-5 (v. 1)

CONTENTS

Dedicated to the Memory of
DR. DAVID GILEAD

ACKNOWLEDGEMENTS

The studies of the prehistory of the Central Negev, Israel, reported in this first of two volumes, began in July, 1969, and are still continuing. To date, four field seasons, totaling twelve months, have been undertaken, as well as many more months of laboratory analysis and manuscript preparation. All this work has been supported generously by a number of National Science Foundation grants (GS-2461, GS-3019, GS-28602X, and GS-28602X1) and is being funded currently by National Science Foundation grant GS-42680.

Numerous professionals and students have worked on the Central Negev Project. Although a number of project members have produced articles for this and the next volume of reports, others also have worked or are working long and hard. All deserve recognition and are listed alphabetically below:

Mr. Michael Askinazi
Ms. Anne Attebury
Ms. Adva Cohn
Mr. Arnon Cohn
Mr. Harvey Crew
Mr. Reid Ferring
Dr. Paul Goldberg
Dr. Don Henry
Dr. Aharon Horowitz
Mr. Peter Jeschofnig
Mr. Harold Juli
Mr. Paul Larson
Dr. Barbara Butler Marks
Mr. Herb Mosca
Mr. Fred Munday
Dr. James Phillips
Mr. Frank Servello
Mr. Tom Scott
Mr. Alan Simmons
Ms. Nancy Singleton
Dr. Eiton Tchernov
Mr. James Webb.

In addition, particular note should be made of Mss. Judith Pines Marks, Toni Kay Ferring, and Margot Munday, who for one or more seasons carried out the job of running the field camp and feeding large numbers of constantly hungry archaeologists.

Even with the handsome support received from the National Science Foundation, the results achieved would not have been possible without the cooperation and active help of many individuals in both America and Israel.

In Dallas much appreciation is due the Institute for the Study of Earth and Man, Southern Methodist University, which not only supplied laboratory space but also funds for this publication. Personnel of the Graphics Lab at the Institute performed the production editing and final typesetting of this volume.

Within the Department of Anthropology, Southern Methodist University, particular thanks go to Dr. Fred Wendorf, who constantly provided encouargement and incentive for this research. No amount of credit is sufficient for the outstanding artifact illustrations done by Mrs. Lucile Addington. Maps and other plans were drawn primarily by Mr. Denny Davis, but appreciation is also due Mr. Lewis Shiner and Mrs. Nancy Sciscenti, both of whom provided some illustrations.

In Israel many members of the Department of Antiquities deserve thanks, particularly Dr. A. Biran, former Director, Dr. Moshe Prausnitz, and Mr. Rudolph Cohen, who offered not only their help but also their friendship. The field work in the Central Negev would not have been successful without the cooperation and help of numerous people in the Israel Defense Forces and in the development town of Mitzpe Ramon. Of the many too numerous to list, who gave of their time, a few deserve particular notice: Mr. Zvi Hassan, former mayor of Mitzpe Ramon, Mr. Hielik Magnus, "park service" inspector for the Central Negev, and Mr. Justus Cohn and his family. These individuals gave their friendship, their knowledge of the Negev, and their help well beyond the call of duty. Three Israeli friends, Drs. Ofer Bar-Yosef, Avraham Ronen, and the late David Gilead not only acted as foils for my own and my students' ideas, but also provided me with much insight into Palestinian prehistory. In addition to the Israelis noted above, much appreciation goes to Dr. Arthur Jelinek, University of Arizona, who read this manuscript and made many useful suggestions. The weaknesses which may occur in this and the next volume, however, are solely mine and those of the other authors.

Anthony E. Marks

Institute for the Study of Earth and Man
Southern Methodist University
September 1974

PREHISTORY AND PALEOENVIRONMENTS
IN THE CENTRAL NEGEV, ISRAEL
VOLUME I

INTRODUCTION

This first of two volumes presents a major portion of the descriptive data on the prehistoric occupations and paleoenvironments of the Central Negev, Israel, gathered over numerous seasons by the Central Negev Project of Southern Methodist University. This project began in 1969 and is still continuing. Therefore, no attempt has been made in this volume either to give an overview of Central Negev prehistory or to relate any portion of it to what is known of the prehistory of adjacent regions. These formidable endeavors will come later, since current field and laboratory work is still adding markedly to the number and variety of prehistoric assemblages, to the understanding of inter- and intrasite relationships, and to the still incomplete paleoenvironmental information.

The genesis of the Central Project lies in the work of the Combined Prehistoric Expedition to Egypt and the Sudan, in which the author took part. As a result of that work (Wendorf, 1968; Wendorf and Said, 1967), questions were raised about possible cultural connections between Palestine and the Nile Valley during the Pleistocene. In fact, by 1967 it had become almost traditional to postulate prehistoric cultural connections between the Levant and North Africa. Such assumed connections had been used to explain the presence of the "Pre-Aurignacian" in both areas (McBurney, 1967), the wide distribution of the Levalloiso-Mousterian (McBurney, 1960), the appearance of Late Paleolithic blade industries in Northeast Africa, the Maghreb, and along the Nile (Huzayyin, 1941; McBurney, 1967), and the introduction of Neolithic traits into Northwest Africa (Clark, 1962; Mauny, 1967; Monod, 1963).

The evidence for these connections, however, was often no more than gross typological or technological similarities between assemblage groups and in no case was there a continuously known distribution of any industry from the Levant to North Africa. If these postulated connections were to be verified or rejected, prehistoric investigations would be necessary in the intervening areas— Northeast Egypt, the Sinai, and the Negev.

In fact, this huge area, from the northern Nile to Beer Sheva, was almost a prehistoric *terra incognita*. In northern Egypt, almost nothing was known of the pre-Neolithic periods, except for small surface collections of some Epipaleolithic materials from near Helwan, which, however, did suggest Palestinian connections (Debono, 1948). Only three poor prehistoric sites had been reported from Sinai (Anati, 1958; Malez and Crnolatac, 1966), while a very limited amount of work in the Central and Southern Negev of Israel was really only sufficient to indicate the presence of prehistoric sites. As early as 1948, Stekelis briefly reported an Epipaleolithic site in the Central Negev (Stekelis 1948). The presence of additional sites, mostly Middle Paleolithic, was noted by Anati (1963) for the Central Negev, but his findings were not published in detail. Yizraeli (1967), again, reported the presence of a few Epipaleolithic sites in the northern Central Negev, but the material was from surface stations which were only briefly visited. Thus, up to 1967 all prehistoric investigations in the Central Negev had been limited in scope and duration, mostly because of the hazardous conditions prevailing in the Negev prior to 1967.

In spite of the numerous indications of prehistoric sites, the consensus was that prehistoric occupation of the Negev had always been ephemeral, at best, since it was held that the Negev had always been desert or semidesert (Perrot, 1962; Anati, 1963). This position was no better documented than the various models postulating North African/ Levantine connections which clearly called for some periods of climatic amelioration, particularly in Sinai. In short, while some prehistoric sites were known from the Negev, they added little to the resolution of the question of North African/Levantine connections.

Of the three regions where North African/ Levantine connections might have been tested—northern Egypt, the Sinai, and the Negev south of Beer Sheva—northern Egypt and the Sinai were not available for field work, while the Negev was sufficiently open to permit such work. A brief trip was made to the Central Negev during the winter of 1968, and the presence of numerous unreported prehistoric sites was confirmed. On the basis of these finds, a project was planned which had three goals: the systematic definition of the various local prehistoric industries in the Central Negev, the mapping of their occurrences within five topographic and environmental zones, and the detailed comparison of these industries with those already defined for the Levant and North Africa.

In the summer of 1969 the first field season began. It did not take long to realize that even a carefully constructed research design can run afoul of reality. Of the five zones chosen for systematic survey, one encompassed a major mine field, another was in the middle of a tank training area, and a third was within an Air Force target range. Such activity areas were not shown on even the best of available maps. Some modification of the research design took place, resulting in the systematic survey of only two zones, both within the Central Negev highlands. While it limited the geographic scope of the project, the modification permitted the remaining areas to be more thoroughly studied; in fact, some six years later these studies are still in progress.

The initial goals of the first field season soon gave way to more complex goals, as the potential of the Central Negev for prehistoric studies was discovered. Major differences between settlement locations through time in the two survey zones focused attention on settlement patterns (Marks, 1971). In addition, because over 20% of the sites in one survey zone were *in situ*, while others only revealed deflation, the question of intrasite patterning came to the fore. Since the sites *in situ* often produced sizable faunal samples, and pollen preservation appeared to be good, it became realistic to attempt a paleoenvironmental reconstruction of the Central Negev throughout the Upper Pleistocene. All of these areas of concern were clearly interrelated and went well beyond the initial interest in typological and technological assemblage groupings. Thus, after each field season additional questions were raised, usually in excess of the answers obtained.

THE AREAS INVESTIGATED

The two areas finally chosen for investigation were both within the Central Negev, which covers an area of ca. 2,000 sq km and has elevations between 500 and 1,021 m (see Munday, this volume for a detailed description). One area was just along the border of Sinai, encompassing part of the Har Harif Plateau, due west of Mitzpe Ramon. This area is the highest in the Negev, with elevations ranging from 900 to 1,021 meters. While the Har Harif was not within any army zone, access to it was through such a zone, so work there was dependent upon the cooperation of the Israel Defense Forces. In spite of their willing cooperation, logistics were difficult and only a 15 sq km block was systematically studied. The results of that work will be presented in the next volume, although some preliminary reports are now available (Marks et al., 1972; Marks, in press).

The second area of systematic survey was ultimately a block of 55 sq km just north of the Byzantine ruins of Avdat, on the northern margin of the Central Negev. This area is typified by markedly broken topography, with elevations ranging from less than 320 to over 600 m, and includes four major perennial springs (Munday, this volume). This zone, referred to as the Avdat/Aqev area was of easy access; this fact partially accounts for the large area surveyed. In addition, the number of prehistoric sites within it was much greater than expected. In fact, the Avdat/Aqev area is as rich in prehistoric sites as any in the Levant. This first volume deals solely with the prehistoric sites in this zone, although additional sites from the Avdat/Aqev area will be reported in the next volume as well.

FIELD METHODOLOGY

In order to overcome the weaknesses of previous work, each study area was systematically surveyed so that every extant prehistoric site would be located and could be tested. Only in this manner could the full range of prehistoric occurrences be documented and the typological and technological parameters of each industry be defined. Systematic survey called for the examination, on foot, of the total surface area within each survey zone. While this was a long and arduous undertaking, it was well rewarded. A total of twenty-one prehistoric sites were located in the Har Harif and thirty-seven in the Avdat/Aqev area. These sites ranged from scattered surface concentrations of derived artifacts to huge *in situ* occurrences.

The testing of sites varied with their condition, but each site was tested so that at least a systematic collection of all artifacts within a portion of the site was obtained. Again, these systematic collections varied with site condition. Those surface concentrations which showed evidence of serious displacement were systematically collected in large, arbitrarily placed squares—usually 25 sq m units. The number of collection areas per site was deter-mined by the density of artifacts. In some cases, even after all artifacts from 100 sq m had been collected, the sample of artifacts would be too small to define the occurrence clearly. In other cases, artifact densities were extremely high, necessitating the systematic collection of only small areas of a site. In general, at each site the area of collection was limited to that necessary for typological and technological definition.

When sites indicated deflation but little lateral movement, the individual collection units were small, 1 to 4 sq m, and placed contiguously so that intrasite patterning could be studied. Again, however, the total area collected was usually held to a minimum so that additional testing by others would be possible and profitable. In a few cases, deflated sites were mapped artifact by artifact over wide areas; the most extensive mapping took place at the Upper Paleolithic site of Sde Divshon (Ferring, this volume), where 235 sq m were mapped.

When logistics, time, and artifactual density permitted, *in situ* occurrences were excavated in either one quarter sq m or one sq m units by natural layers or in 5 cm levels, with all artifacts mapped in horizontal position within each excavation level. This was possible at a number of Middle and Upper Paleolithic sites, but the incredibly high density of artifacts at Epipaleolithic sites made individual artifact mapping impossible. (At one site in the Har Harif, some one sq m, five cm levels produced artifacts at a rate of 37,000 per cubic meter). The area excavated at each site varied. At the extremely large sites with deep deposits, such as Rosh Ein Mor (Crew, this volume), as large an area was excavated as possible, given the other demands of the project. When sites were smaller an attempt was made to excavate most, if not all, of the *in situ* cultural deposits. But in only one case, site Ein Aqev, were the total cultural deposits cleared. Normally, sites were just too large. In the Avdat/ Aqev area, the two *in situ* Middle Paleolithic sites each covers well over 1,000 sq m, while one Epipaleolithic site in the Har Harif has at least 7,000 sq m of *in situ* material.

In short, the approach to data recovery was one of balancing artifact recovery and intrasite patterning data from each site against the goal of acquiring useful data from as many sites as possible. Ony in this way could a regional picture through time be developed.

LABORATORY METHODOLOGY

The development of a regional picture depended not only upon the establishment of a local chronology, but also upon the definition of synchronic patterns of typology, technology, and settlement. While it might have been most expedient merely to borrow the widely accepted and quoted industry sequence for northern Palestine and southern Lebanon, cramming each Negev assemblage into a predetermined slot, it was decided that the materials from the Central Negev would be studied independently of the established industrial sequence from the north, and only when local groups of assemblages had been fully defined would a serious attempt be made to integrate them with the traditional understanding of prehistoric development as seen in the north. The only exception to this occurred when sites obviously containing classic northern assemblages were located, such as the Natufian sites of Rosh Zin, near Avdat, (Henry, this volume), and Rosh Horesha, in the Har Harif (Marks, et. al., 1972), or the Pre-Pottery Neolithic B site of Nahal Divshon, in the Nahal Zin, (Servello, this volume). That is not to say that the total northern framework has been ignored. Levantine Mousterian is recognized as such, as is the Kebaran Complex, but assemblages are rarely dated by reference to northern sites or referred to by specific nomenclature derived from elsewhere in the Levant. Such terms as

Upper Paleolithic III or Levantine Mousterian, Phase B, have been avoided.

As the definition and comparison of industries is one goal of the project, a standardized set of descriptive definitions was adopted for basic artifact classes for the whole of the prehistoric record. These have been used consistently throughout the following reports, unless otherwise noted, and are presented in the glossary at the end of this volume.

For the typological studies, clearly no one type list was appropriate, but within each major period—Middle Paleolithic, Upper Paleolithic, and Epipaleolithic—the same criteria were utilized for every assemblage. Generally, the types recognized in these studies have been defined previously for the Levant or adjacent areas. While a complete glossary of type definitions is not practical, a discussion of some types as well as the definitions used in technological descriptions are presented in the glossary. The only exception to this is the Middle Paleolithic typology which is already extensively referenced in Crew, this volume.

Since the purpose of this volume is to present what is now known of the paleoenvironmental history of the Central Negev and the basic descriptive data of numerous prehistoric occupations, it has been organized into discrete papers, each dealing with a fragment of the total picture. Therefore, some apparent differences are to be found in interpretation, particularly in the sections dealing with paleoenvironmental reconstruction. It must be borne in mind, however, that these interpretations derive from different and fragmentary data bases and differing perspectives on the part of the various specialists. In every case, additional data have been collected during the 1974 field season and more are expected to be recovered during the next few years of field work. While it never may be possible to elucidate fully the whole paleoenvironmental sequence of the Upper Pleistocene for the Central Negev, the present papers provide much new and significant information and the forthcoming data will, it is to be hoped, clarify much of what now is still obscure.

Anthony E. Marks

Institute for the Study of Earth and Man
Southern Methodist University
September, 1974

BIBLIOGRAPHY

ANATI, E., 1958. "Recherches préhistoriques au Sinai." *Bulletin de la Société Préhistorique Française* 55(3-4):209-11.

————, 1963. *Palestine before the Hebrews*. New York: A. Knopf.

CLARK, J. D., 1962. "Africa South of the Sahara." In *Courses toward Urban Life*, edited by R. Braidwood and G. Willey, pp. 1-32. Viking Fund Publications in Anthropology 32. Chicago: Aldine.

DEBONO, F., 1948. "Le paléolithique final et le mésolithique à Hélouan." *Annales du Service des Antiquités de l'Egypte* 48:629-37.

HUZAYYIN, S. A., 1941. *The Place of Egypt in Prehistory*. Mémoires de l'Institut d'Egypte 49.

McBURNEY, C. B. M., 1960. *The Stone Age of Northern Africa*. Harmondsworth: Penguin Books.

————, 1967. *The Haua Fteah (Cyrenaica) and the Stone Age of the Southeast Mediterranean*. Cambridge: At the University Press.

MALEZ, M., and CRNOLATAC, I., 1966. "Two New Paleolithic Sites in Sinai." *Bulletin Science Conseil Académie RSF Yougoslavie, Section A–Zagreb* 11(4-6):102-5.

MARKS, A. E., 1971. "Settlement Patterns and Intrasite Variability in the Central Negev, Israel." *American Anthropologist* 73(5):1237-44.

————; CREW, H.; FERRING, R.; and PHILLIPS, J., 1972. "Prehistoric Sites near Har Harif." *Israel Exploration Journal* 22(2-3):73-85.

————, in press. "The Epipaleolithic of the Central Negev: Current Status." *Eretz Israel* 13.

MAUNY, R., 1967. "L'Afrique et les origines de la domestication." In *Background to Evolution in Africa*, edited by W. W. Bishop and J. D. Clark, pp. 583-99. Chicago: University of Chicago Press.

MONOD, T., 1963. "The Late Tertiary and Pleistocene in the Sahara and Adjacent Southerly Regions." In *African Ecology and Human Evolution*, edited by F. C. Howell and F. Boulière, pp. 117-229. Viking Fund Publications in Anthropology 36. Chicago: Aldine.

PERROT, J., 1962. "Palestine-Syria-Cilicia." In *Courses toward Urban Life*, edited by R. Braidwood and G. Willey, pp. 147-64. Viking Fund Publications in Anthropology 32. Chicago: Aldine.

STEKELIS, M., 1948. "The Prehistoric Collection of Yzkhak Halevi." *Yedioth Hahevra Lahaqirath Eretz-Israel Weathigoteh* 14:1-7. (In Hebrew).

WENDORF, F. (ed.), 1968. *The Prehistory of Nubia*, 2 vols. and atlas. Dallas: Fort Burgwin Research Center and Southern Methodist University Press.

————, and SAID, R., 1967. "Paleolithic Remains in Upper Egypt." *Nature* 215:244-47.

YIZRAELI, T., 1967. "Mesolithic Hunters' Industries at Ramat Matred (The Wilderness of Zin), First Report." *Palestine Exploration Quarterly* 99:78-85.

THE AVDAT/AQEV AREA: ITS HABITAT AND GEOGRAPHIC SETTING

Frederick C. Munday

Southern Methodist University

INTRODUCTION

An understanding of prehistoric sites requires a knowledge of their environmental settings. Before prehistoric environments can be reconstructed, however, it is necessary to undertake an analysis of the present topographic, climatic, and biotic conditions in the site area. This analysis, together with geological, palynological, and paleontological data must be used in any attempt at environmental reconstruction. Only then can sites be placed within their contemporary environmental setting which may allow inferences to be drawn about the reasons for their particular location.

This paper, therefore, will attempt to outline the more important environmental features of the Avdat/Aqev area of the Central Negev as a base from which paleoenvironmental reconstructions may be attempted after all palynological, paleontological, and geological data have been collected. First it is necessary to present a general view of the Negev and particularly of the Negev highlands.

As a general geographic feature, the Negev covers an area of ca. 12,000 sq km and provides a bridge between Sinai to the west and the more expansive Arabian Desert to the east. Shaped like an inverted triangle, the Negev is approximately contained by lines drawn between Khan Yunis, the southern Dead Sea, and Eilat, with the latter station at the apex (fig. 1-1).

THE CENTRAL NEGEV HIGHLANDS

Within the Negev, the Central highlands cover about 2,000 sq km with elevations ranging between 450 and 1,000 m, with the highest point at Har Ramon (1,035 m) on the Negev/Sinai border. These hills experience a continental and desertic climate and have a floral community that is transitional between steppe and desert varieties, consisting mainly of dwarf shrub associations (Hillel and Tadmor, 1962, p. 34). Major nahals (wadis) drain the area toward the Mediterranean via the Nahals Nizzana and Besor, or toward the Dead Sea via the Nahals Zin and Neqarot (fig. 1-1).

In the northwest the highlands slope gently to the Mediterranean, increasing in gradient toward Sinai. On the eastern side of the highlands the region has been dissected deeply by active nahals, including the Nahals Zin and Neqarot, which drain into the Wadi Arava, as well as being sharply demarcated by three erosional depressions, the Makteshes Ramon, Hagodol, and Haqutan. The Nahal Zin is flanked by a steep-sided canyon at its head, expanding into a larger plain as the Arava is approached. The Neqarot drains the flatter, lower southeastern area, beginning near the Maktesh Ramon.

SOILS

Generally, soils fall into three groups (Evenari et al., 1971, p. 51): (1) Gray, loessial soils and brown rocky soils which lie to the south and southwest of Avdat and are thought to have been blown in from Sinai (Evenari et al., 1971, p. 44). They have now accumulated in the nahal beds and depressions, leaving the hillsides somewhat bare; (2) Rock outcrops, hammadas, and shallow desert soils; (3) Reg soils, gravelly slopes, and

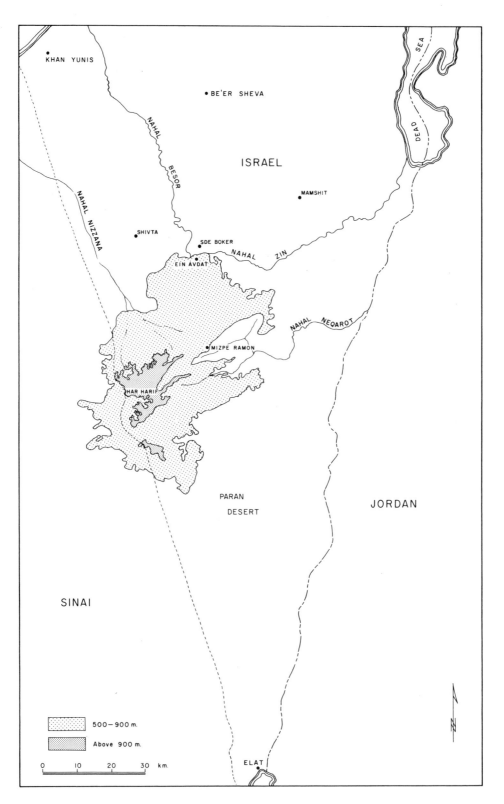

FIG. 1-1—Map of southern Israel, showing Central Negev highlands, major towns, and main drainages.

coarse desert alluvium. These latter two groups lie in the heavily eroded area to the east of Avdat.

CLIMATE

The highlands experience a temperate desert climate (Evenari et al., 1971, p. 34), with warm dry summers and cool moist winters. In general, it can be characterized as one of low, unpredictable rainfall, low humidity, and high evaporation potential (Evenari et al., 1971, p. 33). Table 1-1 illustrates temperature data from three stations, Avdat and Mitzpe Ramon in the central and southern highlands, respectively, and Shivta, which lies to the northwest, just outside of the highlands. The general impression is one of moderate temperature extremes, with ranges of about 40°C. Diurnal changes may be quite extreme, as Marx (1967, p. 17) even reports days on which a low of −5°C (23°F) has risen to 30°C (85°F). July and August are the hottest months and December through March the coolest months, when the mean drops below 15°C. Under conditions of the "khamsin," a dry desert wind blowing in from the east, temperatures may reach 45°C. Occurring in either September to October or May to mid-June, these winds are associated with cyclonic circulation over Libya or Egypt which attracts winds from the east.

Precipitation is variable both in amount and in seasonal distribution. Generally occurring between November and May, it is associated with storm fronts from the eastern Mediterranean, moving to the south and southeast. Increased distance from the Mediterranean results in decreased precipitation. Thus, despite elevational increases, the Central highlands remain relatively dry. Table 1-2 illustrates annual rainfall patterns for several Negev stations.

Total annual rainfall, however, is quite misleading, for its seasonal distribution allows only part of an already meager supply to be

useful. As summarized by Evenari et al. (1971, p. 33), rainfall over 1.0 mm/day falls on only 12 days/year and rainfall over 10 mm/day on only 3 days/year in the Negev highlands (table 1-3).

TABLE 1-1
Elevation and Temperatures
for Selected Stations
in the Central Negev
(Modified from Evenari et al., 1971, p. 34)

	Shivta	Avdat	Mitzpe Ramon
Elevation (m)	350	610	890
Mean annual temp. (°C)	19.5	18.7	17.8
Maximum temperature (°C)	39.8	46.4	38.5
Minimum temperature (°C)	2.2	0.2	0.5
Mean of hottest month (°C)	26.9	25.7	24.7
Mean of coolest month (°C)	11.9	10.8	9.3

The consequences of this particular rainfall regime are realized only when viewed in relation to the moisture requirements of plants. Plant growth is stimulated only by "effective rainfall"; that is, rainfall "that adds moisture to the root zone of plants" (Hillel and Tadmor, 1962, p. 36). With this criterion, effective rainfall occurs no more than three to four times per year in the Negev highlands (fig. 1-2). Its occurrence is important because its onset essentially determines the commencement, quality, and termination of the growing season, although other factors, such as substrate composition, slope intensity and length, and density and roughness of surface cover all affect the availability of moisture to plant life.

A further moisture source in the highlands is dew. For the years 1963-66 surface dewfall at Avdat measured 32 mm, 37 mm, 35 mm, and 26 mm ($\bar{x}$, 33 mm). In fact, during the year 1962-63, the total dewfall of 28.4 mm exceeded rainfall of 25.6 mm (Evenari et al., 1971, p. 37). The effectiveness of such moisture for plant life, however, is negligible (Eve-

TABLE 1-2
Elevation and Rainfall Patterns for Selected Negev Stations
(Modified after Shanan et al., 1967, p. 165 and Evenari et al., 1971, p. 34)

Locations	Distance to Mediterranean (km)	Elevation (m)	Recording Period	Mean Annual (mm)	Maximum Annual (mm)	Minimum Annual (mm)
Mamshit	80	450	1942-63	135	191	58
Shivta	65	350	1960-61	89	n. d.	n. d.
Sde Boker	75	470	1951-63	76	137	23
Avdat	80	610	1960-65	95	159	25
Mitzpe Ramon	100	890	1960-61	65	n. d.	n. d.

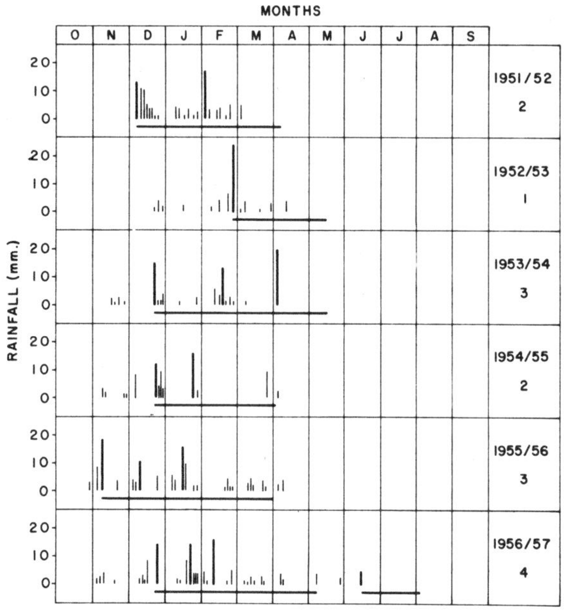

FIG. 1-2—Effective rainfall at Sde Boker, near Avdat (modified after Hillel and Tadmor, 1962). *Heavy to vertical lines*—effective rainfalls; *light line*—ineffective rainfalls; *heavy horizontal line*—observed growing seasons. Large numbers at right signify year and number of effective rainfalls.

TABLE 1-3
Average Number of Days/Year with Rainfall Exceeding Specific Amounts in the Negev Highlands
(Modified after Evenari et al., 1971, p. 33)

Rainfall (mm/day)	Days/Year
0.1	15.8
1.0	12.1
10.0	2.7
25.0	0.5
50.0	0.0

VEGETATION

The Central Negev highlands fall into that area where the Saharo-Sindian region borders on the Irano-Turanian territory (fig. 1-3) (Zohary, 1962). This desert vegetation consists of a large number of plants adaptive to numerous desert microenvironments. (For a more detailed description of desert vegetation adaptation, see Zohary, 1962, and Evenari et al., 1971).

Broadly speaking, the Irano-Turanian territory consists of non-saline gray calcareous soils, loess soil, and rocky hills which receive an annual rainfall between 150 and 320 mm (Zohary, 1952, p. 211). It is generally confined to the higher parts of the highlands and consists of steppe forest, thorny and broom-like brushwoods, and dwarf shrub communities included in the single class *Artemesia*

nari et al., 1971, p. 269). It may, however, be an effective water source for animals who could exploit it during the early hours of the morning.

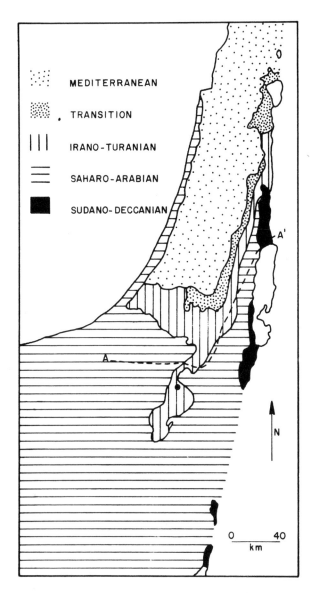

FIG. 1-3—Major vegetal zones of Israel. *A-A'* indicates the "Ramon Line."

the Avdat area only 1-5 trees/sq km are found. Zohary (1962, p. 132) considers these to be but remnant stands of a different plant association.

The Saharo-Sindian territory, surrounding the Irano-Turanian zone on three sides, consists mainly of hammada expanses, slopes with shallow soils, and erosive wadi systems in which the *Zygophyllum dumosum* alliance is dominant. This alliance occupies hammada terrain below 600 m, where rainfall is limited to ca. 75-100 mm per year. Wadi systems are usually occupied by variants of the *Retama raetam—Thymelaea hirsuta* shrub association. These generally contain some Mediterranean floral elements which take advantage of additional moisture present in special soil conditions and runoff patterns (Tadmor and Hillel, 1957, pp. 3-7).

THE AVDAT/AQEV REGION

This section focuses on present environmental conditions specific to the Avdat/Aqev area, within the broader environmental framework of the Negev highlands and their potential in paleoenvironmental reconstruction. Therefore, only that description of the geomorphology necessary to define the various micro-habitats will be presented. Emphasis is placed on moisture availability, soils, flora, fauna, and presently available flint resources. (For a detailed description of the Pleistocene geomorphology of the Avdat/Aqev area, see Goldberg, this volume.)

Within the region of the Central Negev highlands, the Avdat/Aqev area is confined to about 50 sq km located between the Byzantine city of Avdat and the northern edge of the Nahal Zin (fig. 1-4). This area consists of a relatively flat central loessial plain, the Divshon Plain, which has been partially dissected in the west, center, and east by the North/South Nahal Zin and the Nahals Divshon and Aqev, respectively. In addition to the major dissection mentioned above, minor steep-

herba-alba (Zohary, 1962, p. 131). At present, the steppe forest consists of remnant stands of *Pistacia atlantica*, *Rhamnus disperma*, *Rhus tripartita*, and *Amydalus korschinskii* (Danin and Orshan, 1970, pp. 92, 97). Danin reports *Pistacia atlantica* in densities up to 21-30 trees/sq km in parts of the Nahal Loz and on the eastern flanks of Rosh Horesha in the highest parts of the highlands. Density decreases with altitude loss, until in

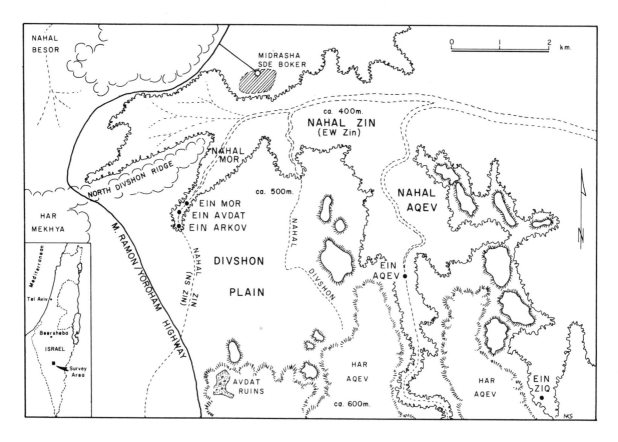

FIG. 1-4—Map of Avdat/Aqev area, showing major features and place names.

sided drainages occur, particularly near the surrounding hillslopes to the south and west. A single depression in the center of the plain heads northward, paralleling the Nahal Divshon. This depression has been used in the past for agricultural purposes, as seen by extant terracing in good condition.

The Divshon Plain is surrounded on the west, south, and east by flat- or round-topped hills (fig. 1-5) rising to ca. 600 m (highest point, 628 m). The flat-topped hills usually have a hammada surface where wind action has removed the lighter material, leaving a pavement of flint, limestone, or other rock, with little soil cover. The slopes falling away from these flat surfaces are normally strewn with stone scree. Often, steep or sheer cliffs drop away from the hilltops, resulting in an inselberg effect. Soil cover on the lower slopes is usually shallow, but where a chalk substratum exists, it tends to be deeper, consisting of well-leached loess containing gravel layers. Hillslopes such as these cover most of the research area.

Another habitat[1] is that of the nahal (wadi) systems. Along most of their length the nahals contain gravel and very little soil. Winding in narrow bands through the hillslopes, they are seasonally filled with floodwater that exerts considerable erosive force. Thus, the dry, summer gravel beds become wider winter torrents that often cover extensive areas within the nahals. This is particularly so in the East/West Zin, where the lower adjacent hillslopes permit a wider spread of water. The wadis themselves may be divided into a number of micro-habitats.

The Nahals Mor and Aqev contain permanent springs: Ein Arkov, Ein Avdat, and Ein Mor in the former and Ein Aqev in the latter.

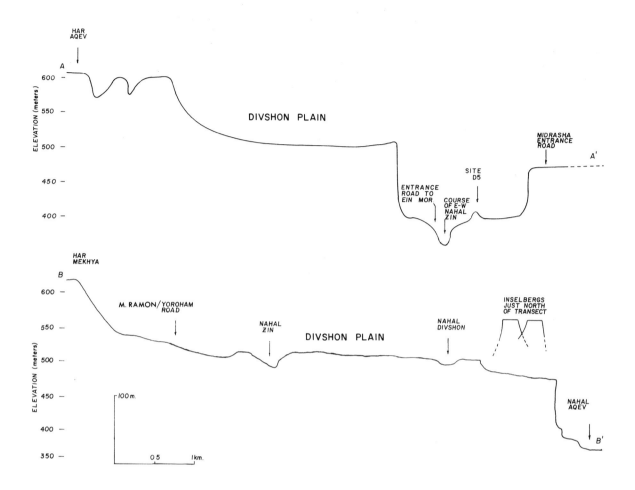

FIG. 1-5—Topographic cross sections through the Avdat/Aqev area. See Fig. 6 for position of transects.

Their water, originating in the upland catchment area, seeps down to an impervious limestone layer and drains, later to emerge at several knickpoints as the springs (see Goldberg, this volume). The spring of Ein Aqev measures approximately 80-90 sq m in area and is about 7 m deep. This spring is contained at the head of a small box canyon, with walls measuring some 10 m in height. The springs at Avdat are located along a long, deep box canyon (Nahal Mor), with sheer walls some 70-80 m in height. Both spring areas contain relatively lush vegetation, in contrast to the somewhat bare hillslopes.

The upper reaches of the Nahals Zin (North/South Zin) and Divshon contain large amounts of soil and more densely packed

vegetation, due mainly to runoff from the gentle slopes bordering the drainage area. The lower reaches of these two drainages, plus the whole length of the Nahal Aqev (with the exception of the spring area) are the more usual gravel-bottomed nahals containing relatively sparse vegetation. The East/West Zin, into which flow all three of the aforementioned, is a major gravel wadi, lined by low loessial hillslopes and alluvial terraces.

In summary, the Avdat/Aqev area consists of the following habitats: (1) the Divshon Plain, a loessial plain; (2) a loessial depression on the Divshon Plain; (3) flat, hammada hilltops; (4) hillslopes; (5) nahals, which may be divided into (a) the upland sections of the Nahals Zin (North/South Zin) and Divshon, and (b) gravel nahals, most of the North/ South Nahal Zin, and the Nahals Divshon and Aqev; (6) permanent springs of Ein Arkov, Ein Avdat, Ein Mor, and Ein Aqev; and (7) steep cliff faces in the Nahals Mor, Divshon, and Aqev, as well as along the East/West Nahal Zin (fig. 1-6).

MICRO-HABITATS

Any description of the present vegetational patterns of the micro-habitats in the research area must consider the effects of overgrazing, of casual cultivation by modern Bedouin, and of agricultural practices of the Nabateans and Byzantines during earlier historic periods. Some hints, however, of the original climax vegetation are indicated where possible.

Hilltops

Shallow soil depth with a high stone content has resulted in low moisture retention. Shanan et al. (1967, p. 169) estimate that the amount of water actually available to plants is equivalent to about 20-30 mm rainfall per year, resulting in very sparse vegetation cover dominated by the dwarf shrub *Zygophyllum dumosum* (bean caper). Surface water is not available except after heavy winter rainfall, when it is usually found in small, shallow depressions. Fauna is generally rare; however, some hares and carnivores have been seen during the summer. Because of the deflation mentioned earlier, it is doubtful that sufficient surface soil would have been present even under climax conditions to maintain a richer vegetation regime than that presently found.

Hillslopes

Two general vegetation associations are found on the hillslopes. On the higher, slightly moister slopes to the south and west of Avdat, the *Artemesia herba-alba* alliance is usually found. On the lower, hotter, and drier foothills to the east and north of Avdat the vegetation is dominated by the *Zygophyllum dumosum* alliance. However, because the research area is located near the Irano-Turanian/Saharo-Sindian boundary, such discrete distributions become somewhat blurred. Thus, it is not unusual to find the two alliances co-existing, with the *Zygophyllum dumosum* occupying the drier lower hillslopes and the *Artemesia herba-alba* the moister depressions between slopes where runoff occurs.

The alliance on the higher, moister slopes, in addition to *Artemesia herba-alba*, consists of other low shrubs, perennial pasture plants, and sedges. The *Zygophyllum dumosum* on the lower, drier hillslopes is accompanied by other perennial browse shrubs and annual pasture plants.

It has to be borne in mind that the vegetation of this habitat is largely the result of extensive grazing of Bedouin herds; thus, many of the original pasture plants have been destroyed. Tadmor and Hillel (1957, p. 3) consider the original climax vegetation to have been a mixture of shrub-grass steppe.

Modern fauna seen in association with this habitat includes rodents, reptiles, gazelle, carnivores, wild goat (particularly when the slopes are at the base of cliffs), and the desert partridge (chukha). This floral/faunal association seems particularly strong when the slopes are close to a nahal.

Loessial Plain (Divshon Plain)

The paucity of runoff drainage patterns and the fine, almost impermeable soil make this a particularly dry habitat. The low gravel content of the soil impedes percolation so that much precipitation is lost to evaporation. Soils dry out soon after the rainy season is over and permanent dryness occurs below 30-50 cm (Evenari et al., 1971, p. 232), resulting in a profusion of annuals which take

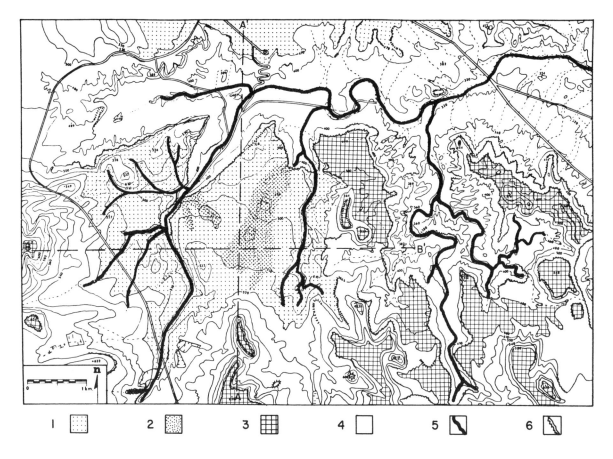

FIG. 1-6—Habitat distributions in the Avdat/Aqev Area. Key: *1*—loessial plain; *2*—loessial depression; *3*—flat hammada hilltops; *4*—hillslopes; *5*—major drainages; *6*—cliffs. *A-A'* and *B-B'* are positions of transects shown in Fig. 5. Springs are not shown on map.

advantage of moisture available only during the wet season.

The major vegetation alliance is dominated by the low shrub *Haloxylon articulatum*. Annual pasture plants, legumes, and sedges are also present. Plant cover, however, is very low, and is mostly consumed early in the year by grazing animals, both wild and domestic. In fact, the modern grazing value of the plain is lower than that of the sparsely covered hillslopes (Tadmor and Hillel, 1957, p. 4). The impermeability of the soil in this habitat would also have controlled the climax vegetation. Therefore, it is expected that vegetation has changed little in recent times.

Loessial Depression

This is a wide, shallow bed occurring where runoff is available from the surrounding loessial plain. The major contrast with the loessial plain is that runoff has increased water availability (equivalent to 30-500 mm of rainfall annually, depending on location). This in turn is reflected in increased plant cover. Two vegetational associations are present. In the shallower, drier, upper reaches *Artemesia herba-alba* predominates, accompanied by pasturage, forbs, and legumes. The deeper, moister, lower parts of the depression are somewhat richer. The perennial shrubs *Thymelaea hir-*

suta, *Retama raetam* (white broom), *Haloxylon articulatum*, *Atriplex leucoclada* and *A. halimus* are joined by legumes and annual and perennial pasture plants.

Whether these associations are representative of the original climax vegetation is unknown; almost assuredly, the proliferation of annual grasses has been influenced by past agricultural practices. Tadmor and Hillel (1957, p. 6) consider that the original climax vegetation "may have been a savanna-type park with trees and an herbaceous ground-cover."

Gravel Nahals

Most vegetation cover in the gravel nahals is confined to their edges, the erosive force of seasonal floods removing soil and plants from the center of the channels. Where silt has been allowed to accumulate, vegetation is similar to the deepest parts of the loessial depression. A second vegetation complex is associated with water found at deeper levels, generally around 3-5 meters. This comprises most elements found in the *Thymelaea hirsuta–Retama raetam* shrub association of the loessial depression. Some *Tamarix* may also occur. This sparse vegetation is largely the result of wood-cutting, overgrazing, and erosion. At one time, this habitat probably enjoyed soil conditions similar to those of the loessial depressions (Tadmor and Hillel, 1957, p. 5). Given possible silt accumulations prior to modern degradation, more extensive pasturage, forbs, legumes, and trees might have been present under climax conditions, making this a relatively rich procurement habitat. Faunal associations include numerous birds and reptiles, carnivores, gazelle, wild goat (particularly when in proximity to cliffs), and desert partridge.

Upland Nahals

These sections of the nahals in the research region contain shallow soils, mixed with gravel that may reach 2 m in depth. Water availability is high due to soil permeability and runoff, resulting in a vegetal association intermediate between the gravel nahals and the loessial depression. This habitat is used extensively for grazing Bedouin herds, resulting in a vegetation association that is a poor reflection of the original climax. Less erosion would probably have resulted in more extensive annual pasturage and legumes, similar to the vegetation now present on the loessial depression.

Springs

The springs are unstudied from a botanical point of view. However, the present vegetation, much overgrazed, probably falls into that category described by Zohary (1962, pp. 146-52) as a northern outpost of the African tropical vegetation, the Sudanian.

Large areas of limestone bedrock have been exposed due to the scouring action of floodwater immediately below the knickpoints. Vegetation coverage varies periodically due to water erosion as well as to burning by Bedouin to encourage new plant growth.

Cliffs

The prime reason for delineating the cliffs as a separate habitat is due to their extensive occupation by the wild goat *Capra ibex nubiana*. Little soil or vegetation is present.

SUMMARY OF HABITATS

It is clear that vegetation type and coverage are greatly dependent on soil composition, which aids or impedes percolation, and slope, where runoff patterns redistribute precipitation. The type of surface cover has also been shown to affect runoff patterns (Evenari et al., 1971, pp. 127-47). Thus, on gentle slopes there is considerable runoff due to the pres-

TABLE 1-4
Summary of Habitat Characteristics of the Avdat/Aqev Region

	Soil Depth (mm)	% Stone Content	% Salinity	Available H_2O (mm)	% Plant Coverage	Plant Association	% of Research Area
Hilltops	20–30	60–90	1–2	10–20	5–20	*Zygophyllum dumosum*	2–6
Hillslopes	30–70	60–90	1–2	20–50	5–20	*Artemesia-herba alba* (higher hills) *Zygophyllum dumosum* (lower hills)	70–80
Loessial Plain	<200		0.5–2.0	30–50	2–15	*Haloxylon articulatum*	10–15
Loessial Depression	<200	–	0.5–2.0	30–500	up to 100	*Artemesia herba-alba* plus annuals, forbs, and legumes or *Thymelaea-hirsuta* association	2–3
Gravel Nahals	Little and isolated	70–100	0–1	15–20 near surface 70–100 at depth	3–40[1]	*Thymelaea hirsuta-Retama raetam* association plus some annuals	3–5
Upland Nahals	<200	30–70	0–1	100–400[2]	30–80[2]	*Retama raetam* plus some annuals	1
Cliffs[1]	–	100	?	–	–	–	1–3
Springs	<100	?	?	High	ca. 35–80	–	<1

[1] Estimate from personal observation.
[2] Estimated from Tadmor and Hillel, 1957, p. 7.

ence of soil cover, which effects a smoother passage to the depression bottom. Steep slopes contain little soil (due to erosion) and the rocky surface impedes runoff, allowing percolation to take place partially on the slopes. Therefore, the nature of slopes adjacent to depressions greatly influences moisture availability in the depression bottom.

In conclusion, it can be said that surface type and slope intensity initially influence runoff patterns. When water reaches the slope bottom, soil composition influences percolation and retention. This in turn determines to a great extent the type of vegetation and even its seasonal distribution (as was noted for the Divshon Plain).

It must be reiterated, however, that none of the present vegetational constituents of the habitats, save perhaps for the hilltops, can be said to represent original climax associations (table 1-4). This is due to past and present grazing and cultivation practices.

FAUNA

While it is possible to define general faunal associations for the Negev highlands, locating most animals within the various habitats of the research area is very difficult.

The fauna of the Negev highlands falls into two groups. One, essentially Mediterranean in character, is located to the northeast of the "Ramon" line (fig. 1-3), while the other, more desertic in character, is found to the southeast of this demarcation (Shkolnik, 1971, pp. 301-3). The fauna of the Avdat/Aqev area falls into the latter category, although the zoogeographic boundary is so close to the research area that *strict* delineation of faunal associations is probably unrealistic. A general, although incomplete, faunal list for the desertic region of the Negev highlands is shown in Table 1-5. The distribution and habits of several species within the research area are of particular interest, as their remains have been found in archaeological context.

Gazelle were generally encountered in the nahal systems and on the low hillslopes adjacent to these drainages. Small groups of less than ten were seen along parts of both the East/West and North/South Zin. Outside of the research area they were noted in upland nahals near Mitzpe Ramon. They were rarely encountered on the Divshon Plain, the higher hillslopes, or hammada hilltops. However, because research was carried on after the end of the growing season, it is possible that gazelle also occupy these habitats during and immediately after the moist season, when mixed shrubs and annual herbage are available. Gazelle have been reported to exist without free water (Cloudesly-Thompson and Ghorbial, 1965; Ghorbial and Cloudesly-Thompson, 1966; Carlisle and Ghorbial, 1968), deriving their moisture from shrubs,

particularly *Acacia tortilis*. Dekeyser (1955, p. 390) has also noted that they split up seasonally into female/young and male groups.

Wild goat, *Capra ibex nubiana*, is found predominantly on steep hillsides and cliff faces. Its eclectic diet is based mainly on grass and shrub consumption. Free water is a daily necessity. They have been seen in herds numbering up to forty in the Avdat/Aqev area. Often it was possible to approach within several meters of an animal on a cliff face before flight ensued, although this may be because hunting has been forbidden for many years. Like gazelle, *C. ibex nubiana* are known to separate seasonally, males occupying higher ground, females and young staying on the lower ridges.

Carnivores were noted on both hammada hilltops and in the nahal systems, although no specific identifications were made, except for a single sighting of a hyena. The large vulture *Aegyptius tracheloitus* was encountered nesting both in the square box canyon to the west of Ein Aqev and on the cliffs of the Nahal Mor. Rodent and reptile distributions are very general, being found in all habitats. They are, however, somewhat limited in distribution on the hammada-covered hilltops because of the lack of soil cover for burrowing. The desert partridge was seen in groups numbering up to two score in the shrub vegetation of the nahals and adjacent hillslopes. In seasons following wet winters, group size and numbers of these birds increased considerably.

RAW MATERIAL (FLINT RESOURCES)

Raw material is common in the research area, and few sites are more than 1-2 km from a source. Flint generally occurs as small nodules, thin, slab-like bands, or as very large cobbles. These can be found either on flat surfaces which have been exposed due to erosion, or bedded in cliffs, hillslopes, and, in the case of the small nodules, in conglomerates (fig. 1-7).

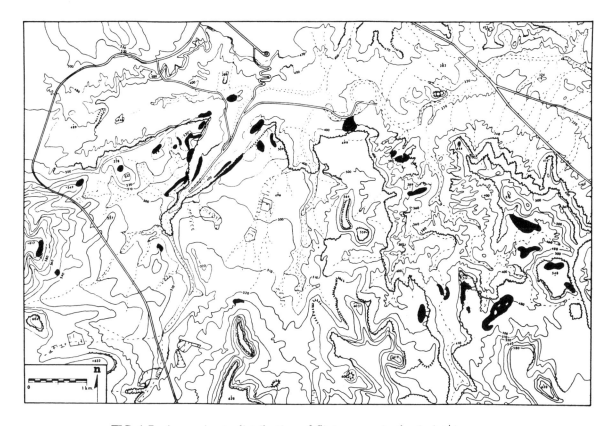

FIG. 1-7—Approximate distribution of flint sources in the Avdat/Aqev area.

In the area near Ein Aqev, raw material is relatively abundant on the cliff tops adjacent to the spring. Extensive surface sources are also present away from the cliff edge, again, where nodular flint is most prevalent. In the Nahal Aqev and adjacent drainages large areas of poor quality, derived flint can be found. In the lower reaches of the drainage isolated sources appear as small nodules in exposed conglomerates, as well as surface occurrences of flint derived from higher elevations.

The area near the Nahal Mor is a source of abundant supplies of excellent flint. Large sources are found in extensive bands of large nodules at the top of the cliffs overlooking the nahal. At the base of these cliffs, on a series of terrace remnants, further supplies of high quality flint are also available, derived from the primary sources above. Several sources are also present on the western edge of the research area, outcropping in narrow bands.

In addition to these major supplies, it should be pointed out that surface occurrences of poor quality flint are available in numerous localities, generally in the form of small, weathered, and broken material. Most of these sources, however, appear to have remained unutilized.

SUMMARY AND CONCLUSIONS

The Avdat/Aqev area has a highly varied topography. This in turn has influenced micro-climatic conditions, particularly moisture availability, resulting in a number of micro-habitats. Vegetation patterns are the result of specific interaction between topographic, soil, climatic, and human factors. These in turn seem to have influenced the dis-

TABLE 1-5
Restricted Faunal List for
the Avdat/Aqev Region
(Modified after Evenari, 1971; Shkolnik, 1971)

MAMMALIA

ARTIODACTYLA
Capra ibex nubiana	Nubian ibex
Gazella dorcus	Dorcus gazelle
Gazella gazella	Gazelle

CARNIVORA
Hyena striata	Hyena
Vulpes rupeli	Desert fox
Felis ocerata	Wild cat
Felis caracal	Caracal lynx

LAGOMORPHA
Lepus capensis	Hare
Lepus arabicus	Arabian hare

HYRACOIDEA
Procavia capensis	Rock hyrax

RODENTIA
Sekeetamys	Bushy tailed jird
Hystrix indica	Porcupine
Acomys russatus	Golden spiney mouse
A. cahirinus	Cairo spiney mouse
Gerbillus dasyurus	Rough tailed gerbil
Meriones crassus	Fat jird
Psammomys obesus	Fat sand rat

INSECTIVORA
Paraechinus aethiopicus	Ethiopian hedgehog

AVES
Pterocles alchata	Sand grouse
Erythrina sinaica	Sinai rose finch
Erythrospize githaginea	Trumpeter bullfinch
Turoides squamiceps	Palestine bubbler
Oenanthe leucopyga	White rumped wheatear
Aegyptius tracheloitus	Lapped faced vulture
Corvus corax ruficollis	Brown-necked raven
Alectoris graeca sinaica	Sinai rock partridge
Ammoperdix heyi heyi	Desert partridge

REPTILIA
Stenodactylus stenodactylus	Elegant gecko
Tropiocoletes studneri	Studner gecko
Agama pallida	Pale agama
A. stellio	Starred gecko
A. sinaita	Sinai gecko
Varanus griseus	Gray monitor
Uromastix aegyptius	Egyptian dabb-lizard
Acanthodactylus boskianus	Bosc's lizard
Ophisops elegans	Menetrie's lizard
Eremius guttulata	Small spotted lizard
Telescopus dhara	Tropical cat snake
T. hoogstraali	Hoogstraal's cat snake
Spalerosophic clifford	Clifford's snake
Coluber rogersi	Roger's snake
C. rhodorhachis	Jan's desert racer

AMPHIBIA
Bufo viridis	Green toad

tribution of fauna. There is no doubt that under natural conditions and with the present climatic regime, this area would be more luxuriant than the present setting. Specifically, the present vegetation of the hilltops and loessial plain is probably as it would be under climax conditions, because of the impermeable soils. The hillslopes, the loessial depression, and the gravel and upland nahals are those habitats which have been most affected by human and domestic animal activity. The extreme overgrazing of these areas has made them highly susceptible to erosion during historic times. Prior to this, they undoubtedly contained greater expanses of soil, which would have allowed a greater concentration of annual plants and slightly more extensive shrub and tree cover. The trees, even under climax conditions, would have been restricted to the larger nahals and perhaps the loessial depression, but then only as relic stands. Thus, without man's interference, the Avdat/Aqev area would have been considerably richer in vegetation and, probably, in fauna, but not radically different from that of today. That the area is still relatively rich in flora and fauna would seem to indicate that slight climatic change could well produce a more abundant environment. Given both the paleozoological (Tchernov, this volume) and palynological (Horowitz, this volume) data now available from prehistoric sites in the Avdat/Aqev area, there is little question that the present environment represents what is probably among the least favorable since the onset of the Upper Pleistocene.

NOTE

[1] The term *habitat* is used in this paper in preference to the more usual *environment* following the terminology of Evenari, Tadmor, Shanan, Hillel, and others who have worked in this region.

BIBLIOGRAPHY

CARLISLE, D. B., and GHORBIAL, L. I., 1968. "Food and Water Requirements of Dorcus Gazelle in the Sudan." *Mammalia* 32:570-77.

CLOUDESLEY-THOMPSON, J. L., and GHORBIAL, L. I., 1965. "Water Economy of the Dorcus Gazelle." *Nature* 207:1313.

DANIN, A., and ORSHAN, G., 1970. "Distribution of Indigenous Trees in the Northern Central Negev Highlands." *LaYaaran* 20(4):115-19. (In Hebrew).

DEKEYSER, A., 1955. *Les mammifières de l'Afrique noire français*. Dakar: Institut Français d'Afrique Noire.

EVENARI, M.; SHANAN, L.; and TADMOR, N., 1971. *The Negev: The Challenge of a Desert*. Cambridge: Harvard University Press.

GHORBIAL, L. I., and CLOUDESLEY-THOMPSON, J. L., 1966. "Effect of Deprivation of Water on the Dorcus Gazelle." *Nature* 212:306.

HILLEL, D., and TADMOR, N., 1962. "Water Regime and Vegetation in the Central Negev Highlands of Israel." *Ecology* 43(1):33-40.

MARX, E., 1967. *The Bedouin of the Negev*. Manchester: Manchester University Press.

ORNI, E., and EFRAT, E., 1966. *Geography of Israel*. Jerusalem: Israel Program for Scientific Translations.

SHANAN, L.; EVENARI, M.; and TADMOR, N. H., 1967. "Rainfall Patterns in the Central Negev Desert." *Israel Exploration Journal* 17(3):163-84.

SHKOLNIK, A., 1971. "Adaptation of Animals to Desert Conditions." In *The Negev: The Challenge of the Desert*, edited by Evenari et al. Cambridge: Harvard University Press.

TADMOR, N. H., and HILLEL, D., 1957. *Natural Conditions and Range Development in the Negev Highlands and Foothills*. Agricultural Research Station, Rehovot, Series 38A.

ZOHARY, M., 1952. "Ecological Studies in the Vegetation of the Near Eastern Deserts." *Israel Exploration Journal* 2(4):201-15.

_____, 1962. *Plant Life of Palestine, Israel, and Jordan*. New York: Ronald Press.

UPPER PLEISTOCENE GEOLOGY OF THE AVDAT/AQEV AREA

Paul Goldberg

The Hebrew University, Jerusalem

INTRODUCTION

The Upper Pleistocene geology of the Avdat/Aqev area includes deposits which represent environments during times of prehistoric occupation. It is important, therefore, to have a clear understanding of the nature of these physical environments in order to make reasonable inferences about those factors which influenced man's behavior, particularly as reflected in specific site locations and in the wider view of settlement patterns. Thus, the purpose of this report will be to describe the Upper Pleistocene geology of the Avdat/ Aqev area, with detailed reference to those deposits associated with archaeological occurrences. Through these deposits, an attempt will be made to determine some of the characteristics of prehistoric man's physical environment. Those characteristics related to specific sediment deposition will be considered, as well as the broader problem of the relationship between these sediments and paleoclimatology.

GENERAL GEOGRAPHIC AND GEOLOGIC SETTING

The Avdat/Aqev area is located along the northern edge of the Central Negev highlands, a plateau consisting of nearly horizontal to gently tilted, very slightly folded and faulted Middle Eocene limestones, chalks, and chert (the Avdat Group—see Bentor and Vroman, 1960). The plateau itself was produced by uplift during the lower Miocene (Garfunkel and Horowitz, 1966) and subsequently underwent two episodes of uplift and erosion during the Pliocene and early Pleistocene (Picard, 1951).

North of the Nabatean city of Avdat and between the Har Mekhya on the west and the Nahal Aqev on the east, two elevationally distinct topographic surfaces can be distinguished: an upper surface between 610 and 630 m, and a lower surface between 495 and 520 meters. The upper surface is present as isolated, flat-topped hills which are erosional remnants of the flat Har Aqev just to the south. On this surface are found numerous Nabatean and Byzantine remains, including the ancient city of Avdat. The lower surface covers most of the area, ca. 14 sq km, and constitutes what is referred to in these reports as the Divshon Plain. This plain is dissected by a number of ephemeral streams. The most important of these are the Nahals Zin, Aqev, and Divshon, all of which flow from south to north through the plain (fig. 2-1).

The Divshon Plain is covered by a variety of sediments. Along the edges of the plain, near the valleys of the Nahals Zin, Divshon, and Aqev are gravels of supposed Neogene age at elevation of around 500 meters. In other localities, usually those above 510 m, are found either highly calcareous silts or, where these have been deflated, patches of chalky bedrock. Vegetation is generally sparse, limited to small shrubs and grasses (see Munday, this volume).

THE NAHAL ZIN

For convenience, it is possible to view the Nahal Zin as having two drainage components, one north/south (NS) and one east/

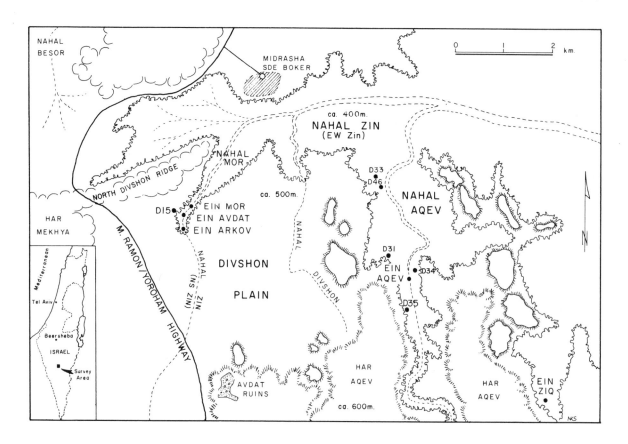

FIG. 2-1—Area map of site locations and features noted in this chapter.

west (EW), which join one-half kilometer due south of the Midrasha Sde Boker.

The North/South Zin

This section of the Nahal Zin is totally south of the juncture below the Midrasha Sde Boker and drains an area of approximately 250 square kilometers. Its origin lies near the Maktesh Ramon, ca. 28 km to the south, from where it flows northward with a gradient of ca. 9.0 m/km in a valley which is relatively broad in comparison to others in this part of the Negev (roughly 1.2 km wide in the area south of the Nabatean city of Avdat). One kilometer north of the city of Avdat, within the Divshon Plain, the stream bed is incised into a more narrow, chalky bedrock channel (ca. 300 m wide). Between this first incision and its junction with the EW Zin, the

stream bed passes over two steep escarpments or knickpoints. These are also formed in chalk and are laterally separated by ca. 0.5 kilometers. At the knickpoints are found the perennial springs of Ein Arkov and Ein Avdat. The knickpoint at Ein Arkov displays a vertical drop of 70 to 80 m into an elongated box-like canyon, the Nahal Mor, at an elevation of about 420 meters. The other knickpoint is similarly confined by vertical canyon walls, but these are only on the order of 10 m, within the larger vertical walls of the Nahal Mor. The Mousterian site of Rosh Ein Mor (D15) is situated directly above the spring of Ein Avdat, along the western edge of the canyon walls in sediments of the NS Zin (fig. 2-2).

From the spring of Ein Avdat, the Nahal Zin flows northeastward for about 3 km, through the Nahal Mor, where it turns toward

FIG. 2-2—Site Rosh Ein Mor (D15) indicated by arrow. Ein Avdat is at the bottom of the cliff.

the east and becomes the EW Zin. Along this northeastward stretch, the canyon walls progressively widen and become somewhat less steep.

The East/West Zin

The main EW portion of the Nahal Zin drainage flows from the above juncture with the NS Zin, below the Midrasha, eastward to the Wadi Arava, with an average gradient of about 8.3 m/km, for that stretch from 380 to 0 m above sea level. Actually, the EW portion of the Nahal Zin begins about 3 km west of the junction with the NS portion, near the Mitzpe Ramon/Yoroham Highway (at an elevation of 500 m), in a badlands topography which is now under active erosion.

Between the junction of the two portions of the Nahal Zin and the point where the Nahal Aqev enters from the south, the stream flows in a meandering course confined to a flat-bottomed valley about 1.5 km wide (fig. 2-3). This portion of the Nahal Zin, west of the Nahal Aqev entrance, is eroding soft, gypsiferous shales and limestones of the Late Cretaceous/Early Tertiary Taqiye Formation. To the south is the Divshon Plain, at 500 m, separated from the stream by steep canyon walls. To the north is the gravel and loess-covered plain on which the Midrasha is situated. This plain, at 475 m, is separated from the stream by somewhat less steep cliffs. In addition, the stream has cut through Upper Pleistocene alluvial and colluvial deposits, resulting in the formation of terraces (fig. 2-4). East of the Nahal Aqev and beyond the eastern margin of the Eocene Plateau, the

FIG. 2-3—Photomosaic of the south side of the Nahal Zin where it meets the Nahal Aqev. Note that the Nahal Aqev Valley flows along the axis of a gently folded syncline.

valley of the EW Zin broadens to a width of several kilometers; this region fell outside the study area.

THE NAHAL AQEV

The Nahal Aqev and its tributaries drain a much smaller area than that of the NS Zin, only about 60 square kilometers. Its head is near the Maktesh Ramon, from where it flows northward, joining the EW Zin about 3 km east of the Midrasha Sde Boker. For most of its length it is within a narrow canyon which broadens to ca. 2 km just north of the spring of Ein Aqev, some 2.5 km upstream from its junction with the Nahal Zin. Along this lower, wider portion the Nahal Aqev flows along the axis of a gently folded syncline (fig. 2-4). The channel of the Nahal Aqev also displays an abrupt break in slope. This is located at the perennial spring of Ein Aqev at an elevation of ca. 400 meters. The escarpment at the spring of Ein Aqev is about 15 to 20 m high and cuts through cherty chalks to form a small elongate box canyon about 75 m wide and 250 m long (fig. 2-5). Capping the chalk and lining the present-day stream near Ein Aqev, at an elevation of ca. 400 m, is a hard, well-cemented conglomerate, consisting of limestone, dolomite, and chert cobbles and pebbles. This conglomerate is found downstream from Ein Aqev on isolated hilltops, the elevations of which progressively decrease in

the direction of the Zin (fig. 2-6). About 0.5 km downstream from Ein Aqev (elevation 370-80 m) the stream has cut below the chalk and has exposed shales of the Taqiye Formation.

It is possible to distinguish three different morphological terraces or sets of terraces near Ein Aqev, one downstream and two upstream from the spring. The downstream terrace is, in reality, a group of three, or possibly four, terraces cut into the same alluvial fill (hence, "set of terraces"). At the north end of the small box canyon holding the spring of Ein Aqev the silty alluvial terrace deposits abut against a northerly sloping chalk face (fig. 2-4), which may represent the back wall of a former box canyon similar to the present one. The Upper Paleolithic site of Ein Aqev (D31) is located within the top 50 cm of these extant alluvial silts (fig. 2-5). The site has been dated by radiocarbon to between 16,000 B.C. and 15,000 B.C. These alluvial deposits and the terraces which have been cut into them can be traced along the present course of the Nahal Aqev and can be correlated with similar well-preserved terraces in the Nahal Zin.

Of the two terraces upstream and altitudinally above the spring of Ein Aqev, one is exposed only over a limited distance, whereas the other extends over a much greater area. The former and lower of the two is approximately 5 m above the present nahal floor and is about 300 m long, beginning about 100 m

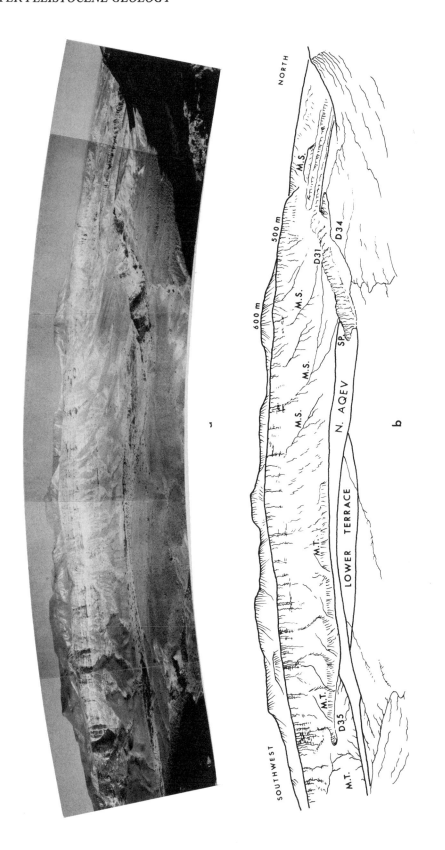

FIG. 2-4—*A*—Photomosaic of the Nahal Aqev, looking northwest. *B*—Schematic drawing made from *A*. Note locations of Sites D35, D31, and D34; also note Ein Aqev (SP), Mousterian Terrace (MT) and lower terrace upstream of the spring, and the Mousterian surface (MS) downstream of the spring. At the top and in the background is the ca. 600 m surface of the Eocene plateau.

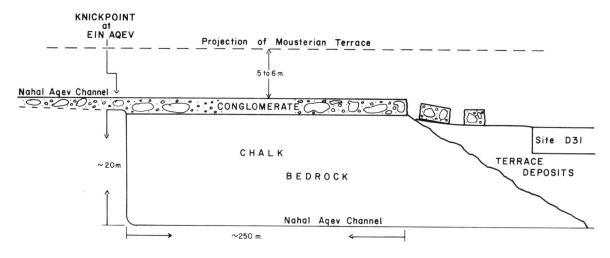

FIG. 2-5—Schematic profile through the small box canyon in the Nahal Aqev.

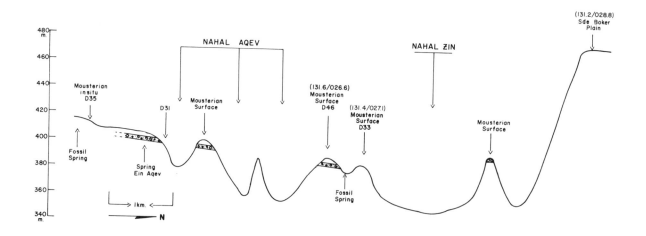

FIG. 2-6—Generalized north/south profile from Site D35 to the Sde Boker plain, showing locations of the Mousterian Sites D35, D46, D33, the Upper Paleolithic Site D31, and the conglomerate outcrops.

upstream from the spring (fig. 2-7). The terrace sediments consist of rounded gravels and silts typical of the nahal alluvium of the region. Although no artifacts were found within it and other definitive temporal criteria were lacking, its height above the nahal floor and the present floodplain seems to rule out the possibility of a very recent age. On the other hand, since the higher terrace unquestionably dates to the Mousterian, this terrace must be *at least* younger than the Mousterian;

perhaps Upper Paleolithic and, so, broadly equivalent to the terrace containing the late Upper Paleolithic site of Ein Aqev (D31). The second, and higher, of the upstream terraces is more clearly defined and more laterally extensive than the lower one. It consists primarily of silt and angular limestone fragments. The top of the terrace ranges from 6 to 8 m above the present nahal floor. The surface morphology of the terrace follows very closely that of the chalk bedrock underneath and, in fact, the break in slope along the terrace edge is mirrored by a similar break in the underlying chalk (figs. 2-4 and 2-7).

Within this terrace, on the western side of the nahal, 1.5 km south of the spring of Ein Aqev, is a large Mousterian site (D35) with artifacts *in situ* in the terrace to a depth of at least 3.0 meters. This upper terrace is well exposed between the Mousterian site (D35) and the Upper Paleolithic site of Ein Aqev (D31), although the latter is not associated with it. The area south of D35 was not extensively studied, but the upper terrace was traced 500 m upstream from the site. North of the Upper Paleolithic site (D31), where the valley of the Nahal Aqev broadens, the terrace is more difficult to trace and virtually disappears, as such. Nevertheless, from a distance (figs. 2-3 and 2-6) it is possible to see what appears to be the northern continuation of this upper terrace.[1]

THE NAHAL DIVSHON

Although only one deflated Mousterian site (D51) was located in the immediate area of the Nahal Divshon, a brief description is necessary in order to characterize the area completely. The Nahal Divshon is by far the smallest of the three ephemeral drainages discussed here, having a catchment area of roughly 8 to 10 square kilometers. It begins relatively close to the northern edge of the Divshon Plain, 3 km into the Har Aqev to the south, and flows northward with an average gradient of 18 meters/kilometer. At the very northern edge of the Divshon Plain, at 500 m elevation, the stream plunges over a sheer vertical escarpment, 150 m high, into a square box canyon (fig. 2-1). The stream then continues NNE for about 1 km where it joins the EW Zin.

Near the very northern edge of the Divshon Plain, the valley of the Nahal Divshon is rather broad, 600 to 700 m, and shows only minor incision into the plateau. In the vicinity of its source, however, the relief is greater and

the valley more narrow. Along the edge of the Nahal Divshon, at an elevation of about 500 m there are gravels similar to those described for the area around the site of Rosh Ein Mor (D15), as well as elsewhere at similar elevations along the drainages and edges of the plateau.

The overall view of the Avdat/Aqev area presents a flat plateau at 500 m elevation, the Divshon Plain, cut by three nahals running south to north (the Nahals Aqev, Divshon, and the NS Zin), sharply defined on the north by the deeply incised EW Zin and demarcated in other directions by hills at 600 m elevation. Within the Nahal Aqev and the NS Zin a terrace system datable to the Mousterian can be defined. Within the Nahal Aqev there are more recent terraces, which are dated by archaeological materials to part of the late Upper Paleolithic and most probably to even later times as well.

Owing to the importance of these archaeological occurrences for the dating of the terraces and, conversely, the importance of the archaeologically associated sediments for environmental reconstruction, detailed description of the geomorphology and sedimentology of the sites is warranted.

STRATIGRAPHY OF THE MOUSTERIAN SITES

ROSH EIN MOR (D15)

Geographic and Geologic Setting

The site of Rosh Ein Mor (D15) is situated in the western part of the Divshon Plain along the west side of the NS Zin, about 70 m directly above the spring of Ein Avdat, at an elevation of 495 m (fig. 2-1). The site is preserved in predominantly fine-grained sediments which fill a shallow bedrock depression probably sculpted by the NS Zin prior to its incision into the bedrock. The fill is part of a more complex terrace system[2] of the NS Zin,

FIG. 2-7—View of the upper reaches of the Nahal Aqev, looking north, showing Site D35 (lower center), the 5
m terrace (to the north of D35), and the fossil spring (indicated by arrow).

one that is particularly clear in the immediate area of the site (fig. 2-8a, b).

In the general locality of Rosh Ein Mor there are two terraces which are visible on both the east and west side of the NS Zin, where it forms the Nahal Mor (fig. 2-9). On the east side of this canyon the lower terrace (fig. 2-10, Section C-C′) has a generally flat surface which slopes up from datum (arbitrarily set as 100 on the surface of Rosh Ein Mor) for 6 m, where it comes into contact with the bedrock. The terrace sediments, about 2 m thick, are composed of well-rounded and slightly cemented gravel which consists of limestone, dolomites, chalk, and some flint. This terrace extends southward from Section B-B′ (fig. 2-10) to a point just north of the major knickpoint in the NS Zin. Between the knickpoint and the Mitzpe Ramon/Yoroham Highway the terrace is more difficult to trace, but does appear in several localities as small remnants.

The higher of the two eastern terraces begins at the bedrock contact at 106 m and slopes westward where it either grades unclearly into the lower terrace or ends against the cliff at a height of 104 m (fig. 2-10, Section B-B′). The sediments of the upper terrace are also gravel and are virtually identical to those of the lower terrace, although they are generally thicker, ca. 3 to 5 meters. This terrace extends northward and ends abruptly ca. 830 m downstream from a point directly over Ein Avdat. To the south this terrace is traceable upstream as far as the highway.

The two terraces also appear on the west side of the canyon of Nahal Mor (figs. 2-8a and 2-9). The lower terrace, in which Rosh Ein Mor (D15) is found, appears as a generally flat, uniformly sloping surface between 99 and 102 meters. These sediments are primarily silts and clays with smaller quantities of coarser (>2 mm) limestone debris. The terrace is only about 200 m long, beginning against the upper terrace on the south and extending to the first major turn of the canyon wall, where it swings to the northwest. The upper terrace occurs between 103 and

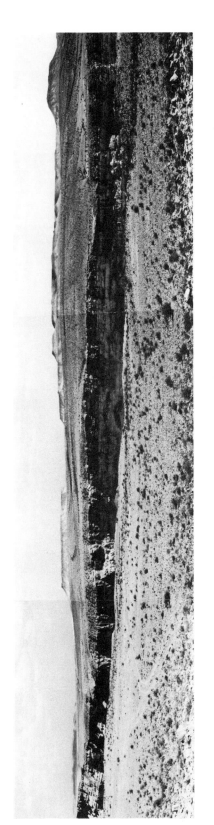

FIG. 2-8—Area surrounding Site D15. A—View across NS Zin to D15 to west. Note well-developed upper terrace just above site. B—View across NS Zin to east taken from upper terrace. Note thick gravel lens left center, above edge of cliff face.

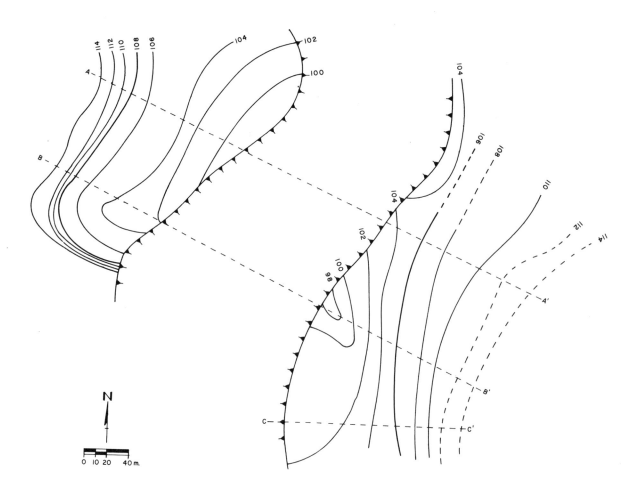

FIG. 2-9–Topographic map of area near Rosh Ein Mor (D15), showing both sides of the Nahal Mor.

106 meters. Unlike the lower one, it consists of gravel which is poorly exposed and which extends northward along the canyon to a point equal to the extension of the upper terrace on the east side of the canyon. To the south the upper terrace deposits abut against a knoblike hill of Eocene chalk about 200 m long; south and upstream of this hill, the terrace can be traced more or less as far as the highway.

Rosh Ein Mor (D15) Stratigraphy

As previously noted, the sediments of the lower, western terrace are situated in a very shallow, elongated bedrock depression. Although these sediments extend for some 200

m along the length of the canyon and are, on an average, 15 m wide, the area containing high concentrations of artifacts (the site of Rosh Ein Mor) only covers 1,200 sq m in area. In general, the sediments average 80 cm in thickness and follow the eastward slope of the bedrock (fig. 2-10).

The sediments are, as a whole, remarkably uniform. Four stratigraphic units, however, were recognized in the field (Samples D-15-0 through D-15-3, from bottom to top), primarily on subtle distinctions of color and hardness. For the most part, these units did not show differences under analysis. Petrographically, all four samples were identical and, thus, the following description applies to all the samples.

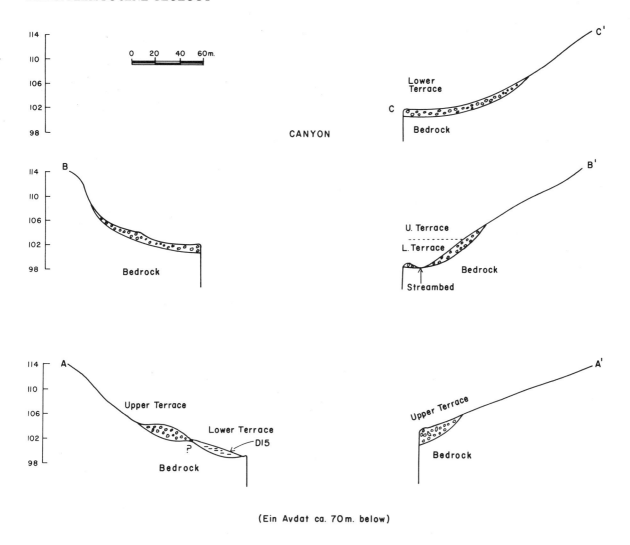

FIG. 2-10—Profiles through the upper and lower terraces near Rosh Ein Mor (D15). See Fig. 2-9 for position of these transects.

The deposits consist primarily (~75%) of light brown (10YR 7/4, dry; 5/4 wet)[3] silt and clay-sized sediment (<0.062 mm) with lesser amounts of sand and other larger sized material.[4] The clay, silt, and much of the sand-sized material are composed of detrital carbonate grains (e.g., bedrock, fossils) or aggregates of grains which are weakly cemented. The coarse silt/fine sand grades contain 10% to 15% angular to sub-angular quartz grains and heavy minerals (mostly hornblende, epidote, tourmaline, and some rutile), reminis-

cent of the loess deposits found in the Beer Sheva Basin (Ginzbourg and Yaalon, 1963). The >2 mm fraction consists of flint artifacts, gypsum and calcite aggregates, and limestone fragments. These fragments are, for the most part, fresh looking, flattish, mostly angular and less commonly sub-angular to sub-rounded. They very much resemble scree weathered from bedrock. The lowest sediments (Sample D-15-0) differed from the others in containing some well-rounded and smooth limestone fragments, ranging in size from 10 to 60 millimeters. The middle sample (D-15-2) also contained similar fragments, but these were usually smaller.

Bedding, laminations, and other sedimentary structures were not discernable in the profiles, although some disturbance from rodent activity was seen in the lower half of the deposits. Bones were rare and only a few microscopic fragments were observed in the thin sections. On the other hand, fragments of ostrich egg shell were plentiful throughout the deposits, within the site area, and these produced three radiocarbon dates ranging between >37,000 B.P. and >50,000 B.P. (Crew, this volume). The excavated artifacts are fresh and normally display sharp, uncrushed edges. Numerous examples were coated on their under surface with a secondary calcium carbonate deposit, while those *in situ* but near the present surface showed a whitish patination typical of surficially buried artifacts in this area.

The sediments are quite soft, although they become harder and more crumbly after exposure to the air. The lowest sediments are particularly soft and moist. Secondary calcium carbonate and gypsum are found in all layers, although the sediments of D-15-2 contain higher percentages of gypsum. The contact with the underlying bedrock is sharp and the bedrock fresh and unweathered.

The Origin and Environment
of Sediment Deposition

It is difficult to determine unequivocally the origin and environment of deposition of the Rosh Ein Mor sediments. The most reasonable environments are eolian, alluvial, colluvial or, as is most likely, a combination of these.

The possibility of an eolian environment is mentioned here primarily because the quartz and heavy minerals are so strikingly similar to those found in the loess of the Beer Sheva area. Being so close to that basin, the Avdat/ Aqev area would be expected to receive some eolian deposits. A strict eolian environment, however, seems unreasonable because of the presence of limestone fragments in the >2 mm fraction. These would require a more competent medium than air for transportation. It is more likely that some of the sediments are of primary eolian origin which have been subsequently reworked by alluvial or colluvial processes, accounting for their present position.

There is good evidence to suggest that the Rosh Ein Mor deposits are mainly alluvial in origin. This is seen in that they are virtually identical, both in composition and texture, to the silty terrace deposits exposed at the junction of the NS Zin and the highway (fig. 2-1). In addition, the silts in which the artifacts are located occur topographically at the same elevation as the lower terrace deposits on the east side of the Nahal Mor Canyon (fig. 2-10), which are unquestionably of fluvial origin. In fact, it is possible to see the D15 sediments as a silty facies of the lower, eastern terrace gravels, deposited prior to the formation of the canyon. This change from a gravel to a silty facies is seen today for the NS Zin in the highway road cut, where gravel grades laterally into silt.

The major drawback to a fully alluvial origin of these sediments lies in the presence of angular limestone fragments distributed throughout the deposits (note, however, the rounded ones in both the lower and middle levels). It is highly unlikely that these fragments are truly alluvial, owing to their angularity and the absence of evidence for battering or rolling. The flint artifacts are also extremely fresh. On the other hand, the fragments could reasonably represent local, low energy deposition of weathered bedrock by surface runoff. As suggested above, this runoff could also carry with it the finer-grained sediments predominantly of eolian origin, such as calcareous and quartz silt and clay, which were deposited on the nearby slopes.

In summary then, the sediments of the lower, western terrace in which the artifacts of Rosh Ein Mor are found, are primarily of alluvial origin (perhaps similar to a floodplain deposit) but sufficiently far from the main channel so that only silts were deposited and not coarser gravels. In addition, by being far from the channel and close to the west side of the valley, the bedrock depression in which the terrace silts occur would also receive both fine-grained sediments and limestone fragments carried by surface runoff, coming from the surrounding low-relief slopes. Such a setting would make an ideal place for prehistoric occupation, for the surface would consist of soft silts, relatively devoid of large rocks which today constitute much of the surface exposure in the area. Also, such a locality would be close to the channel of the NS Zin, without being so close as to be often flooded by high energy flow, which perhaps only occurred during very wet seasons. Perhaps of greatest importance to prehistoric man was the presence of the perennial spring near the site, much closer than the spring at Ein Avdat is today.

As the Rosh Ein Mor sediments correlate with those of the lower, eastern terrace, the relationship between these lower terraces and the upper terraces is of significance. While this is not completely clear, there is some evidence which is suggestive. The gravels of the upper and lower eastern terraces are identical and virtually indistinguishable. Moreover, the upper terrace gravels are most probably equivalent to other gravel deposits which occur on the western edge of the Divshon Plain at the same elevation (ca. 500-510 m), although these gravels cannot be correlated directly with one another. The western Divshon gravels are generally recognized as being Neogene in age, although there is no definitive proof that this is so. In any case, they are certainly older than the Mousterian, as they

are found along the edge of the valley of the Nahal Aqev, which itself contains Mousterian terrace deposits on the nahal floor, some 80 m below the valley edge. It seems that the only reasonable explanation is that the upper terrace gravels are pre-Mousterian, but their exact age cannot be determined.[5] The lower terrace, however, containing the site of Rosh Ein Mor is Mousterian in age and its eastern facies is composed of derived and reworked gravels of the upper terrace, resulting in the similar composition of the two. A Mousterian and/or post-Mousterian age for some gravels is supported by the finding of five artifacts, including two Levallois points, *in situ* in a gravel quarry located east of the highway 1.2 km north of the city of Avdat (coord: 127.1/024.4). Owing to poor exposures and the lack of aerial photographs, however, it was not possible to determine with which of the gravel deposits, if any, this exposure correlated.

Significance of the Mousterian Terrace

The northward extent of the lower terrace clearly suggests that the NS Zin and the spring of Ein Avdat were both very close to the area of occupation, at an elevation much higher than that of the present spring. Given that the NS Zin was flowing at ca. 495 m during the Mousterian occupation and that the northern extent of the terrace represents the Mousterian age knickpoint, then the Nahal Mor has cut back and into the canyon some 600 m since the deposition of the lower terrace. If, for argument's sake, the age of the lower terrace is placed at 60,000 B.P. (a reasonable age for the Mousterian at Rosh Ein Mor), then an average erosion rate of about 1 m per 100 years is obtained. This is generally greater than that which most geomorphologists working in this area are willing to accept (A. Yair, personal communication). Yet, this is not unreasonable if it is kept in mind that in the area of the Avdat springs, erosion of the chalk is not a gradual process. Rather, as a function of the well-developed and closely spaced joints, large blocks of the cliff tend to break off at one time. This is particularly clear both at Ein Avdat and Ein Arkov, as well as at the entrance to the Nahal Mor where large blocks of fallen rubble are present. Although the short-term erosive effects may be rather small, over a long period of time, as a result of this block dislocation, large amounts of material can be dislodged and removed by mass wasting and erosion.

Another significance of the geologic formations immediate to Rosh Ein Mor is that the presence of a Mousterian terrace clearly indicates that alluviation was taking place during this period. Since that time, however, the terraces and the chalk bedrock have been substantially eroded. Whether this change from a depositional to an erosional regime reflects the influences of tectonism, climatic change, or both cannot be determined from the stratigraphic evidence discussed above. A similar sequence of events, however, can be seen in the area of the Nahal Aqev and is beautifully revealed in the vicinity of the sites of Ein Aqev, Ein Aqev East, and D35. In this area, there are indications that the climate was, in fact, somewhat wetter during the Mousterian occupation than at present. This evidence relates to the stratigraphy and geologic surroundings of Site D35.

SITE D35

Geographic and Geologic Setting

Within the Nahal Aqev, on the west side of the valley situated ca. 550 m upstream from the spring of Ein Aqev, at an elevation of roughly 420 m, is the Mousterian site of D35 (fig. 2-4). The site is contained in predominantly silty and gravelly terrace deposits which are well exposed as far north as Site Ein Aqev East (D34). Farther north, the terrace deposits as such are not recognizable,

although there are other stratigraphic and geomorphological features which may represent their continuation (fig. 2-6).

D35 is found on a tongue-shaped portion of this terrace, which owes its shape to dissection of the terrace by a northeastwardly flowing tributary of the Nahal Aqev (figs. 2-4 and 2-7). On this side of the wadi the top surface of the terrace slopes eastward and at D35 the present terrace surface is about 10.5 m above the nahal floor (fig. 2-11).

The artifacts at D35 occur as a loose but large concentration both on the partially eroded surface of the terrace, down the slopes of the terrace, and also *in situ* within the terrace deposits. Two exploratory trenches were excavated, one on the east slope and the other on the west slope of the terrace to determine the position of the *in situ* artifacts and to clarify the terrace stratigraphy (fig. 2-12).

The larger trench, placed on the west slope of the terrace, consisted of a series of steps, 80 cm wide, which reached a depth of 2.5 m below the top of the terrace. A smaller trench, 45 cm wide by 3.3 m long was excavated into the eastern slope to a depth of 1.8 meters. In neither case were the lowermost terrace deposits uncovered, but a number of artifact-bearing deposits were located.

In the western trench, a major artifact-bearing horizon was located between 1.5 and 1.9 m, although a thin scatter of artifacts also occurred in other zones. In the eastern trench, artifacts were primarily restricted to a horizon between 1.0 and 1.45 m, although, again, isolated artifacts occurred elsewhere in the deposit. Thus, these trenches clearly documented that the terrace was occupied during its aggradation.

The sediments which make up the terrace, as a whole, vary lithologically from place to place. At one locality, about 200 m downstream from D35, they are mostly fine-grained but also contain much angular scree. At another locality, 100 m south of D35, the sediments are gravels. At D35, both of these types of lithologies occur and, as a whole, the sediments here are more heterogeneous than those at the other archaeological sites. In general, they may be characterized as silty deposits containing limestone scree with lenses and pockets of fine gravel (granules).

Site D35 Stratigraphy

Although two trenches were excavated, it was not possible to link the sedimentary stratigraphic sequence of one with the other. Nor was it clear which, if any, of the artifact concentrations of one trench related to concentrations in the other. Clearly, a major trenching through the terrace will be necessary before the total stratigraphic picture of the terrace formation can be elucidated. Both trenches, however, give a partial picture of the complexity of the terrace stratigraphy and document multiple Mousterian occupations.[6]

West Trench (see fig. 2-13 for profile)

Layer W1

The deposit is a light tan (10YR 8/4 dry; 10YR 6.5/4 wet), crumbly, loose colluvium consisting mostly of silt, with lesser amounts of limestone fragments and gypsum crystals. The rock fragments are mostly flattish and angular to sub-angular, varying in length from 2 to 45 mm, although clustering around 10 millimeters. These fragments are mostly fresh, although the smaller ones tend to be chalky. This layer rests unconformably on the lower sediments and has the same steep dip as the present hillslope. At the top of the terrace, this colluvium is about 40 cm thick but downslope it generally decreases to 20-25 centimeters. Artifacts with a white patina, but otherwise quite fresh, occur on the surface of and occasionally within the colluvium.

Layer W2

This is a soft, light yellow brown (10YR 7.5/4 dry; 10YR 6.5/4 wet) silt with fresh angular and flat rock

fragments which vary in size from 1 to 6 mm (mode, 1-2 millimeters). Secondary cementation is lacking. The upper contact with Layer W1 is undulating, while the contact with Layer W3 is horizontal. The total layer is 30 to 35 cm thick. A few artifacts were recovered.

Layer W3

This is a gravelly layer in a light yellow brown (10YR 7/4 dry; 10YR 6.5/4 wet) silty matrix. The gravels consist of limestone fragments 2 to 120 mm in length (mode, ca. 10-20 mm) which are flattish to sub-spherical, and are sub-angular to sub-rounded. Limestone fragments are particularly abundant in the northern half of the section, and few gypsum crystals are present. The deposit, 10 to 15 cm thick, is horizontal and the contact with the lower level is sharp. No artifacts were recovered.

Layer W4

This is a pale yellow (10YR 8/3 dry; 10YR 7/3 wet) compact layer, consisting almost exclusively of fine sand/silt-sized grains, with lenses of coarse sand-size calcareous fragments. While there is no apparent bedding, lenses of ash are present. Some gypsum crystals are found, with a few in the form of rootlets. This layer is generally 10 to 15 cm thick, but it increases in thickness at the southern end of the profile, as well as showing a slight dip to the west. No artifacts were recovered.

Layer W5

This layer consists mainly of small limestone pebbles in a very fine sand/silt matrix of yellowish color (10YR 7.5/3 dry; 10YR 6.5/4 wet). The small limestone pieces vary in size from 0.5 to 3 cm, but are generally in the 1.5 to 2 cm range. These are mostly flattish and sub-angular to rounded, unlike the present day scree which is strongly angular. In addition, there are some larger fresh limestone fragments, 10 cm in length, which are mostly restricted to the northern part of the profile. There is no bedding; rather, the deposit seems to be "mixed up." This

FIG. 2-11—View to east side of the Nahal Aqev. *Slanting arrow* shows Site D35, *straight arrow* indicates fossil springs.

layer is generally 20 cm thick, although the upper and lower contacts are undulating. A few unpatinated, fresh artifacts were recovered from the base of the layer.

Layer W6

The deposits of this layer are similar to those of Layer W4 and consist of compact, light yellow brown silt (10YR 8/3 dry; 10YR 7/4 wet) with some limestone and chalk inclusions. The latter are irregularly shaped but mostly flattish, angular to sub-angular.

Near the bottom of the layer are several 1 cm thick bands of chalky, clayey material which may represent weathered chalk fragments. Some gypsum aggregates and microscopic bone fragments were also found. The layer is 35 to 40 cm thick, although the lower contact is very undulatory and seems to fill pockets in the gravelly layer below. A very few fresh artifacts were recovered from the middle of the deposit.

Layer W7 (including W7a)

This is a heterogeneous layer, consisting of two

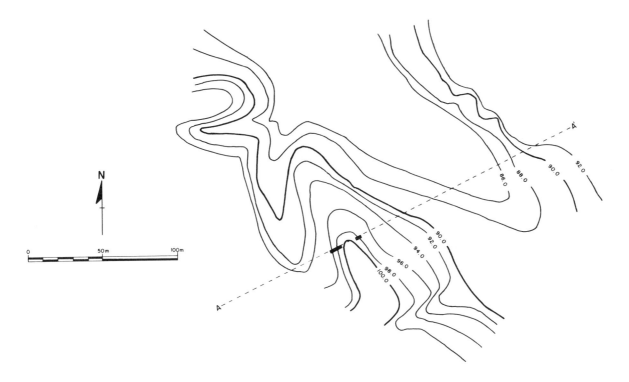

FIG. 2-12–Topographic map of area around D35. *Black rectangles* indicate position of test trenches.

major components: a compact yellow brown (10YR 7/4 dry; 10YR 6/4 wet) silty deposit and two pockets of gravel (Layer W7a) which occur at the top of the layer. The silty deposits are similar to Layer W6, but are somewhat darker and more moist. There are few limestone fragments. The lower contact is sharp and the layer varies between 15 and 25 cm in thickness. No artifacts were recovered. Layer W7a, the two pockets of gravel, consists primarily of fragments 0.3 to 3 cm in length (mostly in the 0.5 to 1.5 cm size range), although some silty matrix is also present. These fragments are generally flat, and are sub-angular to sub-rounded. The northern pocket displays horizontal bedding and seems to be truncated by Layer W6.

Layer W8

This consists of a loose, crumbly gravel deposit with fine-grained, light yellow brown matrix (10YR 8/3 dry; 10YR 6/4 wet). A scattering of limestone blocks range in length from a few centimeters up to 11 centimeters. The larger ones are generally more blocky and more angular than the smaller ones which tend to be flatter. Most fragments are angular to sub-angular and are fresh, although few have weathered surfaces. Gypsum aggregates occur throughout the layer. The deposits are horizontally bedded, 10 to 20 cm thick, while the lower contact is somewhat undulating. A number of fresh, unpatinated artifacts were recovered, but the concentration of these was low.

Layer W9

This is a yellow brown silty deposit, which is compact, moist, and soft, with various-sized limestone fragments and lenses of light yellow gray silt (10YR 8/2 dry; 10YR 7/2 wet). Fine gravel and granules are distributed throughout, some in the form of lenses. Limestone fragments range in length from 4 mm up to large blocks 7 to 8 centimeters. They are mostly flattish and blocky, with angular to sub-angular edges, while the smaller examples tend to be rounded. The layer is horizontally bedded and mainly 55 to 65 cm thick. Its thickness, however, is increased in the southern half of the profile by a gravel lens

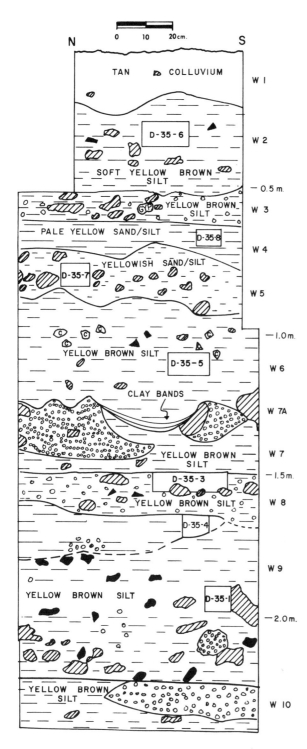

FIG. 2-13—Profile of west trench at D35. Designations (W1, W2, W3, etc.) refer to geological levels. *Black symbols* indicate artifacts.

which is up to 10 cm thick. Small amounts of gypsum crystals are found throughout the silty deposits. At the southern end of the profile the contact with Layer W8 is imperceptible, while between the silty deposits and the lower gravel lens is a 1 cm thick black lens of unknown composition. It is within this layer that the main artifact concentration was located. While fresh, unpatinated artifacts occurred throughout, they were mainly restricted to a 30 to 40 cm band in the middle of the layer. These artifacts showed no sorting by size; the edges of all pieces were pristine, and the vast majority lay flat in the deposits.

Layer W10

This is the lowermost layer exposed by the trench. It consists of soft, moist light yellow brown silts (10YR 8/4 dry; 10YR 7/4 wet). Like Layer W4, it contains very few limestone fragments, although some gypsum is present. It is horizontally bedded and at least 20 cm thick. The true thickness could not be determined, as it was only partially exposed by the trench. No artifacts were recovered.

East Trench (see fig. 2-14 for profile)

The eastern trench, while not as large as the western one, revealed a stratigraphic sequence different from the latter trench, including two clear artifact horizons.

Layer E1 (including E1a and E1b)

These are the uppermost deposits of the eastern trench and consist of two different layers, both of which are conformable to the present topographic slope of the east side of the terrace. They are texturally identical to Layer W1 of the western trench. Layer E1a is a soft, dry, loose, brown (7.5YR 7/4 dry; 10YR 6/6 wet) silty sediment with generally angular limestone rocks of varying size, from 1 to 30 cm in length. The silts have a blocky texture and contain no secondary cementation. They are uniformly 10 cm thick. A few white patinated artifacts were present on the surface of the deposit, as well as within it. Layer E1b is somewhat lighter in color (10YR 8/3 dry;

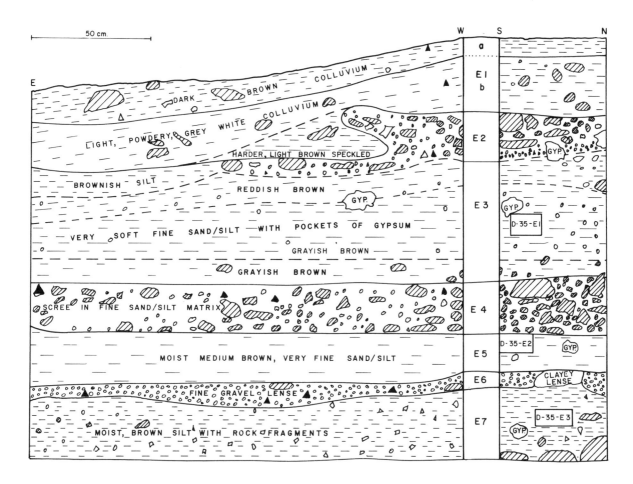

FIG. 2-14—Profile of east trench at D35. Designations (E1, E2, E3, etc.) refer to geological levels. *Black symbols* indicate artifacts, and GYP indicates gypsum.

10YR 7/4 wet) and more powdery than E1a. Along the south face, E1b seems to interfinger with two scree layers, but the contact is unclear because of the very dry nature of the sediment. Layer E1b is generally 25 cm thick and is devoid of artifacts. Both E1a and E1b appear to be colluvial deposits.

Layer E2

This is a scree layer, consisting of limestone fragments 1 to 15 cm in length, with very little fine-grained matrix present. The limestone fragments are fresh, flat to chunky, and mostly angular, with the upper part of the layer being somewhat coarser than the lower part. Gypsum crystals are present throughout. The layer is horizontal, but to the east it either

pinches out or is truncated by the light brown colluvium of Layer E1b. The layer is 15 to 20 cm thick and no artifacts were recovered from it.

Layer E3

This layer is a very homogeneous, moist, and compact deposit of brown (10YR 8/4 dry; 10YR 7/4 wet) soft silts with small limestone fragments distributed throughout. The fragments are flattish to equant, angular to sub-rounded. The sub-rounded examples are somewhat weathered and the larger fragments tend to be toward the bottom of the layer. Some gypsum occurs in the layer, which averages 50 cm thick. The lower contact with the scree of Layer E4 is horizontal and very sharp. No artifacts were recovered.

Layer E4

This is a scree layer of limestone fragments with approximately 20% finer-grained, brown silt matrix. It is similar to Layer E1, but contains a higher proportion of coarse fragments, which are angular to sub-rounded, flattish to chunky. The vast majority of these are fresh, although a few have weathered surfaces. The fragments range in size from 2 to 15 cm, but most fall in the 3 to 4 cm range. The contact with the lower layer is horizontal and sharp. Although some gypsum crystals were found, the deposit is generally soft. A few unpatinated, fresh artifacts were recovered in this layer.

Layer E5

This is a soft, moist, compact, brown (10YR 7/4 dry; 10YR 6/6 wet) and uniform silt which contains small granules in the 1 to 3 mm size range. Pebbles vary from flattish to spherical and angular to round, and all appear to be slightly weathered. Small amounts of gypsum occur throughout. This layer is generally 15 cm thick and the contact with the lower layer is sharp. A very few fresh and unpatinated artifacts were recovered.

Layer E6

This is a 5 to 10 cm thick horizontal deposit of fine gravel with about 30% finer-grained matrix. On the west profile this gravel has been cut and filled with a 10 to 15 cm wide clayey layer which is soft and moist, containing no pebbles. Otherwise, the pebbles in the gravel are mostly sub-equant, sub-rounded to sub-angular, and range in length from 5 to 30 mm (most fall between 5 and 15 millimeters). The gravel is compact but not cemented. This layer produced the largest number of artifacts found. While not comparable in density to Layer W9, the artifacts were as fresh as any found.

Layer E7

This is the lowest layer exposed in the trench. It is a mixed deposit of limestone fragments and boulders,

in a brown (10YR 7/5 dry; 10YR 6/5 wet) silty matrix. It is moist, compact, and quite difficult to dig. The limestone fragments are fresh, flattish, angular, and show no preferred orientation. At the very bottom of the trench are large rounded boulders and angular rock fragments, some of which exceed 30 cm in width. No artifacts were recovered from this layer.

Discussion of the D35 Stratigraphy

In addition to the megascopic descriptions based on field observations, some of the samples (Samples 1-5) were studied petrographically with the aid of thin sections. Aside from the gravelly layers, which were not thin sectioned, the fine-grained components consisted of material which is similar to that found at all other sites: calcareous silt and silt aggregates presumably derived from bedrock, quartz grains, heavy minerals (epidote, hornblende and tourmaline), foraminifera fragments, feldspar, and, rarely, bone fragments.

It would be ideal if the exact sedimentological conditions responsible for producing each layer could be determined. Rarely is this possible and these terrace deposits are no exception. For example, a fine-grained layer exposed in the section may indicate that the entire area was subjected to slightly more eolian deposition, or that this particular section just happened to cut a localized accumulation of silt. In other words, care must be taken to separate the large-scale factors (climatic changes or increased eolian deposition over the area) from localized ones (small channels and cut-and-fill structures).

In a general sense the origin of the sediments at D35 seems relatively clear. The fine-grained component is of combined origin; eolian deposition on the hillslopes, and possibly on the site itself, and downslope accumulation due to surface runoff. The eolian nature of the heavy minerals, quartz grains, and calcareous aggregates bears this out. The coarser fraction (the limestone fragments) has a more local origin, having been moved slowly down-slope as a scree deposit. This is supported by their generally angular and fresh aspect and their close similarity to the scree being produced and deposited on the slopes of the Aqev Valley today. In addition, the mint-like condition of the artifacts indicates that low energy processes were involved and that the artifacts were not moved. The better sorted pockets and lenses of gravelly sediment (Layer W7a, W10, and E6) most probably represent a slightly higher amount of energy such as that which might be found in small drainages developed on the aggrading terrace surface. The horizontal nature of the sediments at D35 should be noted, however. If the sediments were being washed downslope, one might reasonably expect them to have at least some degree of inclination to the east. The most reasonable explanation for the absence of such an inclination seems to be that the terrace sediments at D35 are relatively far from the valley walls. In Layer E7 the large rounded boulders suggest that the main channel of the Nahal Aqev was closer to the west side of the valley during that period of terrace aggradation.

Two additional aspects of the geology around Site D35 require discussion. One is the presence of two fossil spring deposits just southwest of the artifact-bearing portion of the terrace, and the other is the northern continuation of the terrace and its relationship to the conglomerate above Ein Aqev.

The spring deposits are located about 150 m SSW of the trenches at D35 and are about 10 m higher than the present terrace surface (figs. 2-7 and 2-11). They consist of tufas and well-bedded travertines, the largest of which has a circular outline more than 20 m in diameter. At the larger spring there are several artifacts of Levallois technique embedded in the deposit. It is unfortunate that the spring deposits are physically isolated from the terrace and, therefore, not directly traceable to it. The embedded Mousterian artifacts, how-ever, indicate at least some contemporaneity with the terrace sediments. Today, there are no springs active above that of Ein Aqev, strongly suggesting that during the Mousterian occupation the climate was wetter than at present.

Another fossil spring, unfortunately devoid of artifacts, was located at a comparable elevation farther north along the western side of the Aqev Valley with two Mousterian sites (D33 and D46) flanking it (fig. 2-6). While this evidence for dating is not good, the strong association between Mousterian sites and fossil springs is likely to be more than coincidental.

In addition to the springs, there are other sediments which suggest a more moist climate during the Mousterian occupation than at present. About 500 m upstream from D35, along the western side of the valley, there is a cemented deposit of silt and very angular, fresh limestone scree, which is plastered against the chalky wall. This cemented scree contains a few Mousterian artifacts. These deposits grade eastward into the cemented gravels which, when traced northward, are found above the spring of Ein Aqev. This would indicate that the gravels above Ein Aqev are Mousterian in age; and they provide additional evidence for a more moist climate during that period.

All of this suggests that the conglomerate above Ein Aqev is broadly contemporaneous with the D35 terrace. This age assessment is much younger than has been previously postulated. Additional trenching is necessary, however, to document fully whether the terrace does, in fact, grade into the conglomerate, although the available evidence indicates that it should.

THE MOUSTERIAN SURFACE IN THE NAHAL AQEV

While the Mousterian terrace above Ein Aqev does not extend north of the spring, the

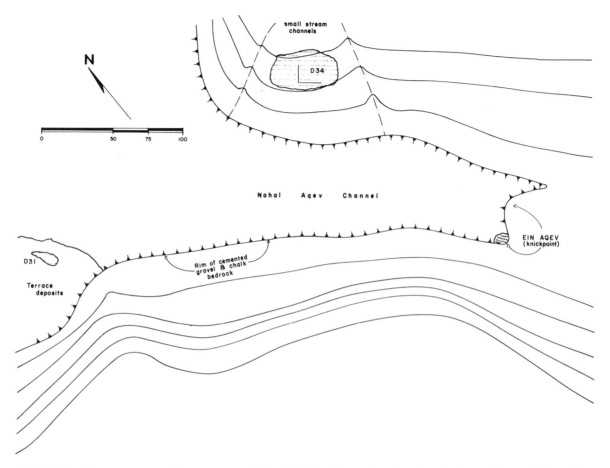

FIG. 2-15—Schematic map of box canyon within the Nahal Aqev, showing the relative positions of the spring
and Sites D31 and D34. Site D34 will be described in volume 2.

probable Mousterian surface itself, represented by the conglomerate, does occur in isolated patches along the whole length of the
nahal (fig. 2-4). This conglomerate decreases
in elevation from south to north and has a
gradient which one would expect for the
Nahal Aqev at the time the conglomerate was
being deposited (fig. 2-6). Beyond that, it is
possible to observe a generally broad, flat
surface on both sides of the valley, at the
same elevation as the conglomerate, which is
presently being dissected by tributaries of the
Nahal Aqev. It is possible, however, that this
surface is conditioned solely by a more resis-
tant underlying chalk layer, but this would
only account for the extant portions, not its
wide distribution. It is striking that all Mous-

terian sites in the Nahal Aqev occur on this
surface, while all younger sites occur on and
in more recent deposits which are lower than
the terrace and the conglomerate.

A major problem arises when an attempt is
made to trace this surface (and the conglomerate) beyond the Nahal Aqev, into the Nahal
Zin. Although one hill in the Nahal Zin Valley
(coord: 131.6/028.2) is capped with both a
conglomerate and a scattering of Mousterian
artifacts, it is not possible to relate this isolated outcrop directly either to others in the
Nahal Zin or to those of the Sde Boker Plain.
Thus, what the Mousterian surface was like in
the Nahal Zin and how it relates to the terrace
deposits south of Ein Aqev and to those at
Rosh Ein Mor could not be determined. There

are, however, terraces or surfaces within the Nahal Zin which are of similar elevation to the Mousterian surface at the mouth of the Nahal Aqev which may be of Mousterian age. Obviously, more work is needed in this area.

STRATIGRAPHY OF UPPER PALEOLITHIC SITES

EIN AQEV (D31)

Geographic and Geologic Setting

The site of Ein Aqev (D31) is located on the west side of the Nahal Aqev, just at the northern end of the box canyon which holds the spring of Ein Aqev (fig. 2-15). The site is situated in the upper portion of a terrace which begins at the northern end of the box canyon and extends northward to the Nahal Zin. This terrace is on a moderate northward slope, with the sediments of the immediate area of the site being slightly higher than those downstream (fig. 2-16). In the site area this terrace is heavily dissected by recent erosional channels, which have isolated the *in situ* portion of the site from the surrounding terrace deposits. At this point, the deposits are ca. 15 m thick, reaching an absolute elevation of ca. 390 meters. The *in situ* artifacts occur in the top part of the isolated deposit, the surface of which is now some 5 m below the surrounding terrace surface. Thus, the occupation of the site took place during the latter, but not the final phase of aggradation. Radiocarbon dates place the occupation between 16,000 B.C. and 15,000 B.C. (see Marks, this volume).

Excavations took place over the entire area which contained *in situ* materials; just under 60 sq meters. Owing to deflation and erosion, the surface of this area was already within the occupation zone. The intact occupation layer ranged from 60 cm thick on the southern edge of the site, to less than 20 cm on the more extensively eroded northern edge. The

excavations revealed a series of small, stratified encampments of relatively low artifact density. The artifacts were absolutely fresh with no edge crushing; bone and charcoal preservation was good. It appears from the archaeological materials that the aggradation of this terrace segment was rapid and of low energy, as no evidence was seen for disturbance of the cultural materials.

Ein Aqev (D31) Stratigraphy

The deposits in which D31 occurs are soft, massive, and lacking in bedding or other sedimentary structures. The sediments are uniform, as a whole, from bottom to top, which is a general characteristic of the whole terrace length. They consist primarily of light brown (10YR 7/4 dry; 10YR 6/4 wet) silts and clays with smaller percentages of limestone/chalk bedrock fragments. The fragments range in size from 8 to 20 mm, with the mode ca. 13 to 15 millimeters. They are generally flat, irregularly shaped, and mostly angular to subangular, although some rounded and subrounded fragments were found. These commonly appear to be weathered, which is probably due to their initial chalky composition.

In thin section, the sediments are quite similar to those of Rosh Ein Mor (D15) and display angular quartz grains, a similar heavy mineral assemblage, microfossils derived from bedrock, and calcareous silt and silt aggregates.

The Origin and Environment of Sediment Deposition

The sediments from D31 and the surrounding terrace most probably accumulated as a combined result of eolian deposition on the superjacent slopes and the later redeposition of this and other material by low energy surface runoff. The particular situation of this terrace segment, banked against the out-

FIG. 2-16—View of the western Upper Paleolithic terrace just north of the box canyon within the Nahal Aqev.
  Arrow indicates location of Site D31.

curving wall of the box canyon at the very head of the channel (where the valley walls are smallest), indicates that the sediments are of a very local origin. This unique location, the presence of very angular limestone fragments, and the absence of gravels all argue against any alluvial component in the sediments. The narrowness of the Nahal Aqev at this point also argues against any lateral facies changes such as those found at Rosh Ein Mor (D15).

It should be noted, however, that in most other locations the northern continuation of this terrace consists principally of gravelly deposits, which are clearly of alluvial origin. The sediments immediately surrounding and incorporating the site of Ein Aqev (D31) and the gravelly alluvial counterparts downstream indicate that, over a considerable area, deposition was going on at least 18,000 to 17,000 years ago and, given the stratigraphic position of the site within the sediments, probably earlier. Subsequent to this aggradation, these deposits were eroded by the Nahal Aqev. It is obvious that during the period of aggradation more sediment was being deposited (whether by eolian, colluvial, or alluvial processes) than could be removed by the Nahal Aqev. Whether this was due to increased or decreased precipitation, or a change in the base level, cannot be determined solely with the stratigraphic data at hand. What is clear, however, is that the upper portion of the terrace at the site of Ein Aqev (D31) rapidly aggraded and is now in the process of rapid erosion.

EIN AQEV EAST (D34)[7]

Geographic and Geologic Setting

The site of Ein Aqev East (D34), like that of Ein Aqev (D31), is located in reasonable proximity to the spring of Ein Aqev. Of all the sites within the Nahal Aqev, however, only this one is situated on the eastern side of the valley, 3 m above the conglomerate, at 403 m elevation, and 140 m downstream from the spring (fig. 2-15). It is situated, therefore, above the eastern edge of the box canyon, 25 m above the nahal floor, on a gentle westward slope between the box canyon and the steep cliffs of the nahal valley. The site itself covers an area of 200 sq m, between two small westward flowing rivulets. These are among many which flow off the east wall of the Aqev Valley and have dissected the westward sloping colluvial cover which drapes the valley wall.

When located, the site had undergone only slight deflation along the edge of the box canyon, although considerable recently arrived scree was present over the whole site surface, as is the case all along this portion of the eastern valley slope.

Ein Aqev East (D34) Stratigraphy

The stratigraphy of the site is divided into three distinct lithologic layers (fig. 2-17), which have been exposed by excavation to a depth of 65 centimeters. The stratigraphy of these layers, from top to bottom, is described below.

"Top Brown" Layer

This layer is considerably different from those underlying it. It consists of brown (10YR 6/6 dry; 10YR 5/6 wet), very soft, powdery silty sediments which very much resemble those of Site Ein Aqev (D31). They are relatively abundant in quartz grains (ca. 15%), calcareous silt and silt aggregates, fossil fragments, and heavy minerals. In addition, they contain many very flat and angular fragments from the nearby bedrock, similar to those which are presently on the surface and are now being carried down the slopes of the valley. The amount of this limestone scree increases upslope and, at the eastern limits of the excavated area, constitute a considerable portion of the sediment. The sediments of this layer are uniformly 15 to 20 cm thick and unbedded; the contact with the lower layer is sharp, although undulating. Some isolated patches of gypsum crystals are found, particularly near the bottom of the layer, but these are much less abundant than in the lower layers. Large numbers of artifacts were recovered from the lower portions of this deposit. While fresh, with sharp uncrushed edges, all have a whitish patination and many are thermally fractured. While no faunal remains were recovered, thin sections showed some microscopic faunal fragments which were heavily corroded and surrounded with calcareous silt.

"Speckled White" Layer

This layer consists primarily of dry, moderately soft, very light brown (10YR 7/4 dry; 10YR 5/6 wet) silt-sized sediments with lesser amounts of angular limestone fragments, similar to those to be described from the bottom layer. In thin section, and in order of decreasing abundance can be seen euhedral gypsum crystals (the major part of the sediment), aggregates of calcareous silt (with quartz), heavy minerals, and foram tests. The contact with the underlying layer is gradual, although distinct, and has an irregular surface. This middle layer varies in thickness from 20 cm to places where it is not at all present, particularly in the eastern portion of the site. In a number of localities fire pits were found beginning at the top of this layer, with only one intruding into the lowest layer. Unfortunately, no charcoal was recovered, although each fire pit contained burned earth. Artifacts are particularly numerous and their condition is fully comparable to those in the top layer.

"Hard White" Layer

This is the thickest of the layers, with an exposed

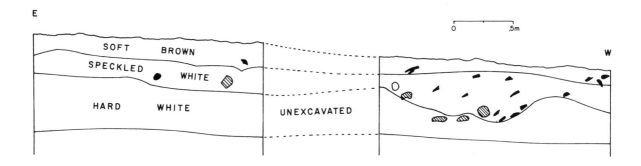

FIG. 2-17—Schematic profile of excavations at Site Ein Aqev East (D34). *Black symbols* indicate artifacts, *striped areas* are natural cobbles.

thickness of between 20 and 30 cm, and consists of an unbedded, very dry, very hard, whitish (10YR 8/4 dry; 10YR 2.5Y 7/4 wet) chalky sediment, the composition of which is difficult to determine megascopically. In thin section, however, it is seen to consist primarily of angular casts of fossiliferous limestone bedrock, 2 to 6 mm in diameter (mode, ca. 3 mm), and more rounded aggregates of euhedral gypsum crystals. The remainder, and minority, of the sediment is generally fine grained and is composed of many individual foram skeletons, quartz grains, very small amounts of heavy minerals (epidote, tourmaline, staurolite, and hornblende), and calcareous silts and silt aggregates. In addition to these fine-grained sediments, this layer contains some very angular and flat pieces of chalky limestone which increase in number upslope, to the east. Very few artifacts were found within this layer, but many were recovered at the contact with the layer above and seem to belong to the latter.

Origin and Environment of Sediment Deposition

As noted above, the top layer is quite similar to the sediments from the site of Ein Aqev (D31). At Ein Aqev most of the sediments were probably reworked eolian deposits washed downhill by runoff. A similar origin seems probable here: eolian, fine-grained sediments which were deposited on the nearby slopes and washed down toward the nahal bottom. Such colluvial deposition is supported by the presence of angular rock fragments, similar to those on the surface today, and by the fact that the number of these fragments increases markedly upslope. The very sharp contact between this "Top Brown" layer and the underlying, harder and less quartz-rich sediments of the "Speckled White" layer also suggests that the upper sediments were deposited rather quickly, over a moderately coherent surface, as no mixing of the sediments is apparent. It furthermore indicates that there was a period of stabilization which occurred between the deposition of the "Speckled White" layer and that of the "Top Brown." Given the extreme unevenness of the "Speckled White" layer and even its absence in small patches, it is most probable that some deflation did, in fact, take place.

The sediments of the lower two layers seem to represent accumulation of precipitated gypsum below a surface which has now been removed. A good source for the gypsum is eolian silt derived from nearby gypsiferous outcrops. Such a source and mechanism of gypsum formation has recently been reported from Tunisia (Page, 1972). Support for subsurface gypsum accumulation by percolation comes from the fact that the contact between the lower two layers is gradational, suggesting capillary movement upward, and that the contact with the top layer is sharp, which implies a period of deflation and/or nondeposition.

The amount of time represented by the unconformity cannot be determined, since it was not possible to date any of the layers. It must be noted, however, that while distinct artifact concentrations appear to be present in each of the top two layers, at the moment there does not appear to be any significant typological or technological difference between the two stratigraphic samples. Thus, the time of the unconformity cannot be very great.

Typologically, this assemblage may be slightly earlier *or* later than that from Ein Aqev, which has been dated between 16,000 B.C. and 15,000 B.C. The geological evidence at this time only permits the conclusion that some time *around* 16,000 B.C. to 15,000 B.C. the sediments at Ein Aqev East (D34) were exposed and subjected to a period of gypsum precipitation at depth. Subsequent to this, the surface was stabilized and slightly deflated and then rapidly covered by the deposition of the "Top Brown" layer.

Two additional points are worth noting. First, no such gypsum deposit was found in the sediments at the site of Ein Aqev (D31). The reason for this is not wholly clear, although it perhaps relates to its special location. Second, the sediments at Ein Aqev East (D34) and the adjacent hillslope do not take on any distinct terrace-like form, such as that found at the other sites, particularly at Ein Aqev (D31) which is not of *radically* different age. This is also perhaps related to the fact that Ein Aqev East (D34) is located above the box canyon of Ein Aqev, where the only erosional effects would be those coming off the slopes in a westerly direction, perpendicular to the channel of the Nahal Aqev, some 25 m below the hillslope. Some deflation has taken place, however, which might have altered an original terrace-like form.

DISCUSSION AND CONCLUSIONS

The description of the Upper Pleistocene geology of the Avdat/Aqev area presented above clearly shows the presence of two terrace systems: one datable to the Mousterian occupation and the other datable to the late Upper Paleolithic (ca. 20,000 B.P. to 17,000 B.P.).

The presence of a Mousterian terrace and associated land surface well above the present floors of the Nahals Avdat and Aqev indicates that considerable erosion and back-cutting has taken place since that time. The down-cutting within the lower Nahal Aqev near the Nahal Zin appears to be on the order of 50 m, while the back-cutting within the Nahal Mor is about 600 meters. Moreover, since the erosion of the Mousterian terrace and conglomerate, the Nahal Aqev underwent a period of aggradation during the Upper Paleolithic, and then another period of degradation in post Upper Paleolithic times. Thus, within the Nahal Aqev there is undeniable evidence for two periods of deposition separated by a period of erosion and followed by another period of erosion.

Determination of the precise causes of these alluvial, depositional and erosional periods within this semiarid zone is a complex problem (Flint, 1971), as universally valid rules are nonexistent (Leopold et al., 1964). Nevertheless, most geologists and geomorphologists would agree that in general the two major factors which are responsible for these processes are base level change and climatic change. Each will be considered here.

Base level control, if any, would have been exerted by the Dead Sea and the tectonics of its graben. This possibility seems quite unlikely, however, because the Avdat/Aqev area is approximately 50 km west of the graben and is sufficiently upstream from it so as not to be affected by tectonic movements or changes in the level of the Dead Sea. Vita-Finzi (1969) reached the same conclusion in his studies of alluvial deposits in Jordan, which are even closer to the Dead Sea than those now under study. This argument is particularly strong for the terrace sediments at Rosh Ein Mor (D15), situated on the elevated Eocene plateau, which forms a temporary base level of its own and is far removed from any possible effects of the graben. In addition, the work of Neev and Emery (1967) provides no indication of any repeated up-and-down movements which would have been necessary to produce the repeated sequence of deposition and erosion found in the Avdat/Aqev area.

Thus, it appears that the terrace sequence found in the Avdat/Aqev area is the result of climatic changes and not those of base level. Given this, the question then becomes, Does deposition represent wetter conditions and erosion, drier ones, or vice versa? As pointed out by Flint (1971), workers have applied both schemes to solve particular problems, and in the area under investigation, the solution is not obvious.

The most significant data which bear on this problem come from the spring deposits, the cemented scree, and wadi conglomerate of Mousterian age found in the upper portion of the Nahal Aqev, near Site D35.[8] These, especially the two springs near D35, point to wetter conditions during the Mousterian, as they are not operating under the present climatic regime. Whether these wetter conditions represented an increase in total annual precipitation or simply a more even distribution of rainfall throughout the year cannot be determined. Both could have resulted in the increased production and downslope movement of material within the Aqev Valley. Vita-Finzi's argument (1964), however, of a relative increase in convective vs. cyclonic precipitation does not seem applicable here, for it would not result in an increased supply of water necessary to bring about flow in the springs.

Evidence of a wetter climate during the formation of the Mousterian terrace receives support from two additional lines of evidence. First, under present climatic conditions this area is undergoing erosion. By analogy, similar dry conditions in the past should have produced the same effect, while moist conditions should have led to deposition.

Second, if the data from Langbein and Schumm (1958), who related sediment yield to mean annual precipitation, are extrapolated, a two-fold increase in effective precipitation (ca. from 75 to 150 mm) could theoretically produce about a three-fold increase in sediment yield. Keeping in mind the many assumptions and possible sources of error in their data and the present extrapolation from it, it still suggests that an increase in annual precipitation would result in an increase in sediment production. As they point out, above 250 mm of effective precipitation vegetative growth increases to the point where it begins to retard sediment yield. It seems probable, however, that the Avdat/Aqev area never experienced that critical amount of rainfall during the Upper Pleistocene, as the presence of gypsum at depth in most sections indicates a precipitation of less than 300 mm, a point above which gypsum does not accumulate in soils (A. Amiel, personal communication).

Unfortunately, there is no other stratigraphic evidence which allows inferences about the climatic factors responsible for the erosion-deposition-erosion which followed the deposition of the Mousterian terrace. By extending the same reasoning used above, however, it is possible to suggest that following the deposition of the D35 terrace, the climate became drier (which resulted in erosion), then wetter (which correlates with the deposition of the Upper Paleolithic terrace), and then came a final period of drier climate comparable to that prevailing today (table 2-1).

Obviously, more detailed and extensive work is needed in the Avdat/Aqev area in order to evaluate these climatic interpretations. Certainly, additional evidence will come from pollen analysis now in progress (see Horowitz,

TABLE 2-1
Tentative Correlation between
Geological Sequence and Climate

Age	Geological Occurrence	Climate
Present	Erosion	Dry
Upper Paleolithic	Deposition	Wetter
Late Mousterian	Erosion	Dry ?
Mousterian	Deposition	Wet
	Erosion	?

this volume), but considerably more geological fieldwork would be desirable.

ACKNOWLEDGMENTS

I would like to thank the Departments of Geography and Geology of the Hebrew University for the use of their laboratory facilities during the course of this research. Drs. O. Bar-Yosef and J. Phillips offered helpful suggestions.

NOTES

[1] The relationship between the sediments in the upper terrace and the well-cemented conglomerate lining the nahal floor near Ein Aqev will be discussed later.

[2] A distinction should be made between the terrace as a geomorphic feature and the terrace as an accumulation of sediment. It is obvious that the sediments making up the terrace must be deposited prior to the erosion which produces their shape. Therefore, any terrace deposit is older than the geomorphic feature itself. The difference in age between them, however, may be variable.

[3] All color determinations were performed on the bulk sample in daylight.

[4] Size analyses, using settling tube and pipette methods, were performed on most of the samples from Rosh Ein Mor (D15) and on the late Upper Paleolithic site of Ein Aqev East (D34). The results, however, are not reported here as they are considered to be of very limited and even doubtful value for several reasons. First, all samples contain secondary calcite and gypsum, the removal of which by acidification would interfere with the analyses. Moreover, if calcite and gypsum were not removed, then, being relatively fragile crystalline aggregates, they would break apart during sample preparation and thereby give an inaccurate picture of the size distribution. Second, many of the detrital fragments in the samples are composed of weathered limestone fragments and cemented aggregates which, likewise, would disintegrate during sample preparation.

Instead, the sediments were studied by means of petrographic thin sections. These were prepared from sample splits cemented with epoxide resin and then cut and sectioned. The advantage of this procedure is that the samples convey, at a glance, much information relating to texture and composition, without destroying or modifying the size distribution.

[5] The author is well aware of the capture of the NS Zin by the EW Zin. It is felt, however, that a discussion of this problem is well beyond the scope and intent of this report.

[6] A major trench was excavated during the summer of 1974. A report on the results of this excavation will appear in the second volume.

[7] The archaeological report for D34 will appear in the second volume. For a preliminary report, see Marks and Ferring, in press.

[8] It is assumed in the discussion that the Mousterian sites of Rosh Ein Mor (D15) and D35 are roughly contemporaneous. Since paleoclimatic criteria are lacking from Rosh Ein Mor, any inferences made for D35 apply equally to Rosh Ein Mor.

BIBLIOGRAPHY

BENTOR, Y. K., and VROMAN, A., 1960. *The Geological Map of Israel Sheet 16, Mt. Sdom*. Jerusalem: The Geological Survey of Israel.

BRAUN, M., 1967. *Type Sections of the Avdat Group, Eocene Formations in the Negev*. Jerusalem: The Geological Survey of Israel, Stratigraphic Section 4.

FLINT, R. F., 1971. *Glacial and Quaternary Geology*. New York: Wiley.

GARFUNKEL, Z., and HOROWITZ, A., 1966. "The Upper Tertiary and Quaternary Morphology of the Negev, Israel." *Israel Journal of Earth Sciences* 15(3):101-17.

GINZBOURG, D., and YAALON, D. H., 1963. "Petrography and Origin of the Loess in the Beer Sheva Basin." *Israel Journal of Earth Sciences* 12(2)(Proceedings):68-70.

LANGBEIN, W. B., and SCHUMM, S. A., 1958. "Yield of Sediment in Relation to Mean Annual Precipitation." *Transactions American Geophysical Union* 39(6):1076-84.

LEOPOLD, L. B.; WOLMAN, M. G.; and MILLER, J. P., 1964. *Fluvial Processes in Geomorphology*. San Francisco: W. H. Freeman.

MARKS, A. E., and FERRING, C. R., in press. "Upper Paleolithic Occupation near Avdat, Central Negev, Israel: An Interim Report." *Eretz Israel* 13.

NEEV, D., and EMERY, K. O., 1967. "The Dead Sea." *Bulletin of the Geological Survey of Israel* 41:1-147.

PAGE, W. D., 1972. "The Paleoclimatic Significance of Gypsum Soils, Southern Tunisia," p. 620. *Abstracts of the Geological Society of America, 1972 Meeting, Minneapolis*.

PICARD, L., 1951. "Geomorphogeny of Israel, I: The Negev." *Bulletin of the Research Council of Israel* 1(1-2).

VITA-FINZI, C., 1964. "Observations of the Late Quaternary of Jordan." *Palestine Exploration Quarterly* 96:19-33.

————, 1969. *The Mediterranean Valleys, Geological Changes in Historical Times*. Cambridge: At the University Press.

LATE QUATERNARY PALEOENVIRONMENTS OF PREHISTORIC SETTLEMENTS IN THE AVDAT/AQEV AREA

Aharon Horowitz

Institute of Archaeology, Tel-Aviv University

INTRODUCTION

The paleoecology of the Negev has received little attention, and no studies directly connected with the subject are available, although some ideas concerning past climates and vegetations have been suggested (Danin, 1970, 1972; Danin and Orshan, 1970). They distinguished Mediterranean flora within the present desert vegetation of the Negev and considered them to be relics of a former, Mediterranean vegetation that covered parts of the Negev which are now desert. Also, paleoclimatic data for the Dead Sea area show that a much more humid climate prevailed during the Würm than that which pertains today (Neev and Emery, 1967). This was indicated through geochemical investigations of Late Pleistocene deposits of the Dead Sea, and is in accord with the results of palynological studies in the northern and western parts of Israel (Horowitz, 1971, 1973).

The pollen diagrams from those current Mediterranean areas of Israel show that the Würm may be divided into three major humid phases, named Würm I, II, and III, separated by interstadials. Würm I lasted approximately from 70,000-65,000 to 40,000-36,000 years ago, Würm II from 32,000 to 22,000 years ago, and Würm III from 18,000 to 11,500 years ago. The following Holocene period may be divided into a humid Preboreal, a dry Boreal, a warm and humid Atlantic, and relatively dry Subboreal and Subatlantic stages (Horowitz, 1971).

In recent times, but prior to the Israeli development of the Negev, which depends mainly upon water transported from the North, the area was inhabited only by a few pastoralist Bedouin, whose economy was strictly limited by the paucity of rainfall. While earlier in the Historic period the Negev was inhabited by farmers, they were able to occupy the area only by using extremely complicated water conservation methods, involving extensive stone constructions.

The recent discovery of widespread remains of prehistoric settlements from Mousterian through Neolithic (Marks, 1971), which were often geologically *in situ*, led to this palynological study, in order to try to determine the paleoclimates, vegetation, and environments during the periods of prehistoric occupation. The results of these studies form the basis of the present report.

MATERIALS AND METHODS

Samples were collected from sites discovered and excavated by Southern Methodist University between 1970 and 1972, around the upper reaches of the eastward-flowing section of the Nahal Zin, near Avdat, a Nabatean site situated on the central Negev road between Yoroham and Mitzpe Ramon. Locations of the sites are shown in Fig. 3-1, and locations of the samples within the excavated profiles may be found in Fig. 3-2, although no profiles are presented for the sites which had only surficial deposits.

Samples were collected from the profiles of two Mousterian sites (D15 and D35), from surficial deposits of three Upper Paleolithic sites (D22, D27A and D27B), from the profiles of two Late Upper Paleolithic sites (D31 and D34), from the profile of a Geometric

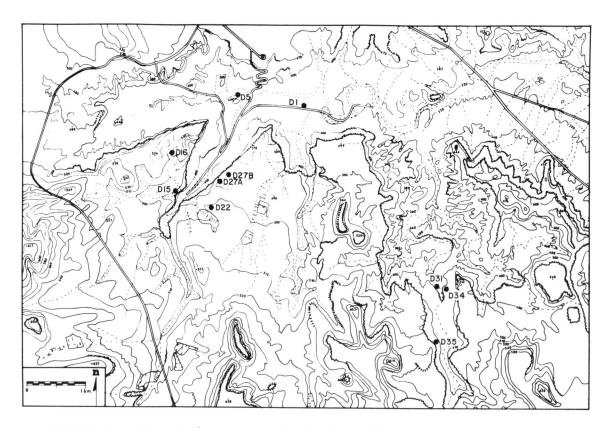

FIG. 3-1–Map of the Avdat/Aqev area, showing sites from which pollen samples were obtained.

Kebaran A site (D5), from the profile of a Natufian site (D16), and from the profile of a Pre-Pottery Neolithic B site (D1). The samples consisted of mainly windblown loess, sometimes containing small amounts of organic materials.

About 500 grams of sediment per sample were treated, utilizing a method developed by Dr. J. Schoenwetter, Arizona State University at Tempe (personal communication, 1971). The yield was surprisingly good for desert sediments: of a total of 34 samples, 11 yielded rich pollen spectra, 4 yielded poor spectra that could be used only to strengthen the better results obtained from other samples from the same sites, 13 samples yielded only organic material with no detectable pollen, while only 3 samples did not yield any material worth mounting.

The residue was mounted on slides with glycerine jelly, and counts were made with

the identifications based upon comparisons with a reference collection. The counts and percentages of the pollen spectra for these prehistoric sites are presented in Tables 3-1 and 3-2, with the percentages calculated on the basis of the total number of counted pollen in a sample equalling 100 percent.

On the basis of these samples two technical conclusions are indicated for the preparation and collection of samples from prehistoric sites. Sediments that are rich in organic material and are gray to black in color should be avoided, since the organic residue masks any pollen which might be present in the sample. Oxidation to various degrees and acetolysis of these samples did not produce usable results. The second point concerns oxidation of the pollen in the sediments during the period of deposition: it was found that samples collected from strata which yielded pollen spectra indicating a humid climate were mostly

TABLE 3-1

Pollen Counts for Prehistoric Sites in the Avdat/Aqev Area

Site	Sample	Culture & Radiocarbon Dates	Arboreal Pollen							Non-arboreal Pollen														Cereals TOTAL
			Quercus	Olea	Amygdalus	Pinus	Pistacia	Tamarix	Other	Gramineae & Cyperaceae	Chenopodiaceae	Compositae	Umbelliferae	Artemisia	Plantago	Liliaceae	Cruciferae	Papilionaceae	Ephedra	Typha	Labiatae	Capparis	Scabiosa	
Recent	Surface			2					Retama 1	20	81		1											105
D1	20-25 cm	PPN"B" 8,500 B.P.		4	1	1	1			19	18	25	1										2	78
D16	10-15 cm	NATUFIAN ca. 11,000 B.P.	6	6	2	1	1		Acacia 1	23	127	44	1	10											224
	15-20 cm		4	4	1	1	4	1	Juniperus 1	26	82	20		16									4	4	169
	30-40 cm						1			9	16	2		1											29
D31	n.d.	LATE UPPER PALEOLITHIC ca. 17,500 B.P.			1				Acacia 1	15	19	7				2									45
	10-16 cm			1				1		17		1			1		16								35
	60-65 cm									6	8	2			3										16
D34	15-20 cm		4				1	25		23	5	6				1									65
D22	ca. 10 cm	UPPER PALEOLITHIC	14	5	1	1	3			18	33	9	3	3			2	4				6		103
D27A	ca. 10 cm		15	1	1	1			Juniperus 1	25	61	18	1	1				4	2	1		3		134
D27B	ca. 10 cm		7	3	1					32	32	19				1					1			95
D15	70-75 cm	MOUSTERIAN <50,000 B.P.	2	2						11	6								1					20
D35	E1,70-77 cm		4					2		10	16		1	2										36
	W1,1.50 cm—1.60 m		22	25	3	5	5	30	Zyziphus 2	43	43	33	1	9			15		6		1	10		253
	n.d.		1	1		3				7	9	26												47

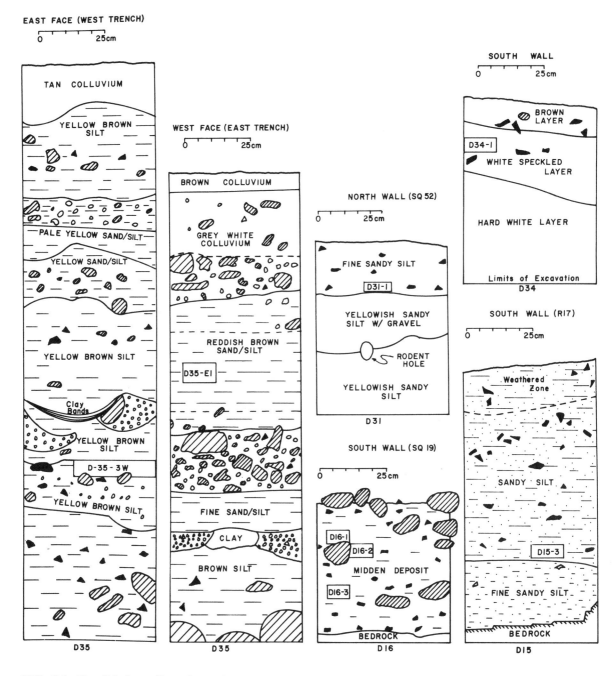

FIG. 3-2—Simplified profiles of sites from which pollen samples were obtained. For greater detail see Goldberg, this volume.

oxidized. Therefore, it was necessary to analyze more than ten Mousterian samples from sites Rosh Ein Mor (D15) and D35 before a good spectrum was obtained, but when a good sample was finally found it yielded more than 500 pollen grains per slide. It appears that higher humidity in times of sediment deposition helps the oxidation processes, probably creating favorable environments for the development of bacteria.

TABLE 3-2

Pollen Counts as Percents for Prehistoric Sites in the Avdat/Aqev Area

Site	Sample	Culture & Radiocarbon Dates	Arboreal Pollen							Non-arboreal Pollen																
			Quercus	Olea	Amygdalus	Pinus	Pistacia	Tamarix	Other	Gramineae & Cyperaceae	Chenopodiaceae	Compositae	Umbelliferae	Artemisia	Plantago	Liliaceae	Cruciferae	Papilionaceae	Ephedra	Typha	Labiatae	Capparis	Scabiosa	Cereals	TOTAL
Recent	Surface			2					1	19	77		1													100
D1	20-25 cm	PPN "B" 8,500 B.P.	3	5	1	1	1			24	23	32												3	9	99
D16	10-15 cm	NATUFIAN ca. 11,000 B.P.	3	3	1	.5	.5		1	10	57	20	.5	4	.5								2			101
	15-20 cm		2	2		.5	2	.5		15	49	12		9	2									2		98
	30-40 cm						3		2	31	55	7		3												99
D31	n.d.	LATE UPPER PALEOLITHIC ca. 17,500 B.P.		3	2				2	33	42	16														99
	10-16 cm									49		3				4	46								101
	60-65 cm									38	50	12													100
D34	15-20 cm	UPPER PALEOLITHIC	6					39	1	35	8	9				2									100
D22	ca. 10 cm		14	5	1	1	3			17	32	9	3	3			2	4				6			101
D27A	ca. 10 cm		11	3	1	1		1		19	45	13		1				3	2	1		2			101
D27B	ca. 10 cm		7	3	1				1	34	34	20				1									100
D15	70-75 cm	MOUSTERIAN <50,000 B.P.		10						55	30								5							100
D35	E1,70-77 cm		11	10				6	1	28	45	3	3	5											101
	W1,1.50 cm—1.60 m		9	2	1	2	2	12		17	17	13	.5	4			6		2		.5	4			101
	n.d.		2	2		6				15	19	55													99

THE RECENT ENVIRONMENT

The area around Avdat comprises a morphological and structural plateau built of Eocene limestones and chalks. The Avdat Plateau is a flat surface, separating the northern Negev anticlines from the Ramon elevated structure to the south. The whole area is presently drained to the Dead Sea by the Nahal Zin (a river that is dry for most of the year, and intermittently flows with strong floods), which breaches the plateau with a number of steep, deep canyons. A number of springs appear on the cliffs of these canyons, but their outflow is very weak, disappearing in the valley floor after a few hundred meters. These are stratigraphic springs, always flowing on the contact between the Eocene chalks and the underlying Taqiye shales.

The area is presently subject to erosion of two types: torrential floods which cause further deepening of the steeply dipping canyon cliffs and backward propagation of the valley heads, and strong winds which cause deflation of the loess accumulations on the plateau. No present deposition of any kind of sediment was observed in the area, except for spring travertines.

The Northern and Central Negev comprise the northern boundary of the subtropical planetary desert. The seasonal climatic variations correspond to those of the northern and western Mediterranean region; namely, a long, warm and dry summer with no rain at all and a short, cool winter during which rainfall is rather limited (see Munday, this volume, for a detailed discussion of the present climatic conditions).

The vegetation of the Northern and Central Negev has been discussed in detail by Danin (1970) and reviewed for the Avdat/Aqev area by Munday (this volume). Most of the vegetation is restricted to the nahal floors and around the rare springs, comprising Chenopodiaceae, of which *Atriplex* is the most abundant, Gramineae and Cyperaceae, and less frequent amounts of Compositae and others. An interesting group of plants comprising trees such as *Pistacia atlantica*, *Amygdalus korschinskii*, *Rhamnus disperma* and *Rhus tripartita*, together with some other shrubs and herbs is mentioned in Danin (1972) and Danin and Orshan (1970) as being relics of a former Mediterranean vegetation in the area.

The mean Recent pollen spectrum of the Avdat/Sde Boker area is the following:

Chenopodiaceae—77%
Gramineae and Cyperaceae—19%
Umbelliferae—1%
Retama roetam—1%
Olea europaea—2%

This pollen spectrum, which is dominated by the Chenopodiaceae, Gramineae, and Cyperaceae, is typical of the desert environment. No naturally occurring arboreal pollen is recorded, and the few isolated trees that grow in the area did not contribute to the spectrum. The closest stands of trees that might have contributed pollen are on the Hebron Mountains, ca. 100 km to the north, but no influence of those was observed. In addition, the influence of trees, such as olive, that were planted in the Sde Boker area can be seen only in samples collected close to the settlement. Samples that were collected south of the Nahal Zin contained only 1-2% of olive grains.

THE LATE QUATERNARY ENVIRONMENTS

THE MOUSTERIAN

Most of the samples that were collected from Mousterian sites yielded no pollen, probably due to oxidation of the grains. Four samples yielded positive results, of which the sample collected from a depth of 1.50 m at Site D35 was especially rich. More than 250 pollen grains were determined and counted in this sample:

ARBOREAL POLLEN:
(total 25%, excluding *Tamarix*)
Quercus calliprinos–9%
Olea europaea–10%
Amygdalus sp.–1%
Pinus halepensis–2%
Pistacia sp.–2%
Zyziphus (or *Rhamnus*)–1%
Tamarix sp.–12%

NON-ARBOREAL POLLEN:
Gramineae and Cyperaceae–17%
Chenopodiaceae–17%
Compositae–13%
Cruciferae–6%
Artemisia–4%
Others–8%

This is a rather surprising pollen spectrum for the Central Negev when compared with the Recent spectrum. It comprises 25% arboreal pollen, not including the *Tamarix*, which is part of the river bank vegetation and does not comprise part of the regional vegetation. The arboreal spectrum is shared between *Quercus* and *Olea* as the major elements, while pollen of those trees mentioned previously as relics of a Mediterranean vegetation also occur. This pollen spectrum resembles that recently obtained from the northern parts of Israel, representing a well-developed Mediterranean maquis of mixed oaks, olives, pistachio, pines, and some other trees. The *Amygdalus*, *Pistacia*, and *Zyziphus* should be considered as comprising a considerable part of the maquis vegetation, since they are always underrepresented in pollen spectra because of poor pollen production, in comparison with oaks and olives (Horowitz, 1971).

The paleoclimate and vegetation of the Central Negev during this Mousterian period were totally different from those of the present day. It seems that the climatic belts were ca. 200-250 km south of their present position, and the desert border was well to the south of the Avdat area. The same shift is seen in the analysis of sediments containing Mousterian artifacts from the north of the country, in the cave of Et-Tabun in Mount Carmel (Horowitz, 1973). The pollen spectra for the Mousterian sediments, Beds C and D, indicate a vegetation that is comparable to that present today in northern Lebanon. The same picture was obtained from the Hula Valley borehole for the Würm I phase, and it seems that during this time Mousterian people occupied Israel. Chronologically, this period may be placed at 70,000-40,000 years ago (Siedner and Horowitz, forthcoming; Horowitz, 1974), although the Negev sites may be dated to more than 50,000 years ago (Crew, this volume).

The Mediterranean climate and rich vegetation of the Central Negev during the Mousterian occupation also resulted in the trapping and deposition of loess sediments. Presently, loess is accumulated only in areas where the annual precipitation is higher than 200 mm (Yaalon and Ganor, 1967), which is probably due to the vegetation cover that helps the trapping of the windblown dust. Without such a vegetation cover, as is presently the situation in the Central Negev, the loess is deflated by strong wind erosion.

The higher humidity and availability of water also raised the groundwater table of the Central Negev, resulting in stronger spring activity. Indeed, some fossil spring deposits containing Mousterian artifacts are present in the area (Goldberg, this volume).

The paleoenvironmental conditions undoubtedly favored hominid occupation and settlement of the Central Negev. The combination of rich flora, and most probably also rich fauna, the somewhat cooler climate, and the less acute diurnal differences of temperature and humidity, all created a most suitable environment.

THE UPPER PALEOLITHIC

Samples were collected and analyzed from three sites that yielded assemblages of Upper

Paleolithic type: D22, D27A, and D27B. The yield was much better than that of the Mousterian samples, but the samples themselves are not so rich, and ca. 100 pollen could be determined and counted in each. The mean spectrum is as follows:

ARBOREAL POLLEN: (total 16.3%)
Quercus calliprinos–10%
Olea europaea–3%
Amygdalus sp.–1%
Pinus halepensis–1%
(and occasional) *Pistacia, Tamarix*
    and *Juniperus*

NON-ARBOREAL POLLEN:
Gramineae and Cyperaceae–25%
Chenopodiaceae–35%
Compositae–15%
Others–3-5%

Compared to the mean Mousterian spectrum, the share of the arboreal pollen in the Upper Paleolithic is lower because of a great drop in the occurrence of *Olea europaea*. The remainder of the arboreal spectrum, and especially the *Quercus calliprinos*, still maintains about the same values as for the Mousterian. Once more, the pollen spectrum for the Upper Paleolithic is markedly different from the Recent spectrum.

It seems that the Upper Paleolithic spectrum indicates a cool Mediterranean climate, somewhat cooler and drier than that of Mousterian occupation. This is indicated by the decrease in the proportional occurrence of olives, which tend to grow in warmer and somewhat more humid conditions than those of the present-day Mediterranean climate of Central and Northern Israel. The oaks, on the other hand, can better resist drier climate, and they still grow naturally as far south as Judea (compare Horowitz, 1971).

The non-arboreal pollen spectrum does not differ essentially from that of the Mousterian. The high Compositae values indicate a higher humidity when compared to the Recent spectrum, in which no pollen of this group is re-

corded (although some Compositae do grow in the area). The Compositae also react in the same way in response to higher humidity in the north of the country (Horowitz, 1971, 1973). The same is probably true for the higher percentages of the grasses and sedges, Gramineae and Cyperaceae, whose share within the non-arboreal spectrum is higher than at present.

Therefore, the paleoclimate and vegetation of the Central Negev during Upper Paleolithic times can be referred to as Mediterranean in nature, most probably resembling present-day northern Judea or Samaria. The climate belts, it seems, were about 100-150 km south of their present positions.

The same climatic and vegetational characteristics were observed in boreholes drilled in the Hula Valley, in northeastern Israel, for the Würm II phase, dated at about 32,000-22,000 years ago. It seems that these Upper Paleolithic pollen spectra might be stratigraphically and chronologically placed within this interval. Unfortunately, no radiocarbon dates are available for these sites as yet, since most of them have only surficial deposits, with no material suitable for absolute dating.

THE LATE UPPER PALEOLITHIC

This group is represented by two sites: D34 and D31. As it appears to be a period of relative climatic deterioration, the pollen spectra for each will be presented separately. While the relative chronology of the sites is not controlled firmly, it now appears that D34 may be somewhat older than D31, which is well dated radiometrically.

The pollen spectrum from D34 is relatively poor, 65 grains, but the pattern represented is not unrelated to the earlier Upper Paleolithic spectra. The D34 spectrum shows the following:

ARBOREAL POLLEN:
(total 7%, excluding *Tamarix*)
Quercus calliprinos–6%

Pistacia sp.–1%
Tamarix sp.–39%

NON-ARBOREAL POLLEN
Gramineae and Cyperaceae–35%
Chenopodiaceae–8%
Compositae–9%
Others–1%

Site D31 has been dated by four acceptable radiocarbon determinations to between 18,000 B.P. and 17,000 B.P. (Marks, this volume). The samples were relatively poor in pollen, the best yielding only 45 grains. The general picture can be outlined, however, since the three analyzed samples show similar characteristics. The mean pollen spectrum shows:

ARBOREAL POLLEN: (total 3%)
Olea europaea–1%
Amygdalus sp.–1%
Acacia sp.–1%

NON-ARBOREAL POLLEN
Gramineae and Cyperaceae–40%
Chenopodiaceae–28%
Compositae–10%
Cruciferae–16%
Other–3%

Compared with the Recent spectrum, both Late Upper Paleolithic spectra are richer in Compositae and arboreal pollen, although only a few of the latter occur. This indicates that the vegetation was probably somewhat richer than today, while the climate was more humid. During this period there appears to be a slight drying between the occupations of D34 and D31, seen in the drop in arboreal pollen, particularly *Quercus*, although it may have been only a minor change, as the level of Compositae remains constant.

The spectra, compared with the preceding Upper Paleolithic and Mousterian spectra, are much poorer, produced by a vegetation that might be compared with that presently in the northwestern Negev. Therefore, the Avdat area was mostly covered by herbs, with some

small stands of trees scattered here and there.

By comparing the pollen spectra of the Avdat area with that of the Hula Valley, and by relying on the radiocarbon dates, it may be determined that the Late Upper Paleolithic occupation of the Negev occurred during the onset of the Würm III wet phase. The better climatic conditions and the richer vegetation enabled settlement of the Central Negev, but it probably had to be much more strongly connected to permanent water sources, which remained only as springs. The paradise of the Mousterian and Upper Paleolithic occupations had ceased to exist.

THE EPIPALEOLITHIC

Prior to the Natufian occupation there is a significant temporal break of several millennia in the pollen record. Although a Geometric Kebaran A site (D5) occurred in the area, it produced no pollen, while earlier Kebaran sites were totally absent. Thus, from ca. 17,000 B.P. to the Natufian occupation at ca. 11,000 B.P. there are no palynological data.

The Natufian site of Rosh Zin (D16) produced excellent pollen spectra from two of three samples processed. The mean pollen spectrum of these samples shows:

ARBOREAL POLLEN:
(total 7%, excluding *Tamarix*)
Quercus calliprinos–2.5%
Olea europaea–2.5%
(rare occurrence of) *Pistacia* sp.,
    Amygdalus sp., *Pinus halepensis*,
    Acacia albida, and *Juniperus* sp.

NON-ARBOREAL POLLEN
Gramineae and Cyperaceae–14%
Chenopodiaceae–53%
Compositae–16%
Artemisia–6%
Others–4%

This spectrum indicates a rather humid climate necessary for maintaining the high Compositae percentage, as well as the indicated level of oaks. It is once more of Mediterranean type, although somewhat drier than during both the Mousterian and Upper Paleolithic occupations. It is clear, however, that it signifies a considerable climatic amelioration over the Late Upper Paleolithic at D31 and is comparable to the environment around the southern Judean Hills today.

THE PRE-POTTERY NEOLITHIC

Samples were collected and analyzed from the Pre-Pottery Neolithic B site (D1), which has radiocarbon dates averaging 8,600 B.P. (Servello, this volume). Stratigraphically, this site falls within the termination of the preboreal stage of the Holocene (Horowitz, 1971). Only one sample from the site yielded pollen, and this was not rich. The results, therefore, should be considered as only preliminary. The pollen spectrum is the following:

ARBOREAL POLLEN: (total 8%)
Olea europaea—5%
Amygdalus sp.—1%
Pinus halepensis—1%
Pistacia sp.—1%

NON-ARBOREAL POLLEN
Gramineae and Cyperaceae—24%
Gramineae, large—9%
Chenopodiaceae—23%
Compositae—32%
Scabiosa prolifera—3%

The large Gramineae pollen exceeded 60 microns in size and are considered to be derived from cereals (Faegri and Iversen, 1964). This seems reasonable as such pollen were not observed in any of the samples collected from older strata.

The pollen spectrum for the time of the Pre-Pottery Neolithic B settlement indicates vegetation and climate that can be compared with those of the northern Negev, around the present Beer Sheva. This is mainly based on the relatively high Compositae percentage.

The trees in the Avdat area most probably were present only as relics, although certainly more abundant than at present. The location of the site adjacent to the streambed of the Nahal Zin may well account for the level of arboreal pollen, since even today relic trees occur most frequently in the larger nahal bottoms (e.g., the Nahal Loz). *Amygdalus* and *Pistacia* are typical of such trees, which can still be found in the Central Negev (Danin, 1970). Pines, however, are not known presently in the area, and it is possible that the olive pollen were produced by trees that might have been cultivated by the Neolithic people. It must be pointed out, however, that there is no difference between wild and domestic olive tree pollen.

It is almost clear, though, that the Neolithic people cultivated cereals of some kind. Whether this cultivation took place within the Nahal Zin, however, is problematic, since even cereals carried to the site from another area could account for the cereal pollen.

CONCLUSIONS

It appears that prehistoric occupation of the Central Negev in Late Quaternary times was highly dependent upon the availability of suitable climatic conditions, which permitted the development of vegetation and, probably, the presence of a rich wildlife. Such suitable conditions are known for the Late Quaternary of Israel during the wet phases of the Würm Pluvials, somewhat in the Preboreal, and also during the Atlantic stage.

Given both the radiocarbon dates and the pollen evidence, it seems clear that the Mousterian occupation of the Central Negev took place during the Würm I Pluvial phase, when the Central Negev maintained a rich Mediterranean environment. Archaeologically, there is a break in the prehistoric record after this occupation which probably encompasses part of the Würm I/II Interpluvial, the period of late Mousterian occupation farther north. The

Avdat area was again occupied during the Upper Paleolithic for which time the presently available pollen indicates a reintroduction of a Mediterranean environment, but one somewhat less developed than during the Mousterian. This may be correlated with Würm II. By late Upper Paleolithic times, however, the environment had deteriorated to a steppic condition and sites are found in very close proximity to perennial springs. This period would seem to encompass parts of Würm II/III and early Würm III. Data are lacking from that point until the Natufian period at ca. 11,000 B.P., when the pollen again suggests a poor Mediterranean environment.

The climatic conditions during Pre-Pottery Neolithic B times were less favorable than during the Würm Pluvials, but somewhat better than at present. While the area was amenable to some habitation there still remains a question as to the nature of it, considering the presence of cereal pollen.

BIBLIOGRAPHY

DANIN, A., 1970. "A Phytosociological-Ecological Study of the Northern Negev of Israel." Ph.D. dissertation, Department of Botany, The Hebrew University. (In Hebrew, English summary).

————, 1972. "Mediterranean Elements in Rocks of the Negev and Sinai Deserts." *Notes from the Royal Botanical Garden* 31(3):437-40.

————, and ORSHAN, G., 1970. "Distribution of Indigenous Trees in the Northern Central Negev Highlands." *La Ya'aran* 20(4):115-19. (In Hebrew).

EVENARI, M.; SHANAN, L.; and TADMOR, N. H., 1968. *Runoff Farming in the Negev Desert of Israel.* Department of Botany, The Hebrew University.

FAEGRI, J., and IVERSEN, K., 1964. *Textbook of Modern Pollen Analysis.* Copenhagen: Munksgaard.

HOROWITZ, A., 1971. "Climatic and Vegetational Developments in Northeastern Israel during Upper Pleistocene–Holocene Times." *Pollen et Spores* 13(2):255-78.

————, 1973. "Preliminary Pollen Analysis of the Tabun Cave Sediments, Mount Carmel, Israel." In "New Excavations at the Tabun Cave, Mount Carmel, Israel, 1967-1972: A Preliminary Report," by Arthur J. Jelinek; William R. Farrand; Georg Haas; Aharon Horowitz; and Paul Goldberg. *Paleorient* 1(2):167-72.

————, 1974. "The Late Cenozoic Stratigraphy and Paleogeography of Israel." Institute of Archaeology, Tel Aviv University, 1-186.

KATZENELSON, Y., 1959. "The Climate of the Negev." *Teva VeAretz* 1:7- 8. (In Hebrew).

MARKS, A. E., 1971. "Settlement and Intrasite Variability in the Central Negev, Israel." *American Anthropologist* 73(5):1237-44.

NEEV, D., and EMERY, K. O., 1967. "The Dead Sea." *Bulletin of the Geological Survey of Israel* 41:1-147.

SHANAN, L.; EVENARI, M.; and TADMOR, N. H., 1967. "Rainfall Patterns in the Central Negev Desert." *Israel Exploration Journal* 17(3):163-84.

SIEDNER, G., and HOROWITZ, A., forthcoming. *Late Cenozoic Chronostratigraphy of Israel.*

YAALON, D. H., and GANOR, E., 1967. *Climatic Influence on Dust Transport in Israel.* The Meteorological Service, Beit Dagon, 8/5. (In Hebrew).

SOME LATE QUATERNARY FAUNAL REMAINS FROM THE AVDAT/AQEV AREA

Eiton Tchernov

The Hebrew University

INTRODUCTION

There has been a lengthy controversy over when and how the Levantine desert came into existence. Among the numerous studies and opinions published to date, very few have been based on paleontological evidence, as such material is very rare in the Near East. Actually, vertebrate remains have never been found before in the Israeli desert.

Although the remains described here are sometimes too limited to draw a complete picture of the desert's history during the Upper Pleistocene, some of the finds are important and permit preliminary suggestions on the nature of the old environments of the Israeli desert.

All the material reported here came from prehistoric sites in the Avdat/Aqev area on the northern edge of the High Negev, in the immediate area of the Nahal Zin, at elevations between 400 and 500 meters. As all sites in that area are open, preservation of bone is generally poor and most material is highly fragmentary and unidentifiable to specific level, although molluscs and land snails are well preserved.

VERTEBRATE REMAINS

The following are tentative lists, with some comments, of the vertebrate remains found at various sites. These are presented in chronological order from most recent to oldest.

Found on the fringe of their distributional range, *Dama* and *Bos* may have been extremely rare during Pre-Pottery times. Shortly thereafter, they apparently became extinct in the Negev, as a result of a severe increase in desiccation.

Nahal Divshon (D1)–Pre-Pottery Neolithic B

Mammalia
  Artiodactyla
    Bovidae
      Bos primigenius: one broken molar
      Capra ibex: a few phalanges, two fragments of mandibles, a maxillary fragment, and a few long bone fragments
      Gazella cf. *dorcus*: various post-cranial fragments, mostly foot bones
    Cervidae
      Dama dama mesopotamica: four horn core fragments (probably belonging to the same individual)

Rosh Zin (D16)–Natufian

Mammalia
  Artiodactyla
    Bovidae
      Capra ibex: phalanges, fragments of mandibles and molars, equaling a minimum of 7 individuals, as well as other post-cranial elements
      Gazella cf. *dorcus*: phalanges, fragments of mandibles and molars, equaling a minimum of 6 individuals, as well as other post-cranial elements
    Cervidae
      Dama dama mesopotamica: one distal metapodium and few long bone fragments in *Dama* size range
  Perissodactyla
    Equidae
      Equus hemionis (onager): tooth fragments

Rodenta
  Spalacidae
    Spalax ehrenbergi (mole rat): three molars and three humeri. These still occupy the Avdat area, but are never found south of the Nahal Zin
    Meriones sp. (?): one ulna, not mole rat, but size of jird

Reptilia
  Lacertilia
    Agamidae
      Agama stellio (hardun): five mandibles. These are widespread all over the country from typical Mediterranean landscape to the extreme arid, rocky zone of southern Sinai

Aves
    Struthio camelus (ostrich): numerous fragments of egg shell

Again, the presence of *Dama* should be noted, while all other forms are either currently present in the area, or were until recent times. In addition, a phalanx of a small carnivore (size range of *Verella*) was recovered, as well as two bird bones in the size range of a hawk.

Ein Aqev (D31)—Late Upper Paleolithic

Mammalia
  Artiodactyla
    Bovidae
      Capra ibex: seven phalanges and a few molars
      Gazella cf. *dorcus*: eight phalanges and a few molars
  Perissodactyla
    Equidae
      Equus hemionis (onager): two metapodials, two terminal phalanges, and one vertebra
  Lagomorpha
    Leporidae
      Lepus cf. *europaeus* (hare): three femur fragments

Reptilia
  Lacertilia
    Agamidae
      Agama stellio (hardun): one mandible fragment

Aves
    Struthio camelus (ostrich): a few egg shell fragments

Rosh Ein Mor (D15)—Levantine Mousterian

Mammalia
  Perissodactyla
    Equidae
      Equus hemionis (onager): eight fragments of metapodials and terminal phalanges, a few teeth, and three vertebrae fragments

Aves
    Struthio camelus (ostrich): a great number of egg shell fragments

COMMENTS

The faunal remains from the Mousterian of Avdat (D15) are too poor for any conclusion. However, open steppic landscape, or a savanna-like area was probably widespread enough to support large populations of onagers and ostriches. Ostriches were known to occur on the Negev Plateau and on the Syrian desert as late as the nineteenth century. It was only at the beginning of this century when the last of these birds were hunted and sold in local markets. Ostrich remains are known as well from the kurkar sandstones along the coastal plain of Israel, part of which is still under a typical Mediterranean climate.

The Late Upper Paleolithic of Site Ein Aqev (D31) is comparatively rich in vertebrate remains, but aside from the *Capra ibex*, which is a cliff dweller, all other megafauna is of steppe variety.

The megafauna from Site Rosh Zin (D16) is quite rich by comparison. Not only are the steppic forms present, but also *Dama*. These occurrences clearly indicate the existence of two different and contradictory habitats in close proximity. The presence of *Dama dama mesopotamica*, a park and wood dweller side by side with a typical savanna dweller—*Struthio camelus*—is quite astonishing from the biogeographical point of view. The remains of *Dama dama mesopotamica* in the Negev is the first paleontolgical evidence for wooded areas which were still sufficiently extended in that region to support a population of this large animal.

The Pre-Pottery Neolithic B site of Nahal Divshon (D1) is also rich in species, and possibly points to man's high skill and technique in hunting. *Dama dama mesopotamica* and *Bos primigenius* still survived in the Nahal Zin area and, thus, wooded areas were extant as late as this period. Relics of plants and animals which are characteristic of Mediterranean climates are still found in a few places in the Israeli and Sinai deserts, such as *Eliomys melanurus (Rodentia)*. The northward retreat of the desert belt in Israel, for a distance of 100 to 200 km, during post-Würmian times, is discussed by Tchernov (1968).

The climatic conditions which prevailed in the Avdat area, during the Natufian and Pre-Pottery Neolithic occupations, were environmentally rich enough to support such a typical wood-dwelling animal as *Dama dama mesopotamica*. However, steppic conditions predominated more or less throughout the Upper Pleistocene (Tchernov, 1968). On the basis of the faunal remains, it seems as if steppic conditions prevailed since Mousterian times, when *Equus hemionis* and *Struthio camelus* were present, although large patches of wooded areas existed as well (see table 1).

As of this time the faunal remains do not clearly point to severe climatic fluctuations throughout the periods in question, with intense desiccation taking place only in post-Neolithic times. More faunal remains are needed, however, before any sure conclusions may be drawn.

TERRESTRIAL SNAILS

Terrestrial snails had penetrated into sites during the sedimentation period, probably *at random* from the vicinity areas (table 4-2). The snails could have been brought in either by natural agencies, like water streams and wind, or by animals. Snails are an obligatory part of the Spinymice (*Acomys*) diet. Very much the same is true for migratory thrushes (*Turdinae*), which might have collected snails from the whole area. Random movements of

TABLE 4-1
Distribution of Large Vertebrates in the Central Negev,
from Mousterian to Recent Times

Species	Early Mousterian	Late Mousterian	Early Upper Paleolithic	Late Upper Paleolithic	Epi-paleolithic	Neolithic	Recent
Dama mesopotamica				? ————————		————————	
Bos primigenius					? ———	———	
Capra ibex			? ————————				————
Gazella cf. *dorcus*			? ————————				————
Equus hemionis	————	— — — —	? — — — — —	— — — —	————	— — ? — —	— —
Struthio camelus	————	— — — —	? — — — —	— — — —	————	— — ? —	————

the snails might have brought them into the sites. Or man himself could have been one of the agents, but this cannot be confirmed.

It seems as if the distribution of the dead snails within the sites (the thanatocoenosus) roughly represents the natural distribution in the near surroundings of the sites. Such distribution may indicate that man had no concern for or interest in collecting terrestrial snails. But if he had had some need for snails, there is no proof that he preferred a particular species.

TABLE 4-2
Occurrence of Terrestrial Snails
at Negev Sites

	D31	D5	D16	D1
Enidae				
Chondrula heptodon	1	3	89	
Petreus sp.	2		1	
Helicidae				
Levantina caesareana		1		1
Helicellidae				
Helicella (Xerocrassa) seetzeni	16		163	4*
Helicella erkeli	3		43	
Helicella sp.	12		37	
Obelus philamnia			15	
Sphincterochillidae				
Sphincterochila fimbriata	2		12	
Sphincterochila zonata	12	1	36	

*
This was a very common occurrence, but no systematic collection was made.

MARINE MOLLUSCS

A considerable number of marine molluscs were unearthed from the late Upper Paleolithic site of Ein Aqev (D31) and the Natufian site of Rosh Zin (D16). A majority of these molluscs consisted of *Dentalium* fragments,

probably used for the production of necklaces and other sorts of decoration (Bar-Yosef and Tchernov, 1967). The function of the other shells is not clear because, with a single exception (Henry, this volume), no marks or holes were left on the shells' surfaces. A few shells from Ein Aqev were covered with red ocher, suggesting a possible ritual function, but this is only speculative.

The shells found at these sites are listed below:

Rosh Zin (D16)—Natufian

Gastrodia
  Cypraea (Erosaria) turdus: One specimen, with the color pattern still preserved. Red Sea species
  Nassa gibberula: 12 specimens, Mediterranean species
  Columbella rustica: 3 specimens, Mediterranean species
  Columbella gibberula: 3 specimens, Mediterranean species

Bivalvia
  Glycimeris lividus: 3 specimens, Red Sea species
  Donax sp.: 1 specimen, Mediterranean species

Scaphopoda
  Dentalium vulgare: 2 specimens, Mediterranean species
  Dentalium elephantinum: 94 specimens, Red Sea species
  Dentalium dentale: 165 specimens, Mediterranean species
  Dentalium (indet.): 20 specimens

Ein Aqev (D31)—Late Upper Paleolithic

Gastropoda
  Nassa sp.: 1 specimen, Mediterranean species
  Nassa gibberula: 11 specimens, three of which were covered with ocher, Mediterranean species
  Mitrella scripta: 1 specimen, Mediterranean species

Scaphopoda
  Dentalium dentale: 4 specimens, Mediterranean
    species

Communication between the Red Sea, Mediterranean, and Negev communities existed since at least the late Upper Paleolithic, although at that early date only contact between the Mediterranean and the Negev can be confirmed. By Natufian times the widespread contacts can be confirmed by the plethora of both Red Sea and Mediterranean *Dentalium. Dentalium elephantinum* is a large Red Sea animal, while *Dentalium dentale* is much smaller in size and is restricted to the Mediterranean Sea. The remaining shells from Rosh Zin show a mixture of both Red Sea and Mediterranean forms, although the Red Sea element is much stronger than that at other Natufian sites. Given Rosh Zin's geographic position, this is not surprising.

BIBLIOGRAPHY

BAR-YOSEF, O., and TCHERNOV, E., 1967. "Archaeological Finds and the Fossil Faunas of the Natufian and Microlithic Industries at Hayonim Cave, Western Galilee (Israel)." *Israel Journal of Zoology* 15:104-40.

TCHERNOV, E., 1968. *Succession of Rodent Faunas during the Upper Pleistocene of Israel.* Berlin: Verlag Paul Parey.

THE MOUSTERIAN SITE OF ROSH EIN MOR

Harvey L. Crew

University of British Columbia

INTRODUCTION

The Mousterian site of Rosh Ein Mor (D15) is located at the western rim of the Nahal Mor cliff, at 500 m elevation, immediately above the spring of Ein Avdat (fig. 5-1). The site is situated in a shallow depression in the bedrock which is filled with up to a meter of predominantly fine-grained sediments and artifacts. These sediments were accumulated in a shallow floodplain situation along an earlier stand of the NS Zin (Goldberg, this volume).

The surface topography of the site is rather uniform, with a moderate slope from west to east, following bedrock contour. The site shape is elongate, stretching ca. 65 m along the edge of the cliff rim, and reaching a maximum of 20 m back from it. The shape makes any detailed estimate of its full area difficult, but surface indications show an areal extent of at least 1,200 square meters (fig. 5-2).

The site was discovered during 1969 (Marks et al., 1971) by a dense concentration of surface artifacts. Initially it was randomly tested by one sq m units, during which time considerable *in situ* cultural deposits were uncovered. Artifacts in very fresh condition were found in a number of pits to depths exceeding 50 centimeters. Also, a single pit produced a few faunal fragments, while all pits contained large numbers of ostrich egg shell fragments. These finds warranted large-scale excavations, which were planned for the following field season.

During the analysis of the pit material, it became clear that two areas of dense *in situ* artifact concentration had been located ca. 15 m apart. Since it was logistically impossible to excavate the total site, it was decided to excavate two areas, one near each concentration, in order to test for intrasite artifactual variability. During 1970, two 3 by 4 m sections, seven meters apart, were excavated. The differential artifactual distributions perceived after the first large-scale excavations necessitated further work, and the unexcavated block between the two sections was removed in 1972. Thus, during 1970 and 1972, a total area of 45 sq m was excavated, forming one contiguous unit, 13 m long by, in places, 3 or 4 m in width (fig. 5-2). As the average depth was 60 cm, a total of ca. 26 m^3 of deposits was removed. After the 1972 season it was clear that intrasite variability was present within the excavated area. Given the huge artifact sample, however, these data have not yet been fully studied. But they will be presented at a later time.

Excavation techniques were based on an interest in intrasite variability tempered by logistical realities. The site was gridded into one sq m units, the areas noted above were excavated in 5 cm ground contour levels, and all artifacts were mapped in their horizontal position within these levels. This was necessary since there was neither visible geological microstratigraphy nor any clear artifactual horizons.

Mapping was carried out by only two individuals, the author and A. E. Marks, in order to maintain comparability. The high density of artifacts necessitated the use of symbols for all debitage classes, but all tools and cores were given individual numbers. Excavated sediments were screened through 1/8 in mesh to increase artifact recovery. While very few large artifacts were seen, numerous small

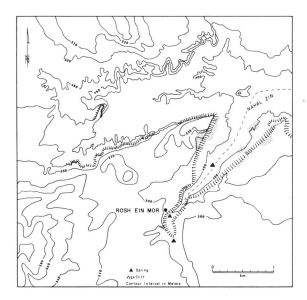

FIG. 5-1—Location of Rosh Ein Mor. *Dotted areas* indicate major flint sources.

chips and ostrich egg shell fragments were recovered. The fill from eight randomly selected units was water-screened at the laboratory to check the efficiency of field recovery, which proved to be more than adequate.

The press of time abroad and academic affairs at home precluded a uniform analysis of the entire excavated artifact sample. Attribute studies were applied only to those artifacts recovered during the 1970 field season. A complete attribute analysis was possible for this sample because the Israel Department of Antiquities permitted its shipment to Southern Methodist University, where the analysis took place during the summer of 1971.

The studies of the artifacts excavated in 1972 were confined to a typological analysis and a detailed counting of the various artifact classes, including cores. Of this material, only that from every other excavation level was shipped to SMU, while the remaining material was given directly to the Department of Antiquities, where it is now stored. The material sent to SMU was studied briefly, to confirm the typological observations made in the field.

Thus, while the total number of each tool type and debitage class is known, as well as the position of each artifact within the deposits, those cores remaining with the Department of Antiquities were not typologically classified, nor were the retouched tools from 1972 treated by attribute analysis. It is unlikely, however, that this would appreciably affect the validity of the present results. Those cores sent to SMU from the 1972 sample contained the same proportional occurrence of types present in the 1970 sample, while the tools did not appear different from the sample studied earlier by attribute analysis.

The measurement of all debitage was not undertaken because of the incredibly large sample. Instead, four of the eight randomly selected units were analyzed. All complete artifacts from these units were measured and their attributes noted, although attributes on broken pieces were taken when possible. This was carried out by a single individual in order to maximize consistency. Measurements were taken as outlined by Bordes (1961).

ENVIRONMENTAL DATA

Three groups of data are available—pollen, fauna, and sediments. While only a poor pollen sample was obtained, it is consistent with better samples recovered from a similar Mousterian site nearby, D35. The samples clearly document the presence of a rich Mediterranean flora in the Avdat area during the Mousterian occupation (Horowitz, this volume). Faunal remains were limited to a few identifiable bones and several hundred unidentifiable fragments of megafauna. Every identifiable bone belonged to *Equus hemonius* and, as the bone distribution was quite restricted, it is possible that only one or two individual animals are represented (Tchernov, this volume). In addition, hundreds of ostrich egg shell fragments were recovered from the deposits, although no bones of ostrich were found.

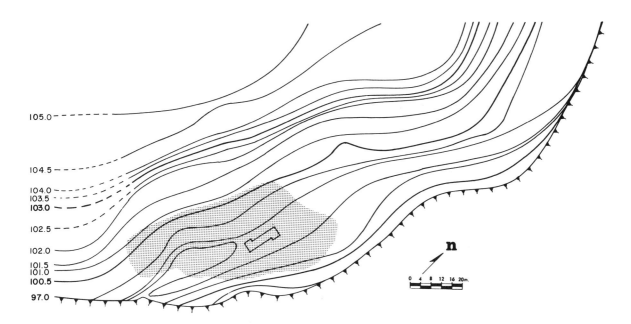

FIG. 5-2—Topographic map of Rosh Ein Mor area. *Dark area* signifies surface concentration and *rectangle* signifies area of excavations.

The sedimentary analysis (Goldberg, this volume) indicated that the sediments were deposited as a lateral facies of a fluvial deposit, demonstrating that the Nahal Zin carried considerable water during this Mousterian period. The data, with the exception of the fauna which is adapted to generally open grassland, are indicative of a Mediterranean biotope of mixed forest and grassy plain quite different from that pertaining near Avdat today (see Munday, this volume). Perhaps Xenophon's description (Warner, 1949, p. 36) of Cyrus's travels through the "aromatic" steppes of northern Syria, with his account of the plentiful Syrian wild asses and ostriches encountered and hunted, would be a reasonable picture of the Negev during the Mousterian occupation.

DATING

The evidence which pertains to the dating of Rosh Ein Mor may be summarized as follows:

1. Three radiocarbon dates have been obtained using ostrich egg shell; the first, from a test pit, by combining fragments from a number of different levels, the second from between 20 and 30 cm below the surface, while the third came from between 45 and 55 cm below the surface. The results of dating these, in sample order, were as follows: > 37,000 B.P. (Tx-1119); >44,000 B.P. (Pta-543); and >50,000 B.P. (Pta-546). As these are all minimal dates, it is likely that the oldest date should be considered the most reliable as a minimal figure for the occupation of Rosh Ein Mor.

2. Both the sedimentary and the pollen analyses indicate a Mediterranean environment during this Mousterian occupation. There have been a number of published paleoclimatic sequences for the Near East in recent years (McBurney, 1967; Farrand, 1971; Horowitz, 1971), all of which agree on a cold/moist period prior to 50,000 B.C., with a warm/dry interstadial beginning anywhere from 47,000 B.C. to 43,000 B.C. Given the southerly position of the Central Negev, the onset of the interstadial is likely to have

occurred somewhat earlier than in the northern Levant, from where most data have been derived.

Thus, both avenues of inquiry converge and are in agreement. Until new data become available, every indication is that Rosh Ein Mor was occupied during a cold/moist period prior to 50,000 B.C.

LITHIC ARTIFACTS

A total of 44,460 counted artifacts were recovered during the two field seasons, and more than twice that number of uncounted chips—those artifacts 25 mm or less in greatest dimension (table 5-1).

All artifacts were made on flint. When completely fresh, the flint exhibits a wide range of colors and grain, from translucent light brown to opaque black, and from very fine-grained to coarse materials with oolites. Most artifacts show some indications of chemical weathering which obscures both their original color and

texture. While there is a flint outcrop immediately west of the site, it is of low quality, and only a very few artifacts might have been made on the material from this source. There are, however, numerous other outcrops of high quality within a kilometer of the site, and any or all of these might have contributed raw material.

TECHNOLOGY

For this study, technology has been assumed to be a set of activities by which a given quantity of raw material is exploited for maximum productivity within the limits of the workers' abilities and habits. This set of activities consists of a number of stages which are not necessarily performed equally or repetitively in each and every activity area, but which can be presented as a series of production steps. First, there is the initial decortication of the flint nodules, producing primary elements. Second, the shaping and prepara-

TABLE 5-1
Total Artifacts by Major Groups

Groups	Number	Percent	Group Percent
Primary Elements	6,522		14.67
Unretouched Levallois	5,123		11.52
a. Flakes	2,218	4.99	
b. Blades	1,241	2.79	
c. Points	1,664	3.74	
Unretouched Non-Levallois	26,206		58.94
a. Flakes	21,266	47.83	
b. Blades	4,629	10.41	
c. Naturally backed pieces	311	.70	
Cores	2,886	6.49	6.49
Retouched tools	3,723	8.37	8.37
	44,460		99.99
Waste and Debris	ca. 125,000		

tion of the core takes place, producing variable debitage, depending upon which production method is being employed—Levallois, discoidal, blade, etc. Third, there is the removal of the desired blanks, either Levallois or non-Levallois, with associated reshaping of the cores until they are no longer useful for the initially intended purpose. The fourth stage is the removal of additional blanks, utilizing a different method, particularly when the Levallois cores become too small for retention of the Levallois method. While it is recognized that this is extremely complex, certain materials can be assigned to the various stages.

The usual practice of placing unretouched Levallois pieces into a tool category and the unretouched non-Levallois pieces into a debitage category has not been followed here. The examination of the technology of this assemblage indicates that Levallois and most non-Levallois pieces are products of a systematic process of core reduction, and the separation of the two would mask this continuity. It is true, however, that the Levallois pieces may be viewed apart from the non-Levallois pieces, as the Levallois material represents what is assumed to be a desired end product. Thus, the Levallois element is still shown in the traditional typological list, although its discussion is in the section on technology.

Technological Indices

In traditional terms, the Rosh Ein Mor assemblage is very low in Levallois pieces, with a Levallois Index (IL) of only 14.6. This needs some explanation, since Mousterian assemblages of non-Levallois facies are not common in the Levantine Mousterian. Copeland has stated (1975) that the IL is affected by how conscientiously one retains all of the excavated pieces, and the high retention level at Rosh Ein Mor undoubtedly had some influence on the low value of the Levallois Index. The main contributing factor, however, was the inclusion into the flake category

of more non-Levallois pieces than are usually placed in this class. Since no tools were found less than 30 mm in greatest dimension, 25 mm was used as the boundary between chippage and debitage. This is probably considerably smaller than is traditional. For example, Fleisch (1970) used the same 25 mm boundary for the analysis of the Naamé assemblage, and his IL values are comparably low. It should be pointed out, however, that collections from open-air sites of Mousterian age have rarely been analyzed, and it is still unknown what IL might be expected at such sites.

The amount of faceting is moderate (IF, 54.6; IFs, 34.7), but it does compare favorably with some Levantine Mousterian assemblages, even those from obviously selected samples (Skinner, 1965, p. 151). The generally high levels of faceting at most Levantine Mousterian sites, again, may be a factor of selection, as smaller flakes tend to have less faceting. The Blade Index (ILame) is computed for only unretouched Levallois and non-Levallois pieces, excluding Levallois points, tools, and all primary elements. These normally included classes do not drastically affect the index, since spot checks have revealed that specimens of blade proportions usually approximate the Blade Index of 19.5. Further, the sample size of these excluded forms is so small that their exclusion would not have had a significant effect.

Unretouched Artifacts

The unretouched artifacts have been divided into seven basic classes: primary elements, non-Levallois flakes and blades, Levallois flakes, blades, and points, and naturally backed pieces. The individual classes may be viewed by specific attributes, so that the similarities and differences between them can become clear.

In terms of length, most non-Levallois debi-

TABLE 5-2
Lengths of the Unretouched Artifacts as Percents

Class	Length (mm)								Mean	N
	40	40/50	50/60	60/70	70/80	80/90	90/100	>100		
Primary Elements	39.4	23.9	14.8	10.6	3.5	4.9	1.4	1.4	47.7	138
Non-Levallois Blades	29.2	24.6	20.0	7.7	13.8	3.1		1.5	53.7	65
Non-Levallois Flakes	68.8	22.3	4.2	1.4	1.4	1.4	.5		36.9	215
Levallois Blades	6.2	9.4	15.2	25.0	18.7	12.5		12.5	78.6	32
Levallois Flakes	10.8	24.1	22.4	19.4	12.9	5.9	2.6	2.2	57.8	232
Levallois Points	11.6	15.9	21.7	19.3	17.9	10.1	1.9	1.4	62.2	207
Naturally Backed Pieces	4.9	5.6	17.4	17.4	13.9	18.7	7.6	14.6	73.9	142

tage, including the primary elements, is considerably smaller than the Levallois classes (table 5-2).

Moreover, the non-Levallois debitage is markedly skewed toward shortness, although there are a few specimens exceeding 100 mm in length. The Levallois element is generally larger, and it is distributed in a normal or near normal fashion. This tendency toward normality would seem to represent a standardization of manufacture not apparent in the non-Levallois debitage. The only exception to this are those pieces with natural backing which are only second in mean length to Levallois blades. This is due to the high percentage of naturally backed blades as opposed to naturally backed flakes.

The distribution of the relative width (W/L) values are normal or near normal for all classes of debitage (table 5-3). The primary elements and non-Levallois debitage do have significantly larger numbers of specimens in the very broad range (>1.00), representing in part *éclat de taille* forms. *Éclats de taille* are derived during the reworking of an edge, and thus are evidence of rejuvenation procedures. The Levallois elements tend to be more lamellar than the non-Levallois, although the proportion of actual blades is similar in all classes. The same tendency for the Levallois pieces to be larger and more standardized has also been noted at l'Hortus, along the Midi of France (Rolland, 1972). The consistent production of about a fifth of blade-

TABLE 5-3
Width/Length Proportions as Percents
of Each Debitage Category

Class	Width/Length									Mean	N
	0-.3	.3-.4	.4-.5	.5-.6	.6-.7	.7-.8	.8-.9	.9-1.0	>1.0		
Primary Elements	2.2	8.8	14.7	11.8	15.4	11.0	11.0	5.9	19.1	.81	138
Non-Levallois Debitage	2.1	8.2	14.3	9.0	14.3	10.1	8.6	10.4	22.9	.73	279
Levallois Flake/Blade	2.5	8.9	12.3	24.2	20.3	14.8	7.6	3.4	5.9	.68	236
Levallois Points	5.7	2.4	12.1	17.4	25.6	21.7	7.2	3.9	3.9	.54	207
Naturally Backed Pieces	6.3	27.3	31.5	24.3	7.7	1.4	1.4			.43	142

proportioned artifacts in all classes must have a correlation with the other features of the total production process, i.e., perhaps the strong tendency toward unidirectional preparation. It is only the naturally backed piece class which has a mean length/width ratio with blade proportions.

The low proportion of cortex platforms in the primary class is evidence that the earliest stages of core reduction were not commonly performed in the area excavated (table 5-4). The few primary elements with cortex platforms could hardly represent all of the decortication flakes needed to supply the amount of raw material manifested in the lithic component. Straight platforms considerably exceed convex platforms in the primary elements. Convex-shaped platforms, however, equal or exceed the straight-shaped platforms in the non-Levallois and Levallois classes. The Levallois pieces in general have a tendency toward salient platforms, which probably has something to do with improving the mechanics of removing pieces from cores. The Levallois points represent the culmination of this tendency toward convexity. Aside from having the highest frequency of *chapeau de gendarme* platforms, many of the convex platforms approach *chapeau de gendarme* form.

Table 5-5 shows an orderly increase in the refinement of faceting from the primary elements to the Levallois debitage. Perhaps, the similarity in the amount of faceting between the primary and non-Levallois blades indicates they were derived during the same decortication and preshaping procedures. The seemingly transitional nature of the non-Levallois flakes should not be viewed as evidence for a sequential progression, since they are likely derived during many different stages of core reduction. Rolland (1972, p. 497) has come to the same conclusion from his analysis of the l'Hortus material.

The debitage of all classes is strongly characterized by dorsal preparation originating from the proximal end (table 5-6). This unidirectional tendency is probably one of the more notable features of the core reduction process. A tendency for unidirectional preparation has been recognized previously (Copeland, 1970; Watanabe, 1968), but it seems to have been noted mainly for the Levallois debitage. In any case, the general similarity in the proportions of the preparation emanating from each direction would seem to show that the controlling factor for the production of Levallois pieces is not the direction of the preparation. The almost complete lack of any

TABLE 5-4
Platform Shapes Shown as Percents of Each Class

Class	Convex	Concave	Straight	CG[1]	Cortex	Unidentifiable	N
Primary Elements	39.7		52.7		2.3	5.3	131
Non-Levallois Blades	42.2		40.7		4.7	12.5	64
Non-Levallois Flakes	51.3	0.5	38.9		2.4	7.2	193
Levallois Blades	65.6	3.1	28.1		3.1		32
Levallois Flakes	73.1	1.9	12.6	9.4	1.9	0.6	309
Levallois Points	74.2	0.4	7.5	17.9			241
Naturally Backed Pieces	57.4	1.4	35.5	5.0	0.7		141

[1] *Chapeau de gendarme.*

TABLE 5-5
Number of Facets of Each Class as Percents

Class	Number of Facets							N	Mean
	1	2	3/4	5/6	7/8	9/10	>11		
Primary Elements	50.4	19.2	17.6	4.8	8.0			125	2.4
Non-Levallois Blades	51.9	17.3	21.1	9.6				52	2.1
Non-Levallois Flakes	36.8	18.7	29.7	9.3	3.8	1.6		182	2.4
Levallois Blades	21.8	1.0	27.6	22.4	13.8	10.6	2.9	312	4.2
Levallois Flakes	9.4	0.9	21.4	26.1	15.8	23.9	2.6	234	6.1
Levallois Points	0.0	1.2	9.5	20.6	17.7	37.9	9.1	243	7.4
Naturally Backed Pieces	23.7	11.5	18.0	24.5	10.8	10.1	1.4	139	4.4

distal preparation in the manufacture of the Levallois points is the only real distinct difference among the classes of debitage.

Primary Elements

Primary elements are derived from the procedure of removing the cortex from flint nodules, either during initial preparation, or subsequent work with cores upon which some cortex still remained. The primary elements tend to be fairly small (table 5-2), although over a fifth exceed 60 mm in length, while a full quarter are of blade proportions (table 5-3). These latter are good-sized pieces approaching Levallois blades in size, and they are generally larger than the non-Levallois blades. Their early stage in the manufacturing process is perhaps best seen in the high numbers of straight-shaped and unfaceted platforms present (tables 5-4 and 5-5). Their dorsal scars indicate they were struck predominantly from the same end from which the piece was then removed (table 5-6). The addition of the naturally backed pieces to the primary elements would increase the amount of faceting and laminarity, but not by much, since these pieces account for less than 5% of the total primary elements.

Non-Levallois Debitage

Overall, non-Levallois debitage is slightly longer than the primary debitage (table 5-2), although pri-mary blades are an exception. As with the primary debitage, the blanks of blade proportions amount to about a quarter of the total (table 5-3). There has been much debate about how to measure the dimensions of artifacts, with most of the fire and smoke centered on how to measure the pieces with an offset axis. The technology at Rosh Ein Mor reveals only a small tendency toward "offsetness," thus its presentation, while measured, was not deemed necessary.

While the degree of laminarity in a class always seems to draw attention and interest, the strong tendency in the non-Levallois debitage toward broadness should not be overlooked. A careful reading of Table 5-3 reveals that a full 41.9% are above .80, and almost a quarter are of sub-flake proportions (>1.00). In short, the non-Levallois debitage exhibits a wide range of sizes and proportions, as befits its multiple origins.

These differences in origin are seen particularly in the platform shapes, and, especially, faceting shows that the non-Levallois blades are closer to the primary elements than to the non-Levallois flakes (tables 5-4 and 5-5). The primary difference is in a definite shift away from single-faceted (unfaceted) platforms in the non-Levallois flake class.

For both blades and flakes, preparation is delivered mainly from the proximal end (table 5-6). Punctiform platforms, indicative of a punch technique, were not noted systematically at the time of examination, but they were not common, and a systematic use of this technique is not present.

TABLE 5-6
Direction of the Dorsal Scars Shown as Percent of Each Class

Class	Directions				Number of Scars	Mean	N
	Distal	Right	Proximal	Left			
Primary Elements	5.3	10.6	78.8	5.3	365	2.60	138
Non-Levallois Blades	10.2	7.4	71.2	11.3	278	4.60	60
Non-Levallois Flakes	8.5	13.8	66.7	11.0	820	3.80	213
Levallois Blades	7.7	4.5	83.3	4.5	156	4.90	32
Levallois Flakes	10.8	9.9	69.2	10.0	977	4.90	198
Levallois Points	0.3	0.4	97.3	1.9	675	3.35	203

Levallois Blades (figs. 5-3*a-d, h*; 5-4*g, h*)

These, as with all Levallois pieces (Bordes, 1961), were distinguished by the preparation on their dorsal surface, uniformity of shape, some dorsal convexity indicative of a Levallois core, but are set apart from Levallois flakes by a width/length of less than .50. The preparation is, of course, the key, and to qualify as a Levallois blade, the preparation had to peel evenly across the surface. The evenness of preparation is necessary to provide evidence of the requisite predetermination.

The Levallois blades are, on an average, the longest debitage (table 5-2). They are generally parallel or lanceolate in shape, although some expanding and triangular forms occur. Levallois blades comprised ca. 23% of the 1970 sample of the Levallois flakes/blades (table 5-3), which matches closely with their overall frequency. The greater majority of their platforms are convex in shape, although the blades do exhibit the highest total of straight-shaped platforms in the Levallois category (table 5-4). The close approximation between straight-shaped and single-faceted platform types is probably a measure of the same feature. The dorsal preparation is, of course, very unidirectional, with only a minimal amount of lateral preparation (table 5-6).

Levallois Flakes (figs. 5-3*e, g, i*; 5-6*a-c*; 5-7*c*)

The definition of a Levallois flake adopted is from Bordes (1961), requiring evidence of predetermination of the size and shape of the piece removed. The sample studied was derived from the three upper and lower levels of the areas excavated in 1970.

A majority of the pieces tend to be under 60 mm in length (table 5-2), their relative width (W/L index) is generally lamellar, although about a fifth are in the broad range (>.80). The dominant platform shapes are salient convex and straight (table 5-4). The few cortex platforms are present on some very "atypical" pieces. The low incidence of unidentifiable platforms is an indication of the increased effort spent in their manufacture. Evidence of increased faceting is manifested by the large number of highly faceted platforms (>9 facets) at the obvious expense of the single-faceted platforms (table 5-5). The direction of the preparation does not differ significantly from the non-Levallois flakes, and the difference between the two is a matter of the care and amount of preparation used.

Levallois Points (figs. 5-3*f*; 5-4*a-f, i*; 5-7*a, b, d*)

The unretouched Levallois point component is large. The definition adopted is that presented by Bordes (1955, 1961), but only to the extent that it is a triangular-shaped flake struck from a triangular-shaped core. Bordes also has defined the Levallois point by a particular sequence of manufacture, and as such, his definition is not fully acceptable in this context.

The shape of the point must be triangular, thus lanceolate pieces with a pointed end have been excluded. Triangular, as used here, means the widest portion of the piece has to be at the platform or near

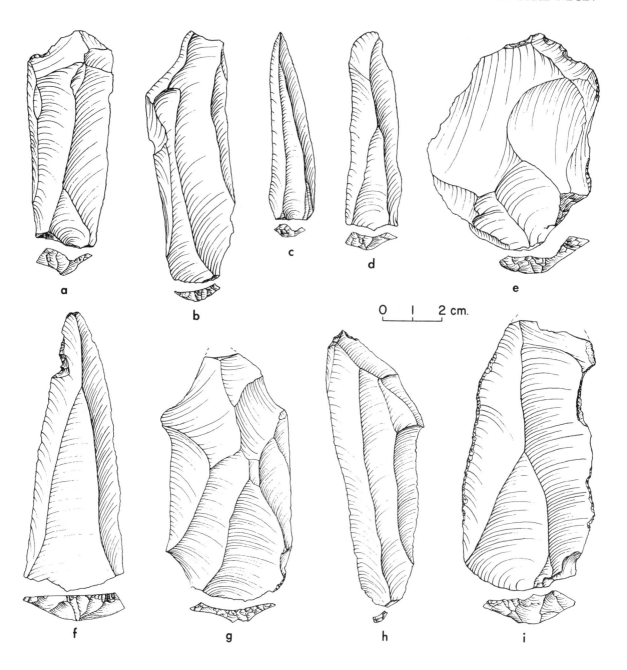

FIG. 5-3—Levallois pieces from Rosh Ein Mor: *a-e, f, i*—points, some with retouch; *g, h*—blades.

to the platform. The "Y"-shaped arrete pattern, in conjunction with the triangular shape, was the rule, although there were some "primary order" points (Bordes, 1961, p. 19). The size of the samples used to measure a particular attribute was not always the same, since these pieces were examined over a two-year period.

There is considerable size range, from 30 mm to in excess of 130 millimeters. Their length averages longer than the flakes but shorter than the blades (table 5-2). The frequency of points of blade proportion is similar to the frequency of blades from all of the classes of debitage (table 5-3), and this must be related to the mechanics of a lithic manufacturing

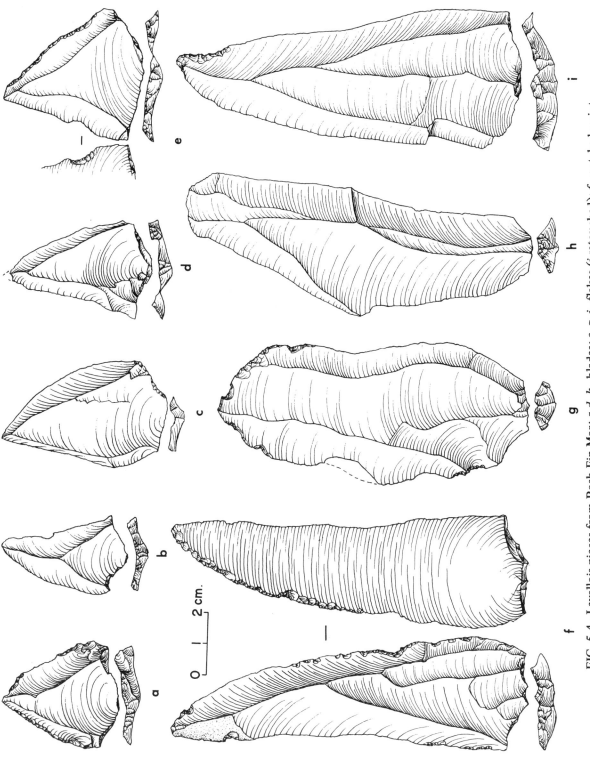

FIG. 5-4—Levallois pieces from Rosh Ein Mor: *a-d, h*—blades; *e, g, i*—flakes (*i* retouched); *f*—notched point.

process in which the majority of the preparation emanates from the same end from which the pieces were removed. The high use of the protuberant platform shapes, and the lack of any cortex platforms whatsoever (table 5-4), are indications of the preparation necessary to remove a point. The increase in the amount of faceting seen parallels the rise in the convexity of the platform shapes (table 5-5). The high increase of platforms with 9 or more facets is, no doubt, a reflection of the amount of faceting necessary to create salient platforms. This saliency of the butts is a major typological feature of the points.

The almost complete lack of distal preparation on the points is the most extreme example of the unidirectional preparation (table 5-6). The points were also examined for the exact order in which their preparatory flakes were removed. Such an analysis was possible because of the comparatively few scars and their strong unidirectional preparation. In brief, an examination of the dorsal arretes revealed that the "Y"-shaped scar pattern on Levallois-point cores can be achieved in three ways (fig. 5-5). This is at variance with Bordes's description (1961, p. 18) of the method. In fact, his method (pattern C) is the least common used at Rosh Ein Mor: of 191 points studied, 57.6% were of pattern A, 29.8% of pattern B, and only 12.6% of pattern C.

The dominance of pattern A, which is blade-like in execution, would probably lend support to Jelinek's belief (1975, p. 22) that Levallois blades are a product of the point preparation.

Naturally Backed Pieces (fig. 5-14h, j)

The placement of unretouched Levallois pieces as debitage logically suggests that the naturally backed pieces should also be considered as debitage, specifically a variant of the primary elements. The criterion used for the selection of these pieces is basically that presented by Bordes (1961, p. 33). The only modification added is the presence of some evidence of use. Specimens without a steep back or with no signs of use on the opposite edge have been included under primary debitage proper. The total of the naturally backed pieces available for study was 186 specimens.

Their lengths range from 30 to 159 mm (table 5-2), with a mean of 73.9 millimeters; however, the majority are between 50 and 80 millimeters. They are very laminar in proportion (table 5-3), and this may be due to their relatively early derivation in the core-reduction process when larger pieces are more likely to be produced. As Table 5-4 reveals, the convex-shaped platforms are dominant, followed by straight-shaped platforms. Cortex platforms are rare (one example), which is a surprise, given the presence of cortex on one edge. The amount of faceting is more similar to the non-Levallois debitage than to the primary elements (table 5-5), probably correlating with the platform preparation necessary to set up the removal of long pieces.

Cores

Cores comprise 6.5% of the artifacts, indicating that a high degree of core reduction took place locally or that large numbers of flakes were carried in from elsewhere (compare this with table 5-5, Munday, this volume). These cores are extremely difficult to classify and describe. While clusters of attributes covary, enabling the recognition of "types," there are many pieces with attribute combinations which preclude easy classification (see Schroeder, 1969, for a discussion of the difficulty of classifying cores from the Levantine Mousterian). The method of analysis adopted for this study is a combination of intuitively derived "types" and metric attributes. The typology has been adapted and modified mainly after Bordes (1961) and Marks (1968), but a few types also have been adopted from de Heinzelin (1962).

It must be realized that the core typology reflects the final state of each core, often at a point when further reduction was useless. Thus, the high percentage of unclassifiable cores (inform) does not mean a paucity of structured core-reduction processes, but merely that these cores have probably been taken beyond recognizable stages (table 5-7).

TABLE 5-7
Core Typology
1970 Sample

Type	Number	Percent
Levallois		14.4
a. Flakes	75	6.5
b. Blades	37	3.2
c. Points	54	4.7
Discoidal		16.4
a. Full	90	7.8
b. Partial	101	8.6
Single Platform		32.0
a. Flake	235	20.4
b. Blade	134	11.6
Opposed Platform		8.8
a. Flake	87	7.5
b. Blade	16	1.4
Other		28.1
a. Change of orientation	64	5.5
b. Globular	55	4.8
c. Unidentifiable	205	17.8
	1,153	99.8
Core Fragments	294	
Untyped (1972 sample)	1,439	
TOTAL	2,886	

Levallois Cores

Levallois cores of all types comprise 14.4% of the complete examples which were classified, comparing closely with the Levallois index of 16.5 for the total assemblage. This has some important bearing on the cores and the amount of debitage they produced. When subdivided by core type, this parallelism becomes even more striking (table 5-8).

As Table 5-8 shows, there is evidence for the importation of some Levallois blanks into the excavated area. The ratio between cores and their associated products runs 1:14.9 for Levallois flake cores, 1:16.8 for Levallois blade cores, and 1:15.6 for Levallois point cores. These ratios are obviously far too high to represent only on-site production. Realistically, three or so Levallois blanks per Levallois core might be expected, and if this is used as a reasonable estimate, it would indicate that for every Levallois blank manufactured on the site, slightly more than five were manufactured elsewhere, at least outside the excavated area. The presence of clearly defined workshops in the Avdat area, however, suggests that these may have been manufactured at totally different kinds of sites. Even with these workshops, however, the figure of five imported blanks for each locally produced one is probably too high, as undoubtedly a number of cores which were originally of Levallois method were finally treated by a non-Levallois process after they became too small to produce usable Levallois blanks. In spite of this, it is clear that many Levallois blanks of all types were manufactured elsewhere and then brought to the excavated area at Rosh Ein Mor.

Levallois Flake Cores (fig. 5-8*b, c*)

These have been classified by the flexible criteria proposed by Bordes (1961), which necessitates only a

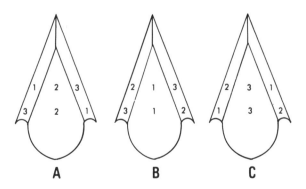

FIG. 5-5—Schematic drawing of sequential Levallois point preparation patterns.

TABLE 5-8

Comparison of Proportional Occurrences of Levallois Cores and Blanks

	Levallois Cores[1]				Levallois Blanks		
Type	1970	1972	Total	Percent	Type	Number	Percent
Flake	75	74	149	45.2	Flake	2,218	43.3
Blade	37	37	74	22.3	Blade	1,241	24.2
Point	54	53	107	32.5	Point	1,664	32.5

[1] The number of Levallois cores from the 1972 sample was estimated by assuming no change in proportional representation in the core sample from that of the 1970 sample.

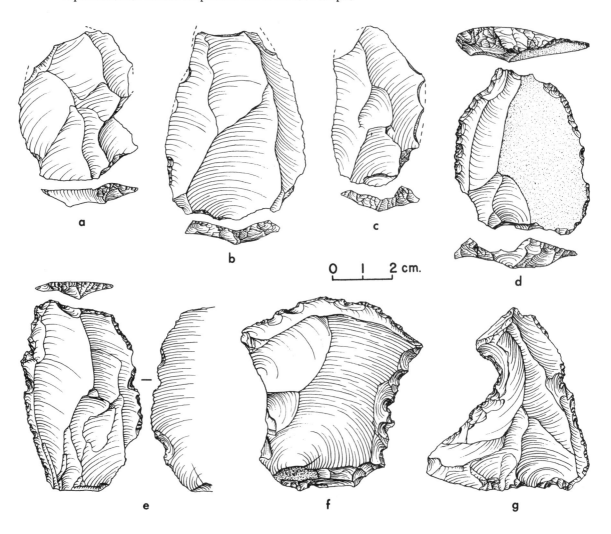

FIG. 5-6—Tools and Levallois pieces from Rosh Ein Mor: *a-c*—Levallois flakes; *d*—double cortex sidescraper; *e*—distal truncated; *f*—denticulate; *g*—notched flake.

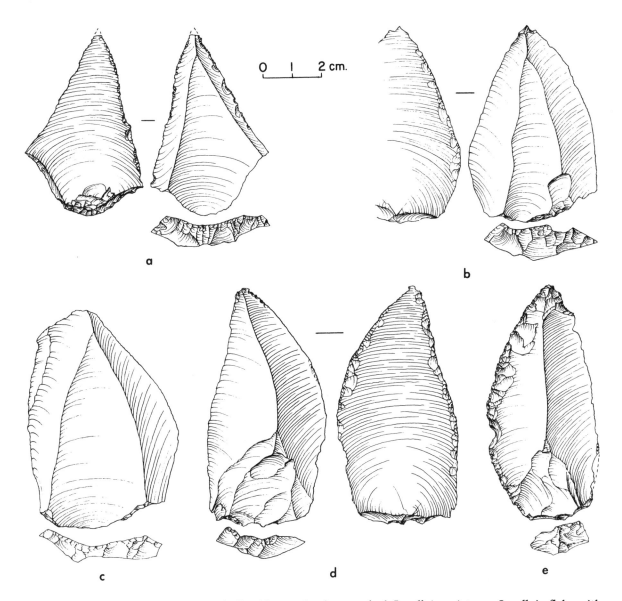

FIG. 5-7—Levallois pieces from Rosh Ein Mor: *a, b, d*—retouched Levallois points; *c*—Levallois flake with point pattern; *e*—convex sidescraper approaching point.

preparation of the dorsal surface such that the shape of the major Levallois piece is predetermined. The more restricted definition of Levallois flake core preparation, that of centripetal dorsal flaking, would necessitate the rejection of a sizable number of both Levallois cores and flakes in the early Levantine Mousterian. Centripetal preparation of the dorsal core surface cannot be regarded even as the norm within the Rosh Ein Mor assemblage.

More Levallois flake cores were unstruck than

were struck. As they tend to be quite small, many undoubtedly proved to be too small for successful flake removal. Some exhibit considerable crushing and battering on their platforms, suggesting that unsuccessful attempts were made to remove the Levallois flake.

The preparation of the primary flaked surface, from which the Levallois flake is struck, has already been discussed in the Levallois flake section and will not be repeated. Some additional observations are

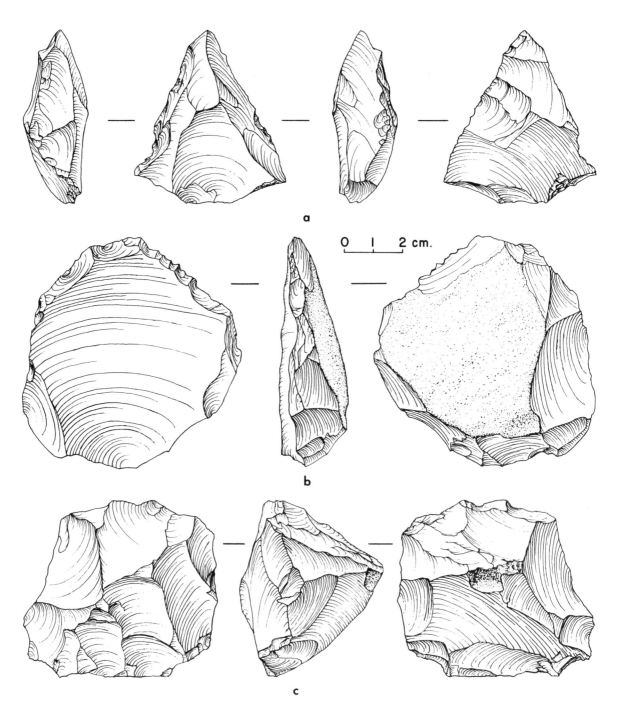

FIG. 5-8—Cores from Rosh Ein Mor: *a*—Levallois point of "Jerf Ajla" type; *b*—typical Levallois flake core;
c—unstruck Levallois flake core.

warranted, however. Levallois flake cores, with a mean length of 49.3 mm, are significantly smaller than the Levallois flakes (tables 5-2 and 5-9), sup-porting the contention that most Levallois flakes were struck during relatively early stages of core re-duction. The mean relative width index (W/L) is 1.04,

TABLE 5-9

Core Length (mm) as Percents of Each Type

Core Type	20-25	25-30	30-35	35-40	40-45	45-50	50-55	55-60	60-65	65-70	70-75	75-80	80-85	85-90	90-95	95-100	>100	N
Levallois Flake		1.6	6.2	12.5	12.5	15.6	20.3	9.4	9.4	9.4				1.6			1.6	64
Levallois Blade			17.1	19.5	17.1	12.2	9.8	4.9	2.4	7.3	4.5	4.9	4.9					41
Levallois Point		2.6	10.2	15.4	17.9	15.4	17.9	2.6	12.8	5.1								39
Discoid			1.4	6.9	12.5	15.3	25.0	11.1	12.5	13.9	2.8							72
Partial Discoid		1.1	5.7	10.2	21.6	19.3	23.9	9.1	6.8		1.1			1.1				88
Single Platform																		
Flake		0.7	4.0	12.1	14.1	19.5	16.8	13.4	8.0	5.4	2.7		2.0	0.7	0.7			149
Blade		1.7	13.6	18.6	22.0	10.2	15.2	8.5	3.4		1.7	1.7	1.7	1.7				59
Change of																		
Orientation	3.6		3.6	10.7	32.1	21.4	10.7	14.3					3.6					28
Opposed Platform			2.8	5.6	8.4	21.1	26.8	12.7	14.1	5.6	2.8							71
Globular		1.5	7.7	21.5	10.8	18.5	16.9	6.1	7.7	1.5	3.1	3.1	1.5					65
Unidentifiable		1.0	3.9	7.8	13.7	17.6	13.7	20.6	8.8	4.9	4.9	2.0				1.0		102
TOTALS	—	0.1	5.0	11.2	14.3	18.2	19.5	12.0	9.0	4.9	2.3	0.7	0.7	0.7	0.1	0.1	0.1	

denoting a roundish plane view. This belies the unidirectional tendency of the preparation, which seemingly would lead to elongated cores.

Levallois Blade Cores (fig. 5-9d)

These are roughly the type figured by Bordes (1961, plate 104), with a flattish upper surface, although the wide specimens illustrated by Bordes are absent. Levallois blade cores in this assemblage tend to be elongate and are the longest cores; about a quarter of them are over 60 mm in length, while a few exceed 80 mm (table 5-9).

Levallois Point Cores (figs. 5-8a; 5-9a-c)

Bordes (1961) is adhered to in the analysis, particularly in the convergence of the preparation to form a "Y"-shaped dorsal pattern which predetermines the triangular point pattern. Point cores, at least those that are extant, were crudely made. They are very small, none larger than 65 mm, and the majority (60%) are under 50 mm in length (table 5-9). The mean length of 44.1 mm is less than the mean of the Levallois points by almost a full 20 millimeters. Cer-

tainly, no point cores were found which could have produced the larger points. There are a few Levallois cores of "Jerf Ajla" type (Schroeder, 1969, p. 121). The characteristic lateral denticulation of the ventral surface, however, is found at Rosh Ein Mor on more core types than just the "Jerf Ajla" variety.

Discoid Cores (fig. 5-10f)

Discoid cores are common, and both full and partial types occur (Bordes, 1961; de Heinzelin, 1962). These cores are usually roughly worked, although some fine specimens exist. The presence of the few finely worked pieces should not be regarded as evidence for a strong presence of a discoid method, since they represent what is really one manifestation of a very flexible core tradition. They range in diameter from 34 to 70 millimeters (table 5-9). They tend to be circular, with a mean relative width (W/L) of 0.95, and are rather flat, with a mean relative thickness (Th/W) of 0.45 (table 5-10). In a sample of discoid cores from the Mousterian layers of the Haua Fteah in Libya (McBurney, 1967, p. 134) which are characterized by a strong radial preparation, the relative thickness (Th/W) is considerably greater, 0.55.

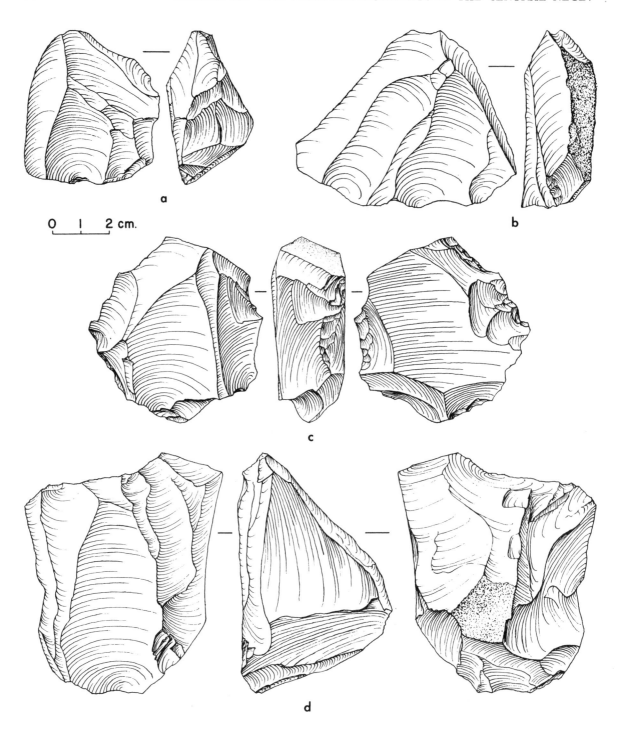

0 I 2 cm.

FIG. 5-9—Cores from Rosh Ein Mor: *a-c*—Levallois point cores; *d*—bidirectional Levallois blade core.

Partial discoids are more common than full discoids (table 5-7). This type was adopted from de Heinzelin (1962, p. 8), having a discoid shape where the platforms extend only around half of the core's circumference, while the dorsal preparation is roughly convergent. Their flaked surface is usually more

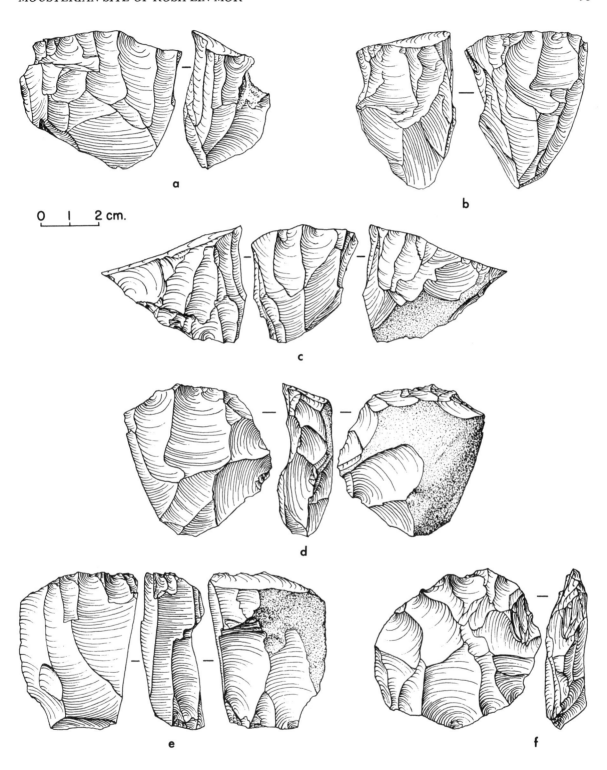

FIG. 5-10–Cores from Rosh Ein Mor: *a, b*–single platform blade; *c*–opposed platform blade; *d*–change of orientation flake; *e*–opposed platform, opposite side blade; *f*–discoidal.

highly raised than on Levallois point cores, although the possibility exists here that a few may be exhausted Levallois point cores. Their mean diameter is 49.3 mm, smaller than that of the full discoids, while relative thickness is about the same (table 5-10).

Single Platform Cores (fig. 5-10a, b)

These are the most numerous in the studied sample, with those having produced flakes more common than those which produced blades (table 5-7).

The blade variety encompasses a great deal of variation, with the only consistent traits being the single platform and a scar configuration indicating that blades were produced. There are a few blade cores with a curved, barrel-shaped surface which could be called prismatic. These account for over half of this group, and for 6.1% of the total of the cores typed. There are also a few cores which could be called pyramidal, which commonly have a very denticulated edge, but have been included here because they are just one expression of this variable core type.

The single platform blade cores range in length from 31 to 78 mm, with a mean under 50 mm (table 5-9). They are slightly elongated (W/L, 0.87), and rather thick (mean = 78.8 mm). Of the sample studied, 74% would have delivered blades under 50 mm in length, again an example of the exhausted state of most of the cores. Over half of the platforms (52%) are unfaceted, a few are cortex, and the remainder are faceted to a minor degree.

The flake variety is relatively short, with a mean length of 51.9 mm but with a wide range (table 5-9). A large percentage of these have cortex opposite the platform.

Change of Orientation Cores (fig. 5-10d)

These are not very common (table 5-7); they match de Heinzelin's "*nucleus à double orientation*" (1962, p. 10), although the description and term are borrowed specifically from Marks (1968). The type can be further subdivided into two varieties, classified by whether the 90° change of orientation is on the same surface or on opposite surfaces. The two varieties appear about equally, but all those studied would have produced only flakes. Since their mean length was under 50 mm, they obviously were nearing the end of their effective use. They tend to be rather wide and flat (table 5-10). Unfaceted platforms account for 38% of the sample, straight-faceted 46%, while the remainder are convex-faceted.

Opposed Platform Cores (fig. 5-10c, e)

Again, these are rare, and they have been subdivided into flake and blade varieties (table 5-7). The definition has been adapted from de Heinzelin's *nucleus bipolaire* (1962, p. 10), and from Marks (1968). The presence of recognizable platforms at the opposite ends of the core is the main diagnostic criterion. They range in length from 35 to 70 mm (table 5-9), with a mean of 51.1 millimeters. They tend to be broad (W/L, 0.90), and rather flat (Th/W, 0.45), as is true for most cores in this assemblage (table 5-10). The majority of the platforms are faceted (81%) and generally convex; only three percent have cortex platforms, while the remainder are unfaceted.

Globular Cores

These comprise only a small percentage of the core component (table 5-7). Flake removals are not oriented in any discernible direction, and cross sections are thick and cubical in shape (de Heinzelin, 1962, p. 8). The cores are not large (table 5-9), although the mean length exceeds 50 mm, and they are considerably thicker than the majority of other cores (table 5-10).

Unidentifiable Cores

These are numerous (table 5-7), as would be assumed given the many permutations available in the core reduction process. These are the cores which could not be placed in the previous categories (de Heinzelin, 1962, p. 18). They generally have multiple platforms, an amorphous shape, or are merely lightly modified fragments of nodules with one or two flakes removed. Such a residual category of unclassifiable cores is not unexpected in a Levantine Mousterian assemblage (Crew, 1975).

TABLE 5-10
Relative Width of Cores as Percents of Each Type

Type	Thickness/Width										N
	.10-.20	.20-.30	.30-.40	.40-.50	.50-.60	.60-.70	.70-.80	.80-.90	.90-1.00	>1.00	
Levallois Flake		17.0	40.0	18.3	15.0	5.0	1.7	1.7			60
Levallois Blade		15.0	34.6	27.0	3.8	15.4	3.8	3.8			26
Levallois Point		13.2	28.9	28.9	23.7	2.6	2.6				38
Discoid		13.7	26.0	30.1	17.8	6.8	4.1	1.4			73
Single Platform											
Flake	1.3	14.2	28.4	29.7	10.8	10.8	4.7				148
Blade	2.2	2.2	8.8	8.8	12.1	23.1	13.2	13.2	8.8	7.7	91
Change of Orientation											
Flake/Blade		20.0	36.0	28.0	12.0	4.0					25
Opposed Platform											
Flake/Blade		14.7	32.0	10.3	5.1	4.0	1.7				75
Globular			11.4	8.6	28.6	22.9	14.3	4.3			35

TYPOLOGY

The retouched tools were analyzed by the typological system presented by Bordes in the early 1950s. Since this system was designed to express the variation in the western European Mousterian, certain modifications have been made here to demonstrate better the variation particular to this assemblage. These modifications are presented in two ways. First, some tool classes are further divided into sub-types to express better intra-class variation. These subdivisions are commonly based upon other typologies, where sub-types have been described. Second, statistically based descriptions of diagnostic intra-class attributes are used to express possible modal changes not apparent in the morphological-type approach. Such dimensional measures of modal values provide possible evidence for time vectored change (McBurney, 1967). The sizes of the samples preclude any discussion of particular artifacts, and qualitative description usually will be relegated to summary observations on a class level.

The frequency of tool types made on Le-

vallois blanks exceeds the latter's overall occurrence, and they must have been a preferred blank form (table 5-11). Levallois flakes, among Levallois blanks, are dominant over points and blades, except for the *bec-burinant*-tool type. Upper Paleolithic tool types (endscrapers, borers, and backed pieces), with the notable exception of the burin, generally have proportionately more specimens made on Levallois blanks than do the Middle Paleolithic types. Of course, the dominant blank form is the non-Levallois flake. It usually accounts for 50% to 60% of all blanks within every tool type, except for the truncations and the backed pieces.

Tool size is not correlated positively with any particular blank form (table 5-12). Thus, Levallois blanks seem to have been preferred blanks for other attributes than size. This confirms what was intuitively apparent during the analysis; the larger Levallois blanks were generally not converted into retouched tools. Also, size does not appear to have any positive correlation with Middle Paleolithic or Upper Paleolithic tool types.

Naturally backed pieces, variously re-

TABLE 5-11

The Association of Tool Type and Blank Form as Percents of Each Type

Blank Form						Tool Type						
	SS	ES	Bu	Br	Tc	Bk	Nt	Dt	Rc	Bc	Rp	Tp
Levallois Flake	24.2	15.0	6.5	14.9	25.3	17.4	13.4	12.4	21.2	11.1		10.7
Levallois Blade		7.5	2.9	12.8	10.3	21.7	4.7	5.4	3.0	3.7		7.8
Levallois Point	3.0	9.6		8.5	9.2	17.4	3.7	3.0	3.0	25.4		3.9
Subtotal	27.2	32.1	9.4	36.2	44.8	56.5	21.8	20.8	27.2	40.2		
Non-Levallois Flake	52.5	54.5	55.0	51.1	43.7	30.4	53.0	51.5	56.1	55.6	57.4	61.1
Non-Levallois Blade	13.1	4.3	11.5	12.8	11.5	13.0	13.1	11.9	4.5	3.7	14.5	13.6
Subtotal	65.6	58.8	66.5	63.9	55.2	43.4	66.1	63.4	60.6	59.3	71.9	
Primary	7.1	9.1	24.1				12.1	13.4	12.1		24.0	
Unidentifiable								2.5			4.0	
Sample	99	187	278	47	87	23	464	202	66	27	420	103

SS–sidescrapers, ES–endscrapers, Bu–burins, Br–borers, Tc–truncations, Bk–backed pieces, Nt–notches, Dt–denticulates, Rc–*raclettes*, Bc–becs, Rp–retouched pieces, and Tp–truncated/faceted pieces (not considered true tools).

TABLE 5-12

Retouched Tools: Length Expressed as Percent of Each Type

Tools	Length (mm)									Mean	N
	20-30	30-40	40-50	50-60	60-70	70-80	80-90	90-100	>100		
Sidescrapers	1.5	3.0	7.6	15.1	27.3	21.3	7.6	7.6	9.1	61.1	66
Endscrapers	11.5	19.2	28.6	18.9	12.8	5.6	1.7	1.3	0.4	49.6	234
Burins	1.7	16.7	19.2	19.2	19.6	13.7	4.7	2.6	2.6	57.2	234
Borers	37.5	27.1	8.3	18.7	4.2	2.1	2.1			39.5	48
Truncations	21.8	29.5	24.4	10.3	7.7	3.8	1.3	1.3		44.8	78
Notches	19.2	25.0	21.8	15.8	10.7	4.5	1.7	1.1	0.2	45.1	468
Denticulates	13.3	27.6	22.1	15.5	9.4	5.5	3.7	0.6	2.2	49.5	182
Raclettes	40.3	29.8	19.4	6.0	3.0	1.5				35.7	67
Becs	20.6	33.3	10.0	16.7	13.3	6.7				46.1	30
Backed Pieces	13.0	21.7	21.7	26.1	13.0	4.3				46.2	23

touched pieces, and truncated/faceted pieces have been excluded from the restricted list. The exclusion of the naturally backed pieces was necessary, since the selection procedures used here are more rigid than is the usual practice. The variously retouched pieces are commonly excluded, and the truncated/faceted pieces are not considered tools. The ILty value above 30 places the Rosh Ein Mor assemblage into a Mousterian of Levallois debitage (Bordes, 1955, p. 490). Typologically, it is characterized weakly by Mousterian tools and strongly by Upper Paleolithic tools, while denticulates are moderate in number (table 5-13).

TABLE 5-13
The Typological Indices

	Unrestricted	Restricted
ILty	60.6	5.3
IR	2.6	8.8
II	3.3	10.8
III	9.2	30.4
IV	4.3	14.3

Notes on the Typology
Sidescrapers (figs. 5-6*d*, 5-7*e*, 5-11*a-g*)

While sidescrapers are a numerically minor element, comprising only 8.8% of the restricted list, the majority of the sidescraper types and the kinds of sidescraper retouch defined by Bordes are present (1961, pp. 8, 9, 25-30).

The most common types are the simple varieties, followed by the double and convergent (table 5-15). Convex-edged specimens dominate in each of the major sub-types. The majority of the specimens are well made, although the single bifacial sidescraper is of poor execution.

The attribute study recognized four retouch types (table 5-16), as defined by Bordes (1961, pp. 8-10). Scaled retouch corresponds to Bordes's *encaille*, and two varieties are recognized, rounded and expanding. The latter form is probably caused by blows delivered almost perpendicular to the edge. There is no true Quina retouch present, although overlapping demi-Quina retouch occurs. Subparallel and parallel retouch is rather invasive, flattish, with generally long edges. Steep retouch is steep in angle, not very invasive, and may be slightly denticulated.

Sidescrapers made on Levallois blanks comprise almost a third (32.7%) of the sample, with the Levallois flakes dominating over the other Levallois forms (table 5-11). There does not appear to be any selection for finely executed Levallois blanks, as both classic and roughly made blanks were utilized. A few sidescrapers were made on primary flakes, but the great majority are made on blanks of more controlled workmanship.

The length of the sidescrapers ranges from 23 to 103 mm, with many falling into the intervals between 50 and 80 millimeters (table 5-12); compared to most other tools, sidescrapers are made on large blanks.

There is a sizable range in sidescraper edge angle (table 5-17), but the majority fall between 40° and 60°, which may be considered a light duty edge. The steep range, >80°, comprises less than 10% of the sample.

The raw material utilized ranged from coarse- to very fine-grained flint, with the majority of specimens made on the finer-grained material. In fact, some of the finer-grained flint observed in the entire collection was in the sidescraper class.

Endscrapers (figs. 5-12*b, c*; 5-13*c, d, f, h*; 5-14*g*)

These are a common tool type, comprising 11.2% of the restricted list (table 5-14). The typology adopted for this study generally conforms to that presented at the London Conference for the endscraper types of the Transitional Industries (Hours and Solecki, n.d.), although this assemblage is certainly not transitional. The "atypical" subtype of Bordes (1961, p. 31), retained by the London Conference, was not used here, since the types recognized account for the variance in the sample (table 5-18).

There is a tendency toward lateralness in the endscrapers; that is, having only one-half of the working edge retouched. The presence of a notch was not utilized as a diagnostic criterion, but deserves some comment. The contiguousness of a notch to a bit is common, with the simple varieties strongest (22%) in this regard. The other endscraper types also have a fair number of notched specimens, usually formed by a single blow.

The use of Levallois blanks is unusually high, 32.1% (table 5-11). The comparatively high use of Levallois points is notable, and it can be compared with the Transitional Industries of Antelias Cave, Lebanon (Copeland, 1970). Flake blanks dominate, but blades, Levallois and non-Levallois, account for 16.2 percent.

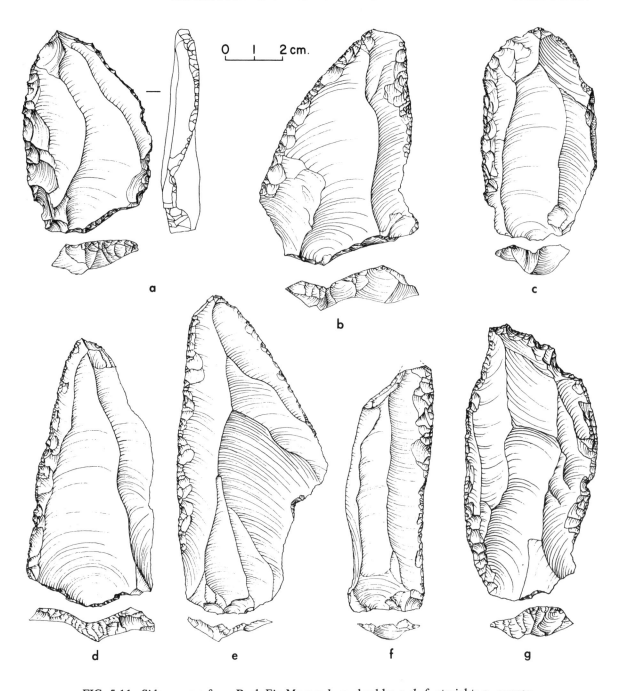

FIG. 5-11–Sidescrapers from Rosh Ein Mor: *a, b, g*–double; *c, d, f*–straight; *e*–convex.

Oval and ogival edge shapes have been combined for this study, since their execution is not so standardized that such a distinction could be justified. These are, by far, the most common (table 5-19). The semistraight shape is merely a very lightly arched edge. The pointed shape has an oval bit with a very narrow, long shank. The irregular shape consists of one piece with an obviously retouched bit which does not conform to the defined shapes.

The arc of the edge was measured by polar grid paper in a manner described by Movius et al. (1968, pp. 10-13). In a sample of 183 pieces, the high per-

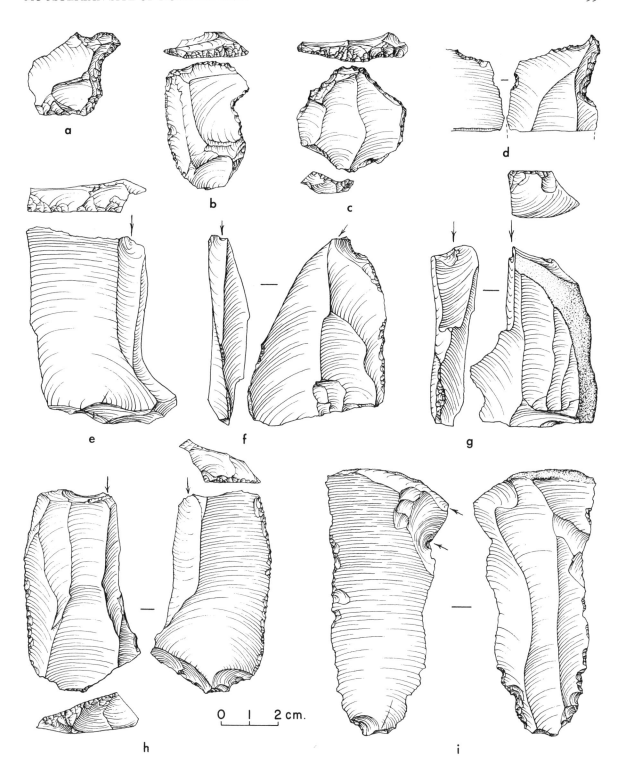

FIG. 5-12—Tools from Rosh Ein Mor: *a, d*—perforators; *b, c*—endscrapers; *e-i*—burins.

TABLE 5-14
Rosh Ein Mor Typology

Type	Number	Percent Unrestricted	Percent Restricted
Levallois Flake	2,218	26.2	
Levallois Blade	1,241	14.7	
Levallois Point	1,664	19.7	
Levallois Point, retouched	136		5.3
Pseudo-Levallois Point	57		2.2
Sidescraper, simple, straight	63		2.5
Sidescraper, simple, convex	89		3.5
Sidescraper, simple, concave	10		.4
Sidescraper, double, straight	3		.1
Sidescraper, double, convex/straight	4		.2
Sidescraper, double, concave/straight	2		.1
Sidescraper, double, convex	7		.3
Sidescraper, double, concave	1		.04
Sidescraper, double, convex/concave	4		.2
Sidescraper, converging, straight	2		.1
Sidescraper, converging, convex	12		.5
Sidescraper, déjeté	3		.1
Sidescraper, transverse, straight	2		.1
Sidescraper, transverse, convex	6		.2
Sidescraper, transverse, concave	2		.1
Sidescraper, inverse	7		.3
Sidescraper, bifacial	1		.04
Sidescraper Total	219		8.8
Endscraper, on flake	156		6.1
Endscraper, on blade	30		1.2
Endscraper, on retouched flake	21		.8
Endscraper, on retouched blade	8		.3
Endscraper, double	5		.2
Endscraper, carinated	7		.3
Endscraper, nosed/shouldered	60		2.3
Endscraper Total	287		11.2
Burin, on truncation	144		5.6
Burin, on snap	152		5.9
Burin, on natural surface	29		1.1
Burin, dihedral angle	55		2.1
Burin, multiple dihedral	16		.6
Burin, multiple on truncation	5		.1
Burin, multiple mixed	2		.1
Burin Total	403		15.5

Borer	56		2.2
Backed Piece	30		1.2
Naturally Backed Piece	311	3.7	
Raclette	84		3.3
Truncation	113		4.4
Notch	752		29.4
Denticulate	364		14.3
Bec, burin	41		1.6
Retouched piece, various	173	5.5	
Notch, end of blade	8		.4
Varia	2		.1
Total	8,458		
Restricted Total	2,554		
Truncated/faceted pieces	699		

<table>
<tr><td colspan="3">TABLE 5-15
Sidescraper Types</td></tr>
<tr><th>Types</th><th>Number</th><th>Percent</th></tr>
<tr><td>Simple, straight</td><td>63</td><td>28.8</td></tr>
<tr><td>Simple, convex</td><td>89</td><td>40.6</td></tr>
<tr><td>Simple, concave</td><td>10</td><td>4.6</td></tr>
<tr><td>Double, straight</td><td>3</td><td>1.4</td></tr>
<tr><td>Double, convex, straight</td><td>4</td><td>1.8</td></tr>
<tr><td>Double, concave, straight</td><td>2</td><td>.9</td></tr>
<tr><td>Double, convex</td><td>7</td><td>3.2</td></tr>
<tr><td>Double, concave</td><td>1</td><td>.5</td></tr>
<tr><td>Double</td><td>4</td><td>1.8</td></tr>
<tr><td>Converging, straight</td><td>2</td><td>.9</td></tr>
<tr><td>Converging, convex</td><td>12</td><td>5.6</td></tr>
<tr><td>*Déjeté*</td><td>3</td><td>1.4</td></tr>
<tr><td>Transverse, straight</td><td>2</td><td>.9</td></tr>
<tr><td>Transverse, convex</td><td>6</td><td>2.9</td></tr>
<tr><td>Transverse, concave</td><td>2</td><td>.9</td></tr>
<tr><td>Inverse</td><td>7</td><td>3.2</td></tr>
<tr><td>Bifacial</td><td>1</td><td>.5</td></tr>
<tr><td>Total</td><td>219</td><td>100.00</td></tr>
</table>

centage of endscrapers in the 160°-200° interval (43.7%) shows how fully many pieces were worked. The tendency toward lateralness is reflected in a high percentage (24.0%) between 50° and 100°, while the remainder falls between 110° and 150°. While the

TABLE 5-16
Sidescrapers—Type of Retouch
N=65

Type	Percent
Scaled	79.0
Demi-Quina	3.1
Subparallel/parallel	7.9
Steep	8.7

workmanship is often poor, the bits are not crudely formed.

TABLE 5-17
Sidescrapers—Edge Angle
N=127

Angle	Percent
30-40	10.2
40-50	34.6
50-60	20.5
60-70	12.6
70-80	13.4
80-90	6.3
>90	2.4

One hundred sixty one-edge angles were also measured by a method outlined by Movius et al. (1968, pp. 13 and 14). A high frequency of the specimens,

TABLE 5-18
Endscraper Types

Types	Number	Percent
On flake	156	54.3
On blade	30	10.4
On retouched flake	21	7.3
On retouched blade	8	2.8
Double	5	1.7
Carinated	7	2.4
Nosed/shouldered	60	20.9
	287	100.0

TABLE 5-19
Endscrapers: Edge Shape
N=180

Bit Shape

	Oval/ Ogival	Semi- Straight	Pointed	Irregular
Simple	112	20	7	1
Nosed/ shouldered	34	3		
Carinated	2		1	
Number	148	23	8	1
Percent	82.2	12.8	4.4	.6

77%, fall into Movius's medium category, 51° to 75°. Acute angled specimens, 26° to 51°, comprise only 1.2% of the sample, while 21.7% have angles which exceed 75°.

Table 5-20 reveals that around half of those pieces from subtypes with adequate samples fall into the thinnest interval (0 to .25), while truly thick specimens, above .50, exist only in small quantities. It is clear that the thick specimens are only the tail end of an asymmetrical curve, which is decidedly skewed toward thinness. The carinated specimens are all thick, by definition. Both bits of the double endscrapers are generally simple, and all were fairly thick. While it was not noted in Table 5-20, the simple endscrapers with the irregular-shaped bits tend to be thicker than the other simple sub-types.

TABLE 5-20
Association of Subtype and Relative Thickness

Th/W	Percent Simple N=102	Percent Nosed/ Shouldered N=40
.15-.25	48.0	52.5
.25-.30	14.7	17.8
.30-.35	6.9	5.0
.35-.40	6.9	10.0
.40-.45	2.9	10.0
.45-.50	2.9	2.5
.50-.55	—	—
>.55	2.0	2.5

Burins

Burins are the second most common tool type in the restricted tool list, accounting for 15.5 percent. The burin classification used here is that suggested by the London Conference on Typology in 1970 (Hours and Solecki, n.d.).

The only other Mousterian assemblage in the Levant analyzed with a typology of burins similar to this one is Jerf Ajla (Schroeder, 1969), and it offers some interesting similarities and differences. The dominance of the burin on snap at Rosh Ein Mor (table 5-21) is paralleled by the upper three layers of Jerf Ajla. The high frequency of burins on truncation is, however, not found at the Syrian site, where dihedral burins are the second most common type. Burins on truncation decrease markedly in the upper layers of Jerf Ajla, and, thus, Rosh Ein Mor appears to be more like the lower layers.

The width of the working bits span a considerable range (table 5-22), but generally they can be characterized as fairly thick (mean width, 13 millimeters).

Burins are made only occasionally on Levallois pieces (9.4%), contrasting with the majority of other tool types (table 5-11). The use of primary blanks, however, is the highest for any tool type, except the variously retouched pieces.

A transverse burin spall removal is considered an attribute. It is not a common trait, being present on only 26 of the 278 specimens studied. Burins on old

TABLE 5-21
Burin Subtypes

Type	Number	Percent
On truncation	144	35.7
On snap	152	37.7
On natural surface	29	7.2
Dihedral	55	13.7
Multiple dihedral	16	4.0
Multiple truncation	5	1.2
Multiple mixed	2	.5
	403	100.0

TABLE 5-22
Width of Burin Bits
N=172

Width (mm)	Percent
0-5	6.4
5-8	17.4
8-11	20.9
11-14	12.2
14-17	13.4
17-20	14.5
>20	15.1

surfaces have the most transverse examples (21%), followed by dihedral (14.5%), burins on truncation (11%), and lastly, the burins on snap (5.4%). As a number of burin types are recognized, each will be discussed separately.

Burins on Truncation (fig. 5-12e-h)

Ninety-six were studied. Edge angles tend to be very steep, with over 80% above 70° (table 5-23). Retouch on the truncated edges varies from coarse to fine, although those which are proximally located are definitely the coarsest. Straight truncations are dominant (71.2%), followed by convex (18.2%) and concave (10.6%). Some of the latter may be considered burins of "Adlun" type. The majority are distally located (73), in comparison to the lateral (7), and proximal (14). Only 10 examples are on oblique truncations.

Burins on Snap (fig. 5-13b)

This is the most frequent burin type (table 5-21). The majority have edge angles over 70°, but are second to the truncated burins in this respect (table 5-23). Over half, 53%, have bits formed by two or more facets, while eleven have four or more.

Burins on Old Surface (fig. 5-12i)

This is not a common type. Edge angles are very similar to those on burins on truncation.

TABLE 5-23
Burins: Edge Angles

Type	Edge Angle						N
	30°-40°	40°-50°	50°-60°	60°-70°	70°-80°	80°-90°	
On truncation	2.6	1.3	5.1	7.9	20.5	62.8	90
Dihedral	2.4	21.4	16.7	28.6	12.0	19.0	48
On snap		4.3	13.0	23.9	15.2	43.5	92

Burins, Dihedral[1] (fig. 5-13g)

The burin bit is usually formed by three or four acutely intersecting burin facets, and in a few cases it is as many as six. A single example approaches busked form with eight facets on one side. Edge angles have a restricted range, indicating some standardization; the mean is 70°, which is considerably lower than is the case for the other burin types.

Borers (figs. 5-12a, d; 5-13i-k)

Borers are not a common tool in the Mousterian, and they are no exception here (table 5-14). One type is recognized, and its variability is expressed by attribute analysis. The borers were studied as to the location, the curvature, and dimension of the borer bits.

The association of Levallois forms and borers is the highest noted for any of the retouched tools (table 5-11). These blanks tend to be rather elongated, since the use of blades and points surpasses that of Levallois flakes.

The high percentage of frontally located bits (59.2%) is similar to the endscrapers. Over half of these bits are made on Levallois blanks, and there is a strong tendency for them to be made on blanks of blade proportions (37%). The bits located on the distal, midsection, and proximal portions of the blanks account for only 22.4%, 8.2%, and 10.2%, respectively. Distall located bits are primarily made on non-Levallois blanks (63.6%), and there is no tendency for blanks of blade proportion. The other two bit forms are too few to judge, but they likely follow the distally located forms in these respects.

The shape of the bit is determined strictly by the presence or absence of bit curvature. As shown in Table 5-24, straight bits surpass curved forms by a considerable margin.

The workmanship is generally very good, and there are a number with very finely made, long narrow bits. This comes as a surprise in a Mousterian context, but Esh-Shubbabiq, in northern Israel, also seems to have equally well-made specimens (Binford, 1966, p. 30, fig. 8).

TABLE 5-24
Shape of the Bit and Blank Form
N=44

Type of Blank	Shape			
	Straight		Curved	
Levallois flake	4		1	
Levallois blade	5	36.7%	4	50.0%
Levallois point	2		2	
Non-Levallois flake	17		5	
Non-Levallois blade	2	63.4%	2	50.0%
	30		14	

Truncations (figs. 5-6e; 5-13e)

This is a comparatively uncommon tool (table 5-14). The definition presented by Bordes (1961, p. 34) was used without modification.

The utilization of Levallois blanks is quite high (table 5-11), with flakes most common. The moderately high use of blanks of blade proportion resembles the situation with the endscrapers.

The location of the truncation was studied on 102 specimens. Distal truncations were the most common (63.7%). Over half of the truncations are slightly convex in shape, approaching poor endscrapers, while the remainder are straight. Truncations tend to be rather thick, with the majority falling into the 4 to 7 mm range, and with proximally located specimens being the thickest. The execution of the truncations is rather crude, some are formed by as few as three blows, and inverse retouch is not uncommon.

Backed Pieces (fig. 5-14e)

These are very rare (table 5-15). The requirement of Bordes's definition (1961, pp. 32 and 33) for steep to semisteep backing was rigidly adhered to in the analysis. The sample studied was very small—only 23 specimens.

The use of Levallois blanks exceeded that of the non-Levallois blanks, and more flakes were backed than blades (table 5-11). They are normally fairly small (table 5-12), and the mean of their Th/W index is .26, indicating they tend to be thicker than most Levallois pieces. The majority have an arched profile (54%), and on 71% the backing is located toward the distal extremity. Only four specimens have continuously backed edges, qualifying as "typical" backed pieces. The backing itself is variable in quality. Eighteen have obverse backing, but there are three examples each of inverse and bipolar backing (sur enclume). Six with frontally located backing would seem to be morphologically similar to de Lumley-Woodyear's San Remo points (1969, p. 56).

Denticulates (figs. 5-6f; 5-14a, b, d, f)

These are comparatively common (table 5-14). A piece was defined as a denticulate if it had three or more contiguous notches (Bordes, 1961, p. 36), but were further subdivided into three sub-types, based upon the number of notches along a standardized 50 mm length of edge. The notches were counted and the length of the retouched edge measured. The number of notches per 500 mm length of edge was then computed. Given a 50 mm edge, micro-denticulation has eleven or more notches, normal denticulation has

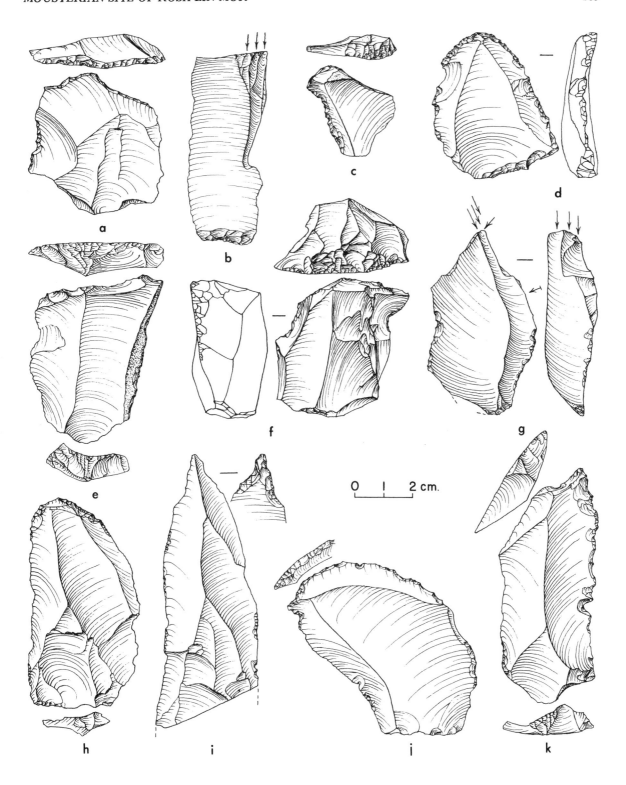

FIG. 5-13—Tools from Rosh Ein Mor: *a—raclette*; *b, g—*burins; *c, d, f, h—*endscrapers; *e—*truncation; *i-k—* borers.

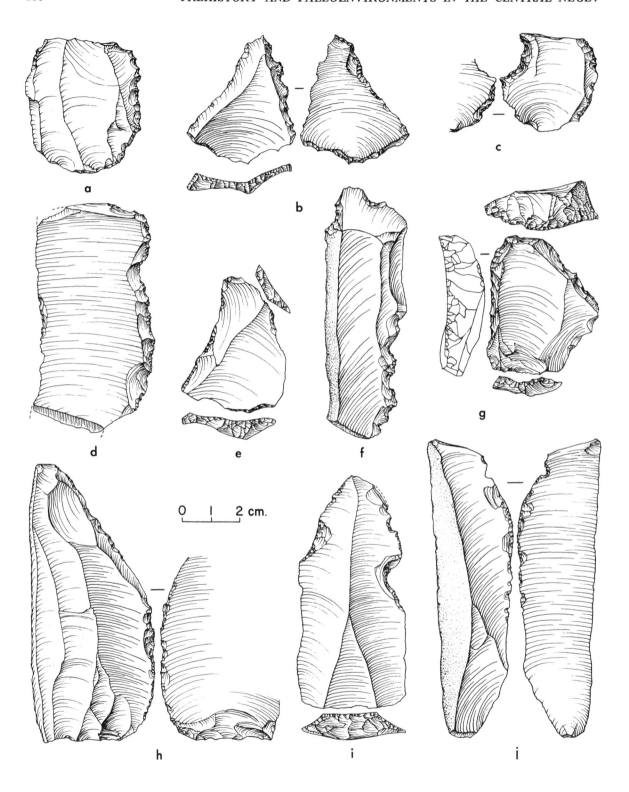

FIG. 5-14–Tools from Rosh Ein Mor: *a, b, d, f*–denticulates; *c, i*–notched pieces; *e*–backed piece; *g*–end-scraper; *h, j*–naturally backed knives (*h* on truncated/faceted piece).

between 6 and 10, and macro-denticulation has 6 or less. If a continuous retouched edge was not present, then an averaging system similar to de Heinzelin's (1962, p. 39) was utilized; i.e., micro-denticulation averages less than 5 mm per notch, normal averages between 6 and 10 mm per notch, and macro would average 11 mm or larger. The sizes of the denticulates are distributed in a near normal curve, with 28.9% micro-denticulated, 49.1% normal, and 22.0% macro-denticulated (N=159), suggesting there was no selective factor for a particular size range.

The association between denticulates and Levallois blanks is about average, 20% (table 5-11). Since the use of blanks of blade proportions approximates the total frequency of blades, their selection was probably fairly random, while the use of the primary elements is rather low.

As Table 5-12 shows, they are rather small, with a mean length of 49.5 mm, and almost two-thirds are under 50 mm in length. The longer specimens are likely made on blanks of blade proportions discussed earlier, since the frequency of pieces above 60 mm (21%) is similar to the frequency of the blanks of blade proportion (ca. 20%).

The location of denticulated edges, each counted individually and, thus, given equal priority, shows that from a sample of 278 edges, 17.3% were frontal, 31.7% were distal (denticulate endscrapers), 33.8% were on a midsection, while only 17.3% were near the proximal extremity. The low percentage of frontally positioned denticulates contrasts with most other tool types.

Edge angles of the notches forming denticulations tend to be steep: abrupt retouch (80° to 90°) accounts for 40.1%, steep to semisteep (50° to 70°) comprises 53.8%, and shallow-angled edges account for only 6.1 percent. Given the difficulties of replicating the exact procedures of measurement each time, measurements of steepness are acknowledged as rough categories. A little over half of the retouch is inverse (52.8%), but spot checks indicate there is no significant correlation with the type of retouch.

Notched Pieces (figs. 5-6*g*; 5-14*c, i*)

This is the most common retouched tool type in the assemblage (table 5-14), which is exceptional in the Levantine Mousterian. The types of notches recognized correspond to Bordes's definition (1961), although they have been further defined by metric criteria. In particular, Bordes acknowledges two types as being valid tools; true notches which are formed by retouch, and Clactonian notches, formed by single blows. The acceptance of the Clactonian forms has been modified to include only those with widths exceeding 10 millimeters. Following Bordes (1961, p. 35), notches on thick flakes with alternating steep retouch have been rejected.

Single notches are most frequent (84.8%), followed by double- (14.0%) and triple-notched pieces (1.2%). Unlike single blow notches, all retouched notches of any size were counted and studied.

Notches are rather commonly made on non-Levallois pieces, on blades (ca. 20%), while the use of primary elements is higher than usual for other types (table 5-11).

The effect of the size threshold against single-blow notches is apparent in the low percentage of notches less than 10 mm wide (17.4%). Even granting this, the small notches are still not as common as those in the 10 to 20 mm range (68.3%). The majority of notches above 20 mm in width are the retouched variety and account for 14.5% of the sample.

The location of the notches was recorded on 67.3% of the entire sample and should be representative: distal portion, 32.1%; medial, 46.3%; and proximal, 21.6%.

Raclettes (fig. 5-13*a*)

The definition of this tool is based solely upon the criteria presented by Bordes (1961, p. 37). A continuous line of retouch is required for the classification of *raclettes*, since accidental flaking can easily result on the requisite thin edge. The size of the sample examined by attribute was sixty-six.

The use of Levallois blanks is only moderately high; few are made on blades, 10%, but a considerable number occur on primary blanks.

There is a high incidence of edges located on the forward (frontal) end of the piece, 37.9 percent. Eight of the twelve frontally located edges have a convex shape. Five of the distally located edges (22.7%) are convex, and seven are straight. The laterally located edges (36.4%) show more variety, since five are convex, four are concave, and five are straight. The one proximally located edge (3.0%) is convex. Four of the twelve frontal edges have a notch associated, perhaps suggesting some affinity with the endscrapers. The retouch is usually obverse, although there are seven inverse examples which are all poorly executed.

Becs Burinants Alterne

Becs are not a common tool, accounting for only 1.2% of the restricted tool list (table 5-14). The definition is Bordes's (1961, pp. 37 and 38), and no modifications have been made.

Levallois blanks comprise 37.9%, with the Levallois point the most common (table 5-11). The high use of Levallois points is exceptional, although the regrettably small sample (29) does not permit much discussion of significance. They are also rather small (table 5-12), with a mean length of 46.1 mm, and moderately thick (Th/W = .26). Nineteen of the bec bits are located frontally, three are located distally, and one is located toward the midsection of a side.

Variously Retouched Pieces

These account for 5.5% of the unrestricted tool list (table 5-14). Under this type is subsumed Bordes's miscellaneous retouched pieces, numbers 45 to 50 (1961, pp. 45-56). They have not been separated into types, since the meagerness and crudity of their retouch generally did not warrant it. In essence, retouched pieces are a collection of retouched artifacts, the edges of which are too amorphous to classify satisfactorily as anything else. The retouch may be due to use in some cases, although this would probably not account for the majority of the specimens. Accidental crushing, whether by trampling underfoot, or postdepositional factors, may account for a fair share of the more irregular pieces. Bordes's caution (1961, pp. 45-56) concerning these types is shared and they are not believed to be useful for comparative purposes.

The relative scarcity of Levallois blanks, at least in a recognizable form, precluded distinguishing between Levallois and non-Levallois blanks in the retouched tool class, although blanks of flake proportion were most common. The proportion of blades corresponds to the frequency of their occurrence for most of the tool types, and perhaps their use is more a function of the blanks' availability than a matter of preference.

The forms of retouch recognized are flat inverse, steep, semisteep, bifacial, flat-invasive, weak denticulation, and nibbling. Flat inverse retouch is self-explanatory, steep has edge angles which range from 80° to 90°, and semisteep from 60° to 80°. Bifacial retouch, while present, is almost invariably crudely executed. Flat-invasive retouch is sidescraperlike but of only limited extent. The same caveat applies to the weak-denticulated retouch, which is also of such a limited extent that it cannot be called continuous. The nibbling retouch is believed to be caused by use rather than purposeful modification. To insure that pieces with nibbling caused by post-depositional factors would stand the best chance of being removed, a piece was not placed in this class if more than one edge revealed nibbling.

The high incidence of steep and semisteep retouch (table 5-25) is suspect since accidental crushing creates such angles. Bordes (1961, p. 46) attributes such retouch to the trampling of animals, at least for one North African site. The same may hold true for the weak denticulation and notches. The remainder of the pieces have retouch that is unlikely to have been caused accidentally, and they at least can be considered marginally retouched. For example, pieces with flat invasive retouch are probably just insufficiently retouched sidescrapers, and, in fact, their relative scarcity parallels that of those tools.

As to the terms used in describing the origin of the retouch, alternate is the English equivalent of the French "*alterne*" (Brezillon, 1968, p. 110), and alternating the English equivalent of "*alternate*" (Bordes, 1961, p. 29). Inverse is on the ventral or bulbar surface, and obverse is normal. The relative frequency of each "type" is about what would be expected: alternate, 7.1%; alternating, 2.5%; obverse, 68.7%; and in-

TABLE 5-25
Type of Retouch
N=324

Type	Percent
Flat, inverse	12.7
Sidescraper	8.6
Steep	17.9
Semisteep	36.4
Bifacial	.03
Weak notch	4.0
Weak denticulate	13.3
Nibbling	6.8

verse, 21.9%. Alternate and alternating retouch usually are the steeply angled types.

Truncated/Faceted Pieces

Truncated/faceted pieces have only recently been described by Schroeder (1969, pp. 397-404), Solecki and Solecki (1970, pp. 138-42), and noted by others (Copeland, 1970; Fleish, 1970). To date, it seems confined to the Levantine Mousterian, although a re-examination of some steeply retouched pieces and truncations in the assemblages from other Mousterian complexes may find it is more widespread (Schroeder, 1969, p. 398).

These pieces cannot validly be called tools, since it is their mode of manufacture which sets them apart. A blank is first roughly truncated, and the truncated surface then serves as the platform for subsequent flake removals. The removed flakes are generally quite small and on the dorsal surface. While the technique is the same as the process of removing a flake off a core, the resulting pieces are usually so small that it is difficult to see any use for them. The assumption is that it represents a technique to thin a piece, perhaps to facilitate hafting. A close examination of a number of the worked edges, however, did not reveal any traces of wear.

The total sample was 699, which excludes those on tools, while the sample studied was 148. This sample was classified during the initial stages of the examination, and it was treated in a manner similar to the

cores. The earlier and preceding works of Solecki and Solecki and Schroeder were at the time unavailable, but it is hoped that the typology presented will adequately display the variation of these pieces, so that the sample can be compared with these earlier analyses. The technique was not measured on the tools, although its occurrence on them is presented in Table 5-27.

Levallois blanks comprise about a quarter of the sample, and as Table 5-11 shows, it was applied to all three Levallois forms. This low use contrasts with Jerf Ajla, where the use of Levallois pieces was closer to 60% (Schroeder, 1969, p. 401).

The classification of these pieces has caused some problems, since they cross-cut many types. Again, the pieces measured and examined are from the nontool class. Basically, three types have been recognized: single platform, opposed platform, and change of orientation.

The dominance of proximally modified pieces (74.8%) is similar to Jerf Ajla (Schroeder, 1969, p. 401) and Nahr Ibrahim (Solecki and Solecki, 1970, p. 139). The dominance of proximal specimens is usually seen as evidence for the need to thin these pieces for hafting; however, if the small chips are the desired product, the thickness of the proximal end is still likely to be optimal. Distal modification is rare (13.7%), as is opposite (6.1%) and change of orientation (5.3%).

The length of these pieces is generally longer than those of the cores (table 5-26). The mean is 58.4 mm, which is the approximate mean length of the Levallois blanks.

These pieces cannot be regarded as distinct tool forms. They cline into burins on the one hand and cores on the other. The distinction between a burin *à face plan* and some of these pieces is almost arbitrary, determined by a judgment as to whether a removed piece originated from a lateral edge or from the inward surface, although only a small fraction of the sample poses such problems.

No distinction was made between a truncated platform and a truncated/faceted piece in the retouched tool class during the examination of the 1970 material. The only other site which presents the association of tool form and this technique is Jerf Ajla

TABLE 5-26
Length of Truncated/Faceted Pieces
N=148

Length (mm)	Percent
0- 10	2.7
10- 20	.7
20- 30	6.1
30- 40	14.2
40- 50	27.0
50- 60	22.3
60- 70	18.9
70- 80	4.1
80- 90	3.4
90-100	0.0
>100	.7

(Schroeder, 1969, p. 401). The results of the two analyses are probably comparable, since only truncated/faceted platforms and not truncations are mentioned. Thus, the same attribute was noted, but viewed from a different perspective.

As Table 5-27 shows, the differences between the two samples is considerable, and it may reflect a basic

TABLE 5-27
The Association of Tool Form and T/F Technique
A Comparison between Rosh Ein Mor and Jerf Ajla

TOOL TYPE	Rosh Ein Mor N=250	Jerf Ajla N=139
Sidescraper	6.4	34.8
Endscraper	11.9	7.6
Burin	23.2	15.1
Naturally backed piece	5.6	21.2
Notch	33.2	4.5
Denticulate	9.2	12.1
Other	10.0	4.5

difference in technology. Hopefully, when the analysis of the material from Nahr Ibrahim is finished (Solecki and Solecki, 1970), it will add data to the apparent significant difference between these two samples.

CONCLUSIONS

The Rosh Ein Mor collection represents a series of Levantine Mousterian occupations which likely occurred during the first major cold/wet phase of the last glacial cycle, ca. 60,000 to 50,000 years ago. Technologically, it is a Mousterian of non-Levallois facies (a low IL), but of Levallois debitage (a high ILty). Typologically, it is characterized by a high percentage of Upper Paleolithic tool forms and a low percentage of Mousterian types.

The present analysis of the Rosh Ein Mor lithic material has been designed to describe the implements themselves and the variable techniques by which they were fabricated. The author recognizes that the measurements and counts of artifacts cannot be used merely to refine the descriptive analysis. Their purpose is ultimately to supply insights about the behavior of the people who made them. There is no pretense here that his objective has been attained. Obviously, many other measurements have not been recognized, although they have been applied elsewhere, so that they have no comparative value at present. Those used in this analysis were designed to show attributes of the debitage and tool classes which are believed to express best the diagnostic variability representing local stylistic traditions.

NOTES

[1] The burin types not mentioned here have samples too small to warrant attribute analysis.

BIBLIOGRAPHY

BINFORD, S. R., 1966. "Mearat Shovakh (Mugharet esh-Shubbabiq)." *Israel Exploration Journal* 16:18-32; 96-103.

BORDES, F., 1955. "Le paléolithique inférieur et moyen de Jabrud (Syrie) et la question du Pré-Aurignacien." *L'Anthropologie* 59:486-507.

————, 1961. *Typologie du paléolithique ancien et moyen.* Bordeaux: Mémoire 1, Publication de l'Institut de Préhistoire de l'Université de Bordeaux.

BREZILLON, M., 1968. *La dénomination des objets de pierre taillée.* Paris: CNRS.

COPELAND, L., 1970. "Early Upper Paleolithic Flint Material from Levels VII-V, Antelias Cave, Lebanon." *Berytus* 19:99-143.

————, 1975. "The Middle and Upper Paleolithic of Lebanon and Syria in the Light of Recent Research." In *Problems in Prehistory: North Africa and the Levant*, edited by F. Wendorf and A. E. Marks. Dallas: Southern Methodist University Press.

CREW, H., 1975. "An Evaluation of the Relationship between the Mousterian Complexes of the Eastern Mediterranean: A Technological Perspective." In *Problems in Prehistory: North Africa and the Levant*, edited by F. Wendorf and A. E. Marks. Dallas: Southern Methodist University Press.

FARRAND, W., 1971. "Geological Correlation of Prehistoric Sites in the Levant." In *The Origin of Homo Sapiens*, edited by F. Bordes. Paris: UNESCO.

FLEISCH, S., 1970. "Les habitats du paléolithique moyen à Naamé (Liban)." *Bulletin du Musée de Beyrouth* 23:25-98.

de HEINZELIN, J., 1962. *Manuel de typologie des industries lithiques.* Bruxelles: Institut Royal des Sciences Naturelles de Belgique.

HOROWITZ, A., 1971. "Climatic and Vegetational Developments in Northeastern Israel during Upper Pleistocene—Holocene Times." *Pollen et Spores* 13(2):255-77.

HOURS, F., and SOLECKI, R. L., MS. *Proceedings of a Symposium on the Terminology of the Paleolithic of the Levant, London, 1969.*

JELINEK, A. J., 1975. "A Preliminary Report on Some Lower and Middle Paleolithic Industries from the Tabun Cave, Mount Carmel (Israel)." In *Problems in Prehistory: North Africa and the Levant*, edited by F. Wendorf and A. E. Marks. Dallas: Southern Methodist University Press.

de LUMLEY, H., 1969. *Le paléolithique inférieur et moyen du Midi méditerranéen dans son cadre géologique* 1. Paris: CNRS.

McBURNEY, C. B. M., 1967. *The Haua Fteah (Cyrenaica) and the Stone Age of the Southeast Mediterranean.* Cambridge: At the University Press.

MARKS, A. E., 1968. "The Mousterian Industries of Nubia." In *The Prehistory of Nubia*, edited by F. Wendorf, 1:194-314. Dallas: Fort Burgwin Research Center and Southern Methodist University Press.

_____; PHILLIPS, J.; CREW, H.; and FERRING, R., 1971. "Prehistoric Sites near En-Avdat in the Negev." *Israel Exploration Journal* 21(1):13-24.

MOVIUS, H.; DAVID, N.; BRICKER, H.; and CLAY, R., 1968. *The Analysis of Certain Major Classes of Upper Paleolithic Tools.* American School of Prehistoric Research, Peabody Museum, Harvard University, Bulletin No. 26.

ROLLAND, N., 1972. "Etude archéométrique de l'industrie moustérienne." In *La Grotte de l'Hortus, Etudes Quaternaires*, Mémoire 1, edited by H. de Lumley, pp. 489-508. Marseille: Université de Province.

SCHROEDER, B., 1969. "The Lithic Industries from Jerf Ajla and Their Bearing on the Problems of a Middle to Upper Paleolithic Transition." Ph.D. dissertation, Columbia University (Ann Arbor: 72-19, 087).

SKINNER, J., 1965. "The Flake Industries of Southwest Asia: A Typological Study." Ph.D. dissertation, Columbia University (Ann Arbor: 65-9177).

SOLECKI, R. S., and SOLECKI, R. L., 1970. "A New Secondary Flaking Technique at the Nahr Ibrahim Cave Site, Lebanon." *Bulletin du Musée de Beyrouth* 23:137-42.

WARNER, R. (translator), 1949. *The Persian Expedition*, written by Xenophon. Harmondsworth: Penguin Books.

WATANABE, H., 1968. "Flake Production in a Transitional Industry from Amud Cave, Israel: A Statistical Approach to Paleolithic Techno-Typology." In *La Préhistoire, problèmes et tendances*, edited by F. Bordes, pp. 499-509. Paris: CNRS.

INTERSITE VARIABILITY IN THE MOUSTERIAN OF THE CENTRAL NEGEV

Fred C. Munday
Southern Methodist University

INTRODUCTION

This paper will both describe and analyze the relationships between a series of Middle Paleolithic assemblages encountered in the Avdat/Aqev area of the Central Negev, Israel. Its aim is to move beyond the descriptive level to an analysis of the technological adaptation, as it is reflected in the site data.

The unique opportunity arises to deal with a large number of Mousterian sites, of which eleven, from a restricted 50 sq km area, are utilized here. This should allow for the testing of a number of propositions related to behavioral adaptation. Not only can much information be gained by studying site location in relation to some basic resources (water and flint), but the high site density should permit an insight into technology as an adaptive system.

The particular advantages offered by high site density in the Avdat/Aqev area are somewhat offset, however, by a lack of specific chronological control over most of the sites. Only two stratified sites were located, Rosh Ein Mor (D15) and D35, of which only Rosh Ein Mor has been dated (Crew, this volume). All other Mousterian sites are surface occurrences, exhibiting variable degrees of post-occupational artifact movement. Given these conditions, this study will consider the following: (1) location, condition, and field-work at each site; (2) artifactual content of samples recovered; (3) technological and, where possible, typological relationships and comparisons between sites; (4) relationships between site content, location, and distribution of natural resources; and (5) how technology was adapted to aid in the economy of

energy expenditure within the environmental system of the Avdat/Aqev area.

It is necessary to relate these sites technologically, so that the large number of assemblages without specific chronological controls can be treated as parts of the same industry. This relationship has to be established before sites can be viewed as operating under a single resource procurement system. The assumption is that people in the same area, operating within the same technological system, essentially respond in similar ways to subsistence and other procurement problems.

Once the technological integrity of the assemblages has been determined, the following section will be concerned with adaptation of technology as it minimizes energy expenditure in movements across the landscape. Energy expenditure, particularly as it relates to raw material use and transportation, will provide a focal emphasis. It is not the opinion of the author that Levantine Mousterian core technology was oriented solely to the production of a specific blank form, i.e., Levallois pieces. Rather, it is felt that this technological pattern is a method which tends to emphasize maximum debitage production. This view is similar to that expressed by Binford and Binford (1966, p. 265), where they refer to an interest in flint working "as an index of economizing behavior and as a clue to site utilization on the part of Neanderthal populations." Thus, essentially, technology is considered to be one means by which populations can efficiently adapt to a set of environmental conditions which involve movement between habitation areas and resource localities.

In order to maintain consistency in the numerous technological observations made throughout this paper, all tables show the sites listed in the same order. This order was determined by putting first those sites very close to water sources but far from flint sources, and last those sites on flint sources but far from water sources. The other sites are positioned relative to these two resources, although the exact position of any site in the table ordering is not of major significance.

LOCATION, CONDITION
AND FIELDWORK:
THE AVDAT AREA (fig. 6-1)

The materials recovered from the following sites, on the Divshon Plain, consist mainly of lithic assemblages. Faunal and/or floral information is available from only two sites (Rosh

Ein Mor and D35), which is to be expected since all other sites are surface occurrences.

Rosh Ein Mor (D15)

While already described in detail (Marks and Crew, 1972; Crew, Goldberg, this volume), a number of observations are particularly pertinent to this study. This site has deep continuous artifactual deposits containing large numbers of tools, much debitage, and numerous exhausted cores.

The major resource association (table 6-2) seems to have been water, which at the time of occupation was probably less than 300 m distant. Raw material (flint) was available from a number of sources, ranging from 20 to 30 m for very poor supplies, to 600 to 2,000 m for very good supplies. The site commands an excellent view of the NS Zin, but only limited areas of the

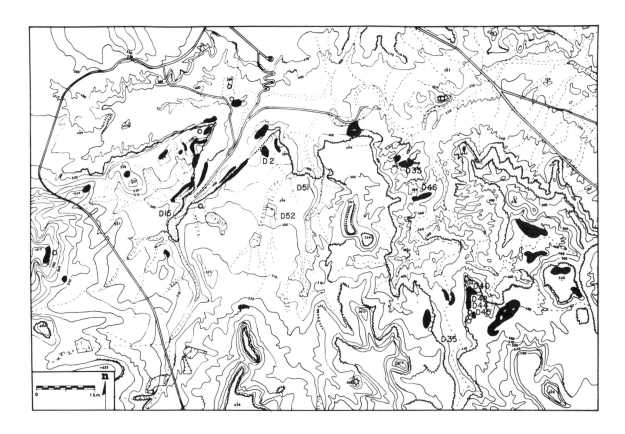

FIG. 6-1–Location of Middle Paleolithic sites in the Avdat/Aqev area. *Black areas* show flint sources, *open circles* are sites not yet studied, while all studied sites are shown by survey number prefixed with a "D."

Divshon Plain on the far side of the Nahal Mor. The site is in primary context, the good condition of the artifacts attesting to minimal artifactual movement.

Dimensional statistics and distances to resources of this site and other sites are shown in Tables 6-1 and 6-2. While a complete study of portions of the excavated material have already been undertaken (Crew, this volume), this paper will deal only with a very restricted sample. The 12 sq m examined for this study come from a 1 m band across level 10 (45 to 50 cm below the surface).

D2

This is an elongated, oval surface concentration of ca. 2,500 sq m which has undoubtedly undergone considerable artifactual movement. Situated near the edge of the cliff overlooking the EW Zin, the site is located on a raw material source that slopes downward to the southeast. Artifacts are heavily concentrated on the lower slopes of the site, with lighter concentrations upslope and along its eastern and western sides.

The raw material source consists of a large amount of cracked, slab-like flint with little cortex, which has been exposed through erosion and deflation. The closest permanent water source was probably at Ein

Mor, 1,600 m away. The closest seasonal water resource would probably have been in the Nahal Divshon, some 1,100 m to the east. The site commands an excellent view of the Divshon Plain, and, by moving a few meters to the cliff edge, of the EW Zin and the lower reaches of the NS Zin within the Nahal Mor.

Artifact movement has resulted in considerable edge damage, causing many problems with tool identification. In many ways, the dispersed nature of the site controlled the collection techniques. In the less dense upper reaches of the site, a single 36 sq m unit was collected. Five additional units of 4 sq m each were collected in a line through the denser, middle, and lower reaches of the slope, so that the full range of artifacts would be recovered.

D51

This site is located close to the junction of the Nahal Divshon and the cliff of the EW Zin. Originally, the site was probably quite small, but with the aid of deflation, the artifacts have spread out over a sizable area (table 6-2). The site is on a gently sloping surface of soft loess with only a small percentage of rocky debris. The fineness of these sediments probably accounts for the relatively good condition of the arti-

TABLE 6-1
Summary of Site Dimensional Data

Site	Area(sq m)	Depth(cm)	Area Analyzed(sq m)	Density per sq m	Degree of Movement[a]
D15	1,200	45-120	12	68.92	1
D35[b]	2,000	300	50	17.58	2
D52	0.25km	0	all	1.00	4
D51	1,000	0	all	0.50	4
D44	750	0	19	36.31	1–2
D45	24	0	12	25.66	1–2
D40	650	0	136	5.00	3
D46	450	0	125	2.81	3
D33	600	0	150	2.17	3
D42	270	0	36	25.61	2
D2	2,225	0	56	11.69	4

[a]*1*–Little or no movement; *2*–Little significant movement; *3*–Significantly moved; and *4*–Extensively moved.

[b]This sample comes from a surface sample.

facts, considering the movement that has occurred, although tool identification still was difficult in some cases.

The closest raw material is ca. 900 m away, to the northwest, along the cliff edge overlooking the EW Zin. Permanent water was probably closest at Ein Mor, ca. 2,100 m away, while seasonal water may have been available in the Nahal Divshon, 200 m to the east. The site offers an excellent view of both the Nahal Divshon and parts of the eastern Divshon Plain.

All surface artifacts were collected in a series of 10 by 20 m strips running down the slope, since smaller units seemed impractical given the post-occupational artifact scatter.

D52

Located on a relatively flat portion of the Divshon Plain, this assemblage has long since spread radially and somewhat downslope toward the northeast. In spite of this extensive movement, the lithic material is in relatively good condition, and possibly not too much material has been lost. Original site area remains unknown, however. All artifacts were collected

as a single unit over ca. 0.25 sq kilometers. The general location of the assemblage has a good view of most of the Divshon Plain and the Nahal Divshon. It is, however, some distance from both raw materials and permanent water. Raw material is closest along the cliff overlooking the NS Zin (ca. 1,200 m), while permanent water at Ein Mor is ca. 1,750 m distant. Seasonal water in the Nahal Divshon would have been only about 300 m away.

LOCATION, CONDITION, AND FIELDWORK: AQEV AREA (fig. 6-1)

Within the Aqev area, Middle Paleolithic sites occur in two major zones: within the Nahal Aqev, either within the Mousterian terrace, D35, or on the old Mousterian surface, D33 and D46; and, on the eastern extension of the Divshon Plain on the far side of the Nahal Aqev (D42, D40, D44 and D45). Those sites within the Nahal Aqev range in elevation from 410 to 380 m, while those on the plain are all at about 500 m elevation. These latter sites posed logistical problems, since access

TABLE 6-2
Relationship between Sites and Resources

Site	Distance to Raw Material[1]	Altitude Difference[2]	Distance to Water[3]		Altitude Difference[2]
D15	600 m	-15 m	300 m		-20 m
D35	600 m	+80 m	150 m		+10 m
D52	1,200 m	+20 m	1,750 m	(300 m)	- 5 m
D51	900 m	+15 m	2,100 m	(300 m)	- 5 m
D44	75 m	0 m	800 m	(300 m)	-80 m
D45	25 m	- 5 m	950 m	(350 m)	-80 m
D40	10 m	0 m	800 m	(425 m)	-80 m
D46	0 m	0 m	300 m		-10 m
D33	0 m	0 m	200 m		-10 m
D42	0 m	0 m	600 m	(350 m)	-80 m
D2	0 m	0 m	1,600 m		-20 m

[1] Distance to closest substantial raw material source.
[2] Negative sign indicates resource is downslope of site. Positive sign indicates resource is upslope of site.
[3] Distance is given to probable supply of permanent water. Figure in parentheses refers to distance to possible seasonal supply.

was only by a steep trail up the eastern Nahal Aqev cliff and, therefore, the size of each site collection was determined by how much lithic material could be transported down the steep 80 m cliff face.

SITES IN THE NAHAL AQEV

D35

Located on and in a terrace remnant at 410 m elevation, about 500 m upstream of the present Ein Aqev, this site of ca. 2,000 sq m appears to contain several strata of Mousterian artifacts *in situ* and in mint condition, separated by relatively sterile layers[1] (see Goldberg and Horowitz, this volume). In order to minimize mixing of artifacts from originally different artifact levels, the artifacts utilized in this study were only the surface material from ca. 50 sq m at the very top of the terrace. While the artifacts were in generally good condition, tool identification was undertaken somewhat cautiously, since some edge damage was present.

Two fossil springs occur ca. 150 m upstream from the site and appear to have been active at the time of site occupation (Goldberg, this volume). No raw material is present at the site, and the closest good resource is ca. 600 m away, but involves a steep climb of some 80 meters. Poor quality material is available along the terrace downstream from the site, but it is questionable whether it was present at the time of site occupation, because it appears to be recent scree from the western cliff top overlooking the Nahal Aqev.

The surface of the site has a slightly rounded profile, and consequently, it is possible that some of the smaller debitage and lighter, smaller cores have been lost.

The site commands a good view of both the upper and lower reaches of the Nahal Aqev, and access to all parts of the Nahal is relatively easy. Reaching the 500 m plateau, however, is somewhat difficult, due to the cliffs flanking the sides of the Nahal Aqev.

D33

Located on the top of an eastward sloping, soil-capped limestone remnant within the Nahal Aqev, this 600 sq m site is relatively close to the base of the western Nahal Aqev cliff face. The site is located on an exposed outcrop of hammada flint. About 200 m to the southwest, a fossil spring was possibly active at the time of occupation (Goldberg, this volume). The site commands an excellent view of the lower reaches of the Nahal Aqev, as well as parts of the EW Zin. Therefore, it seems to possess a number of advantages: immediately available raw material; possible water supplies; and access to two drainage areas.

Artifact movement has undoubtedly occurred, although artifact density is highest at the top of the slope, which would seem to mitigate against extensive movement. A total of 150 sq m was collected in six 25 sq m units from all parts of the slope.

D46

This site of ca. 450 sq m is located on the flanks and in the saddle of a Mousterian surface remnant north of Ein Aqev, within the Nahal Aqev. The density of artifacts in the trough of the saddle indicates that considerable artifact movement probably occurred, although topography of the site prevented significant artifact loss. Given these conditions, 5 units of 25 sq m each were collected in various parts of the site.

Raw material is available on the site where erosion has exposed the Mousterian conglomerate. About 300 m to the northwest lies the fossil spring mentioned for D33. Thus, permanent water may well have been close by, and the site offered the same advantages as did D33. Access to the 500 m plateau would have been difficult, however, owing to the steep cliffs.

SITES ON THE EASTERN DIVSHON PLAIN

D42

Located directly at the top of the only modern path up the eastern cliff of the Nahal Aqev, this site of ca. 270 sq m is placed directly on a source of flint cobbles and hammada flint exposed by erosion. As the site surface slopes gently away to the east, there is some uncertainty as to how much artifactual movement has taken place. Artifact density is relatively homogeneous across the site, and even somewhat higher on the upslope portion of the site, suggesting that little lateral movement has occurred, although deflation may well have caused some lowering of artifacts. The surface raw material, however, suggests that if the site was originally located on the flint source, then deflation has been minor.

The present bedrock location has resulted in considerable damage to artifact edges, again making tool identification difficult. Given the possible movement of artifacts at the site, two areas totaling 36 sq m were collected in 1 sq m units. One area was located downslope of the other and slightly to the south, in order to gather data on artifact distributions, as well as to check for downslope movement of artifacts.

Despite its location, the eastward slope of the site prevents a view of the Nahal Aqev. The view is generally of the slightly undulating hammada-covered surface to the east. The closest permanent water supply at the time of occupation was probably the spring near D35, some 600 linear meters away and 80 m lower in altitude. Seasonally, water may have been available in a shallow, rocky drainage channel on the surface to the east; however, the ability of this drainage to retain water subsequent to rainfall is doubtful.

D40

This site of ca. 650 sq m is located at the base of a knoll at a northern promontory of the 500 m high hammada plain, overlooking the Nahal Aqev. The location on a semisteep slope has undoubtedly resulted in artifact movement. Just how much has occurred cannot be determined precisely because artifact densities remain quite high across the site, and there are two concentrations at different points along the slope. Artifact condition is quite good, and it is possible that the site has only recently been exposed, since some pieces exhibit relatively little patination. Again, caution was exercised in tool identification because of some edge damage.

A flint source is close at hand, ca. 10 to 15 m downslope, and a larger raw material source is ca. 200 m away, near D42. Permanent water was available from the spring near D35, some 800 m away and 80

m lower in altitude. Should seasonal water have been available in the drainage mentioned above, it would have been about 425 m distant.

The site commands a good view of most parts of the northern Nahal Aqev and the whole of a major eroded box canyon to the east of the main Aqev drainage, although access to these areas would have been limited by steep cliffs. A view of the southern reaches of the Nahal Aqev is prevented by the knoll.

Samples from a total of 136 sq m were collected in 4 sq m units; samples were taken from both concentrations, as well as from a section connecting the two concentrations.

D44

This site of ca. 750 sq m is located back from the cliff edge overlooking the Nahal Aqev, and has an excellent view of the hammada surface to the east of that drainage. Its location on a very gentle slope has probably resulted in little artifactual movement, as seen by both definite core clusters and debitage concentrations along various parts of the slope. Again some deflation may have occurred.

The rocky surface of the site has caused edge damage to artifacts, and consequently tool identification is difficult. A total of 96 sq m was mapped artifact by artifact; however, owing to logistic problems discussed earlier, material from only 19 sq m was recovered for metric analysis.

No raw material is immediately available, but a source is only 75 to 100 m away. Permanent water was available from the springs near D35 (800 m distant and 80 m lower), while seasonal water may have been present in the rocky drainage on the plain to the east some 300 m distant.

D45

This very small site of 24 sq m in area is located near D44, but is farther south along the cliff edge. The site surface is flat, and probably little artifact movement has occurred. The rocky surface has caused considerable edge damage, however, with consequent effects on tool identification. Due to the seemingly small amount of artifactual movement, 12 sq m were mapped and completely collected.

Raw material is not directly associated with the site; however, hammada flint is located ca. 25 m east of the site. Permanent water is some 950 m away, and, again, involves a descent of about 80 meters. If present, seasonal water may have been in the rocky drainage on the plain about 350 m away.

METHODOLOGY AND SITE DATA

Of all the sites described, only Rosh Ein Mor (D15) has lithic material in sufficiently good condition that all tools, debitage, and cores can be described and classified with certainty. Even at D35, where edge damage was not too significant, it is considered best to be cautious in tool identification. At all other sites, the varying degrees of edge damage precluded sure tool identification, particularly for retouched pieces, notches, denticulates, and endscrapers.

One should not despair, however, for it is the opinion of the author that tool typologies have, at best, a limited use in studies relating intersite variability to settlement location. Since tool types are but morphological constructs, they add little to analytic approaches to site function.

Given the paucity and poor condition of the tools, as well as their questionable usefulness in integrating a series of sites, it was essential to utilize debitage and core information to a maximum. Therefore, much of this study will center around debitage and core relationships, both within and among sites. Where possible, and useful, tool assemblages will be utilized to clarify and refine conclusions. It is obvious that debitage characteristics are largely the result of capabilities and intensity in raw material reduction within a given technological method. Because of the direct relationship between debitage and cores within a reduction sequence, particularly useful information may be gained by a study of

shifts in these relationships with changes in site location.

The set of relationships between debitage and cores should covary, depending on behavioral attitudes toward core reduction and debitage production. It is expected that within a technological method, sufficient flexibility should exist, such that behavior toward the reduction of raw material will change, depending on the relationship of site location to resource availability and the amount of work involved in moving raw material between sites.

Given that relationships between debitage and cores are expected to change during Mousterian core reduction, a model for this sequence is proposed (table 6-3).

Generally, the early stages of the reduction sequence are expected to be dominant at sites on or very near raw material sources, since raw material must be on hand. The absence of water would not allow anything other than very short occupation; therefore, later reduction stages normally would not be reached (table 6-4). If water also is nearby, debitage characteristics are expected to reflect additional, later stages of the reduction sequence, since there are possibilites for extended site occupation. It is expected, however, that raw material usage will be relatively wasteful. The later, intensive stages of the reduction sequence, which require more work, might well be eliminated by the utilization of fresh cores after the intermediate stages.

The intermediate stages of the reduction sequence are expected to be dominant at sites located away from both raw material and water sources, although the former may be relatively close by. Because raw material has to be transported to these locations, it becomes necessary to maximize its usage. However, the lack of water lessens the possibility of extensive occupation, so that the really late reduction stages might not be attained. Where the distance to flint is relatively

TABLE 6-3

Proposed Core/Debitage Relationships during Core Reduction Sequence

STAGE	CORE CHARACTERISTICS	DEBITAGE CHARACTERISTICS
Initial	Raw material, nodule or chunk, with size dependent upon available raw material.	No debitage.
Early	Core partially developed, with few scars on the major removal face and simple scar patterns. Cores are generally large and heavy. Major removal face is large.	Primary debitage prevalent. Low dorsal scar counts and simple dorsal scar patterns. Debitage thick and large to enable rapid development of core. Debitage size and weight relatively high.
Middle	Core size (weight) and removal face area reduced. Removal face is more complex both for scar count and pattern. Little primary material remaining on core.	Less primary cortex on dorsal surface of debitage. Higher dorsal scar count relative to surface area. Size of debitage reduced but more complex scar patterns. Debitage thin in order to increase blank production. Mean size and weight lower.
Late	Cores are small, light, somewhat amorphous and exhausted. Very complex scar patterns and high scar count.	Little, if any, primary debitage. Surface area of debitage reduced and scar count high. Most complex scar patterns, very thin debitage to maximize blank production. Debitage size and weight very low. High dorsal scar count relative to surface area of blank.

short, raw material usage is expected to be more wasteful.

These intermediate stages of the sequence should not normally be dominant close to permanent water because this resource allows intense, long-term occupation and thus, the potential for working raw material to exhaustion, although exceptions may occur.

The later stages of the reduction sequence are only expected to be dominant where a single resource, water, is to be found. As suggested above, this is because of the possibility for long-term occupation and, hence, the scarce commodity, flint, has to be maximally utilized.

While this sequence has been described as a series of "stages" in raw material reduction, it should not be thought of as a series of discrete steps but, rather, as a continuous pro-

TABLE 6-4

Relationship between Core Reduction Stages and Resources

RAW MATERIAL

		On Site	Close	Far
	On Site	4	3–4	1
		(D46,D33)		(D15,D35)
WATER	Close	4–5	3	1
		(D42,D2)	(D44,D45,D40)	(D52,D51)
	Far	5	2–3	1–2

Key: Site numbers in parentheses. *1*–Late stage; *2*–Intermediate to Late stage; *3*–Intermediate stage; *4*–Early to Intermediate stage; and *5*–Early stage.

cess, one stage passing into another. Using the above criteria, it is possible to relate sites to this reduction sequence to test its validity. It should also be emphasized that this study is concerned more with the emphasis in reduction activity at sites and does not preclude all stages of the reduction sequence being present at any single location no matter what its resource associations.

METHODOLOGY AND DESCRIPTION

The proposed model for Mousterian reduction sequence necessitates the following observations on debitage and cores[1] :

I. Debitage (fig. 6-2)
  A. Maximum length measured parallel to the percussion axis .
  B. Maximum width measured perpendicular to maximum length
  C. Maximum thickness anywhere along artifact, excluding bulbar area
  D. Platform type utilizing the following categories:
    1. Cortex
    2. Unfaceted
    3. Dihedral
    4. Multifaceted straight
    5. Multifaceted convex
    6. *Chapeau de gendarme*
    7. Crushed
    8. Thinned
  E. Dorsal scar pattern, regardless of number of scars involved in the pattern (see fig. 6-3)
  F. Number of scars on dorsal surface of artifact
  G. Artifact weight in grams
  H. General debitage categories:
    1. Non-Levallois flake
    2. Non-Levallois blade
    3. Primary flake (more than 50% cortex)
    4. Primary blade (more than 50% cortex)
    5. Naturally backed flake (included in non-Levallois flakes)
    6. Naturally backed blade (included in non-Levallois blades)
    7. Levallois flake

    8. Levallois blade
    9. Levallois point
    10. Core-trimming elements

Cores

Typologically, the variety of core morphology is shown in Fig. 6-4. For the amount of use and relative placement in the reduction sequence, the following observations were made:

II. Cores
Typologically, the variety of core morphology is shown in Fig. 6-4. For the amount of use and relative placement in the reduction sequence, the following observations were made:
  A. Debitage category removed from core prior to its abandonment. While it cannot be determined what kind of general debitage had been removed during the core reduction process, this observation is but a statement of the final condition of the core with regard to debitage removed. Four general categories were utilized:
    1. Predominantly flake
    2. Predominantly blade
    3. Flake and blade
    4. Point
  B. Surface area of removal face measured in square centimeters
  C. Core weight in grams
  D. Removal face shape. The following categories were utilized:
    1. Circular
    2. Oval
    3. Square
    4. Rectangular
    5. Triangular
    6. Irregular
  E. Core type

Where more than one removal face was present on a core, observations II-A., B., and D. were repeated. In addition, cores were typed according to morphology, the general range of types being illustrated in Fig. 6-4 and Table 6-14.

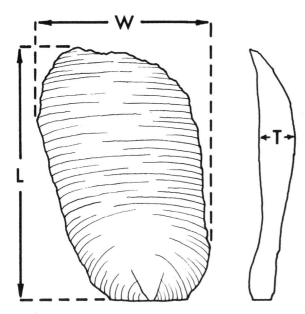

FIG. 6-2—Schematic illustration of major artifact measurements.

It must be reiterated that the most that can be expected of the data is the detection of trends through which both quantitative and qualitative attributes move. In this respect, the data have been tabulated with the sites ordered in terms of general resource relationships.

Table 6-5 presents a general summary of numbers of tools, cores, and debitage for each site. The highest artifact densities are at those sites where minimal movement of artifacts has taken place, while lowest densities are at those sites exhibiting maximum artifact movement (table 6-1). Site D2 is the single exception, where the surface configuration forced artifact congregation in certain localities.

DEBITAGE ANALYSIS

Mean debitage length tends to increase as the raw material association becomes stronger (table 6-6). Site D42 seems to be slightly aberrant, but this may be a function of the generally small, cobble flint found at that site. It should also be noted that the variability around the mean also increases as the mean increases. The range of variability is also relatively large with a maximum to minimum variance of 5.46. Certainly though, the seven sites closest to raw material, D44, D45, D40, D46, D33, D42, and D2, tend to have the longest debitage.

A similar pattern emerges for width (table 6-6). Sites D40, D46, D33, D42, and D2 have

TABLE 6-5
Group Summary of Artifacts from Studied Sites

Site	Debitage	Retouched Tools	Cores[1]	Total	Debitage and Tool to Core Ratios
D15	681	79	67	827	11.34:1
D35	778	59	47	879	17.80:1
D52	232	18	36	284	6.94:1
D51	412	43	64	497	7.11:1
D44	589	48	91	690	7.00:1
D45	268	16	26	308	10.92:1
D40	504	28	163	681	3.26:1
D46	292	19	61	352	5.10:1
D33	271	11	44	326	6.41:1
D42	746	61	126	922	6.40:1
D2	422	57	176	655	2.72:1

[1]
Includes broken cores.

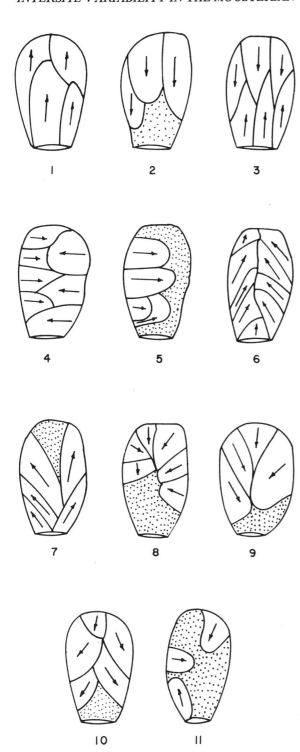

FIG. 6-3—Dorsal scar patterns. Key: *1*—unidirectional from base; *2*—unidirectional from distal end; *3*—bidirectional on axis; *4*—bidirectional perpendicular to axis; *5*—unidirectional perpendicular to axis; *6*—converging from base; *7*—expanding from base; *8*—peripheral and partial peripheral; *9*—converging from distal end; *10*—expanding from distal end; *11*—random.

the widest sets of debitage, and increased variability with increased width occurs again. A relatively large range of variability also occurs with a maximum to minimum variance ratio of 4.69.

A very definite pattern emerges with thickness. Increased mean thickness of all debitage occurs with an increased relationship to raw material sources. Again, increased variability around the mean occurs as the mean increases. The range of variability is the smallest of the three attributes with a maximum to minimum variance ratio of 4.26.

In addition to these general observations, it should be noted that Site D52 exhibits the tightest range of variability in all three attributes—length, width, and thickness. Site D40 exhibits the largest range of variability for length and width, and the second largest for thickness.

When the means of the length, width, and thickness are expressed in relative proportions to each other and plotted on a tri-polar graph a very tight cluster occurs (fig. 6-5). In general, the implication of this tight cluster is that there is a general trend to produce debitage of a particular shape, with the attributes being interdependent. While there is a consistency of debitage shape, there is certainly no consistency of size for complete pieces (table 6-7).

The largest debitage seems to be associated with those sites having a strong relationship with a raw material source. Thus, while there seems to be a general concept of shape, sufficient flexibility exists within the technological system to allow for larger or smaller pieces. The possible behavioral phenomena operating behind this flexibility will be returned to later.

While it was not mentioned in the model,

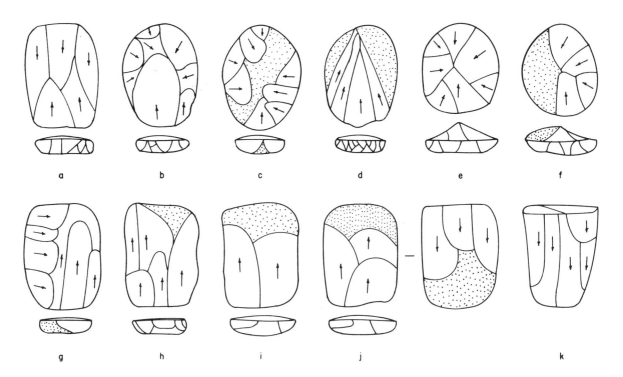

FIG. 6-4–Major core forms. Key: *a*–bidirectional Levallois; *b*–typical Levallois; *c*–unfinished Levallois; *d*–Levallois point; *e*–discoidal; *f*–partial discoidal; *g*–change of orientation; *h*, *i*–single platform; *j*–opposed platform, opposite side; *k*–single platform blade core (pyramidal).

it was suspected that platform morphology also might well change according to site resource association. This is the case where increased platform complexity is present at those sites located away from raw material sources (table 6-8). Unfaceted and cortical platforms are proportionately higher at those sites located on raw material sources, while dihedral platforms only weakly follow the increase in complex forms. These data suggest that at those sites where debitage size is thin, small, and light, the degree of platform preparation is very high. The implication is that when raw material becomes scarce, the approach to technology becomes more deliberate and exacting.

The reduction model proposed that dorsal scar patterns should become more complex as the reduction sequence progressed. In general, as site relationships to resources change and with changes in reduction stage emphasized,

dorsal scar patterns do, in fact, become more complex. This is best indicated by the indices of scar pattern complexity, which have been computed from the combined percentages of complex scar patterns (table 6-9). That Sites D42, D2, D46, and D33 have the simplest scar pattern indices is in line with the proposed model, since at those sites raw material is immediately available and the early stages of the reduction sequence should occur. By the same token, it is not surprising that Sites D15 and D35 have very complex patterns. It was proposed that it is only in the later stages of the reduction sequence that complex scar patterns would predominate. Water is not an easily transportable commodity, hence intensively occupied sites (as exhibited by the deep lithic deposits) should be associated with permanent water resources. It is at these sites that the later stages of the reduction sequence would be reached.

TABLE 6-6
Mean Debitage Length, Width, and Thickness from Studied Sites (mm)

Site	Length			Width			Thickness		
	N	Mean	S.D.	N	Mean	S.D.	N	Mean	S.D.
D15	264	49.1	18.0	513	33.9	10.8	679	8.9	4.3
D35	408	55.4	20.5	504	41.7	13.7	688	8.9	4.3
D52	48	45.4	11.5	142	33.8	9.3	231	9.6	3.6
D51	116	56.2	18.3	175	42.7	15.5	396	10.4	4.9
D44	156	54.1	21.0	251	39.6	13.1	562	11.3	5.2
D45	48	55.9	25.3	117	38.0	14.3	264	11.9	5.9
D40	251	70.3	26.9	341	49.8	20.2	462	12.4	6.8
D46	95	68.1	24.9	147	45.8	15.5	280	12.5	5.5
D33	143	71.6	24.8	192	46.5	15.4	269	13.1	6.3
D42	424	57.8	21.5	611	43.7	15.9	771	13.7	6.2
D2	217	66.3	25.5	301	49.5	19.0	405	15.6	7.5

It was also proposed that dorsal scar count should pattern according to the reduction sequence. Table 6-10 presents data on the mean dorsal scar count for all sites; as can be seen at first glance, no clear pattern appears. It has to be considered, however, that surface area of debitage is reduced as the reduction

TABLE 6-7
Mean Size of Intact Debitage[1]

Site	Mean	Standard Deviation	Number
D15	20.3	19.4	248
D35	27.4	27.7	372
D52	21.4	21.3	40
D51	38.4	30.2	96
D44	39.3	43.1	112
D45	45.5	49.2	30
D40	66.0	73.1	216
D46	64.5	57.5	68
D33	60.7	51.1	124
D42	47.3	52.5	398
D2	74.6	79.3	206

[1] Size computed as follows: $\dfrac{\text{length} \times \text{width} \times \text{thickness}}{1{,}000}$

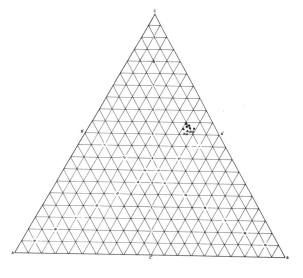

FIG. 6-5—Tripolar graph, showing the relationship between mean length, width, and thickness by assemblage. *A'-A*—thickness; *B'-B*—width; and *C'-C*—length. Key to resource associations: *x*—raw material; *square*—raw material and water; *triangle*—close to raw material; *circle*—close to water; *open circle*—far from raw material and water.

sequence progresses. Therefore, debitage surface area has to be introduced. When this is taken into consideration, a trend does occur.

TABLE 6-8
Summary of Platform Types for Debitage

Site	N	Simple		Total Simple	Dihedral	Complex (Multifaceted)			Total Complex	Other[1]
		Cortex	Unfaceted			Straight	Convex	C.D.[2]		
D15	456	3.3	35.7	39.0	14.5	20.8	18.0	3.3	42.1	4.4
D35	502	7.0	30.1	37.1	13.9	10.4	34.9	2.2	47.5	1.6
D52	138	6.5	28.3	34.8	15.2	20.3	21.0	–	41.3	8.8
D51	258	14.7	29.5	44.2	11.2	10.9	30.2	1.6	42.7	1.9
D44	305	12.8	32.1	44.9	15.7	14.8	21.0	0.7	36.5	2.9
D45	129	11.6	29.5	41.1	10.1	31.0	12.4	–	43.4	5.5
D40	360	12.8	29.5	42.3	11.4	13.7	27.5	3.6	44.8	1.7
D46	188	13.3	38.3	51.6	12.8	13.8	16.5	3.2	33.5	2.1
D33	208	16.4	41.8	58.2	9.6	10.6	18.8	1.9	31.3	1.0
D42	532	15.4	48.1	63.5	12.2	8.9	13.2	–	22.1	2.3
D2	296	19.6	47.3	66.9	10.8	6.4	12.2	0.7	19.3	3.1

[1] Other includes crushed and thinned.
[2] C.D.–*Chapeau de gendarme.*

TABLE 6-9
Dorsal Scar Patterns of Debitage by Sites

Site	Scar Patterns[1]												N	Index[3]
	None	1	2	3	4	5	6	7	8	9	10	11		
D15	0.5	15.2	0.5	13.3	–	2.4	24.1	–	35.8	0.3	–	7.9	369	83.5
D35	0.5	20.0	1.1	18.3	0.7	0.7	30.0	–	27.1	–	–	1.6	436	76.1
D52	2.1	17.8	–	18.5	–	1.4	10.3	–	42.5	–	–	7.5	146	71.3
D51	3.2	21.7	–	18.9	–	4.1	15.7	–	29.5	–	–	6.9	217	64.1
D44	1.1	18.5	1.1	19.2	0.4	3.6	14.2	–	37.0	–	–	5.0	281	70.8
D45	1.4	23.2	0.7	16.2	–	4.2	7.0	0.7	30.3	–	0.7	15.5	142	54.9
D40	1.4	20.2	0.9	22.5	0.6	2.0	12.8	0.3	32.8	0.3	–	6.8	155	68.7
D46	3.0	26.2	1.8	20.7	–	1.8	10.4	–	32.9	–	–	3.0	164	64.0
D33	2.7	29.2	0.5	10.8	1.6	2.2	19.5	–	27.0	–	–	6.5	185	58.9
D42	3.4	44.0	2.7	10.3	0.8	3.7	14.2	0.3	14.8	0.2	–	5.6	593	40.3
D2	3.6	33.6	1.8	11.9	1.8	5.7	9.8	0.3	24.1	–	–	7.4	336	49.7

[1] See Fig. 2 for drawings of these types.
[2] No dorsal scars.
[3] Percentage of complex patterns (3, 4, 6, 7, 8, 9, and 10).

At those sites where intensive core reduction has taken place (i.e., sites away from raw material sources), dorsal scar count remains high even though debitage size is reduced. Thus, the scar count is increasing relative to decreasing debitage surface area. This rela-

TABLE 6-10
Dorsal Scar Counts by Site and
Surface Area of Debitage

	Scar Count			Surface Area[1] and Scar Count	
Site	Number	Mean	S.D.	Area	Area/Dorsal Scar Count
D15	270	4.3	2.0	1,664.0	387.1
D35	441	4.5	2.3	2,310.2	513.4
D52	66	3.9	1.9	1,534.5	393.5
D51	140	3.9	2.1	2,399.7	615.3
D44	168	3.9	2.1	2,142.4	549.3
D45	50	3.7	2.1	2,124.2	574.2
D40	286	4.7	2.3	3,500.9	744.8
D46	118	3.7	2.1	3,119.0	843.0
D33	142	4.0	2.1	3,329.4	832.4
D42	554	3.3	1.9	2,525.9	765.4
D2	327	3.7	2.0	3,281.9	887.0

[1] Approximated from mean length x mean width.

tively small area per dorsal scar indicates a higher intensity of core reduction and, hence, fits the proposed model. At sites closely associated with raw material sources, the large surface area per dorsal scar indicates that it is probably at these sites that the early reduction stages occur, because the large dorsal scar size facilitates rapid core preparation.

A final technological variable to be examined at the general site level is that of debitage weight.

Generally, those sites with direct raw material associations have heavier mean debitage weights and larger variances (table 6-11). Lighter debitage is found at those sites away from raw material sources. Intermediate weights are found at sites close to, but not on, raw material sources. Again, Site D40 is an exception to this pattern, although it by no means disturbs the trend. It should also be noted that D40 has by far the largest variance around the mean. This seems to be caused by a few outliers in the general distribution pat-

tern for weight. Clearly, the pattern seen for weight is related to debitage size and, as such, merely provides a slightly different perspective.

TABLE 6-11
Mean Weight of Debitage by Site (gms)

Site	Number	Mean	Standard Deviation
D15	246	19.0	16.3
D35	157	27.0	20.7
D52	38	18.8	18.6
D51	95	39.0	26.9
D44	112	38.1	38.1
D45	27	36.7	34.9
D40	204	57.7	58.3
D46	56	49.7	36.1
D33	123	58.1	41.2
D42	n.d.	n.d.	n.d.
D2	47	55.3	31.5

DEBITAGE CATEGORY ANALYSIS

The proportional occurrence of debitage categories is shown in Table 6-12. For a number of these there is little variation from site to site. For example, non-Levallois flakes only range from 44% to 69% and no trend can be seen. Sites D15 and D35 have proportions similar to D42 under different resource conditions, although some sites with similar resources do exhibit only minimal variation (e.g., D51 and D52, D15 and D35, etc.).

No apparent trend is present for non-Levallois blades, and there are some large variations seen for similar resource associations (i.e., D15 and D35).

For primary flakes, sites away from raw material have fewer primary flakes as compared with those sites where raw material is present or close. The same pattern holds for primary blades. Site D2 is an exception to this pattern, but this is probably due to the lack of cortex on the parent raw material at the site.

TABLE 6-12

Major Debitage Classes by Site as Percents

Site	Primary		Non-Levallois		Levallois			Core Trimming Elements	N
	Flakes	Blades	Flakes	Blades	Flakes	Blades	Points		
D15	6.6	1.3	54.3	20.5	7.9	3.8	3.4	2.1	681
D35	5.9	2.2	58.0	11.1	11.1	4.5	7.1	0.3	778
D52	9.5	1.3	63.4	10.0	5.6	4.7	0.4	5.2	232
D51	11.2	0.7	62.8	9.2	5.8	5.6	1.7	2.9	412
D44	12.6	2.7	61.3	13.4	7.3	1.7	0.3	0.7	633
D45	16.8	2.6	50.4	12.3	6.0	4.9	0.4	6.7	268
D40	6.3	2.0	48.6	12.1	13.9	11.3	2.6	3.2	504
D46	18.0	5.1	45.1	14.0	9.9	5.8	1.4	0.7	292
D33	15.1	4.1	46.8	15.8	8.9	5.9	1.8	1.5	271
D42	16.5	5.6	55.1	16.5	2.5	2.0	0.6	1.2	846
D2	10.7	1.7	69.0	10.9	5.2	2.6	—	—	422

In the Levallois categories, very little patterning is obvious. At all sites Levallois flakes are most common, followed by Levallois blades and, with a single exception, by Levallois points. It is noticeable, however, that Sites D15 and D35 have proportionately high point components within the Levallois class.

Sites D2 and D42, located on raw material sources, have the lowest proportion of Levallois elements, while D40 exhibits a very large Levallois component (27.8% of all debitage). It is interesting that this site has the smallest primary component and a very large mean core weight (see table 6-15). Thus, the relatively large Levallois component might be merely the result of well-prepared cores being brought to the site (as exhibited by the low primary component) which are then minimally reduced, as exhibited by the high core weight (table 6-15). The net effect would be to produce relatively large amounts of Levallois-related debitage as opposed to non-Levallois material.

So far, debitage attributes have been considered for each assemblage as a unit, without any breakdown by artifact class. When this is done, the patterns described continue to pertain in a general sense. Size appears to be most consistent in retaining the general trends, although Levallois points are clearly an exception (table 6-13). Nondimensional attributes, however, show trends only for the non-Levallois pieces, with the Levallois types being highly consistent regardless of resource availability. Certainly, this is partially caused by the qualitative criteria used in the definition of Levallois pieces, although the highly uniform stylistic attributes for these Levallois pieces must be considered part of prehistoric cultural patterns.

Qualitative comparisons of debitage between sites reveal a homogeneous series of assemblages. Of the diagnostic elements, i.e., the Levallois categories, only one site, D40, exhibits any significant variation. At D40 a series of very elongated Levallois points were recovered; these, however, were technologically similar to points found at other sites, only their numbers were excessive.

CORES

This section will deal primarily with the descriptive aspects of core technology. As this only becomes particularly revealing when considered in conjunction with general debitage characteristics, a section on core/debitage relationship will also be included.

TABLE 6-13

Index of Mean Debitage Size by Major Artifact Classes[1]

Site	Primary		Non-Levallois		Levallois		
	Flakes	Blades	Flakes	Blades	Flakes	Blades	Points
D15	24.4	–	17.3	22.4	20.2	18.6	22.4
D35	35.6	35.1	27.7	28.8	22.4	30.1	23.1
D52	44.6	–	16.2	8.8	27.3	31.2	–
D51	31.0	–	37.4	58.9	27.4	16.6	41.3
D44	27.7	34.2	40.8	47.0	34.5	–	36.0
D45	67.1	–	28.1	13.8	–	32.7	–
D40	134.5	154.3	65.7	82.7	44.7	31.4	37.7
D46	88.0	112.8	60.4	73.5	33.8	26.0	33.4
D33	81.6	115.4	55.0	64.4	40.1	52.6	18.1
D42	63.8	65.7	42.0	39.2	48.7	71.8	34.7
D2	111.1	149.4	62.9	90.3	50.8	56.7	–

[1] Size Index computed by $\dfrac{\text{length x width x thickness}}{1{,}000}$ on complete pieces.

Table 6-14 presents a summary of the core types found at each site. In general, these cores at first appear to be composed of a multitude of discrete types (fig. 6-4). As has been suggested earlier, however, several of these types probably represent nothing more than a series of continuous stages of core reduction. Thus, early stage Levallois cores, typical Levallois, bidirectional Levallois variants, and irregular cores may be just cores at different parts of the reduction sequence. Also, it must be noted that a core is typed on the basis of its final morphology, rather than by the process of reduction.

Levallois Cores, Early Stage

These have shapes similar to the typical Levallois cores, but tend to be thicker, to exhibit little flake removal on the upper surface; marginal preparation is often complete, and large areas of cortex are usually still present. Often these show hinging, which may account for their abandonment. It is notable that these are found most often at sites with direct raw material association.

Levallois Cores, Typical

These tend to be circular to oval in shape, and rather thick. Scar patterns tend to be radial, although true centripetal patterning is rare. Of all the Levallois cores, these come closest to the classic western European variety (fig. 6-6*a*).

Levallois Cores, Bidirectional

These usually have a square-to-rectangular upper surface shape, exhibiting a relatively large area. Often these may have cortex on the under surface and minimal lateral preparation, although platforms are always well made and usually multifaceted. From the existing scar patterns, this type of core could produce Levallois flakes, blades, or more rarely, points.

A variation of this type is rectangular, very thin, and has bidirectional removal planes at right angles to each other. Normally, these exhibit very careful preparation and skillful workmanship. All of these bidirectional Levallois cores may be considered typical for the Levallois method in the southern Levant (fig. 6-6*b, d*; fig. 6-7*a-d*).

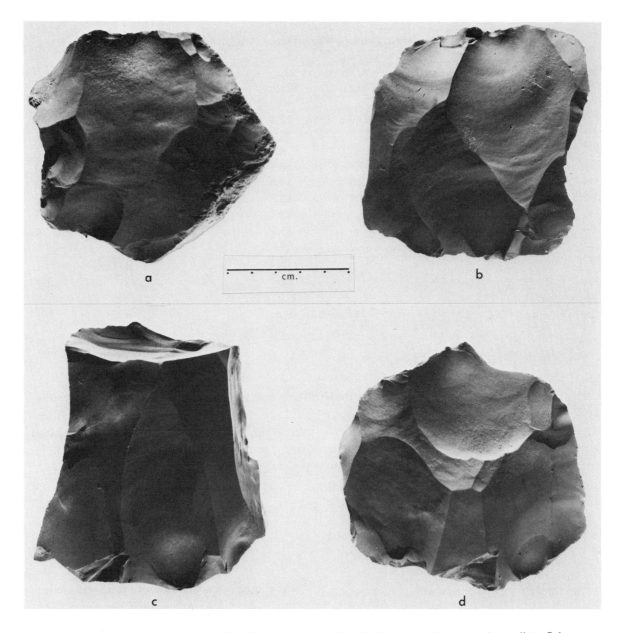

FIG. 6-6–Levallois cores: *a*–typical Levallois flake core (Site D42); *b, d*–bidirectional Levallois flake cores (Sites D44 and D40); *c*–unidirectional Levallois point core (Site D40).

Levallois Point Cores

These normally exhibit minimal preparation, as they often take advantage of the natural shape of the raw material (fig. 6-6c). Thus, it is not uncommon to find a core on which fracture planes have been utilized in the production of a point.

A number of point cores are of the Nubian, Type II variety (Guichard and Guichard, 1965) on which deep, oblique scars originating from the distal extremity help shape the removal face. These exhibit considerable preparation along their lateral edges, which are almost denticulate. In general, point technology can be best described as opportunistic, with minimal preparation prior to point removal.

TABLE 6-14
Core Typologies for Studied Sites as Percents

Types	Sites										
	D15	D35	D52	D51	D44	D45	D40	D46	D33	D42	D2
Levallois											
a. Early Stage	0.0	0.0	2.8	3.6	10.0	0.0	0.7	6.3	0.0	8.0	3.1
b. Typical	6.0	7.7	2.8	10.9	5.0	4.2	9.3	6.3	12.1	7.0	6.9
c. Bidirectional	3.0	10.3	8.3	23.6	27.6	20.8	32.9	14.6	27.3	30.0	20.0
d. Bidirectional, double	—	—	—	—	—	—	—	—	—	3.0	—
e. Bidirectional, opposed	3.0				1.3	4.2	2.9	4.2			3.2
f. Point	1.5	7.7	2.8	7.3	12.5	8.3	7.1	8.3	12.1	2.0	4.4
Subtotal	13.5	25.7	16.7	45.4	56.4	37.5	52.9	39.7	51.5	50.0	37.6
Non-Levallois											
a. Single Platform <3 scars	13.5	7.7	8.4	5.6	18.8	4.2	14.2	14.6	3.0	7.0	11.2
b. Single Platform >3 scars	25.4	23.1	27.8	20.0	18.8	37.5	17.8	22.9	24.3	22.0	25.6
c. Pyramidal	—	—	—	—	—	—	—	—	—	1.0	—
d. Ninety-Degree	1.5	2.6	2.8	1.8	1.3	4.2	2.9	2.1	15.2	8.0	3.7
e. "Nahr Ibrahim"	11.9	20.5	13.9	7.3	5.0	4.2	4.3	—	3.0	5.0	6.8
f. Discoidal	9.0	5.1	8.3	1.8	—	—	2.1	8.3	3.0	2.0	5.0
g. Partial discoidal	7.5	—	—	—	—	4.2	—	—	—	—	—
h. Irregular	17.9	15.4	22.2	18.2	—	8.3	5.7	12.5	—	5.0	10.0
Subtotal	86.5	74.4	83.4	54.7	43.9	62.6	47.0	60.4	48.5	50.0	62.3
Sample	67	39	36	55	80	26	140	48	33	100	160
Fragments	—	8	—	9	11	—	23	13	11	26	16

Ninety-Degree Cores

In some cases it was difficult to distinguish these cores from partially prepared Levallois cores. Generally, however, they are small, more angular and thinner than Levallois cores, with less upper face preparation, and this face generally consists of two sets of scars intersecting at right angles.

Single Platform Cores

These simple cores vary greatly in size and inten-

sity of reduction. The category with less than three scars is essentially arbitrary, but there are large numbers that appear to have been only partially utilized. Shape is highly irregular, as is weight.

Discoidal

These cores are the classical discoidal cores, well prepared marginally and with peaked, almost pointed upper removal surfaces. They are generally not present in any great number and tend to be of variable size.

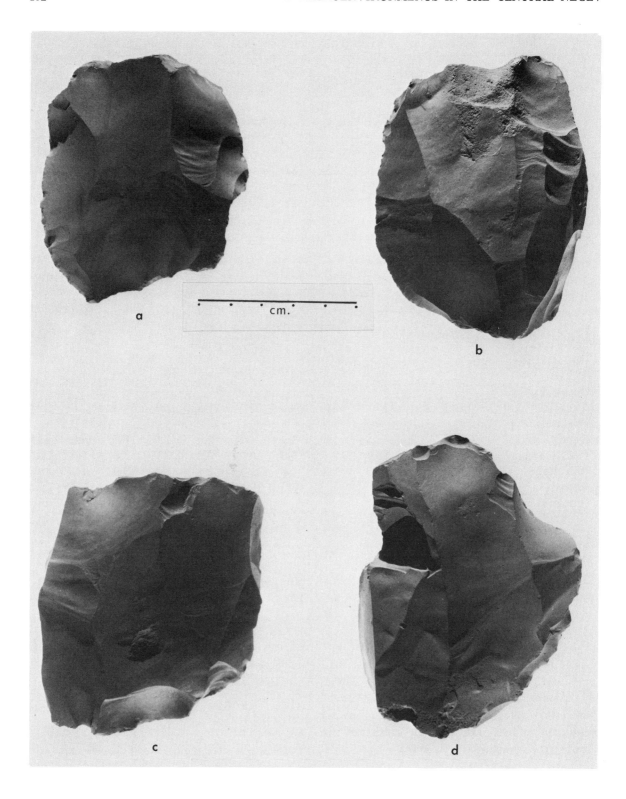

FIG. 6-7—Cores: *a-d*—bidirectional Levallois cores (Sites D42, D46, and D44).

Irregular

For the most part, these cores are very small, exhausted varieties. A few, however, are flint nodules from which several flakes have been removed from various parts of the core, seemingly without pattern. In general, these cores are marked by small size, with edge angles exhibiting extensive crushing, which precludes further debitage removal (fig. 6-8*a-i*).

Nahr Ibrahim Cores

These have been adequately described elsewhere (Solecki and Solecki, 1970). They generally occur in two basic varieties, unidirectional and bidirectional, although additional subdivisions are possible.

Partial Discoidal

In many respects, these cores resemble discoidal cores, although parts of the major, upper removal face have not been intensively worked, nor is the center of the face so peaked.

Summary of the Analysis

In a more general sense, the following observations are of interest when examining Table 6-14.

1. There seem to be relatively higher proportions of Levallois core types at those sites on or close to raw material sources than at those sites with weak raw material associations. This can partially be explained with the proposition that cores are partially prepared at raw material sources. If some of these are discarded, they remain at the site. Those Levallois cores removed from the site are reduced at other sites (i.e., D35, D15, etc.) where they may lose their Levallois character, resulting in either struck Levallois cores or those irregular in nature. At those sites away from raw material sources, irregular core types are proportionately high. Again, this pattern is what was expected from the proposed model.

2. The Nahr Ibrahim cores are not equally represented at all sites. They are proportionately higher in those sites away from raw material sources and are weakly represented where raw material is close by. A

possible explanation for this is that where raw material is not immediately available it becomes economical to utilize pieces of debitage as sources for fresh blanks.

3. While it is not evident from Table 6-14, a number of the Levallois cores at Sites D42 and D2 have had large Levallois flakes struck from them. However, analysis of the Levallois debitage at those sites has failed to reveal these pieces. It has to be surmised, therefore, that some selective debitage removal from these sites has occurred.

4. From Table 6-15 it can be seen that the trends for core weight and surface area of removal face are as expected in the reduction sequence model, given the resource associations for each site. Both weight and surface area generally increase as raw material associations become stronger and water associations weaker.

TABLE 6-15
Weight and Surface Area of Cores

Sites	Core Weight (gms)			Core Surface Area (sq cm)		
	Mean	S.D.	N	Mean	S.D.	N
D15	46.9	30.7	67	15.8	6.5	46
D35	78.4	51.1	36	23.8	12.1	30
D52	43.7	35.4	36	14.6	7.9	30
D51	108.9	156.0	52	26.6	11.1	45
D44	159.6	125.2	77	30.3	15.9	64
D45	87.5	46.0	24	23.2	9.8	20
D40	190.0	151.4	140	42.2	23.8	108
D46	156.0	115.8	47	33.0	17.5	42
D33	253.4	160.7	32	44.6	19.4	30
D42	124.7	90.2	89	30.0	14.4	75
D2	154.9	139.4	159	32.9	18.8	122

Sites D42 and D2, however, seem to be smaller than might be expected. It should be remembered that sites located on raw material sources probably served, among other functions, as reservoirs for cores to be used at other sites. Thus, one might expect cores with more potentially removable debitage (i.e., the larger cores) to be taken from the site. This would

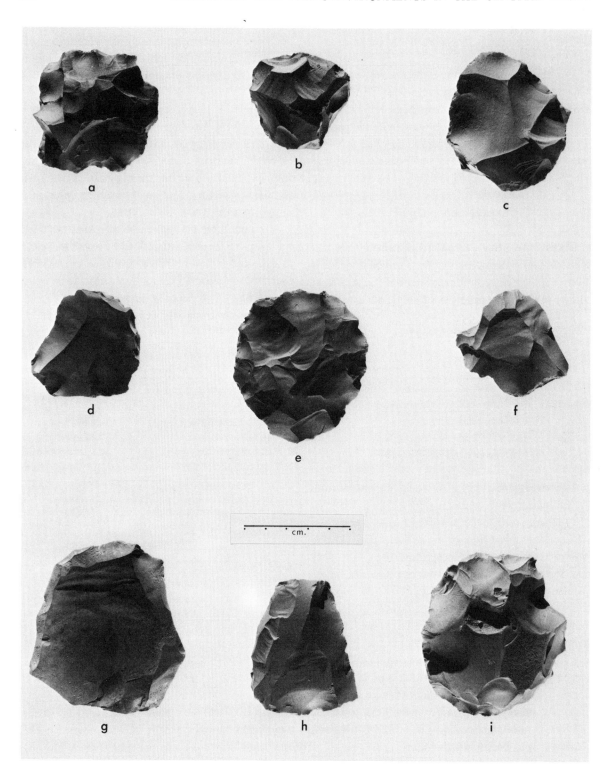

FIG. 6-8—Cores: *a, b, e*—exhausted discoidal (Sites D40, D42, and D44); *c, i*—discoidal (Site D52); *d, f, g*—small Levallois cores (Site D35); *h*—Levallois point core (Site D44).

have the effect of depressing these means of the cores initially produced at the site.

Cores from Site D45 also have a mean weight and surface area somewhat lower than expected. In part, this may be due to more extensive core reduction, as exhibited by the high debitage and tool-to-core ratio (table 6-5).

Core preparation at each of these sites indicates the technological homogeneity of these series of assemblages, with most core types exhibiting little morphological variability. The pragmatic and opportunistic preparation of all point cores is striking in this respect. Bidirectional Levallois cores are also very consistent morphologically at all sites, as are "Nahr Ibrahim," ninety-degree, and bidirectional variants.

DEBITAGE/CORE/RESOURCE RELATIONSHIPS

In the reduction sequence model (table 6-3), it was proposed that certain co-variation in core and debitage characteristics should occur. Further, it was proposed that these relationships could be even better understood when relationships between sites and resources were taken into consideration.

In general, it was expected that as core size decreased, there would be consequent changes in debitage morphology and size. Table 6-16 summarizes some of the data already presented, and documents those trends expected in the model.

Admittedly, these trends are not absolutely consistent; however, they are strong enough to indicate that the sites under discussion do conform to certain basic patterns within a technological system of core reduction. This, together with other general technological observations (e.g., Levallois-related cores at all sites generally have the same morphology), would indicate that all the sites discussed are part of the same technological tradition. This point should not be taken lightly, as it is something that has to be ascertained before further integrations of the sites on a behavioral level can be undertaken.

Thus, despite what might have appeared initially to have been considerable and unrelated variability, is, when examined, within the framework of a reduction sequence model, quite consistent and predictable. In terms of the trends noted in Table 6-16, core weight and the percentage of primary debitage show the least consistent trends. Possibly the variation in the primary debitage has been greatly influenced by the parent raw material available on each site. At sites where small, nodular flint is present, considerable primary debitage might be expected, while at sites where large boulders of raw material are available, one might expect selection of that material requiring minimal core reduction, i.e., material with minimal cortex. Site D2 seems to fit the latter pattern and D42 the former. At Sites D46 and D33, where cortex-covered tabular flint is exposed on the surface, the incidence of primary elements in the debitage is again high.

The anomalies in the trends for cores might well be due to some form of selective factor wherein cores are moved from site to site. This has already been suggested in reference to D2 and D42. At the other sites, the trend is more deliberate, and this may be the result of little core removal.

In general, there is a large range of ratios of debitage and tools to cores (table 6-5). However, this is not totally without patterning. Sites D15 and D35, which exhibit core and debitage characteristics of the end of the reduction sequence, have relatively high ratios. Alternately, D52, which also exhibits characteristics of the end of the reduction sequence, has a low ratio. Thus, low mean core and debitage weights combined with low debitage and tool-to-core ratios suggest that cores brought to this site were initially quite small. Considering the distance of D52 from both raw material and water, there is indication that there was some concern for the size of raw material carried between sites.

Certainly, the relationships between debi-

TABLE 6-16
Summary of Selected Core and Debitage Characteristics for Studied Sites

Site	Core Weight (gms)	Primary Debitage Percent	Debitage Area/ Dorsal Scar Count	Complex Dorsal Scar Pattern Percent	Complex Platform Percent	Debitage Weight (gms)
D15	46.9	7.9	390.6	83.5	42.1	19.0
D35	78.4	8.1	511.3	76.1	47.5	27.0
D52	43.7	10.8	394.1	71.3	41.3	18.8
D51	108.9	11.9	613.2	64.1	42.7	39.0
D44	159.6	15.3	555.8	70.8	36.5	38.1
D45	87.5	19.4	580.3	54.9	43.0	36.7
D40	190.0	8.3	743.4	68.7	44.8	57.7
D46	156.0	23.6	832.0	64.0	33.5	49.7
D33	253.4	19.2	823.5	58.9	31.3	58.0
D42	124.7	22.1	764.7	40.3	22.1	n.d.
D2	154.9	11.7	890.7	39.6	19.3	55.3

tage and cores are very complex, as illustrated by Site D40. It would appear that comparing sites solely on the basis of the debitage or core component leads to a loss of understanding of the relationship between the two. It might be argued that Levallois pieces were imported into D40 in large numbers because of their high frequency (27.8% of the flake debitage). If this is so, then one has to account for the very low debitage and tool-to-core ratio (3.32:1). If Levallois elements were brought to the site, they would presumably account for a large proportion of this ratio. The question then is, why were the cores brought to the site? It seems reasonable to propose that D40 consists of a site into which well-prepared cores were brought and minimally reduced. The site might be viewed, therefore, as one in which multiple, short-term occupations occurred.

TOOL ANALYSIS

There is no doubt that the tools were the least valuable part of the assemblages examined from this area, as their condition demanded that they be classified with extreme caution. This is primarily due to the extensive movement which occurred at a few sites and to the generally poor condition of all artifacts at surface sites of this age. Some comments, however, are useful, particularly for sites where artifact movement was minimal and/or where the tools were in good condition.

As Table 6-17 indicates, at all sites a large percentage of the tools are notches and/or denticulates. These types must be considered of questionable validity, given the surface position of the assemblages. Only such types as sidescrapers and burins are always the result of clearly purposeful retouch. Also, the sample size is so small that any attempt to characterize any tool assemblage is useless.

The tools from Site D35 are among the best recovered, since all were only recently deflated. Perhaps this is the one site where denticulates, at least, were probably purposefully formed, although notches could still be accidental. The sidescrapers are only rarely made on Levallois pieces, but all show a rather flat, invasive retouch of the type typically present at Rosh Ein Mor (D15). The Levallois element at this site tends to be finely produced, and complete Levallois flakes and points are the rule.

TABLE 6-17

Tool Typologies from Studied Sites as Percents

Type	Sites									
	D35	D52	D51	D44	D45	D40	D46	D33	D42	D2
Levallois flake	36.3*	28.9*	22.2*	40.2*	33.3*	40.0*	37.2*	39.3*	18.1*	22.7*
Levallois blade	14.8*	24.4*	21.3*	9.8*	27.1*	32.6*	21.8*	26.2*	14.7*	11.4*
Levallois point	23.2*	2.2*	6.5*	1.8*		9.1*	5.1*	8.2*	4.3*	
Levallois point, retouched			5.9				6.3			
Pseudo-Levallois Point	2.0		2.9			4.5	18.8			1.9
Sidescraper, simple straight	6.1			2.4	15.4	4.5	12.5		6.1	5.8
Sidescraper, simple convex	2.0	6.3		4.8			6.3		4.1	3.8
Sidescraper, simple concave	2.0									3.8
Sidescraper, concave/straight	2.0									
Sidescraper, double convex	2.0									1.9
Sidescraper, transverse		12.5								1.9
Sidescraper, bifacial				2.4					2.0	
Sidescraper, double straight									2.0	
Endscraper	4.1	12.5	5.9	9.1	23.1	4.5			2.0	11.5
Endscraper on retouched piece	2.0									1.9
Burin on truncation		12.5	2.9		7.7					1.9
Burin, dihedral	10.2		5.9	19.0		13.6	12.5	33.3	8.7	5.7
Perforator	6.1		2.9	2.4		4.5				
Backed pieces	2.0			2.4						
Naturally backed knife	2.0*					0.6*	2.6*		0.9*	
Raclette	2.0									
Truncation			5.9	4.8		4.5		16.7	6.1	1.9
Notched piece	34.7	43.8	38.2	21.4	15.4	50.0	31.3	50.0	34.7	25.0
Denticulate	12.2		17.6	14.3	30.8	13.6	12.5		22.4	25.0
Bec burin			5.9							3.8
Retouched piece	4.2*	4.4*	9.3*	5.4*	6.3*	2.3*	5.1*	8.2*	9.8*	6.2*
Varia	6.1	12.5	5.9	7.1	7.7				2.0	3.8
Sample Totals	237	45	108	112	48	175	78	61	116	97
Restricted Totals	49	16	34	42	13	22	16	6	49	52

*Percentage based on total samples, all others based on restricted samples.

Only five tools at D44 were made on Levallois pieces. Tools here are generally larger and thicker than those from D35, and only rarely exhibit the fine workmanship seen at the latter site. Levallois pieces are normally fragmentary and rather crude. This attribute may be applied to all the sites on or near raw material sources. The single exception is Site D40 where the Levallois pieces are rather well made and many complete examples were recovered, including numerous, long Levallois blades.

The relatively large tool samples from Sites D42 and D2 are of interest, as a site on a raw material source might not be associated with camp site activities. These tools, however, are all within the "atypical" range, and a large number are fragmentary or incomplete, suggesting they were rejected during manufacture.

To date, the only good tool sample from this area is from Rosh Ein Mor (D15). Since it has already been described in detail (Crew, this volume), no further discussion is warranted.

CONCLUSIONS

Initially, it was pointed out that the large number of Middle Paleolithic sites in the Avdat/Aqev region had very few chronological controls. Because of this, these sites had to be related technologically through the use of morphological similarity and a core reduction sequence model. Given that human behavior is somewhat flexible, the general trends detected in most of the material presented here seem remarkably consistent, which leads to the conclusion that these sites are relics of the same technological system. While it is agreed that the trends detected do show some fluctuation, this should by no means be taken as an invalidation of the model. Certainly, there are inherent properties of raw material, size, shape, and composition that might well influence the results, but in general, there are no major contradictions to the model.

Since sites generally have the characteristics expected at different stages of the reduction sequence, it would seem to indicate that complete core reduction rarely, if ever, took place at a single site. It appears as if some initial preparation may well have taken place where raw material was present, then cores and blanks were moved to secondary sites where further reduction took place. From a behavioral point of view, this pattern suggests there was some conception of how raw material could be processed in order to minimize the volume moved between sites. That is, in an ideal sense, only desired raw material was moved between sites. Thus, if the cores taken to D52 were small, as proposed earlier, this may well be merely a function of distance to be traveled between the raw material source and the site.

In many respects, this problem can be derived from discussions of the economy of work such as that proposed by Zipf (1949, p. 346), in which behavior is oriented to "most economically procuring raw materials and fabricating them into consumable goods" (Zipf, 1949, p. 348). In this instance, the raw materials would be flint, and consumable goods the artifacts utilized by prehistoric man and derived from the flint. In a technological sense, this can be related to the Binfords's (1966) "economizing behavior" mentioned earlier.

If this behavior structure is present in the archaeological material, it should be possible to relate sites to the specific resources mentioned in this paper, i.e., distance to water and raw material (flint), as well as topographic variables such as altitude and slope. In this respect, variables such as mean debitage size and core weight should be those that vary according to changes in distance, altitude, and slope of sites to resources.

To test this relationship, a multiple stepwise regression was conducted for all sites in which the dependent variables (debitage size and core weight) were related to several independent resource variables. These independent variables were: (1) distance to permanent water; (2) distance to the nearest substantial flint source; (3) altitudinal change between site and permanent water; (4) altitudinal changes between site and raw material; (5) site upslope or downslope of permanent water; (6) site upslope or downslope of raw material.

The results of this analysis can be seen in Table 6-18.

TABLE 6-18
Regression Analysis of Debitage Size and Core Weight with Resource Variables

	Simple R	Multiple R	R Square
Dependent Variable—Debitage Size			
Independent Variables—			
Raw material distance	-.70021	.70021	.49030
Raw material slope	-.75568	.80118	.64190
Distance to water	-.03167	.86221	.74341
Slope to water	-.32987	.88684	.78649
Altitude to water	.18563	.90842	.82523
Altitude to raw material	-.55994	.94718	.89714
Dependent Variable—Core Weight			
Independent Variables—			
Raw material distance	-.69632	.69632	.48486
Raw material slope	.74002	.78933	.62304
Distance to water	.24623	.79815	.63704
Slope to water	.25718	.80264	.64423
Altitude to water	.16074	.75186	.56529
Altitude to raw material	-.48594	.90443	.81800

For the variable debitage size almost 90% of the variability is accounted for by these six independent variables which essentially control the amount of work involved in moving raw material between sites. More precisely, distance of a site from its potential raw material source controls about 50% of the variability alone.

Core weight is also greatly affected by these same factors. Over 80% of the variability in mean site core weight is accounted for by the six independent variables, again with raw material distance being responsible for almost 50% of this variability. It is interesting that the amount of altitudinal change has more effect on core weight than on debitage size, as can be seen by the large increase in the R square.

Those independent variables associated with water have minimal effect on both debitage size and core weight. It would seem, therefore, that water, as an independent variable, does not effect debitage size, but effects other site characteristics, such as occupational intensity (contrast Sites D15 and D35 with Sites D51 and D52).

The high predictability factor indicates that site placement with respect to these two resource variables, as well as the subsequent treatment of raw material, was of considerable concern to the Mousterian inhabitants of the Avdat/Aqev area. Through the mechanism of a very flexible technology, raw material was differentially treated so as to minimize the number of trips to flint sources. In this way, energy expenditure and work were minimized in moving raw material between sites. In order to do this, it became necessary to work raw material more intensively to maximize debitage production. Thus, in sites far from flint sources, more intensive core preparation took place, as exhibited by the more complex qualitative technological variables (platforms, scar pattern, scar count) found on the resultant debitage. This would certainly seem to fall within the concept of economizing behavior.

To some extent, these concepts of economizing behavior are supported by other aspects of site characteristics mentioned earlier. For instance, the probable small size of cores taken to D52 and the high instance of Nahr Ibrahim cores at sites away from raw material sources certainly fall into this same energy conservation framework.

From a traditional point of view, variation in site assemblages is often seen as reflecting cultural differences. However, in this analysis, albeit a simplified one, a large number of sites with a high degree of variability between them can be seen to fit into a consistent technological pattern. It is, therefore, unfortunate that the condition of the tool assemblages was not of the quality required to make detailed typological comparisons. This would have been of considerable interest for the Near East, where most past research has been done with tool classification and comparison.

NOTES

[1] Excavations in 1974 confirmed three artifact horizons in 3 m of terrace deposits. This site will be described in detail in the second volume of these reports.

[2] All measurements were taken in millimeters.

BIBLIOGRAPHY

BINFORD, L. R., and BINFORD, S. R., 1966. "A Preliminary Analysis of Functional Variability in the Mousterian of Levallois Facies." *American Anthropologist* 68(2,2):238-95.

GUICHARD, J., and GUICHARD, G., 1965. "The Early and Middle Paleolithic of Nubia: A Preliminary Report." In *Contributions to the Prehistory of Nubia*, edited by F. Wendorf, 157-166. Dallas: Fort Burgwin Research Center and Southern Methodist University Press.

MARKS, A. E., and CREW, H., 1972. "Rosh Ein Mor, an Open-Air Mousterian Site in the Central Negev, Israel." *Current Anthropology* 13(5):591-93.

SOLECKI, R. S., and SOLECKI, R. L., 1970. "A New Secondary Flaking Technique at the Nahr Ibrahim Cave Site, Lebanon." *Bulletin du Musée de Beyrouth* 23:137-42.

ZIPF, G. K., 1949. *Human Behaviour and the Principle of Least Effort: An Introduction to Human Ecology*. New York: Hafner Publishing Company.

UPPER PALEOLITHIC SITES NEAR EIN AVDAT

Anthony E. Marks
Southern Methodist University

and

C. Reid Ferring
Southern Methodist University

INTRODUCTION

A sizable number of Upper Paleolithic sites were located during the surveys undertaken between 1969 and 1972. The sites reported in this chapter, however, fall into only two categories: those which amounted to little more than sparse surface scatters of artifacts, where meaningful samples either could not be obtained or where there was some serious mixture from other periods; and those which were dense surface concentrations without apparent admixture from other periods and with, perhaps, small amounts of material still *in situ*. Given the large number of prehistoric sites in the Avdat/Aqev area, it was only possible to accord these sites moderate attention. In the case of the sparse scatters, systematic surface collections were made over large areas but without any attempt to control for horizontal distributions. At times, even large collections failed to recover significant samples of tools which could be clearly identified as Upper Paleolithic, much less provide a sample for detailed typological and technological definition. Those sites with dense concentrations were treated in more detail. Systematic collections were made utilizing small collection units (from 2 sq m to 4 sq m), and deposits were excavated to bedrock when *in situ* material was present. At each site, however, only a minimum of the total area was collected—just enough to provide sufficient samples for detailed typological and technological analysis, and to test for intrasite varia-

bility, although no attempt was made to define fully such variability. A single exception to this was the site of Sde Divshon (D27B), which was mapped artifact by artifact over 235 sq m and will be reported in a following chapter (Ferring, this volume). Thus, while typological and technological descriptions of the assemblages recovered from these sites will be presented, it should be fully realized that the larger sites still have considerable potential for further work, particularly in the study of intrasite patterning.

The Upper Paleolithic sites of concern here occur in two major geographic zones: on and along the edges of the Divshon Plain and in the lower portion of the North/South Zin (fig. 7-1). Those sites on the Divshon Plain are situated in three sub-zones: along the north-central border of the plain, where it is truncated by the southeastern cliff of the Nahal Mor (Sites D22, D26 and D27A); those which occur along the western margin of the plain on small ridges which finger onto the plain (D20 and D28); and those which occur in an east/west line along the North Divshon Ridge and the northern end of the Har Mekhya (D14, D18, D21, and D29). Only two Upper Paleolithic sites were located within the Nahal Zin (D100 A and B) and, owing to their very recent discovery, only a very brief preliminary note will be presented.

Because these sites represent only a portion of all the Upper Paleolithic sites recorded and studied in the Avdat/Aqev area, and because there are still many problems with the

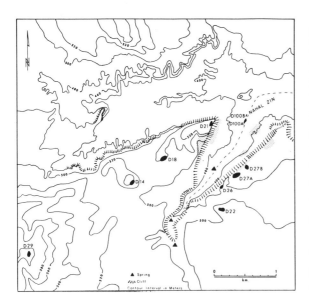

FIG. 7-1—Map of Upper Paleolithic sites near Ein
Avdat. *Stippled areas* indicate raw material
sources.

local relative chronology of the Upper Paleolithic occupation of the Central Negev, no attempt will be made to order the site descriptions by assumed temporal priority. Rather,
they will be grouped by their geographic location.

SITES ON THE NORTHERN
DIVSHON PLAIN

The edge of the Divshon Plain, where it
meets the southeastern cliff of the Nahal Mor,
provides a number of attractive resources for
prehistoric man. Paramount among these is
the presence of a band of large flint cobbles
outcropping just at the contact between the
plain and the cliff. In addition, this rim of the
plain is some 5 m higher than the major portion of the plain to the south, thus permitting
a complete, uninterrupted view for over 2 km
in an arch of about 135°, taking in all of the
plain and most of the slopes of the surrounding high ground.

While surface water from perennial springs
is less than one km distant from this rim, it is

at the bottom of a ca. 80 m cliff, within the
Nahal Mor. The present topographic situation
prohibits easy access from the rim to the
springs, but only minor block-faulting could
have obliterated prior paths down the cliff
face. The position of the rim above the
springs also presented a favorable hunting
lookout for megafauna which had to pass
through the Nahal Mor in order to reach the
water and which, once within the canyon,
would have been limited in movement by the
steep walls.

It is not surprising, considering these advantages, that a number of Upper Paleolithic
sites were located along this rim. Two of
these, D26 and D27A, were situated within a
few score meters of the cliff edge, while the
third, Arkov (D22), was some 300 m to the
south.

ARKOV (SITE D22)

The site of Arkov is located 300 m south
of the cliff edge above the Nahal Mor, at an
elevation of 500 m (fig. 7-1). The site is situated on a flat surface about 100 m east of a
minor drainage which flows toward the cliff.
It was recognized by a large surface concentration of ca. 1,500 sq m of which only about
500 sq m was dense. Within this smaller zone,
three sub-concentrations were visible, separated by areas of low artifactual densities. All
three concentrations included a fair number
of large limestone cobbles. While no pattern
could be discerned for these, it is most likely
that they were carried from the rock outcrops
some tens of meters away. The artifacts lay
on and in a fine eolian deposit from 20 to 30
cm deep.

A total of 32 sq m was systematically collected and excavated: 16 sq m in the largest
sub-concentration, Area A; 12 sq m within
the middle sub-concentration, Area B; and 4
sq m within the smallest sub-concentration.
The materials from 4 sq m of Area A and the
total collection from the smallest sub-

concentration were given to the Department of Antiquities without study, while the remaining 24 sq m form the basis for this report.

After the systematic surface collection of each 2 sq m unit block, each unit was excavated to bedrock. The high surface density, however, was not paralleled sub-surface, and it appears that it is the result of deflation with the attendant lowering and concentration of artifacts. In Area A, 36.06% of all artifacts were recovered sub-surface, while in Area B this increased to 47.66%, suggesting somewhat less deflation of the middle sub-concentration.

The surface artifacts have a whitish-brown patina but show no signs of edge damage. The sub-surface material ranges from unpatinated to the same patina found on the surface artifacts, and the edges of all the artifacts are in fine, fresh condition. Owing to the shallow depth of the deposits, only lithic material was found during the excavations.

Lithic Artifacts

Technology

Raw material consists of mostly thin tabular to kidney-shaped flint nodules, the source of which was not located. While a major source of fine flint is available 300 m away at the cliff edge, it is in the form of large cobbles unlike those present at Arkov. A total of 3,463 artifacts was recovered, excluding debris; 1,850 from Area A and 1,163 from Area B. Their distribution by artifact class shows no significant difference between Areas A and B, indicating that the same pattern of raw material exploitation took place in each (table 7-1). Blade production is clearly a normal part of the basic technology, and from the relatively sizable percentages of cores and core-trimming elements, it seems that much primary flaking took place at the site.

Again, platform preparation indicates a

strong homogeneity between the two areas (table 7-2), although there is considerable variation between the three different classes of artifacts under consideration. Most striking is the high percentage of lipped and crushed blade platforms, as compared with those on flakes and primary elements. This is suggestive of two basic techniques being utilized: a hard hammer for the roughing out of the cores and most of the production of flakes and primary elements, and a soft hammer or punch for the actual removal of blades. Given the percentage of lipped platforms on primary elements, however, it seems likely that a soft hammer technique is involved and that it was not exclusively used for blade removal, although that appears to have been its main function.

There is considerable size variation within the artifact sample. Flakes range in length from 15 to 88 mm, although the majority fall between 25 and 40 millimeters. Flake widths show a somewhat similar pattern, although the distribution is slightly skewed toward the lower end of the range (fig. 7-2a). Blades show an equally wide range, from 15 to 87 mm in length, but there is considerably less clustering (fig. 7-2b). Blade widths range from 11 to 34 mm, but these measurements may be somewhat misleading, as only complete blades were measured (fig. 7-2b). There are large numbers of fragmentary blades which have widths under 12 millimeters. In Area A, for instance, 39.36% of all blades, complete and fragmentary, are less than 12 mm in width. These, however, are almost never found complete, and it is quite possible that the vast majority broke during their removal. All blades tend to be fairly long, narrow, with thin platforms, while 66.54% of their distal extremities are naturally blunt. A majority (57.97%) have parallel lateral edges, 28.02% are converging, while only 14.01% have lateral edges which expand toward the distal extremity.

The length/width ratios of the blades show a majority falling between 2:1 and 3:1, but

TABLE 7-1

Occurrence of All Artifacts by Class of Tool Blanks and Proportional Utilization by Class

	Area A					Area B				
Type	Total		Tools		Percent Utilized	Total		Tools		Percent Utilized
	Number	Percent	Number	Percent		Number	Percent	Number	Percent	
Cores	107	5.78	4	2.41	3.74	120	7.44	11	7.38	9.71
Core Trim-ming Elements	137	7.41	6	3.61	4.38	85	5.27	7	4.70	8.24
Core Tablets	66	3.57	3	1.81	4.55	65	4.03	1	0.67	1.54
Primary Elements	341	18.43	26	15.66	7.62	277	17.17	30	20.13	10.83
Flakes	738	39.89	87	52.41	11.79	657	40.73	72	48.32	10.96
Blades	461	24.92	40	24.10	8.68	409	25.36	28	18.79	6.85
	1,850	100.00	166	100.00		1,613	100.00	148	99.99	
Burin Spalls, etc.	56					n.d.				
Chips and Chunks	887					n.d.				
	2,793									

TABLE 7-2

Platform Types on Primary Elements, Flakes and Blades as Percentages

Platform Types	Primary Elements		Flakes		Blades	
	Area A N=184	Area B N=158	Area A N=527	Area B N=435	Area A N=233	Area B N=219
Unfaceted	47.28	42.41	54.08	50.80	28.76	26.94
Dihedral faceted	6.52	6.33	8.73	9.66	5.58	4.57
Multiple faceted	4.89	1.27	4.74	2.53	2.15	1.37
Lipped[1]	10.87	13.92	5.12	6.67	35.19	37.44
Cortex	10.33	18.35	13.66	18.85	3.43	2.74
Crushed	20.11	17.72	13.66	11.49	24.89	26.94
	100.00	100.00	99.99	100.00	100.00	100.00

[1] As noted in the glossary of terms, faceting and lipping are not mutually exclusive. However, for the Upper Paleolithic sites in the Avdat/Aqev area virtually all lipped platforms are unfaceted.

with some examples exceeding 4:1. Flakes tend to cluster between 1:1 and 1.5:1, with as many falling between 1:1 and 1:1.5 as fall between 1:1 and 1.5:1. On a more general level, 33.2% of all flakes are wider than they are long, while only 25.3% approach blade proportions with length/width ratios falling between 1.5:1 and 2:1. A similar pattern

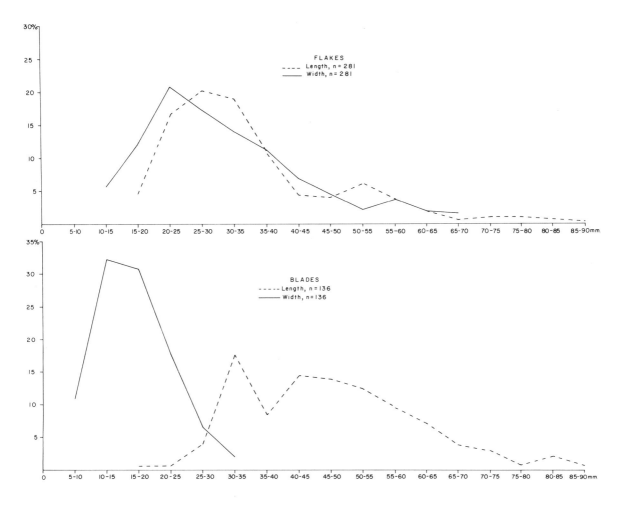

FIG. 7-2—Length and width of flakes and blades at Site D22.

occurs for tool blanks (fig. 7-3*a, b*), although the latter category is more heavily represented.

Typology

A total of 166 retouched tools were recovered in Area A and 148 in Area B, representing 8.97% and 9.18% of the available blanks in each area. The blanks utilized in tool production (table 7-3) for both areas are weighted toward flakes, in that they were used to a proportionately greater extent than they were available in the total assemblage. Other blank forms seem to have been selected in approximately the same proportions as they were present.

There is a clear differential distribution of a few tool types between Areas A and B, perhaps giving some indication of spatial variations in activity patterning.

Notes on the Tool Typology

The differences between Areas A and B do not pertain to manufactural style or to blank utilization. The main difference lies in the proportional occurrence of certain tool types and in the larger number of specific types which occur in Area B as opposed to Area A;

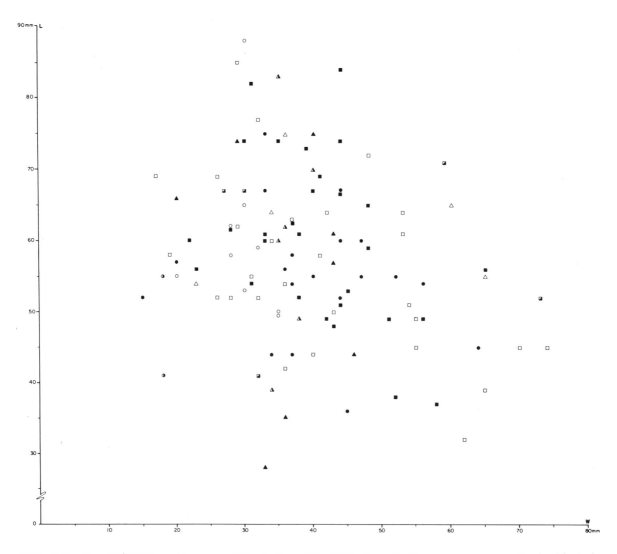

FIG. 7-3a—Length/Width scattergram of tools from Site D22, Area B. Key: *open square*—simple dihedral burins; *closed square*—multifaceted dihedral burins; *half-closed square*—other tools; *open triangle*—retouched pieces; *closed triangle*—notched pieces; *half-closed triangle*—denticulates; *dot*—thin endscrapers; *open circle*—thick scrapers; *half-closed circle*—truncations.

33 types in Area B as opposed to 27 in Area A. The majority of these, however, are variations on types present in both areas. The only exception is the presence of a single perforator in Area B.

Endscrapers

The heavy use of flakes and primary elements as blanks in endscraper production is notable (fig. 7-4a). In Area A the range of thin endscrapers is quite lim-ited (three varieties) and their manufacture is some-what irregular. In Area B, however, there are five vari-eties and the retouch tends to be of better quality (fig. 7-4d).

Thick-nosed, thick-shouldered, carinated (fig. 7-4h), and lateral carinated (fig. 7-4i) types occur in small numbers, with the lateral carinated form most common. A number are made on chunks and are dif-ficult to distinguish from exhausted cores. There are two origins of retouch present on the thick scrapers. The majority of pieces show retouch originating from

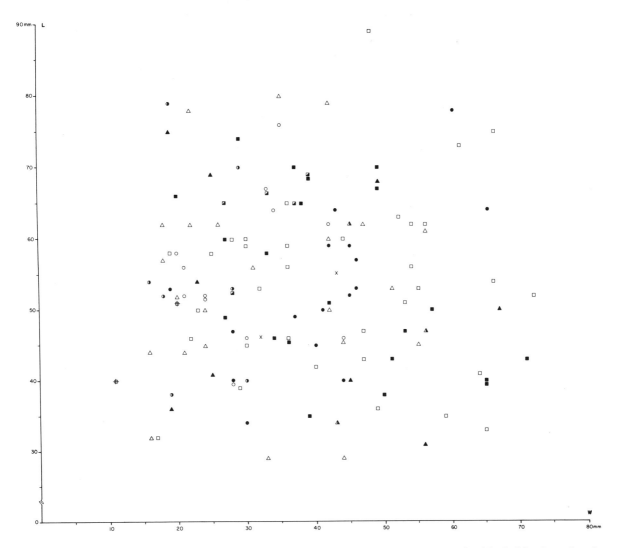

FIG. 7-3b—Scattergram of tools from Site D22, Area A. Key: *open square*—simple dihedral burins; *closed square*—multifaceted dihedral burins; *half-closed square*—other tools; *crossed square*—burins on truncation; *open triangle*—retouched pieces; *crossed triangle*—notched pieces; *half-closed triangle*—denticulates; *dot*—thin endscrapers; *open circle*—thick endscrapers; *half-closed circle*—truncations; *x*—multiple tool.

the ventral surface, but on a significant number the retouch originates from a lateral face. The few double endscrapers are all noncarinated varieties, and are often poorly formed (fig. 7-4*f*).

Multiple Tools

There are three endscraper/burin combinations. All are thin endscrapers, one denticulated, while all the burins are dihedral, one of which is multifaceted.

The other multiple tool is a convex sidescraper combined with a dihedral, multifaceted burin.

Burins

Burins show considerable type variability. Dihedral forms predominate with simple and multifaceted examples rather evenly divided. Of the simple dihedral burins, 25 are asymmetric and all five of the symmetric examples come from Area A. Those with only two burin facets (fig. 7-5*g*) are uncommon, as most

TABLE 7-3
Typology of Site Arkov (D22)
a. Area A

Type	Blank Forms							Total	Percent
	Bladelet	Blade	Flake	Primary Element	Core Trimming Element	Core Tablet	Core		
Simple endscraper		1	4	2		2		9	5.42
Unilateral endscraper			3					3	1.81
Thin-nosed scraper			2					2	1.20
Thick-nosed scraper			2	1	1			4	2.41
Carinated scraper, typical			2			1		3	1.81
Carinated scraper, atypical			1					1	0.60
Lateral carinated scraper			6					6	3.61
Double endscraper			2					2	1.20
Endscraper/Burin			1	1				2	1.20
Sidescraper/Burin			1					1	0.60
Burin, dihedral		2	9	5				16	9.64
Burin, dihedral, multifaceted		2	8	4		1		15	9.04
Burin, dihedral, angle			5	1	1			7	4.22
Burin, on old surface			2	1				3	1.81
Burin, on snap		1	2	1				4	2.41
Burin, on snap, multifaceted			1					1	0.60
Burin, on truncation	1	1						2	1.20
Burin, transverse on lateral truncation			3	1				4	2.41
Burin, multiple dihedral			3					3	1.81
Burin, multiple mixed			1	1			2	4	2.41
Truncated piece		5	2					7	4.22
Retouched piece	2	15	12	3	5			37	22.28
Denticulate	1	1	1	2				5	3.01
Denticulate endscraper			1					1	0.60
Notched piece		7	7	3				17	10.24
Pièce à mâchures		1	1					2	1.20
Varia			5					5	13.01
Total Blank Forms	4	36	87	26	6	3	4	166	
Percent	2.41	21.69	52.41	15.66	3.61	1.81	2.41		100.00

b. Area B

Type	Blank Forms							Total	Percent
	Bladelet	Blade	Flake	Primary Element	Core Trimming Element	Core Tablet	Core		
Simple endscraper			5	10	2			17	11.49

								Total	Percent
Unilateral endscraper				1				1	0.67
Endscraper on retouched piece			1	1				2	1.35
Ogival endscraper				1				1	0.67
Thin-nosed scraper			1		1			2	1.35
Thick-nosed scraper							1	1	0.67
Thick-shouldered scraper				1				1	0.67
Carinated scraper, typical			1	2				3	2.04
Carinated scraper, atypical				1				1	0.67
Lateral carinated scraper							4	4	2.70
Double endscraper			1					1	0.67
Endscraper/Burin			1					1	0.67
Burin, dihedral		2	4	4		1	3	14	9.46
Burin, dihedral, multifaceted		1	12	6	2		1	22	14.86
Burin, dihedral, angle			1	1	1			3	2.04
Burin, dihedral, angle, multifaceted			2	1				3	2.04
Burin, on old surface			5					5	3.38
Burin, on old surface, multifaceted			1					1	0.67
Burin, on snap				1				1	0.67
Burin, on straight truncation			1	1				2	1.35
Burin, on oblique truncation			2					2	1.35
Burin, on oblique truncation, multifaceted			1					1	0.67
Burin, transverse on lateral notch			1					1	0.67
Burin, busquoid		2	2					4	2.70
Burin, multiple dihedral							1	1	0.67
Burin, multiple mixed			1					1	0.67
Truncated piece	1	3						4	2.70
Perforator			1					1	0.67
Retouched piece	1	6	4	2				13	8.78
Denticulate		1	4		2			7	4.73
Denticulate endscraper			2	1				3	2.04
Notched piece	1	5	10	1				17	11.50
Sidescraper			1	2				3	2.04
Pièce à mâchures				2				2	1.35
Varia			1		1			2	1.35
Total Blank Forms	3	25	72	30	7	1	10	148	
Percent	2.01	16.78	48.32	20.13	4.70	0.67	7.38		99.99

have three. There is often a lack of balance between the burin facets on the simple examples, with one burin facet quite short, and the other very long. Burin bits show considerable range in width, from 4 to 17 mm, although 18 of the 30 examples have bits between 8 and 11 mm wide. Dihedral burins which have multiple facets are overwhelmingly asymmetric; 30 as opposed to only 7 symmetric. A high propor-tion of the asymmetric examples are "transverse" in that the majority of the burin facets are struck transverse or highly oblique to the axis of the piece (fig. 7-5*i*). In fact, there is a strong tendency for the multi-faceted burins to have as many as five burin facets present, four of which are on one plane, opposed by only a single facet on the other (fig. 7-5*m*). In this regard, they are similar to cores, and some examples

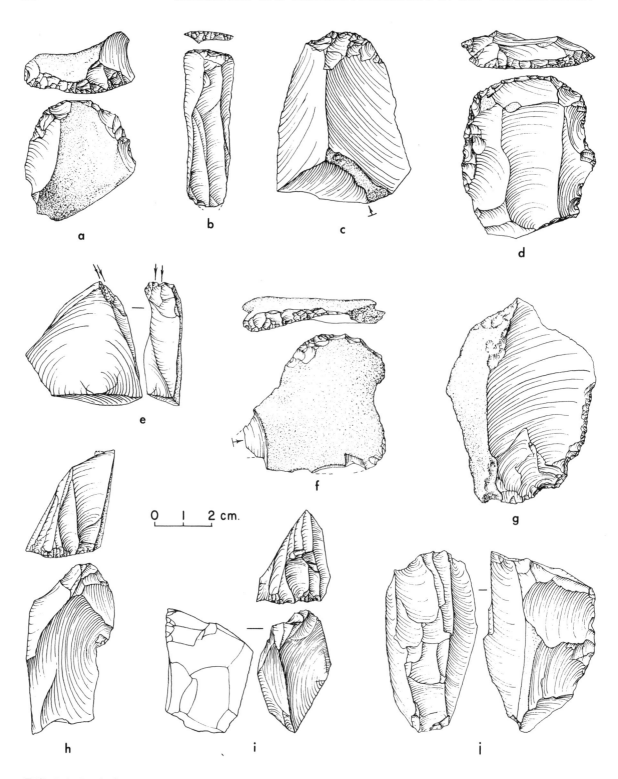

FIG. 7-4—Tools from Site D22: *a, c*—endscrapers; *b*—truncation; *d*—unilateral endscraper; *e*—burin on oblique snap; *f*—double endscraper broken; *g*—notch on retouched flake; *h, i*—carinated scrapers; *j*—blade core with lateral preparation.

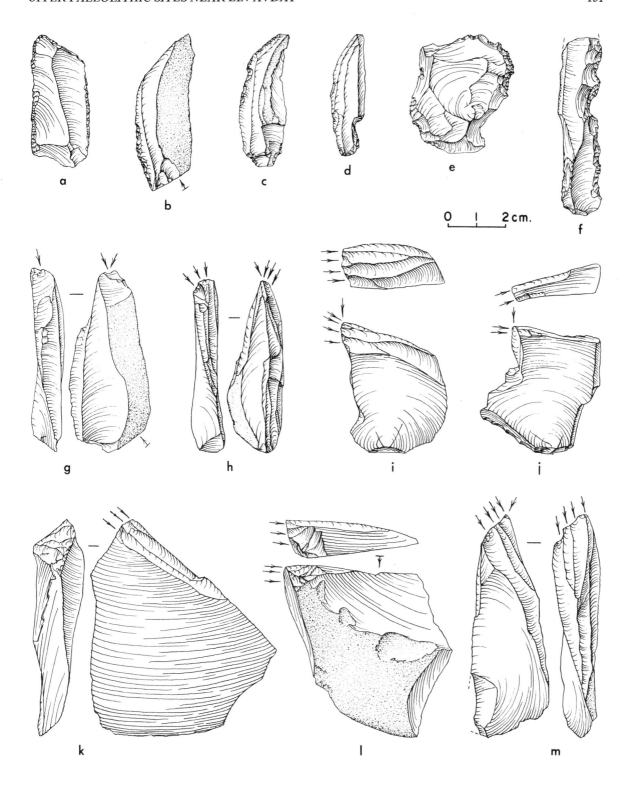

FIG. 7-5—Tools from Site D22: *a-c*—retouched blades; *d*—notched blade; *e*—denticulate endscraper; *f*—denticulate; *g-m*—various burins.

might well have been classified as either. Another aspect of these multifaceted burins is the presence of some lateral battering just below the terminal portions of the burin facets. This is clearly suggestive of a retouched preparation of the blank edge prior to the burin blows. In spite of the multiple burin facets, the bits on most pieces are not appreciably wider than on the simple dihedral forms; from 6 to 20 mm, but with 64.9% clustering between 8 and 12 millimeters.

Dihedral angle burins are not so common, but they show the same variation in the number of burin facets as do the other dihedral forms (fig. 7-5*j*). The same is true for burins on snap and, in many cases, the snap or break is oblique (fig. 7-4*e*) or even parallel (fig. 7-5*l*) to the long axis of the piece, rather than perpendicular to it.

Burins on truncation are rare and tend to have burin facets which are either transverse or strongly oblique to the long axis of the piece (fig. 7-5*k*).

Truncations

These are among the few tool types which occur more regularly on blades than on flakes or primary elements. The majority are distal oblique truncations, although a single distal straight truncation is also present (fig. 7-4*b*).

Perforators

This is a unique piece. It has a very sharp tip formed by bilateral obverse retouch, with a single small flake taken off the ventral surface to sharpen the tip.

Retouched Pieces

Of the retouched pieces, 37 have continuous light retouch along a single lateral edge (fig. 7-5*b, c*); 21 obversely and 10 inversely retouched. The remaining examples include one bilaterally retouched blade (fig. 7-5*a*), and nine pieces with distal end retouch which are too weak to form true scraping edges.

Denticulates and Denticulate Endscrapers

These show considerable variation in size and position of the denticulation. Of the simple denticulates, six are lateral, including one very fine example on a blade (fig. 7-5*f*). The remaining denticulates are evenly divided between those which are transverse and those which are bilateral. The denticulate endscrapers parallel the simple endscrapers in that they are generally well retouched but usually exhibit only moderate serration (fig. 7-5*e*).

Notched Pieces

Of the 34 notched pieces, 21 are single lateral notches which occur on a wide variety of blank forms, including blades (fig. 7-5*d*). The remaining notches are either distal (6) or multiple (6), and in one case, there is a multiple notch on a retouched flake (fig. 7-4*g*). Notch size varies from 6 by 1 mm to 15 by 4 mm, with the larger notches occurring on the thicker blanks. Most notches, however, tend to be quite shallow—less than 2 mm deep—and are formed by careful retouch.

Pièces à Mâchures

These are large blanks which exhibit bifacial battering along a single lateral edge. They are more or less comparable to those illustrated for Site Ein Aqev (Marks, this volume), although not nearly as heavily utilized.

Varia

This group includes mostly pieces which appear to be unfinished carinated or thick tools. Whether they were originally intended as burins or scrapers could not be discerned. In addition, there is an atypical oblique endscraper which has been unsuccessfully modified into a burin-like object, a pick-like piece on a thick flake, and a flake with two notches, a poor truncation with a bec burin at one end.

Cores

A total of 107 cores was recovered from Area A and 120 from Area B. The basic manufactural technique employed was relatively simple: a thin slab or flake had a platform produced on it by a single blow, and then this platform was utilized as a base from which a series of blades were struck, primarily along one narrow edge of the piece. Often, however, the removal of blades would continue around the edge onto one of the lateral faces of the core. This technique is not significantly different from that used in the production of many dihedral burins and, without question, there is a gradation between the two.

There is little evidence for initial preparation of the core surface to be flaked, but when occurring, it normally is restricted to either unifacial flaking, perpendicular to the intended axis of blade removal, or a retouch along the lower portion of the core, which appears to be a remnant of more extensive retouch along the original edge to be flaked (fig. 7-6a). Very occasionally, there is evidence for the shaping of the back of the core, so that the core cross section is triangular (fig. 4j).

The core classification (table 7-4) recognizes three basic classes: those where only a single platform is present, those with two or more platforms, and those which are discoidal and do not really exhibit easily definable platforms. In addition, there is a group for those cores which are highly fragmentary or do not fit into the detailed classification. A second level of differentiation is based on whether the core produced blades or flakes, with no distinction made here between blades, *sensu stricto*, and bladelets.

Notes on the Core Typology

Most identifiable cores from both areas produced blades. Of these, single platform types strongly dominate, with simple blade cores in the vast majority (fig. 7-6b, d, f). These were produced mainly on fairly thin flint nodules, with one or both lateral faces still exhibiting cortex. There are, as well, a number where it is clear that either flakes or primary flakes were utilized (fig. 7-6a, b). The true number of such cannot be estimated, as it is quite possible that some of those pieces with only one cortex face may have started as thick primary flakes, then the bulb of percussion subsequently eliminated by flake or blade removals. On those which are identifiable as flakes or primary flakes, however, most have the flaked surface transverse to the original axis of the piece.

Simple single platform cores vary in length from 28 to 106 mm, but of 58 examples only two fall below 42 mm and only six exceed 75 millimeters. Both areas show similar core sizes: a mean of 61.5 mm in Area A, and a mean of 59.8 mm in Area B. Platform angles show considerable variability, from a low of 40° to a high of 79°. Most cores, however, have rather acute platform angles; in Area A the mean is 64.3° and in Area B it is 62.9° (given a margin of error of about 5°).

Those single platform cores with some initial preparation of the flaked surface exhibit the same size and platform characteristics as those on the simple single platform core. They are, however, on the average slightly smaller (Area A mean is 57.3 mm; Area B mean is 56.0 mm), although the sample size is not large enough to warrant significance.

One aspect of the single platform cores worth noting is the presence of what might be called stepped platforms. On about 24%, the platform has been formed by a blow from the flaked surface which has hinged a short way behind that surface. In some cases, this is clearly a technique of platform rejuvenation, as it has removed the very tops of older blade scars, while on others it appears to be initial preparation.

There are a small number of carinated cores which approach scraper form. Seven of the

TABLE 7-4
Core Classification for Site Arkov (D22)

Type	Area A				Area B			
	Blade	Flake	Total	Percent	Blade	Flake	Total	Percent
Single Platform								
a. Simple	45	11	56	60.22	60	9	69	66.99
b. Prepared	8		8	8.60	8		8	7.77
c. Carinated	8		8	8.60	10		10	9.71
Subtotal	61	11	72	77.42	78	9	87	84.47
Multiple Platform								
a. Opposed, simple	7		7	7.53	6	1	7	6.80
b. Opposed, opposite side	4	1	5	5.38	4		4	3.88
c. Ninety Degree	2	2	4	4.30	1	1	2	1.94
d. Opposed, twisted	2		2	2.15	3		3	2.91
e. Globular		2	2	2.15				
Subtotal	15	5	20	21.51	14	2	16	15.53
Discoidal		1	1	1.08				
Total	76	17	93	100.01	92	11	103	100.00
Percent	81.72	18.28			89.32	10.68		
Unidentifiable and Fragments	2	12	14		6	11	17	

eighteen are more similar to lateral carinated scrapers than to typical ones, but all appear to be just on the core side of the continuum. These also exhibit a tendency toward stepped platforms (33%), all have rather marked convex-flaked surfaces, and most are keeled. Their size and platform-angle range roughly correspond to those of the single platform cores, although the carinated cores average two or three mm shorter and have a mean platform angle of 57.1°.

The sample sizes for the various multiple platform cores are so small that metric observations are of questionable value. There are two groups: those with opposed platforms (fig. 7-4*j*) and those where the platforms are not opposed. Of the first group, most utilize the same surface for flaking, a small number

of which show a slight shift in plane, resulting in a twisted appearance. Others, including a few on flakes, have two opposed flaked surfaces (fig. 7-6*c, e*). Those without opposed platforms include a few where the orientation of the flaked surface has been changed, resulting in flaked surfaces which are about 90° to each other.

There are a very few globular cores, while other flake cores seem to represent more unsuccessful attempts at blade cores than any real technological variation.

SITE D26

Site D26 is the most southwesterly occurring concentration above the eastern cliff of the Nahal Mor (fig. 7-1). It is situated on a

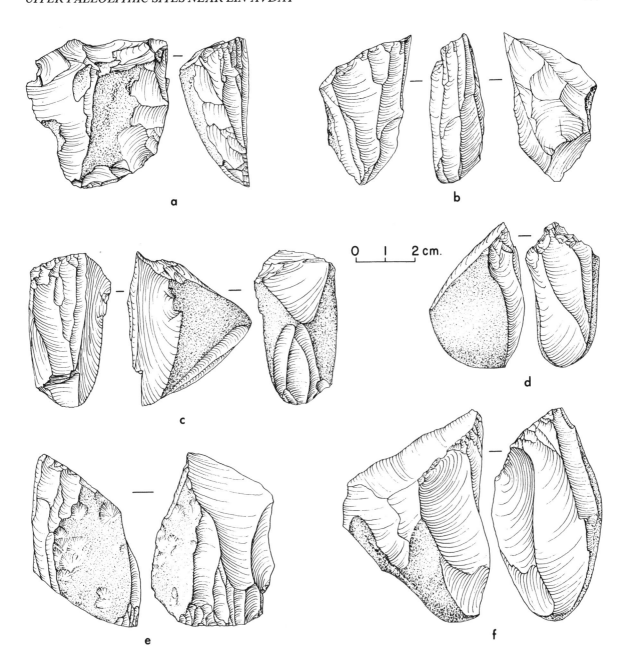

FIG. 7-6—Cores from Site D22: *a*—prepared blade core; *b, d, f*—simple blade cores; *c, e*—opposed platform, opposite side blade cores.

slight slope, some 65 m from the cliff edge, with artifacts resting on both bedrock and small patches of eolian deposits. The whole area of this section of the cliff top is littered with artifacts of various periods, within which the site forms an island of some 500 sq m of a relatively clear concentration of Upper Paleolithic artifacts. The density of concentration was extremely low, with the exception of an area of some 30 sq m, where a sizable concentration of cores and other artifacts were present. The condition of the scatter and of the artifacts themselves indicate a fair amount of movement through slopewash, particularly for that material outside the 30 sq m sub-concentration.

An initial collection was made of the 30 sq m sub-concentration and then, to increase the artifact sample, another 100 sq m were collected. Even this, however, failed to provide a significant tool sample.

Lithic Artifacts

Technology

While certain variability exists in the material, most artifacts were made from a fine-grained flint of the kind available along the cliff edge. Most showed a brown patination, although some pieces were only partially patinated, while others exhibited little or no patination. This might well be explained as the result of differential deflation of the artifacts out of the eolian deposits, although no artifacts were recovered from *in situ*.

A total of 618 artifacts was collected, and their distribution by artifact class shows a pattern quite distinct from other Upper Paleo-lithic sites in that the percentage of cores is extremely high (table 7-5).

The distribution by artifact class must, in this case, be viewed with some caution, owing to the apparent movement of artifacts, as shown by the number of fragmentary pieces and the paucity of truly small chips. Only the larger artifacts, particularly the cores, show little evidence of movement, which may account for their proportionately high occurrence.

The extremely small samples for each major artifact class makes many observations of dubious value. Some, however, do give indications of technological proclivities. Of the 18 proximal blade fragments, one-half had lipped platforms, only two bladelet fragments were present, and a number of the fragments exceeded 75 mm in length. All of this is suggestive of a developed blade technology, utilizing a soft hammer or punch technique. This is consistent with the core morphology, since the vast majority are long, well-formed blade cores.

Typology

A total of 84 retouched tools was recov-

TABLE 7-5

Occurrence of All Artifacts by Class of Tool Blanks and Proportional Utilization by Class

Artifact Class	Total		Tools		Percent of
	Number	Percent	Number	Percent	Class Utilization
Cores	67	16.88	0	0.00	0.00
Core Trimming Elements	27	6.80	6	7.14	22.22
Core Tablets	11	2.77	2	2.38	18.18
Primary Elements	58	14.61	12	14.29	20.69
Flakes	154	38.79	43	51.19	27.92
Blades	76	20.15	21	25.00	27.63
Totals	393	100.00	84	99.99	
Chips and Chunks	225				
	618				

TABLE 7-6
Typology for Site D26

Type	Blade	Flake	Primary Element	Core Trimming Element	Core Tablet	Total	Percent
Simple endscraper	1	3	1			5	5.95
Unilateral endscraper		2				2	2.38
Endscraper on retouched piece	1	1				2	2.38
Thin nosed scraper		3	1	1		5	5.95
Thin shouldered scraper		1				1	1.19
Thick shouldered scraper		2				2	2.38
Carinated scraper, typical		1				1	1.19
Lateral carinated scraper		2	1			3	3.57
Endscraper/burin	3					3	3.57
Burin, dihedral	2	3	2			7	8.33
Burin, dihedral, multifaceted		1				1	1.19
Burin, busqouid			1			1	1.19
Burin, on old surface		2				2	2.38
Burin, on old surface, multifaceted			1			1	1.19
Burin, on straight truncation		1				1	1.19
Burin, on oblique truncation	2	1		1		4	4.76
Multiple burin, dihedral	1		1			2	2.38
Multiple burin, dihedral, multifaceted		1				1	1.19
Perforator		1				1	1.19
Backed piece		1				1	1.19
Truncation, straight	1				1	2	2.38
Truncation, straight, oblique	2	1				3	3.57
Retouched piece	2	4	3	3	1	13	15.48
Denticulate	1	4	1			6	7.14
Denticulate endscraper	1	2				3	3.57
Notched piece	4	4		1		9	10.71
Bec burin		1				1	1.19
Raclette		1				1	1.19
Total Blank Forms	21	43	12	6	2	84	
Percent	25.00	51.19	14.29	7.14	2.38		99.97

ered, representing 21.37% of the available blanks. Clearly, there was a selection against cores for tool production but a selection for both flakes and blades (table 7-5). The very high proportional utilization within each blank class for tool production suggests that this site perhaps represents a special activity facies. There does appear to be a contradiction in the combination of a high blank utilization and also a high percentage of cores in the assemblage. It is difficult to project the effects of slopewash, however, which may have artificially sorted the artifacts.

The typology shows a rather even distribution of scrapers and burins, with a number of specific types occurring in each class (table 7-6).

Notes on the Tool Typology

Owing to the extremely small sample sizes for specific types, detailed notes are not ap-

propriate. A few comments, however, may be useful. The endscrapers are generally well formed (fig. 7-7*d, i*), and thick scrapers are all quite classic (fig. 7-7*j*), including a few quite small lateral carinated examples (fig. 7-7*f*). The burins are well made (fig. 7-7*g*), including ones thinned by retouch (fig. 7-7*e*). There is one atypical busquoid example (fig. 7-7*b*),

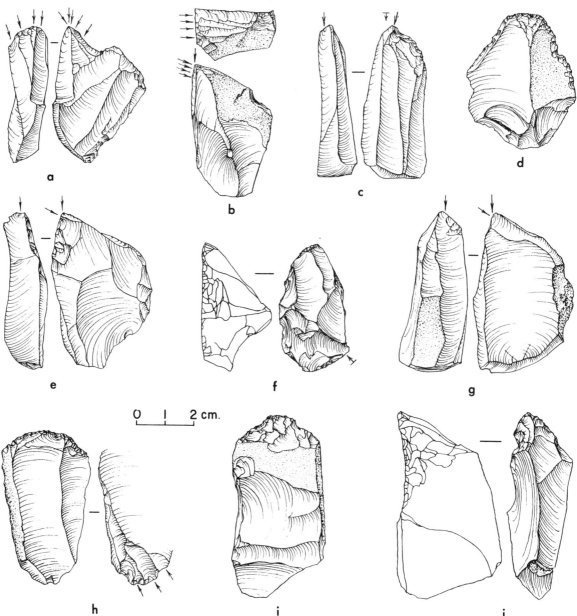

FIG. 7-7—Tools from Site D26: *a-c, e, g*—various burins; *d*—simple endscraper; *f*—lateral carinated scraper; *h*—multiple tool; *i*—thin nosed endscraper; *j*—carinated scraper.

and the multifaceted forms approach cores (fig. 7-7*a*). Those on truncation are poor, with only minimal retouch (fig. 7-7*c*). The backed piece is highly atypical and there is no evidence for any truly backed blades. The remaining tools are generally well made, including three scraper/burin combinations (fig. 7-7*h*).

Cores

While the tool sample is poor, the core sample is sufficiently large to provide a reasonably clear view of the techniques employed and the resulting core morphology. A total of 67 cores were recovered, the vast majority of which are finely formed blade cores, some of considerable size. The typology (table 7-7) shows a preponderance of simple, single-platformed cores.

Notes on the Core Typology

The cores show a high degree of control in the removal of blades and the occasional use of some complicated core preparation. This preparation seemingly relates to initial core shaping and takes two forms: a unifacial flaking from one or both edges, perpendicular to the intended axis of the blade removal, and the same pattern but with the use of bifacial flaking (fig. 7-8*b*). It is clear that this preparation can be obscured by subsequent blade removals and will appear only on those cores which have been moderately utilized or where the preparation was carried out on the back of the core. There is a large group of cores, however, where no preparation was necessary. These are mostly formed on rather thin tablets (fig. 7-8*c*), on chunks, or thick flakes.

There is a small series of carinated cores, which approach tools. These are distinguishable by the removal of blades around one end and two lateral edges, a use of the shorter dimension of the core for flaking, and a

TABLE 7-7
Core Typology for Site D26

Type	Blade	Flake	Total	Percent
Single Platform				
a. Simple	26	4	30	49.18
b. Prepared	9		9	14.75
c. Carinated	9		9	14.75
Subtotal	44	4	48	78.68
Multiple Platform				
a. Opposed, simple	2	2	4	6.56
b. Opposed, prepared	1		1	1.64
c. Opposed, twisted	1		1	1.64
d. Opposed, opposite side	3	1	4	6.56
e. Ninety degree	2	1	3	4.92
Subtotal	9	4	13	21.32
Total	53	8	61	
Percent	86.89	13.11		100.00
Unidentifiable		6	6	

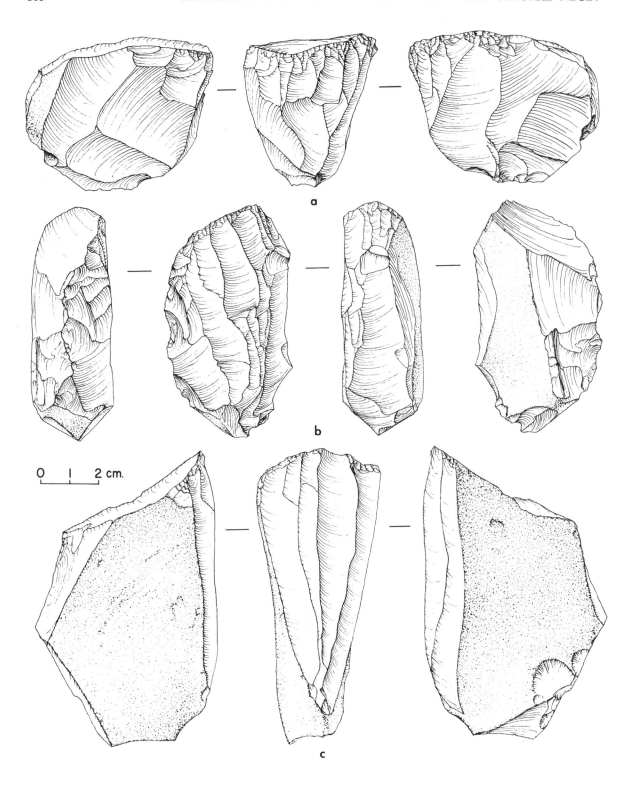

FIG. 7-8–Cores from Site D26: *a*–carinated core; *b*–bifacially prepared blade core; *c*–simple blade core.

marked convex keel (fig. 7-8*a*). These are relatively small compared to the other cores, with flaked surfaces which range in length along the flaked axis from 33 to 45 mm as compared to single platform blade cores which range from 47 to 102 mm (mean, 68.6 mm).

In addition, there are small numbers of opposed platform cores of various types, which range in length from 47 to 78 millimeters. Almost all blade cores have simple platforms which are acute to the flaked surface (mean angle, 61.5°). This is less true for the flake cores, where the angle between the platform and the flaked surface often approaches 90°.

SITE D27A

Site D27A is located just at the edge of the eastern cliff above the Nahal Mor, at an elevation of 505 m (fig. 7-1). The site consists of an oval concentration of artifacts resting on both bedrock (along the cliff edge) and on and in 15 to 25 cm of eolian deposits which cover the bedrock back from the cliff. The artifactual density was greatest at the center of the site, in an area of ca. 80 sq m, with a progressive decrease in density toward the edges of the concentration. A block of 24 sq m was collected in 4 sq m units from the dense concentration, and each unit was excavated to bedrock. Artifacts from one unit were given to the Department of Antiquities, while those from the remaining 20 sq m were used for this report. The surface artifacts were mostly patinated a dark brown, although a small percentage showed the typical sub-surface condition—a light brown and white. All artifacts were extremely fresh and little edge damage was apparent. The condition of the artifacts and the presence of mottled artifacts on the surface indicates both that little or no horizontal movement has taken place and that the site is presently in a state of active deflation. While no attempt was made to test for intrasite variability, the surface

indications suggest that such is probably present.

Lithic Artifacts

Technology

Most artifacts were made on the fine-grained flint that is available along the edge of the cliff, although a few were on a coarse-grained flint which is now available 200 m to the northwest.

The collection recovered a total of 2,991 artifacts, of which 32.4% were found sub-surface. Since the site was actively deflating and the depth of the *in situ* deposits minimal, both surface and sub-surface materials were combined and are presented as a single collection.

The distribution of artifacts by class shows a dominance of flakes (table 7-8). The core-trimming elements indirectly point to blade production, as almost all are highly elongated. The cores are also heavily dominated by those which produced blades. Core tablets, while rare, show all necessary characteristics, although the number of scars tends to be fewer than those on tablets from some other sites.

Blade platforms differ considerably from those of flakes and primary elements, with the lipped form accounting for over one-third of those identifiable (table 7-9). This high occurrence suggests the use of a soft hammer or punch in blade removal, although the consistent presence of lipped platforms on other artifact classes indicates that the technique was possibly not utilized exclusively during the final stage of blade production. The number of blades with multifaceted platforms is an anomaly. It is possible that these are really long core tablets rather than true blades, as the faceting is usually extremely fine at the platform edge but less so on the face of the platform.

This assemblage includes some of the larger

TABLE 7-8

Occurrence of All Artifacts by Class of Tool Blanks
and Proportional Utilization by Class

Artifact Class	Total		Tools		Percent of
	Number	Percent	Number	Percent	Class Utilization
Cores	115	5.85	12	2.63	10.43
Core Trimming Elements	80	4.08	13	2.84	16.25
Core Tablets	13	0.66	1	0.22	7.69
Primary Elements	338	17.18	67	14.66	19.82
Flakes	1,054	53.58	229	50.11	21.73
Blades	367	18.66	135	29.54	36.78
	1,967	100.01	457	100.00	
Burin Spalls	15				
Chips and Chunks	1,009				
	2,991				

artifacts recovered from Upper Paleolithic sites in the area. Flakes range in length from 18 to 100 mm and in width from 10 to 91 mm, although there are clear clusters in the intermediate ranges (fig. 7-9*a*). Most flake blanks chosen for tool production cluster between 40 and 70 mm in length, and in width from 18 to 43 mm (fig. 7-10). Blades tend to be large and, while only 40 unretouched examples were complete, range in

TABLE 7-9

Platform Types on Primary Elements,
Flakes, and Blades as Percentages

Platform Types	Primary Elements	Flakes	Blades
	N=103	N=142	N=100
Unfaceted	44.66	54.22	44.00
Dihedral faceted	10.68	11.97	2.00
Multiple faceted	0.97	5.63	8.00
Lipped	9.71	9.86	37.00
Cortex	20.39	13.38	4.00
Crushed	13.59	4.93	5.00
	100.00	100.00	100.00

length from 25 to 89 millimeters. Blade widths, from a much larger sample, vary from 6 to 43 mm (fig. 7-9*b*). Those modified into tools, again, tend to be large: from 31 to 124 mm in length and from 16 to 43 mm in width, although the main cluster is between 40 and 70 mm in length and 18 to 30 mm in width (fig. 7-10).

Blades fall into two groups: those which are often complete are fairly thick, normally with large unfaceted platforms, while the remainder tend to be quite thin, although broad, and, where proximal pieces are found, to have small, thin platforms of crushed or lipped type. Blade shape shows a majority (66.34%) with parallel sides, while the remainder are evenly divided between those with converging and those with expanding lateral edges.

All but one of the length/width blade ratios fall between 2:1 and 3:1 and, given the tendency toward thickness, they give the impression of heavy, rather massive pieces. Flakes exhibit a length/width pattern in which only 18.88% approach blade proportions, between 2:1 and 1.5:1; 41.33% fall into the 1.5:1 to

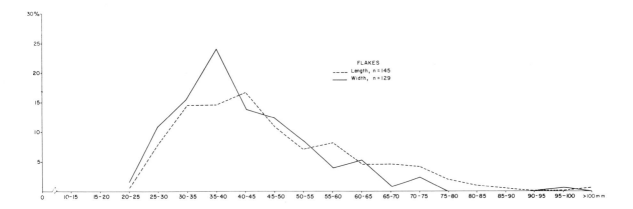

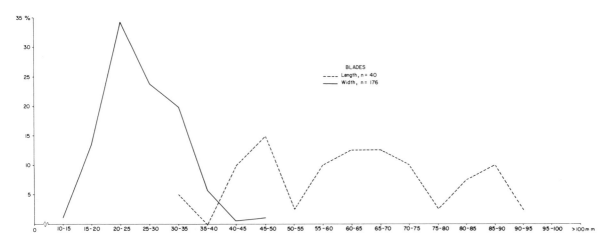

FIG. 7-9—Length and width of flakes and blades at Site D27A.

1:1 category; 31.63% are between 1:1 and 1:1.5, and 8.16% fall between 1:1.5 and 1:2.

Typology

A total of 457 retouched tools were recovered, representing 23.23% of the total available blanks. The blanks utilized in tool production (table 7-8) show only a selection for blades, with other classes being utilized in more or less the proportions in which they were available.

The retouched tools can be characterized by the high number of burins (36.36%), their strong tendency toward multifaceted forms (43.10% of all burins), and the considerable variation in specific burin types. While scrapers are present in significant percentage

(24.52%), and while there are numerous specific forms, only simple endscrapers and those on retouched pieces occur with any frequency. Other tools, aside from simple retouched pieces and notched pieces, are rare and show little type variation (table 7-10).

Notes on the Tool Typology

Endscrapers

As a general rule, the simple endscrapers on blades are better formed than those on flakes, although those on blades are mostly on fragments and there is considerable variation in the form of retouch—from flat and invasive to steep. A single huge specimen has inverse retouch. Those on flakes are generally poor, due to both the somewhat irregular retouch and to

TABLE 7-10
Typology of Site D27A

Type	Blank Forms						Total	Percent
	Blade	Flake	Primary Element	Core Trimming Element	Core Tablet	Core		
Simple endscraper	15	20	5	2			42	9.19
Unilateral endscraper		2	1				3	0.66
Bilateral endscraper		1					1	0.22
Endscraper on retouched piece	7	7	2				16	3.50
Ogival endscraper	3	4					7	1.53
Thin nosed scraper	3	3		1			7	1.53
Thin shouldered scraper	2	1					3	0.66
Endscraper on notch			1				1	0.22
Thick nosed scraper		1					1	0.22
Carinated scraper, typical	3	2	1			2	8	1.75
Carinated scraper, atypical	6	3				3	12	2.63
Lateral carinated scraper	2	1	2			3	8	1.75
Double endscraper		2		1			3	0.66
Endscraper/Burin	1	3					4	0.88
Burin/Truncation			1				1	0.22
Burin/Sidescraper		1					1	0.22
Burin, dihedral	8	17	11				36	7.88
Burin, dihedral, multifaceted	9	35	8				52	11.38
Burin, dihedral, angle		1	4	1			6	1.31
Burin, on old surface	1	3	1	1			6	1.31
Burin, on old surface, multifaceted		5					5	1.09
Burin, transverse on old surface	2	1					3	0.66
Burin, busquoid, atypical		1		1			2	0.44
Burin, on snap	10	7	5				22	4.82
Burin, on snap, multifaceted				1		1	2	0.44
Burin, on straight truncation	1	2					3	0.66
Burin, on oblique truncation	3	7	1	1			12	2.63
Burin, on oblique truncation, multifaceted		3	1				4	0.88
Burin, on convex truncation	2	1					3	0.66
Burin, transverse on lateral truncation		1	1				2	0.44
Bruin, transverse on lateral notch		1					1	0.22
Burin, multiple dihedral		2	1				3	0.66
Burin, multiple dihedral, multifaceted		3	1				4	0.88
Perforator	2	3	1	1		1	8	1.75
Truncation, straight	2	1	1				4	0.88
Truncation, oblique	8	1	1				10	2.19
Backed piece	1	1		1			3	0.66
Double-backed piece	1						1	0.22
Retouched piece	24	32	5		1		62	13.57
Denticulate	5	21	3			1	30	6.56
Denticulate endscraper	1	4					5	1.09

Notched piece	12	18	8	2		40	8.75
Sidescraper		4				4	0.88
Core scraper					1	1	0.22
Bec burin		1	1			2	0.44
Scaled piece	1					1	0.22
Varia		2				2	0.44
Total Blank Forms	135	229	67	13	1	12	457
Percent	29.54	50.11	14.66	2.84	0.22	2.63		100.06

the tendency for minimal treatment of the scraping edge.

The unilateral and bilateral scrapers show some of the heaviest retouch of any scrapers (fig. 7-11*i*). The ogival endscrapers on blades are among the most beautifully made, including one with lateral retouch (fig. 7-11*j*). Again, however, those on flakes are atypical. Endscrapers on retouched pieces conform to the general observations made above. The additional retouch on these pieces is normally a lateral denticulation, 10 of 16 pieces (fig. 7-11*c*), while the remainder include those with continuously and partially retouched edges (fig. 7-11*a*).

The thin-nosed and shouldered scrapers have very thin protrusions, at times approaching perforators. The single endscraper on notch is well formed with a major inversely retouched notch which forms a bec at one end of the scraping edge.

The thick scrapers are, with a single exception, various carinated forms. The typical carinated examples include some small examples (fig. 7-11*b*), as well as a few which approach cores. The atypical examples are mostly on thick-keeled blades and are, perhaps, best described as semicarinated (fig. 7-11*d*). Those on flakes are atypical owing to the lack or irregularity of the lamellar scars. The lateral carinated scrapers are typical, with the scraping edge clearly lacking symmetry (fig. 7-11*f*; fig. 7-13*j*).

The double scrapers include an atypical carinated scraper with a simple scraper, a double simple scraper on a retouched flake (which approaches a bilateral scraper), and a combined ogival and simple endscraper on an elongated core-trimming element.

Multiple Tools

The endscraper/burins all combine flat endscrapers

with forms of dihedral burins, one on a snapped blade (fig. 7-11*h*), and three dihedral, multifaceted examples (two asymmetric), including two where the burin facets extend onto the ventral surface of the pieces (fig. 7-12*h*). The burin/truncation has an oblique proximal truncation and an asymmetric, dihedral, multifaceted burin, while the burin/sidescraper has the same type of burin combined with a convex sidescraper.

Burins

The majority are dihedral forms (82.63%), of which 41.07% are multifaceted. Of the simple dihedral burins, 20 are symmetric and 16 are asymmetric, while 32 of the 52 multifaceted dihedral examples are asymmetric. The burin bits on the simple dihedral forms are quite narrow; from 3.5 to 15.5 mm (mean, 8.06 mm), with only 5 of 36 bits wider than 10 millimeters. On the multifaceted examples the bits range from 4.5 to 22 mm in width (mean, 9.5 mm), with 16 of the 52 wider than 10 millimeters.

While normal examples dominate (fig. 7-12*e*), on both the simple and multifaceted forms there is a strong tendency for the thinning of the burin bit by one of the two techniques: a third burin blow is struck on the simple forms, so that the negative bulb is strongly concave, forming a minor shoulder and thus narrowing the bit (fig. 7-12*d*); the same technique may be used on the multifaceted forms (fig. 7-12*b*, *c*; fig. 7-13*g*), or one or more burin facets are struck off one face of the blank, forming *plan* facets which thin the bit (fig. 7-12*g*). In addition, on the multifaceted forms there are also examples where these *plan* removals are quite short, more like retouch than burin blows (fig. 7-12*f*).

The two busquoid burins are highly atypical in

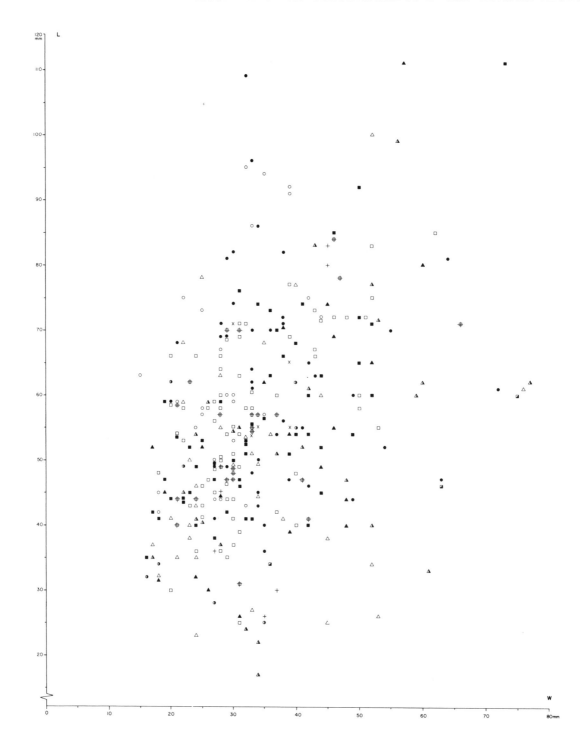

FIG. 7-10–Length/Width scattergram of tools from Site D27A. Key: *open square*–simple dihedral burins; *closed square*–multifaceted burins; *crossed square*–burins on truncation; *dot*–thin endscrapers; *circle*– thick scrapers; *half-closed circle*–truncation; *open triangle*–retouched pieces; *closed triangle*–notched pieces; *half-closed triangle*–denticulates; *cross*–perforators; *x*–multiple tools; *half-closed square*–other tools.

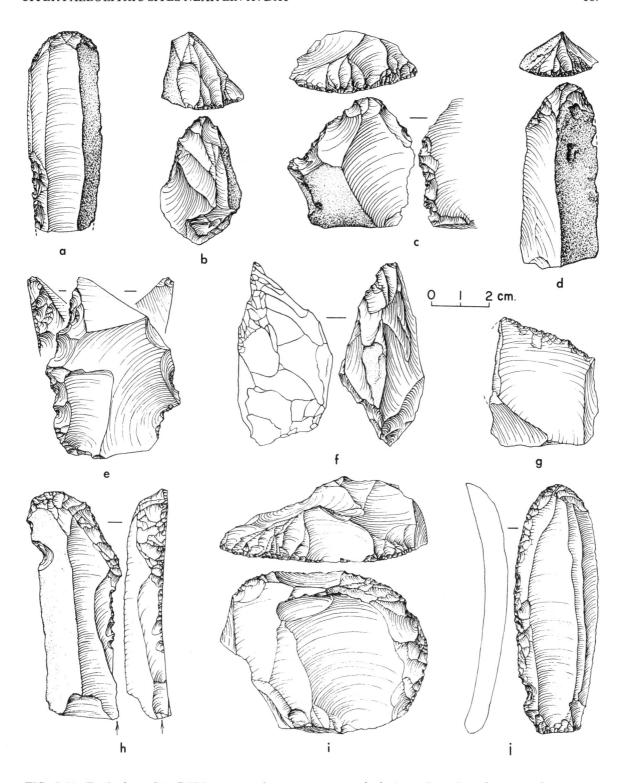

FIG. 7-11–Tools from Site D27A: *a, c*–endscrapers on retouched pieces; *b*–carinated scraper; *d*–semicarinated scraper; *e*–denticulate; *f*–lateral carinated scraper; *g*–retouched piece; *h*–multiple tool; *i*–unilateral endscraper; *j*–ogival endscraper on retouched blade.

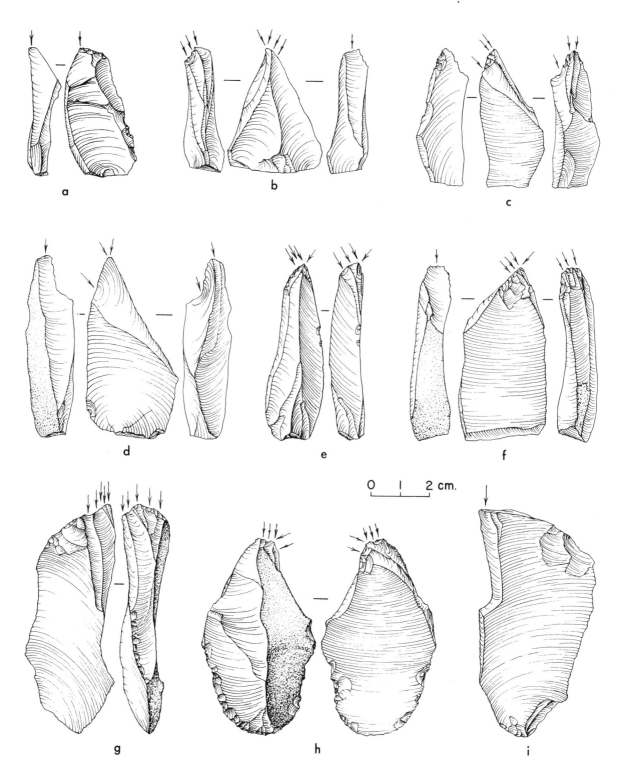

FIG. 7-12—Tools from Site D27A: *a-g, i*—various burins (see text for specific types); *h*—burin/endscraper.

that the burin blows are very small and poorly applied. Both, however, have clear notches where the burin facets terminate.

The only other dihedral burin form which occurs in reasonable number is the burin on snap. These are overwhelmingly simple, formed by only one or two burin facets struck off a snapped edge (fig. 7-12*i*). The vast majority of these have oblique snaps (fig. 7-13*f*) and relatively short burin facets. The burin bits range in width from 2.5 to 9.5 mm, with a mean of 5.7 millimeters. The narrowness of the bits is to a large extent the result of the high proportion of thin blades used as blanks (fig. 7-13*i*). Also, a few show additional *plan* retouch which thins the bit (fig. 7-13*k*).

The burins on truncation are generally poor, owing to rather weak truncations (fig. 7-12*a*). The exceptions to this are those with convex truncations, where the truncations approach scraping edges. It appears as if these pieces were actually endscrapers, subsequently modified into burins rather than burins produced at a single time.

Perforators

These are various blanks and blank fragments which have a single sharp tip produced by bilateral retouch. The tips are small, straight, and quite pointed.

Truncations

This is the one tool class which is heavily dominated by the use of blade blanks. While a few have straight truncations, most have straight oblique truncations formed by normal abrupt to semisteep retouch (fig. 7-13*c*), although one has a straight truncation (fig. 7-13*d*).

Backed Pieces

These are all atypical and cannot be classified as any specific backed type. Two are proximal flake fragments with abrupt retouch, while the third is a core-trimming flake which has some abrupt retouch along the same plane as the preparatory flake scars.

Double-backed Piece

This is a proximal blade fragment with bilateral abrupt retouch extending from the platform to the break (fig. 7-13*a*). It might have been a large atypical el Wad point, but the absence of complete examples makes this purely conjectural.

Retouched Pieces

These are all classed here, owing to the absence of other specific tool forms. Many may well be unfinished tools, some are tool fragments which are not clearly identifiable, but the majority appear to be pieces with simple retouch. A breakdown of the blanks and position of retouch is shown in Table 7-11.

TABLE 7-11
Position of Retouch on Retouched Pieces

Position of Retouch	Blade	Flake	Primary Element	Core Trimming Element	Total
Unilateral					
a. Obverse	15	24	3	1	43
b. Inverse	3	4			7
Bilateral					
a. Obverse	6	2	2		10
Alternate	1	2			3
Total	25	32	5	1	63

Retouch on blades varies from quite flat (fig. 7-13*b*) to semisteep on the bilaterally retouched pieces (fig. 7-13*e*). These may be bases of el Wad points but, as noted above, no complete examples or even distal extremities were recovered. Retouch on flakes tends to be heavier than that on blades, and numerous examples look like unfinished scrapers or broken tools (fig. 7-11*g*).

Denticulates and Denticulate Endscrapers

The majority of denticulates (20) are simple lateral forms produced by rather coarse retouch, including

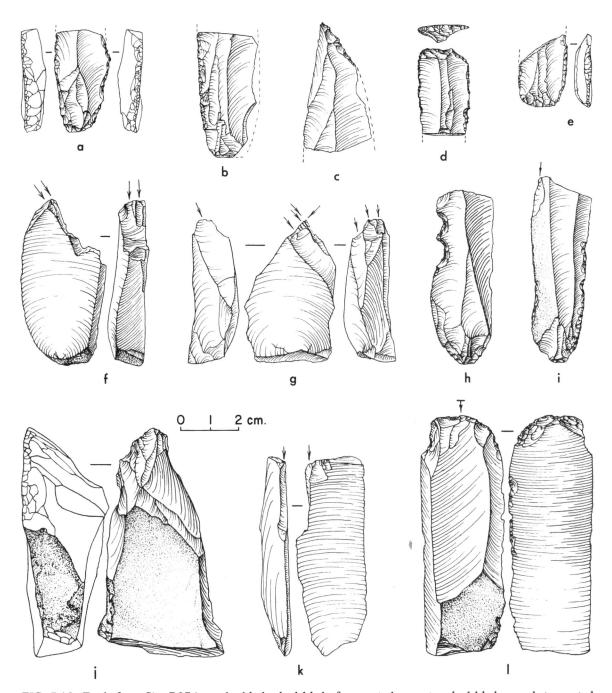

FIG. 7-13—Tools from Site D27A: *a*—double backed blade fragment; *b, e*—retouched blades; *c, d*—truncated blades; *f, g, i, k*—burins; *h*—double notched blade; *j*—lateral carinated scraper; *l*—scaled piece.

one with a perforator-like tip (fig. 7-11*e*). There are, as well, four converging denticulates, four which are bilateral, and two which approach transverse sidescrapers. The denticulate endscrapers are not typical, as the denticulations tend to be weak.

Notched Pieces

Twenty-six of the 40 are single retouched notches, ranging in size from 6 by 1 mm to 25 by 5 millimeters. Most, however, range between 10 and 15 mm in length and 2 to 3 mm in depth. In addition, there are 12 pieces with double notches (fig. 7-13*h*) and 2 with three notches. The notches on these pieces are comparable to single notches.

Varia

Included are two convex sidescrapers, one of which is inversely retouched, a questionable core scraper which does not approach a *rabot*, two classic bec burins, and a scaled blade (fig. 7-13*l*). In addition there are two flakes which combine notches, bec burins, and partial truncations.

Cores

A total of 103 cores and core fragments was recovered, apart from those modified into tools. Overall, two aspects are striking: there is wide size variation and most, even the smaller examples, tend to be chunky. In spite of this lack of elegance in form, the majority produced blades (table 7-12).

Notes on the Core Typology

Single platform cores, without obvious initial preparation beyond platform formation, dominate. In almost all cases, they have apparently been abandoned due to hinge fracturing just below the platform. Scars are deep and there is little evidence for a soft-hammer technique, at least on the large examples. There is considerable range in platform angle on blade cores from ca. 50° to almost 90° (mean angle, 73.4°), while flake cores exhibit even less acute angles. Blade cores show a wide length range, from 31 to 96 mm (mean, 64.4 mm), with little clustering.

Only 11 examples were produced on thick flakes and none approach tools, as there is a strong tendency for all cores to have flaked surfaces across one wide side of a piece, rather than along a narrow edge (fig. 7-14*c*). Stepped platforms were present on only 5 out of 34 single platform blade cores (fig. 7-14*a*).

The multiple-platformed cores parallel the single-platformed varieties both in size and

TABLE 7-12
Core Classification for Site D27A

Type	Blade	Flake	Total	Percent
Single Platform				
a. Simple	29	19	48	59.26
b. Prepared	2		2	2.47
c. Carinated	3		3	3.70
Subtotal	34	19	53	65.43
Multiple Platform				
a. Opposed, simple	10	1	11	13.58
b. Opposed, opposite side	8	1	9	11.12
c. Globular		1	1	1.23
d. Ninety Degree	3	4	7	8.64
Subtotal	21	7	28	34.57
Total	55	26	81	
Percent	67.90	32.10		100.00
Unidentifiable and Fragments	2	20	22	

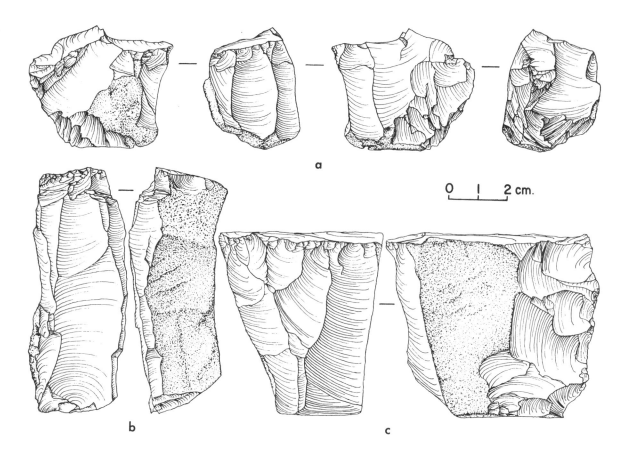

FIG. 7-14—Cores from Site D27A: *a*—flake core; *b*—opposed platform blade core; *c*—change of orientation core.

tendency for abandonment only after extensive hinge-fracturing (fig. 7-14*b*).

One noticeable aspect is the relatively large number of core fragments and unidentifiable cores, which is a sign of intensive utilization, as is the paucity of those blade cores amenable to further flaking.

SITES ON THE NORTHERN DIVSHON RIDGE AND THE HAR MEKHYA

The North Divshon Ridge forms a minor barrier between the Divshon Plain and the upper reaches of the Nahal Besor where it merges into the badlands of the east/west Zin. The ridge originates in the northern end of the Har Mekhya, at an elevation of 634 m, and extends northeastward to a point (at 537

m) where the badlands of the Zin and the canyon of the Nahal Mor join. The ridge, however, is not a solid block there being a 200 m wide pass through the ridge, at 510 m, connecting the Divshon Plain to the Nahal Besor. Both portions of the ridge have steep slopes covered by minimal vegetation, numerous bedrock outcrops, and a thin layer of loess cover.

The apparent advantages for occupation of the ridge rest mostly with the view it affords of the whole Divshon Plain and the northern portions of the Nahals Zin and Besor. While there are some flint sources along the ridge, these tend to be limited in comparison with the massive quantities of flint cobbles available along the northwest cliff of the Nahal Mor. While surface water is not available on the ridge, the ridge does afford a view of the upper, western accesses into the Nahal Mor.

The Har Mekhya, the western anchor of the North Divshon Ridge, runs north/south along the western edge of the Divshon Plain. While only a very small portion of it was surveyed, a single site (D29) was located at 610 m, where the Har Mekhya transforms itself into the North Divshon Ridge. The specific advantages of this location appear to be both the extremely wide view of the Divshon Plain which it affords and a large flint outcrop which occurs a few meters from the site.

The Upper Paleolithic sites on the North Divshon Ridge, D14, D18, and D21 are situated on the upper southern slope of the ridge, overlooking the plain. Originally (Marks et al., 1971), an additional site (D13) was listed as Upper Paleolithic. Since that time, much more experience has been gained concerning the range of Proto-Historic lithic assemblages in the Central Negev and, while the assemblage from D13 lacks the highly characteristic tabular flint scrapers, there are elements which strongly suggest that it is, in fact, Proto-Historic.

SITE D14

Site D14, located at the center of the North Divshon Ridge, is situated on the uppermost portion of its southern slope at an elevation of 530 m (fig. 7-1). The site is ca. 850 m northwest of the spring of Ein Avdat, although actual access to it would require traveling a considerably greater distance, owing to the cliff of the Nahal Mor.

The site is a roughly oval 400 sq m surface concentration of variable artifact density, occurring on both bedrock and on shallow pockets of sterile eolian deposits. A total of 40 sq m was systematically collected in 4 sq m units, covering both dense and sparse areas of concentration. Thus, the collection well reflects the average artifactual density for the

site as a whole. Of the 40 sq m collected, the material from 8 sq m was given to the Department of Antiquities without study, while that from the remaining 32 sq m forms the basis for this report.

Lithic Artifacts

Technology

The vast majority of the artifacts recovered were made of a light brown, fine-grained, unpatinated flint. While major flint sources are available along the western edge of the Nahal Mor and other sources are present on the North Divshon Ridge itself, no flint of this specific type was located.

The collection recovered a total of 4,114 artifacts. The distribution of artifacts by class is indicative of considerable blade production, and a rather low proportional occurrence of core-trimming elements and cores (table 7-13). It is probable that this reflects the tendency for full core utilization, thereby increasing the ratio of flakes and blades to cores.

Platforms are mostly unfaceted with marked bulbs of percussion. Faceting does occur, but it is mainly of simple dihedral form. Evidence for the use of a soft hammer, even on blades, is negligible. The platforms suggest that much initial core formation took place at the site, since the proportional occurrence of cortex platforms on primary elements is quite high (table 7-14).

A major characteristic of the assemblage is the overall small size of the artifacts. They range in length from 17 to 65 mm, but just under 66% of the flakes and just over 60% of the blades fall between 25 and 40 mm (fig. 7-15a, b).

The length/width ratios of the artifacts show a strong cluster, 54.35%, between 1:1 and 2:1. Only 18.34% of the artifacts are wider than they are long, but 27.31% do attain blade proportions. These, however, are

TABLE 7-13
Occurrence of All Artifacts by Class of Tool Blanks
and Proportional Utilization by Class

Artifact Class	Total		Tools		Percent of
	Number	Percent	Number	Percent	Class Utilization
Cores	79	2.89	1	0.38	1.27
Core Trimming Elements	103	3.77	8	3.11	7.77
Core Tablets	5	0.18	2	0.77	40.00
Primary Elements	480	17.58	23	8.94	4.79
Flakes	1,484	54.33	132	51.41	8.89
Blades	580	21.25	79	35.39	15.69
Totals	2,731	100.00	257	100.00	
Microburins	8				
Chips and Chunks	1,375				
	4,114				

clustered between 2:1 and 3:1, with only a very few exceeding 3:1.

There is little standardization in blade shape, with a rather random distribution between those which have converging (30.61%), expanding (28.79%), or parallel (40.60%) dorsal shape, while the distal extremities are heavily dominated by blunt forms (77.64%).

There does not appear to have been any selective factor operating which chose blanks for tool production outside the normally available size distribution (fig. 7-16).

It must also be noted that eight microburins were recovered (fig. 7-17d). These are fully consistent with the assemblage, both in terms of the raw material utilized and the absence of patination. Their small number (Microburin Index, 3.11), however, suggests that they were fortuitously produced and that no purposeful microburin technique was employed.

Typology

A total of 257 retouched tools was recovered, representing 9.41% of the available blanks. The blanks utilized in tool production (table 7-13) show that primary elements were selected against, blades were used in excess of their overall proportional occurrence, while other major artifact classes were utilized in about the same proportions as they were available. The only major artifact class showing a massive proportional utilization is the core tablet, but the sample size is so small that no significance can be drawn from the observation.

TABLE 7-14
Platform Types on Primary Elements,
Flakes, and Blades as Percentages

Platform Type	Primary Elements N=237	Flakes N=434	Blades N=257
Unfaceted	50.21	53.92	52.15
Dihedral faceted	8.02	13.18	7.39
Multiple faceted	1.69	5.12	1.95
Lipped	–	0.44	2.33
Cortex	24.47	7.19	7.39
Crushed	15.61	20.15	28.79
	100.00	100.00	100.00

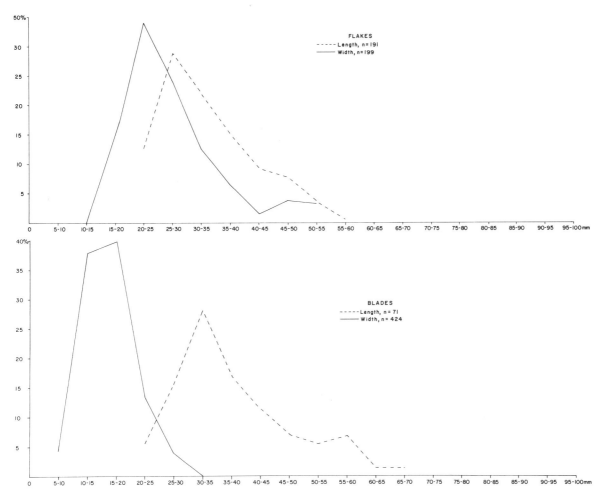

FIG. 7-15—Length and width of flakes and blades at Site D14.

Typologically, no class of tools strongly dominates the assemblage. While retouched pieces are most numerous, most other tool classes occur with some frequency. Notable is a small series of backed tools and truncations which are produced on both blades and bladelets. While none is truly geometric, two do approach lunates (table 7-15).

Notes on the Tool Typology

In general terms, retouch tends to be carefully applied, but on pieces other than backed forms and scrapers it is often marginal.

Endscrapers

Simple forms predominate, with only light, moderately invasive retouch. All are small, but only a few approach the size and shape of a thumbnail scraper (fig. 7-17*a,f*). Modified forms of simple endscrapers—those on retouched pieces, or unilateral and bilateral endscrapers—are not common but quite well made (fig. 7-17*q*). It appears that the larger the blank, the heavier and more invasive the retouch. Again, thin-nosed or shouldered scrapers show the general characteristics of the simple forms, particularly the tendency to be produced on quite thin flakes or blades (fig. 7-17*m, n*).

Thick scrapers, including nosed and carinated

TABLE 7-15
Typology of Site D14

Type	Blank Forms							Total	Percent
	Bladelet	Blade	Flake	Primary Element	Core Trimming Element	Core Tablet	Core		
Simple endscraper		2	11	1	2			16	6.22
Endscraper on retouched piece		1		1				2	0.78
Unilateral endscraper			2					2	0.78
Bilateral endscraper			2					2	0.78
Ogival endscraper		1						1	0.39
Thin nosed scraper			2					2	0.78
Thin shouldered scraper		2	2					4	1.56
Thick shouldered scraper		1	1					2	0.78
Carinated scraper, atypical			1			1		2	0.78
Burin, dihedral			1					1	0.39
Burin, dihedral, multifaceted	1							1	0.39
Burin, dihedral, angle	1		1					2	0.78
Burin, dihedral, angle, multifaceted	1		1					2	0.78
Burin, on snap		3	5	1				9	3.50
Burin, on old surface		1	1	1				3	1.17
Burin, on straight truncation		2	1		1			4	1.56
Burin, on oblique truncation		1	2					3	1.17
Burin, transverse on lateral truncation				2				2	0.78
Multiple burin, on snap			2					2	0.78
Perforator		3	4			1		8	3.11
Double-backed perforator	1	1						2	0.78
Double backed piece		1						1	0.39
Truncation, distal straight		2	2	1				5	1.94
Truncation, distal oblique	5	3	7					15	5.83
Truncation, proximal oblique			3	1				4	1.56
Truncation, distal concave oblique			1					1	0.39
Arch backed pieces		4						4	1.56
Arch tipped pieces		3						3	1.17
Straight backed pieces	2	1	1					4	1.56
Shouldered piece		3						3	1.17
Lunate, atypical	2							2	0.78
Retouched piece	1	19	30	2	2	1		55	21.38
Denticulate		6	8	7				21	8.17
Denticulate endscraper		1	10	1	1			13	5.05
Notched piece	1	14	27	4	2			48	18.67
Sidescraper, simple			3					3	1.17
Varia		1		1				2	0.78
Total Blank Forms	12	79	132	23	8	2	1	257	
Percent	4.66	30.73	51.41	8.94	3.11	0.77	0.38		100.00

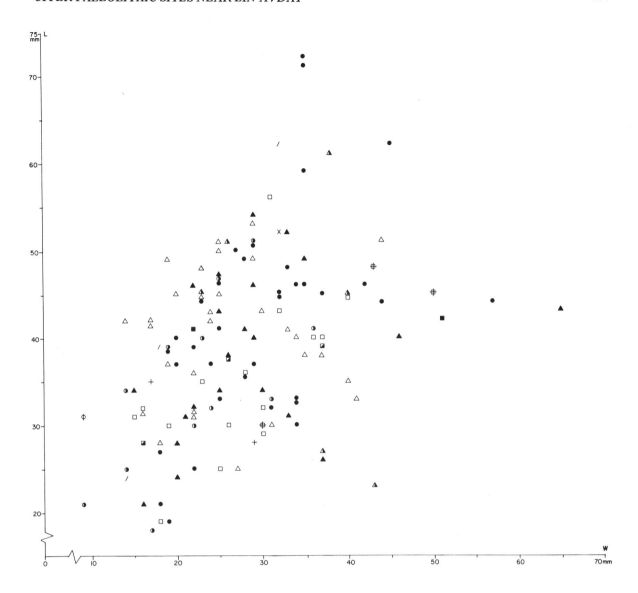

FIG. 7-16—Length/Width scattergram of tools from Site D14. Key: *open square*—simple dihedral burins; *closed square*—multifaceted dihedral burins; *crossed square*—burins on truncation; *dot*—endscrapers; *half-closed circle*—truncations; *lined circle*—atypical lunate; *open triangle*—retouched pieces; *closed triangle*—notches; *half-closed triangle*—denticulates; *cross*—perforators; *diagonal line*—backed pieces; *half-closed square*—other tools.

forms, are very rare. The larger examples are made on old reutilized flakes (fig. 7-17*p*). The carinated forms are atypical by virtue of the absence of true bladelet scars, although they are both quite symmetrical. The thick-shouldered examples have shoulders created initially by large notches with subsequent modification by additional retouch.

Burins

Considerable typological variety is present, although dihedral forms, including those on snap, are twice as numerous as those on truncations (figs. 7-17*o*; 7-18*c*). A striking aspect is the paucity of examples with multiple facets; only 3 out of 29. The

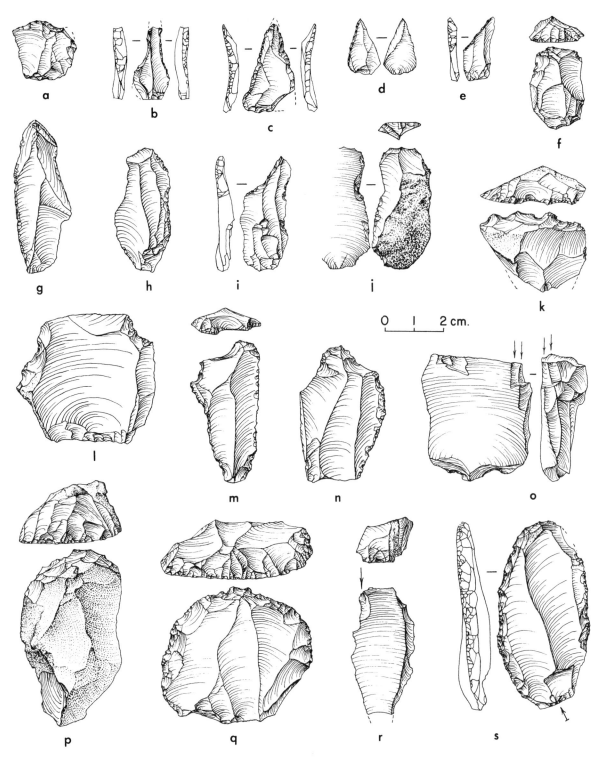

FIG. 7-17—Tools from Site D14: *a, f, m, n, p, q*—various endscrapers; *b, c*—double backed perforators; *d*—microburin; *e, j*—truncations; *g, h*—retouched pieces; *i*—shouldered blade; *k*—denticulate; *l*—notched piece; *o, r*—burins; *s*—backed blade.

dihedral angle burins are notable in that the main burin facets are transverse or markedly oblique to the axis of the pieces. This is also seen on those struck from old surfaces where the burin facet on each is transverse.

The burins on truncation are morphologically variable, but the truncations are all well formed and the burin edges are produced by only one or two burin facets (fig. 7-17*r*). Again, the transverse tendency is present on two of the nine. While most burin bits tend to be quite narrow, reflecting the small, thin blanks on which they were made, a number of examples are somewhat *plan*, with bits from 9 to 11.5 mm wide. Most, however, range from 2.0 to 7.5 mm (overall mean, 6.25 mm).

Perforators

The simple examples are produced on small flakes or blade fragments and have small, straight-pointed tips formed by bilateral obverse retouch (fig. 7-18*b*).

The double-backed perforators are formed by converging steep to semisteep obverse retouch and both have broken tips (fig. 7-17*b, c*).

Double-backed Piece

As this is a medial fragment, it is impossible to tell whether it is a section of a double-backed perforator or merely a double-backed blade.

Truncations

The quality of truncation is mixed. Those on bladelets tend to have abrupt retouch (fig. 7-17*e*), while those on blades at times show partial retouch, although typical examples do occur (fig. 7-17*j*). Those on flakes are poorly formed, irregular, and the flakes are often quite thick.

Backed Pieces

The predominant style is abrupt arched backing. Included here are four distal blade fragments with arch tips, which might also be considered convex oblique truncations. The arch-backed blades all have pronounced convex backs, with the backing extending the whole length of each piece. These all approach Chatelperron form, while one example, particularly wide, has some additional retouch along the cutting edge (fig. 7-17*s*).

The straight-backed pieces are clearly distinct from those which are arch-backed, with no evidence of any gradation. Those on bladelets are typical, while one on a blade is only partially backed with irregular abrupt retouch. All of the straight-backed pieces are much smaller than the arch-backed examples.

A distinct form of backed piece is seen in the shouldered blades. Two are typical, formed by obverse abrupt retouch (fig. 7-17*i*), while the third is formed by abrupt inverse retouch.

Two artifacts have been classified as atypical lunates. One is fragmentary, while the other is quite elongated (length/width ratio, 3:1). Both show irregular backing, and one example still has a portion of the bulb of percussion intact. They may be no more than variations of the arch-backed blade class.

Retouched Pieces

These continuously retouched pieces exhibit considerable variations as to the position of the retouch and blank form utilized (table 7-16).

Two aspects are noticeable: retouched pieces occur only rarely on primary elements, and retouch tends to be very regular and normally occurs over one-half of one or more edges (fig. 7-17*g, h*). Of some interest are five leaf-shaped flakes with bilateral or alternate retouch. These approach some form of point, although their small number makes such a conclusion only impressionistic.

Denticulates and Denticulate Endscrapers

These are quite common and generally well formed (fig. 7-17*k*). A sizable portion are made on primary elements as compared with other tool classes. There is considerable size range in the denticulates and a few are among the largest tools in the assemblage (fig. 7-16).

The denticulate endscrapers fall into two size groups: one of relatively large flakes with heavy ser-

TABLE 7-16
Position of Retouch on Retouched Pieces

Position of Retouch	Bladelet	Blade	Flake	Primary Element	Core Trimming Element	Core Tablet	Total
Unilateral							
a. Obverse	1	10	18	2	2	1	34
b. Inverse		4	4				8
Bilateral							
a. Obverse		2	4				6
Alternate		3	4				7
Total	1	19	30	2	2	1	55

rated retouch along rather broad edges, while the second group occurs on very small flakes and blade fragments and has fine but rather steep retouch.

Notched Pieces

While notches are quite frequent, they rarely occur on primary elements and only a single example was found on a bladelet. The number and position of notches on both blades and flakes show no clear patterns. The majority are simple obversely retouched notches (flakes, 20; blades, 7), although inverse notches are present (flakes, 5; blades, 6). Multiple notches are also present in significant numbers (fig. 7-17*l*). The most common are pairs of unopposed, obversely retouched notches (flakes, 6; blades, 1), but unopposed alternately retouched notches also occur (flakes, 2; blades, 1). Notches range in size from a few very small examples 5 by 0.5-1.0 mm to one which measures 16 by 3.5 millimeters.

Varia

There is a blade with heavy bilateral retouch with one shouldered side which converges to a point at the distal end and a flake with distal and proximal notches which approach truncations and a heavily denticulated lateral edge.

Cores

A total of 79 cores was recovered. All are small and numerous examples show extensive utilization. Core types parallel those from other Upper Paleolithic assemblages (table 7-17), although very few give any indication of initial preparation and a number have rather coarsely faceted platforms. It is most likely, however, that these platforms reflect a type of rejuvenation rather than a planned platform type.

Notes on the Core Typology

In comparison with other Upper Paleolithic assemblages, the cores here not only are smaller but also have platform angles which are considerably less acute.

The single platform blade cores exhibit a strong tendency toward the utilization of a large portion of the core surface for blade removals. Of the 33 examples, only two are utilized along one narrow edge, most have at least one wide face (fig. 7-18*f, h*) and often as much as three-quarters of the total platform circumference flaked, while a few have been struck around the total circumference (fig. 7-18*g*). Platform angles range from ca. 40° to

TABLE 7-17
Core Classification for Site E22D14

Type	Blade	Flake	Total	Percent
Single Platform				
a. Simple	25	9	34	46.58
b. Prepared	4		4	5.48
c. Pyramidal	4		4	5.48
Subtotal	33	9	42	57.54
Multiple Platform				
a. Opposed, simple	5	5	10	13.70
b. Opposed, opposite side	2	2	4	5.48
c. Ninety Degree	10	4	14	19.18
d. Globular		2	2	2.74
Subtotal	17	13	30	41.10
Discoidal		1	1	1.37
Total	50	23	73	
Percent	68.94	31.51		100.00
Unidentifiable and Fragments		6		

a high of ca. 85° (mean, 75.3°), but only four have angles of less than 70°.

The lengths of single platform blade cores range from 21 to 49 mm (mean, 35.3 mm). Clearly, in their present state, none could have produced blades, *sensu stricto.* This size is fully paralleled by the multiple platform cores (fig. 7-18a) so the larger blanks used in tool production either were brought to the site already struck or considerable core rejuvenation and reduction took place at the site.

Owing perhaps to the small size of the cores and the lack of use of a single narrow edge, there are only five flakes which have been modified into cores. For the most part, cores were made on small cortex-covered nodules or nodule fragments, and some cortex is often present on the unflaked core surfaces.

The number of multiple platform cores, particularly the ninety-degree variety, again is suggestive of intensive core utilization. These

often have utilized a number of platforms, so that there are opposed platforms, flaked surfaces at 90° to each other, although numerous forms occur (fig. 7-18a, d, e, i).

Overall, this is a curious assemblage. The small size of the artifacts, the presence of double-backed perforators, and the rough cores perhaps indicate a very late phase within the Upper Paleolithic of the Levant. The minor backed tool component argues against an Epipaleolithic affinity, while the absence of diagnostic Proto-Historic tools and cores places the assemblage outside that period.

SITE D18

Site D18 is located on the uppermost part of the southern slope of the North Divshon ridge, at an elevation of 525 m, 1.9 km almost due north of the spring of Ein Avdat (fig. 7-1). The site consists of an 1,800 sq m sur-

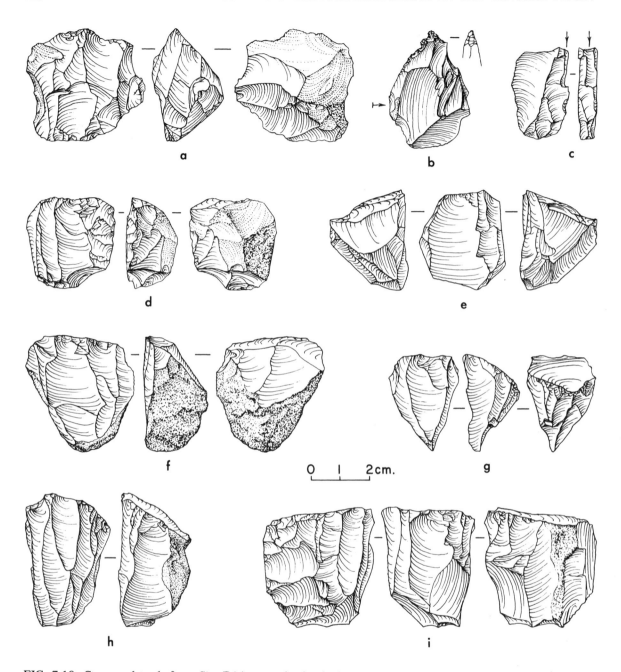

FIG. 7-18—Cores and tools from Site D14: *a*—multiple platform cores; *b*—perforator; *c*—burin on snap; *d, e, i*—ninety degree cores; *f-h*—single platform cores.

face concentration of lithic artifacts resting both on bedrock and on thin, scattered pockets of sterile eolian deposits. The total size of the site is most likely the result of low energy slopewash over a considerable period, as a small area of 150 sq m near the top of the slope contained the only dense concentration. From this concentration, a total of 53 sq m was systematically collected in 13 four sq m units and one 1 sq m unit. Of these, the collection from 12 sq m was given to the Department of Antiquities without detailed analysis, while the artifacts from the remaining 41 sq m form the basis of this report.

Lithic Artifacts

Technology

The artifacts are made on variable qualities of flint: from light colored, very rough grained to dark, very fine grained. Almost all exhibit a heavy reddish brown patination and their edges often show some minor crushing, both suggestive of a considerable time on the surface. The nearest major source of flint is 0.5 km to the southeast at the edge of the western cliff of the Nahal Mor, although minor outcrops also occur some 350 m eastward along the top of the ridge.

The collection from the 41 sq m recovered a total of 1,977 artifacts. The proportional occurrence by artifact class is shown in Table 7-18, where an outstanding feature is the paucity of blades. The apparently high occurrence of core-trimming elements is, perhaps, partially accounted for by a number of small elongated examples with triangular cross sec-

tions which might actually be burin spalls. This is reinforced by the number of burins which show bilateral battering just below the burin facets, a sign of initial edge preparation.

While no true core tablets were recovered, a series of very small flakes similar to core tablets were found. These have been classed as scraper tablets, appearing to have been produced during resharpening of thick-nosed or shouldered scrapers.

Platforms are largely unfaceted with marked bulbs of percussion (table 7-19). The apparent lack of a true blade technology is seen not only in the paucity of blades, but also in the total absence of lipped platforms, suggesting that a soft hammer or indirect percussion method was not employed. It is also clear that no distinction was made in platform preparation for blades as compared with flakes, again suggesting that blade production was probably not distinct from flake production.

There is considerable size range for artifacts, with flake lengths mainly clustering between 20 and 65 mm and widths between 20 and 55 mm (fig. 7-19a). The length/width

TABLE 7-18
Occurrence of All Artifacts by Class of Tool Blank
and Proportional Utilization by Class

Artifact Class	Total		Tools		Percent of Class Utilization
	Number	Percent	Number	Percent	
Cores	99	7.74	2	0.96	2.02
Core Trimming Elements	69	5.39	3	1.44	4.35
Scraper Tablets	11	0.86	–	–	–
Primary Elements	276	21.58	44	21.05	15.94
Flakes	730	57.08	124	59.33	16.99
Blades	94	7.35	36	17.22	38.30
Total	1,279	100.00	209	100.00	
Burin Spalls	10				
Chips and Chunks	688				
	1,977				

TABLE 7-19

Platform Types on Primary Elements,
Flakes, and Blades as Percentages

Platform Type	Primary Elements N=141	Flakes N=140	Blades N=39
Unfaceted	51.78	59.44	58.97
Dihedral Faceted	5.67	7.51	10.26
Multiple Faceted	4.26	9.66	7.69
Lipped	—	—	—
Cortex	14.18	5.58	5.13
Crushed	24.11	17.81	17.95
	100.00	100.00	100.00

ratios for the artifacts show that 83.59% fall between 1:1 and 2:1, only 6.96% are wider than they are long, and only 10.05% attain blade proportions, with over 90% of these being less than 3:1.

While the blade sample is poor, half have parallel dorsal outlines, while 32% are converging and 18% expanding. In terms of distal extremity, 80.56% are blunt. Blades tend to be quite large and, while only 11 were measurable, they ranged in length from 42 to 92 mm and in width from 17 to 38 mm (fig. 7-19b).

Blanks chosen for tool production were not randomly picked; the tools show both lengths and widths which fall into the higher ranges of the debitage sample (fig. 7-20).

Typology

A total of 209 retouched tools were recovered, representing 16.21% of the totally available blanks. There is a clear preference for blade blanks, as almost 40% of those available were utilized (table 7-20).

Typologically, the dominant tool class is the endscraper (40.12%), with burins next most common (14.12%), while retouched pieces, notched pieces, and denticulates occur with some frequency.

Notes on the Tool Typology

The tools tend to be on rather large, thick blanks and show somewhat coarse retouch. The general impression is one of chunky, mediocre pieces formed by strong retouch carried out by direct percussion.

Endscrapers

Simple endscrapers are on a variety of blanks, which are usually roughly quadralateral in shape (fig. 7-21c). The blanks are occasionally thick, resulting in scraping ends which are almost semicarinated. Endscrapers on retouched pieces are all on thick-keeled blanks. The retouch along the lateral edge of each piece tends to be irregular and, in three cases, is clearly denticulated (fig. 7-22h). Unilateral and bilateral endscrapers are also on thick blanks and all show rather steep retouch which transverses the distal end and extends down over one-third of the lateral edge or edges. Retouch on these pieces is heavy and occasionally even somewhat scaled. The ogival endscrapers are generally atypical, on thick short pieces. The thin-nosed scrapers have very restricted scraper edges, approaching perforators.

The thick scrapers are, perhaps, the most typical aspect of the scraper class. The thick-nosed scrapers are on very thick flakes or core remnants (fig. 7-22i), except for two which are retouched from lateral faces of thinner flakes and approach carinated burins. The general pattern is either a very steep, narrow nose (fig. 7-22g) or a very thick, steep but not particularly projecting nose (fig. 7-21d). The thick-shouldered scrapers parallel the nosed variety and are occasionally difficult to distinguish from carinated burins. They all have a very pronounced keeled form and are narrow and steep (fig. 7-21e). Retouch is extremely lamellar, as is typical for the nosed variety. The carinated scrapers are all produced on flakes or primary elements. The resemblance to cores is notable, as many cores are also made on thick flakes. On these pieces, retouch originates from the ventral surface, except for two where it begins on a lateral face. A few show very weak nosing, while others are ogival (fig. 7-21f) or rounded. Again, retouch is lamellar and

TABLE 7-20
Typology for Site D18

Type	Blank Forms						Total	Percent
	Blade	Flake	Primary Element	Core Trimming Element	Scraper Tablet	Core		
Simple endscraper	7	9	1	1			18	8.61
Endscraper on retouched piece	1	3	4				8	3.83
Unilateral endscraper		5					5	2.39
Bilateral endscraper	1						1	0.48
Ogival endscraper	1	2					3	1.44
Thin nosed scraper	1	2	1				4	1.91
Thick nosed scraper		4	3	1		2	10	4.78
Thick shouldered scraper		2	2				4	1.91
Carinated scraper, typical		8	7				15	7.18
Carinated scraper, atypical		2	1				3	1.44
Carinated scraper, lateral		1	1				2	0.96
Double endscraper	2						2	0.96
Endscraper/Burin		1	1				2	0.96
Endscraper/Truncation	1	1					2	0.96
Burin, dihedral	1	2					3	1.44
Burin, dihedral, multifaceted	1	5	2				8	3.83
Burin, on old surface	1						1	0.48
Burin, on snap		1	1				2	0.96
Burin, on snap, multifaceted	1	4	1				6	2.87
Burin, on straight truncation			1				1	0.48
Burin, on straight oblique truncation		1	1				2	0.96
Burin, transverse on lateral truncation		2	1				3	1.44
Multiple burin on truncation			1				1	0.48
Multiple burin, mixed			1				1	0.48
Perforator		5					5	2.39
Backed blade fragments	4						4	1.91
Truncation, distal straight	1	1	1				3	1.44
Truncation, distal oblique	1	1	2				4	1.91
Retouched piece	7	15	2	1			25	11.96
Notched piece		14	2				16	7.66
Denticulate	3	13	2				18	8.61
Denticulate endscraper		5	2				7	3.35
Sidescraper, simple		7					7	3.35
Sidescraper, transverse		1					1	0.48
Sidescraper, double		1					1	0.48
Scaled piece		1					1	0.48
Varia	2	5	2				9	4.31
Total Blank Forms	36	124	44	3	0	2	209	
Percent	17.22	59.33	21.05	1.44	—	0.96		100.04

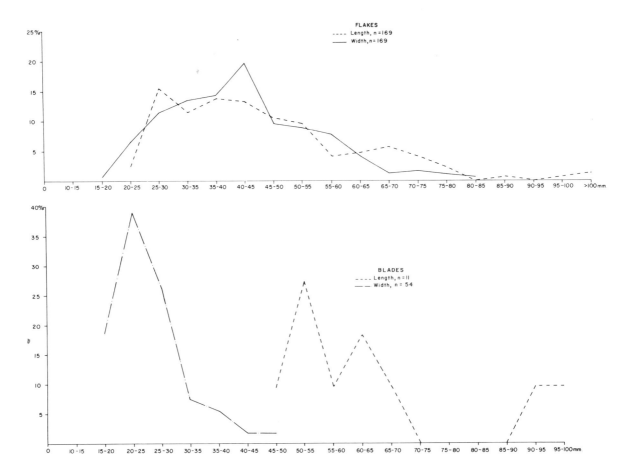

FIG. 7-19—Length and width of flakes and blades at Site D18.

several pieces exhibit unifacial or bifacial preparation along the keel. The atypical examples either lack the lamellar scars or the distinct keel (fig. 7-21*b*). The lateral carinated forms are well made, with the vast majority of retouch off to one side of the distal extremity, resulting in an oblique scraper edge. Of the two double scrapers, one is a typical carinated scraper on a thick blade with a normal endscraper on its flat, proximal extremity, while the other is a thick-nosed scraper on a flake, again with a normal endscraper at its proximal end.

Multiple Tools

Of the two endscraper/burin combinations, each has a flat endscraper at its distal end and a burin at its proximal extremity. On one it is a simple dihedral burin, while on the other it is a burin on a straight

truncation. The endscraper/truncation is not typical with the scraper poorly made, while the proximal truncation is inversely retouched.

Burins

One striking element is that 14 of the 17 dihedral burins are multifaceted, showing four or more burin facets. It is also noticeable, however, that a sizable proportion of all burins are on truncation—7 out of 29.

The simple dihedral burins are all on large blanks and have wide burin bits (from 16 to 19 mm). Of these, one shows battering below the longest burin facet (fig. 7-23*f*), while two do not (fig. 7-23*a, h*). The dihedral burins with multiple facets are somewhat smaller and quite classic (fig. 7-23*g*). These

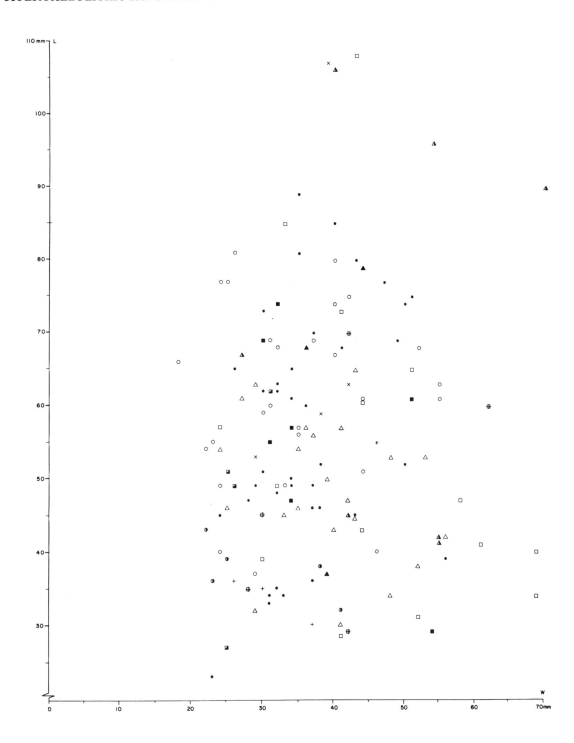

FIG. 7-20—Length/Width scattergram of tools from Site D18. Key: *open square*—simple dihedral burins; *closed square*—multifaceted dihedral burins; *crossed square*—burin on truncation; *dot*—thin endscrapers; *open circle*—thick scrapers; *half-closed circle*—truncations; *open triangle*—retouched pieces; *closed triangle* —notched pieces; *half-closed triangle*—denticulates; *cross*—perforators; *x*—multiple tools; *half-closed square* —other tools.

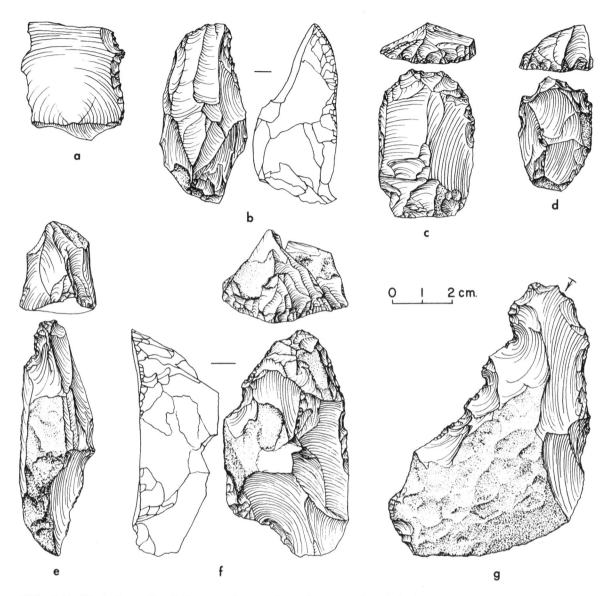

FIG. 7-21–Tools from Site D18: *a*–perforator; *b, e, f*–carinated and thick scrapers; *c*–endscraper; *d*–thick nosed scraper; *g*–denticulate.

burin bits range in width from 6 to 18 mm, but most fall under 11 millimeters.

Burins on snap are for the most part multifaceted. The snap is normally oblique to the axis of the piece, rather than perpendicular, and one even approaches a carinated scraper (fig. 7-23*b, d*). The bits on all these burins tend to be narrow, from 3 to 13 mm in width.

The burins on truncation are all simple with the burin edge formed by one or two burin facets intersecting with a truncation. The truncations are gener-

ally irregular but the burin bits are standard, from 8 to 12 mm in width. A single transverse example is somewhat oblique and is produced on the only blank which might be interpreted as being of Levallois manufacture (fig. 7-23*c*).

The multiple burins include one with two truncations and a single *plan* burin facet off each truncation, one with a dihedral multifaceted burin combined with a simple dihedral example, and one very

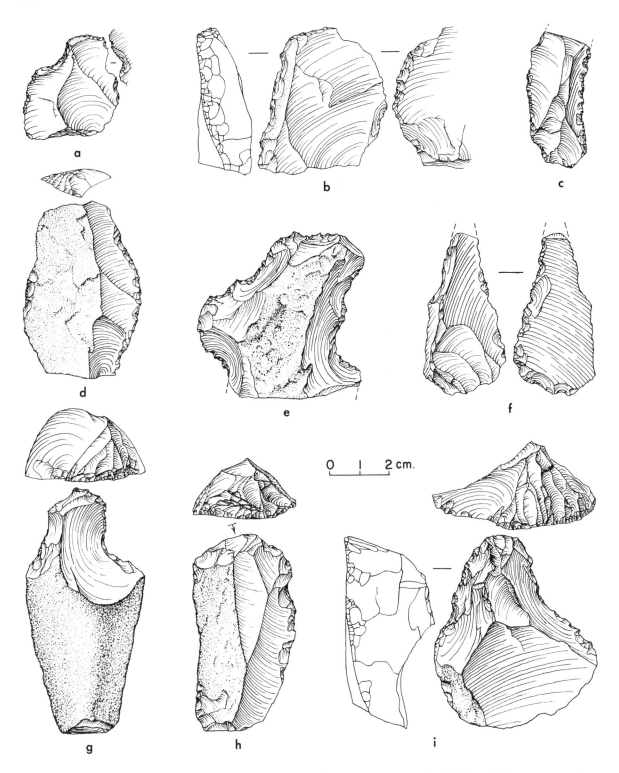

FIG. 7-22–Tools from Site D18: *a*–notched piece; *b*–sidescraper; *c*–retouched blade; *d*–inverse truncation; *e*–denticulate; *f*–varia; *g*–thick shouldered scraper; *h*–endscraper on retouched piece; *i*–thick nosed scraper.

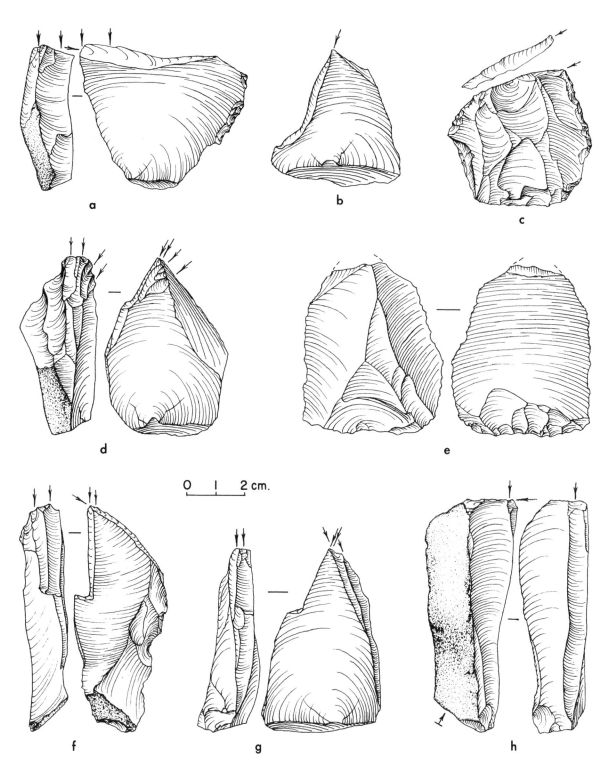

FIG. 7-23—Tools from Site D18: *a-d, f-h*—various burins (see text for types); *e*—varia.

chunky example with a burin on snap combined with a burin on a wide, irregular truncation.

Perforators

The perforators are formed on rather thin flakes and flake fragments by bilateral retouch which, on one example, is inverse (fig. 7-21*a*). In all cases, the tips are short and quite pointed.

Backed Pieces

These are all rather poor, including two distal fragments of thick blades which have marked but rough, irregular convex backing. A third piece is a wide, blunt-backed blade fragment with straight but irregular backing. The final piece, a small pointed flake with partial straight backing, is, perhaps, intrusive.

Truncated Pieces

All truncations are distal. While most have typical abrupt retouch, there is one primary piece which has a partial inverse truncation, as well as some light continuous lateral retouch (fig. 7-22*d*). In addition, there is one example on a massive primary flake where the truncation approaches a scraper.

Retouched Pieces

Owing to the slight edge damage on most pieces, the recognition of simple retouch has been restricted to that which is very regular. With a single exception, the retouched blades are fragmentary. The retouch is always obverse and, in one case, possibly bilateral (fig. 7-22*c*). The retouched flakes show considerable variation. A few approach transverse sidescrapers, but the retouch is too marginal and weak. On others it is bilateral, but on the majority, it is only on a single lateral edge. Four of these flakes approach Levallois form, but the absence of Levallois cores and the great rarity of such flakes makes it unlikely that a true Levallois technique was practiced at this site.

Notched Pieces

All tend to be on thin flakes or primary elements (fig. 7-22*a*). The notches all show retouch, although some of the larger examples were initially formed by a heavy, single blow. The notches range in size from 6 by 2 mm to one that is 25 by 5 mm, with most clustering between 9 and 15 mm in length and 2 to 3 mm in depth.

Denticulates and Denticulate Endscrapers

These show considerable variation in size and treatment. Among them are some of the largest tools in the assemblage, formed on primary elements with large irregular serrations (figs. 7-21*g*; 7-22*e*). There are, as well, small flakes with finely retouched serrations and blade fragments with bilateral denticulation.

Sidescrapers

Of the eight examples, three are simple convex, one simple straight, two straight inverse, one straight transverse, and one multiple straight/convex inverse. They are all on flakes and retouch varies from semi-steep to invasive on the inverse examples. The multiple scraper approaches a backed piece, but the opposed inverse scraper edge is too well developed to be considered minor retouch (fig. 7-22*b*).

Scaled Piece

Only a single example on a thick flake was recovered. It approaches a small core, although the bifacial battering is much more developed than is normal on even bipolar cores.

Varia

Included here are six small scraper fragments which could not be further classified. Another piece approaches a transverse multifaceted burin, but the burin facet along the dorsal plain has been heavily retouched, and there is steep retouch along much of the lower portion of the lateral edge from which the burin facets were struck. In addition, there are two very curious tools. One is a flake with clear bifacial thinning of the base (fig. 7-22*f*). The other, on a poor Levallois point, exhibits clear ventral thinning of the base, but without any dorsal modification taking it out of the range of an Emireh point (fig. 7-23*e*).

Cores

A total of 97 cores were recovered (table 7-21). They are consistent with the rest of the assemblage in size range, patination, and form.

Notes on the Core Typology

Overall, the cores exhibit a rather poor and rough manufacture, although a majority managed to produce blades. Part of this roughness is due to extensive utilization, so that a core was rarely abandoned prior to serious crushing of its platform or hinge fracturing of its face (fig. 7-24*d*). Cores were made mostly of chunks or nodule fragments, although some were on thick flakes or primary flakes.

Of the simple, single platform blade cores, nine were made on flakes, of which six primarily utilized only one narrow face (fig. 7-24*c*), while of those on chunks, 6 of 23 were similar. There is a small tendency toward flaking both a single narrow edge and then bending around onto a broad face: a technique which parallels many of the burins. The carinated cores, including the two multiple examples, approach tools. Multiple platform cores follow the pattern described above, although they tend to be somewhat smaller than the single platform varieties (fig. 7-24*a*).

Cores show considerable size variation. For

TABLE 7-21
Core Classification for Site D18

Type	Blade	Flake	Total	Percent
Single Platform				
a. Simple	32	16	48	58.54
b. Prepared	4		4	4.88
c. Carinated	6		6	7.32
Subtotal	42	16	58	70.74
Multiple Platform				
a. Opposed, simple	5	3	8	9.76
b. Opposed, opposite side	2	1	3	3.66
c. Globular		4	4	4.88
d. Ninety Degree	1		1	1.22
e. Double Carinated	2		2	2.44
Subtotal	10	8	18	21.96
Discoidal		6	6	7.32
Total	52	30	82	
Percent	63.41	36.59		100.02
Unidentifiable and Fragments		15	15	

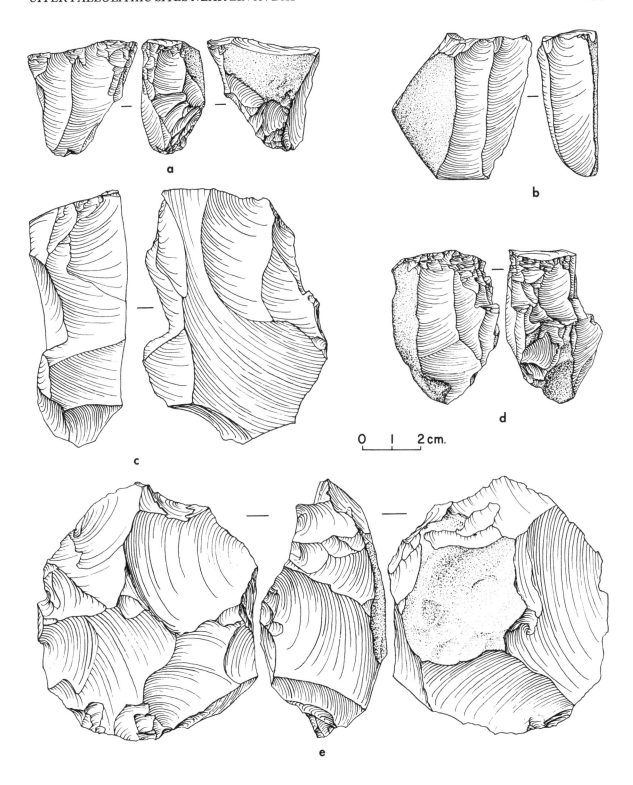

FIG. 7-24–Cores from Site D18: *a*–opposed platform blade core; *b-d*–single platform blade cores; *e*–discoidal core.

the single platform blade cores, the range in length is from 35 to 90 mm with a rather tight cluster between 45 and 58 mm and a mean of 53.6 millimeters. Platform angles on the simple cores vary from ca. 47° to ca. 87°, with a mean angle of 65.8°. The stepped platform is only present on 15.6% of the single platform blade cores.

Of particular note are a few very well-made unifacial discoidal cores (fig. 7-24*e*), two of which approach unstruck Levallois form, but could not be so classified.

SITE D21

Site D21 is located at the tip of the North Divshon Ridge at 537 m elevation overlooking the Nahals Mor and Zin. The site contains mainly Middle Paleolithic artifacts, although there is a small but clear Upper Paleolithic admixture, including typical blade cores, blanks, and tools. A very small collection was made which recovered a few typical carinated scrapers. Additional collection is necessary before anything more definite may be said.

SITE D29

Site D29 is located at the point where the Har Mekhya becomes the upper end of the North Divshon Ridge (fig. 7-1). It is situated on a flat shelf at an elevation of 610 m, near the top of the quite steep and broken hill complex. The site consists of a surface concentration of artifacts covering ca. 1,000 sq m, which is densest in the center of the shelf and becomes sparse toward the east, where it dips into the slope of the hill. About 10 m below to the east is a band of outcropping flint and a scattered concentration of large cores and flakes. These, however, are separated from the site, not only by the elevational distance, but also by some 30 m of slope. The artifacts around the flint outcrop consist of two clear elements: a dominant Middle Paleolithic component of heavily

whitish yellow patinated Levallois cores, broken Levallois and non-Levallois debitage, and a minor component of blades, flakes, and blade cores which have a dark brown patination, most of which appear to be of Upper Paleolithic technology.

The concentration on the shelf initially appeared to lack significant Middle Paleolithic components, while a brief examination of the retouched tools showed them to be of Upper Paleolithic type. A total of 100 sq m was systematically collected in six large areal units, from 10 sq m to 25 sq m, in the central portion of the concentration. The materials from 25 sq m were given to the Department of Antiquities, while that from the remaining 75 sq m were retained for study.

Upon close examination of the collections, it was apparent that the artifacts could not be considered representative of a single assemblage. There was a small but clear Middle Paleolithic component fully comparable to that found at the flint outcrop below, there was a definite Upper Paleolithic component, and there was a small, possible Proto-Historic component. This mixture was not solely restricted to tools, but to debitage as well. About 40% of those tools which were clearly Upper Paleolithic in form (e.g., multifaceted burins, thick and carinated scrapers, etc.) showed double patination. The blanks had the whitish yellow patination of the Middle Paleolithic cores and Levallois flakes, but the retouch showed either a brown patination or almost no patination. Thus, it was clear that considerable reutilization of Middle Paleolithic artifacts had taken place during the Upper Paleolithic occupation, and that studies of the lithic technology would not produce useful information.

The retouched tools also posed a problem. While there were few which could be attributed to the Middle Paleolithic component, there were a number of extremely fresh tools with or without multiple patination, particularly large heavily retouched perforators and multiple denticulates which are most commonly found in Proto-Historic context. As the denticulates, at least, are common in both Upper Paleolithic and Proto-Historic assemblages, it was felt that the various components could not be safely separated to isolate the Upper Paleolithic tools. Yet there was, without question, an Upper Paleolithic occupation. In order to give some idea of its nature, as reflected in the artifacts, those which can be unquestionably identified as Upper Paleolithic will be briefly discussed.

Lithic Artifacts

There are a few technological observations possible. Of the clearly non-Middle Paleolithic cores, 57% produced blades, suggesting considerable blade orientation. The blade cores are largely simple single platform types, although a few poor carinated examples occur. The vast majority of these cores are flaked along one wide face, but a few flakes were utilized along a narrow edge. Core length varies considerably from 29 to 83 mm, falling into the range for most other Upper Paleolithic assemblages. Blade debitage is common and of those with the proximal extremity intact, most are unfaceted; only rarely does a faceted platform occur, and about one-quarter have lipped platforms.

Scrapers form the major class of tools attributable to Upper Paleolithic manufacture. Among these is a series of thick-nosed scrapers (7), thick-shouldered scrapers (3), carinated (4), and lateral carinated (2) forms. Of 46 flat scrapers, 20 are on blades, including three double scrapers.

Burins are not common but include, within the 21 recovered, 5 asymmetric dihedral, multifaceted examples, one multifaceted piece on a snap, two transverse burins on lateral truncations, two atypical carinated burins, and four simple asymmetric dihedral burins, two of which have the shouldered bit common at Site D27A.

The remaining tools, including denticulates, retouched pieces, truncations, etc., are not sufficiently diagnostic to be sure that they are not of Proto-Historic origin. Also, no evidence was found for el Wad points, *lamelles Dufour*, or other specialized Upper Paleolithic blade tools.

It is obvious that this site throws little additional light on the Upper Paleolithic occupation of the Avdat area. It is possibly significant, however, as it is located well away from the perennial springs and is well above the Divshon Plain. As such, it represents a different kind of site locality from that of all other Upper Paleolithic sites.

SITES ON THE WESTERN EDGE OF THE DIVSHON PLAIN

The western edge of the Divshon Plain is defined by the steep slope of Har Mekhya, which is deeply cut by numerous drainages. While most of this slope ends at the edge of the plain, two small, low fingers extend several hundred meters onto the plain, terminating along the western edge of the incised North/South Zin channel. From each of the ridge ends, a good view is afforded of the Zin channel and the main portion of the Divshon Plain to the east.

The surfaces of these two ridges are flat, covered with a thin layer of eolian deposit, while their sides are defined by eroded bedrock and loose boulders derived from bedrock. On the eastern extremity of each finger sparse surface concentrations of artifacts were located (D20 and D28).

Originally (Marks et al., 1971) both of these sites were classified as Upper Paleolithic but lack of study prevented any additional characterization. Since that time materials from both sites have been analyzed and, while some hints of Upper Paleolithic occupation are present at both, the bulk of the materials must be attributed to some Proto-Historic industry.

SITE D20

A systematic collection was made from 150 sq m along the southern edge of the finger, at an elevation of 520 m (fig. 7-1). While numerous artifacts were recovered, only eight may be classified safely as Upper Paleolithic. These include two typical carinated scrapers, three multifaceted dihedral burins, two fine burins on oblique truncations, and one bifacially prepared blade core. The remaining artifacts are of Proto-Historic type or are non-diagnostic. While there are many small, rough blade cores, lipped platforms on blades are almost nonexistent, and the propensity for thick, unfaceted, highly oblique platforms on both blades and flakes points to a non—Upper Paleolithic technology.

SITE D28

A similar situation exists for this site (fig. 7-1). A total of 50 sq m was collected, and detailed analysis indicates that almost all the artifacts can be attributed to a Proto-Historic occupation. In addition, however, are a very few multifaceted burins and carinated scrapers which appear to be Upper Paleolithic. At best, all that can be said is that very ephemeral Upper Paleolithic occupations were probably present on these two fingers. The lack of typical Upper Paleolithic cores and significant numbers of Upper Paleolithic tools, however, makes this observation at best tentative.

SITES IN THE NORTH/SOUTH ZIN

As so often happens, as much in reality as prophetically, an Upper Paleolithic site complex, D100, was found eroding from the northern terrace of the Nahal Zin about one kilometer from the mouth of the Nahal Mor (fig. 7-1), during the last day of the 1972 field season. It was discovered during an afternoon trip by P. Goldberg and R. Ferring, who were making some final geological observations on the terrace system in that area.

This terrace system had been surveyed during the 1969 field season, but the heavy rains of the past few winters apparently cut additional exposures which brought these sites to light. The complex consists of two *in situ* artifactual deposits about 50 m apart. It is of importance as it will provide the first instance of two Upper Paleolithic occurrences in clear stratigraphic relationship.

One occurrence, D100A, is eroding from a low terrace of the Nahal Zin. The cultural horizon is clearly discernable as a distinct living floor some five meters above the present nahal bed. This floor, with a dense concentration of artifacts, including one firepit, could be traced in profile for about ten meters. The other occurrence, D100B, is located about 50 m downstream, *in situ*, within the upper part of the terrace alluvium. This latter occurrence is just visible and artifacts could not be recovered easily.

Eroding out of the first occurrence was a dense concentration of fresh, unpatinated artifacts. Five square meters of this was systematically collected, yielding a sample of over 2,000 artifacts. It was impossible at that time to analyze or transport them from Israel, however, and thus the only information on this assemblage is that gained from a very preliminary sort undertaken at Hebrew University. A small sample of tools was returned to Southern Methodist University, some of which are illustrated in Fig. 25.

Technologically, this assemblage is characterized by the production of blade cores and blades similar to but smaller than those at site Sde Divshon (Ferring, this volume). A soft hammer or punch technique is suggested by an exceedingly high proportion of blades with lipped or crushed platforms. Also, the overall proportion of blades to other artifact classes appears extremely pronounced. The core tablet technique is used extensively, and other core-trimming elements are very com-

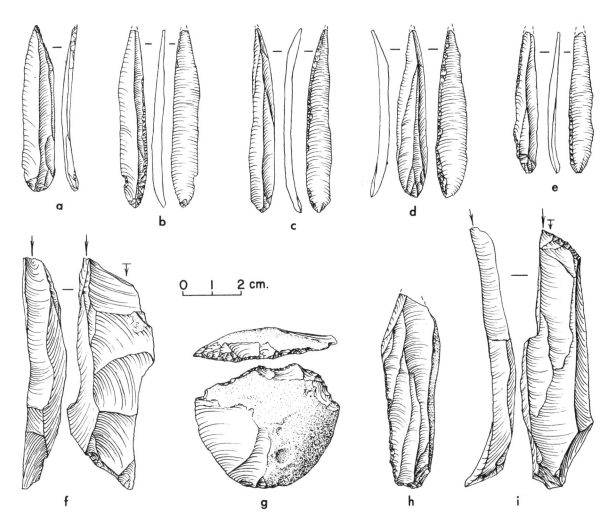

FIG. 7-25—Tools from Site D100A: *a*—el Wad point; *c, d*—inversely retouched blades; *b, e*—alternately retouched blades; *f*—burin on snap; *g*—endscraper; *h*—retouched blade; *i*—burin on truncation.

mon. Elongation of blades is marked, with a small sample yielding length/width ratios up to 7:1.

Typologically, a very common tool form is a long, incurvate blade with inverse, semisteep retouch along one margin (fig. 7-25*c, d*). Other similar blades have alternate, semisteep retouch (fig. 7-25*b, e*), while also present, but in less numbers, are some typical el Wad points (fig. 7-25*a*). Burins are common, including both simple and multifaceted dihedral forms, those on snap (fig. 7-25*f*) and on truncation (fig. 7-25*i*). These burins are most frequently made on long blades, as is a series of continuously retouched pieces (fig. 7-25*h*). From the total surface collection only two poorly made endscrapers were recovered (fig. 7-25*g*).

While this description is largely impressionistic, it is clear that the assemblages from D100A represent yet another Upper Paleolithic manifestation. It is hoped that excavations will not only permit the radiometric dating of the occurrence but also firmly place it stratigraphically in relation to the other, as yet undefined, nearby occurrence.

The other occurrence, D100B, is still largely unknown. There was little material eroded from the terrace face and no time for even test excavations. What few artifacts were seen, however, indicate that blades are minimally represented and that scrapers are present.

CONCLUSIONS

The Upper Paleolithic sites in the Avdat area represent a number of discrete occupations. At present, it seems as though only two sites, D26 and D27B (Ferring, this volume), may represent the same cultural manifestation. It must be remembered, however, that other Upper Paleolithic sites are present in the total survey zone, and these must be integrated with those reported here prior to any detailed comparisons or synthesis of the Upper Paleolithic occupation of the Avdat/Aqev area.

In spite of the fragmentary nature of the evidence, as seen from around Ein Avdat, a number of observations may be useful. Technologically, there is considerable variation from assemblage to assemblage, particularly in the wide range in occurrence of lipped platforms on blades. It should be noted, however, that all assemblages indicate similar blade emphasis, as seen through cores, although considerable differences are present in the percentage of blades actually utilized in tool production.

Typologically, the range of tools from these assemblages parallels those from Upper Paleolithic sites in the northern Levant. On the other hand, the proportional occurrence of specific classes and types shows considerable variability even on an intrasite basis. It is most likely, therefore, that the proportional occurrence of tool classes within any assemblage will reflect, however darkly, activity patterning rather than a strict cultural bias toward any group of tools. Only additional work will clarify this point, however.

In the most general terms, it is clear that the area around Ein Avdat was one focal point for Upper Paleolithic occupation in the Central Negev. Another was clearly around Ein Aqev, just to the east. Unfortunately, too little of the prehistory of the Central Negev is known to judge whether this type of density is typical or whether the presence of the perennial springs acted as a magnet to Upper Paleolithic peoples.

NOTE

[1] Additional excavations did take place in the summers of 1974 and 1975. The site, now referred to as Boker, including D100A and D100B, is much more complex than thought at the time this manuscript was prepared.

BIBLIOGRAPHY

MARKS, A. E.; PHILLIPS, J.; CREW, H.; and FERRING, R., 1971. "Prehistoric Sites near En-Avdat in the Negev." *Israel Exploration Journal* 21(1):13-24.

SDE DIVSHON: AN UPPER PALEOLITHIC SITE ON THE DIVSHON PLAIN

C. Reid Ferring
Southern Methodist University

INTRODUCTION

The site of Sde Divshon (D27B) was located during the 1969 field season. Work commenced during that season and was completed the following year. The site is a surface and *in situ* concentration of lithic artifacts some 800 sq m in area, lying about 30 m south of the edge of the Zin cliff line, on the northern periphery of the Divshon plain (fig. 8-1). The immediate terrain is one of a very gentle slope (grade = 1:33) away from the cliff toward the center of the plain (figs. 8-2 and 8-3). Vegetation is slight, owing to the shallow soil cover (15-20 cm). The surface is relatively unbroken by cobbles other than the artifacts. Some limestone cobbles do occur, although no patterns among them could be discerned.

The position of Sde Divshon relative to major landforms and resources is important. Its absolute elevation at ca. 505 m permits a clear view of the entire Divshon Plain and the slopes of the surrounding high ground. A similar commanding view of the floor of the Nahal Zin, which begins to broaden sharply some 100 m directly below, is afforded from the cliff edge, just a few meters from the site. The spring of Ein Avdat is 1.5 km to the southwest, and Ein Aqev is some 4.2 km to the southeast. Although considerable elevational differences separate the springs from the site, walking times to both are not excessive: approximately one hour to either. These are the only nearby sources of permanent water, yet seasonal water was undoubtedly available on the plain, in the Nahals Divshon and Zin, both only 1.5 km away. These two drainages also support fairly dense growth of perennial vegetation, while the Divshon Plain has a thick growth of annuals after the rainy season (see Munday, this volume). The most immediate resource is flint. High quality Eocene flint outcrops in the form of small to medium-sized nodules at the cliff edge, some 30 m from the site. The amount of flint taken from this source was massive, as indicated by the dense cover on and in the site. Yet, an abundant deposit of flint is still available at the cliff edge, indicating the permanence of the source. Other sites in the area undoubtedly utilized this source as well.

When assessing the spatial relationship of Sde Divshon to local resources, then, several factors must be considered. It lies within the Divshon Plain proper, yet its proximity to other zones, such as the cliffs and the annual drainages, gives its location a more centralized aspect. It seems that the flint outcrop is the resource with "locational priority," yet the presence of other suitable flint sources in the Avdat/Aqev area support the view that this particular flint source was chosen for its relationships to certain other resources. That relationship seems to be one of efficient, multiple-resource utilization.

The present condition of the site is one of a partially deflated deposit. About one-third of the material is still *in situ*. No faunal remains or evidence of firepits were found, but some burned ocher was recovered. The condition of the artifacts on the surface is extremely fresh, with little patination or edge damage. The *in situ* artifacts are unpatinated and in very fine condition. Both the condition of the artifacts and the very minor slope at the site are regarded as support for the view that the site structure (i.e., artifact positions) had not been

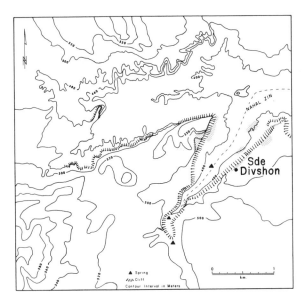

FIG. 8-1—Location of Sde Divshon on the edge of the
Divshon plain.

significantly disturbed by deflation or erosion. The slope was sufficient, however, to
carry most of the very small chips some distance below the site where they remain today.
This accounts for the small number of chips
in the collected assemblage (table 8-1).

The main objective of the work at Sde Divshon was the mapping of a large area of the
site so that artifact distribution studies could
be undertaken. The *in situ* material was tested
in several locations and was found to be in
continuous distribution with the surface material. Since it appeared that the total artifactual deposit represented overlapping single
occupation clusters, and that there was no
stratification of the material, the recovery of
a large area of the *in situ* material was deemed
too costly in time, given the amount of return
toward the primary objective. Thus, the surface material provided the area sample for distribution studies. This surface deposit is characterized by both differential densities of artifacts, as well as differential distributions of
specific artifact classes. The differential densities could be detected visually and prompted
the methodology employed in the field.

A total of 235 sq m was systematically
collected in the following manner. A site grid
system, composed of one-square-meter units,
was laid down and the location of each nontool artifact was mapped within each unit by
coded symbol. Each tool was located exactly
and numbered so that classification could be
done in the laboratory. The artifact classes
noted by symbol only were: cores, blades,
flakes, primary elements, core-trimming elements, core tablets, chips, and unutilized raw
material. After mapping, the artifacts from
each unit were bagged separately and analyzed by unit in the laboratory to provide
control over the field technique. Only two
workers were used in the field to control sub-
jective differences in field coding. A small
portion of tools, primarily retouched pieces,
was found in the laboratory once the debitage
had been washed, and hence slight discrep-
ancies arose in some cases. The location
of these pieces was known within the square
meter, and these tools were added to the
maps according to the density of their
mapped debitage class. Both the typological
and technological data presented here are
those obtained from the laboratory analysis,
not the field counts.

FIG. 8-2—Profile of surface through Sde Divshon.

Considerable work has been done on the
locational analysis of the artifacts from Sde
Divshon. These efforts have verified the existence of both artifact density clusters and
clusters of specific artifact classes. The current impression (tests of significance have not
yet been completed) is that Sde Divshon consists of several occupations. These occupations exhibit the same typological and technological characteristics, indicating close cul-

TABLE 8-1
Composition of Sde Divshon Lithic Assemblage

	Total		Debitage		Tools		Percent of Utilization
	Number	Percent	Number	Percent	Number	Percent	
Blades	4,320	23.18	3,669	21.45	652	42.64	15.07
Flakes	9,176	49.24	8,568	50.09	609	39.83	6.64
Primary Elements	2,575	13.82	2,426	14.18	151	9.88	5.86
Core Trimming Elements	538	2.89	508	2.97	28	1.83	5.20
Core Tablets	722	3.87	655	3.83	67	4.38	9.28
Cores	1,303	6.99	1,279	7.48	22	1.44	1.69
Total	18,634		17,105		1,529		
Chips and Chunks	6,708						
Total	25,342						

tural and temporal affinities, yet the character of each specific occupation is expressed by different proportions and distributions of specific artifact classes. The problems encountered in dealing with spatial analysis are complex, however, and statistical verification of these observations is necessary.

LITHIC ASSEMBLAGE

Both technological and typological data presented here are those from the complete surface assemblage. This cumbersome sample of over 25,000 artifacts was analyzed for the areal sample needed for distributional studies, not because a smaller sample would not have sufficed for descriptive purposes. The sample is reported *in toto* here, owing to the intermediate stage of those studies, and the present lack of precise definition of intrasite clusters.

While the total assemblage is dominated by flakes (table 8-1), the production of blades and the selection of blades for retouched tools characterizes the assemblage. These aspects are reflected in the core technology, the debitage, and in the tools, which show a markedly higher frequency of blade forms

than that found in the debitage. This emphasis on specialized blade production will be examined in terms of the core technology, the removal techniques, the character of the debitage, and the selection of blanks for tool production.

CORE TECHNOLOGY AND TYPOLOGY

The emphasis on blade production is best seen in the specialization of the core technology, which is of quite classic Upper Paleolithic character. Ten core types were recognized for this study, eight of which produced blades and which accounted for 90.79% of all classifiable cores (table 8-2). The standardization of cores, as well as the removal techniques is exceptional. About 67% of all cores are single platform, simple or prepared. There is a high degree of standardization of core size (table 8-3), as well as platform angle. While for some types there is a slight tendency for cores made on flake blanks to be somewhat longer, this is probably due to their earlier exhaustion owing to smaller initial mass than is true for cores on nodules. Platform angles show little variability among types (compared to burin angles in table 8-10), although each

FIG. 8-3—Sde Divshon, showing extreme density of surface artifacts.

type shows a fair range. The quite consistent mean length of blade core types correlates well with the mean length of blades (65.42 mm). Ninety-degree and pyramidal forms have smaller size, but are quite negligible in frequency (2.3% of all cores). Since almost all of the cores have sufficient mass remaining for the removal of more blades, it seems that the mean lengths of the cores and the blade debitage may be taken as estimators of the optimum size for blades.

The observations on core blanks (table 8-2) indicate a consistent use of nodules, but also the occasional use of flakes for most of the types. The estimation of the ratio of this use is most likely biased toward the nodules to some degree. A core blank was classified as "flake" only when evidence such as platform, bulb, or ripple marks was present. Many of

the cores have had most of their surfaces worked, thereby preventing any accurate judgment as to the identification of the blank. In such a case, the blank was classed as a nodule. The general pattern of core reduction and core form indicate that many of the single platform prepared and twisted type cores, especially those with back keels, have been made on large thick flakes. This practice, based just on the frequency of identifiable flake blanks, indicates complete use of the raw material available at the flint outcrop, not simply the nodules which were the correct size for direct preparation as cores. The larger nodules were consistently reduced into large flakes which were subsequently prepared for core use. The preparation and reduction of these cores, and the obliteration of blank features prohibits any accurate assessment of the original blank frequencies.

TABLE 8-2
Core Typology of Sde Divshon

Type	Percent on Nodule	Percent on Flake	Number	Percent
Single Platform, simple	80.21	19.79	187	17.22
Single Platform, prepared	83.92	16.08	541	49.82
Twisted	95.90	4.10	122	11.23
Opposed Platform	93.85	6.15	65	5.99
Alternate Platform	94.74	5.26	19	1.75
Pyramidal and Sub-pyramidal	100.00		20	1.84
Carinated	77.78	22.22	27	2.49
Ninety Degree	100.00		5	0.46
Flake Core, single platform	71.25	28.85	52	4.79
Globular	100.00		48	4.42
Subtotal			1,086	100.01
Unclassified[1]			120	
Unidentifiable			75	
Total			1,281	
Percent	87.82	12.28		

[1] These were given to the Department of Antiquities without detailed analysis.

NOTES ON THE CORE TYPOLOGY

The terminology employed to describe the cores takes as an ideal a single platform blade core. This is a core which is elongated along the axis of blade removal, and which has a relatively restricted area exhibiting the negative scars of blade removal; i.e., only a small portion of the platform circumference has been utilized to strike off blades. The proximal end of the core is the end with the platform. The distal end of the core is that opposite the proximal end, along the axis of blade removal. The back of the core is that surface opposite the surface of blade removal, which is referred to as the face for the core. The lateral sides are those which connect the back and the face of the core. The terminology obviously cannot be used for all of the core forms. Clearly, a pyramidal core has no lateral sides or back since the total surface, aside from the platform, shows the negative scars of blade removal. In such a case, the core only has a platform and a face, although a very extensive one. In spite of these difficulties, this terminology is expedient to use as it is applicable to the vast majority of core forms found in this assemblage.

Single Platform, Simple

These exhibit no preparation other than the formation of a platform (fig. 8-4d), which is done most commonly with a single blow. Little use is made of the lateral margins of the platform for blade removal as is seen in the other core types. These cores may well represent those made on the smaller blanks, for which initial preparation was simple, or where no elaborate preparation was warranted, owing to the smaller size. The larger blanks probably needed more

TABLE 8-3
Lengths and Platform Angles of Cores

Core Type Blank	Sample Size	Length		Platform Angle	
		Mean	S.D.	Mean	S.D.
Single Platform, simple					
Nodule	149	62.15	.72	61.05	.49
Flake	37	61.64	3.77	64.19	.85
Single Platfrom, prepared					
Nodule	452	66.76	.55	63.80	.06
Flake	87	64.35	1.65	67.89	.31
Twisted					
Nodule	117	63.88	.63	61.30	.58
Flake	5	71.60	16.70	67.00	6.00
Opposed Platform					
Nodule	61	62.77	1.77	63.27	1.51
Flake	4	69.00	7.50	62.50	10.10
Carinated					
Nodule	21	64.19	4.06	59.52	.10
Flake	6	66.50	2.01	56.66	.74
Ninety Degree					
Nodule	5	50.60	4.80	67.00	1.50
Alternate Platform					
Nodule	19	65.31	1.72	66.57	3.16
Pyramidal/Sub-pyramidal					
Nodule	21	42.23	.39	—*	

*Not taken.

Single Platform, prepared

preparation as they were reduced to allow control of blade morphology. Very simple preparation, such as *lame à crête* removal in many cases would not be evidenced on these cores, but the relatively low frequency of this core-trimming element suggests that it was restricted in use, and probably was more commonly associated with the prepared types, where evidence of initial bilateral trimming is present.

In many cases, it is apparent that only one platform was prepared, and only a few blades removed. This would not call for platform rejuvenation by the removal of a core tablet, but rather a single primary flake, which helps to explain the low tablet-to-core ratio.

Single Platform, Prepared

Six forms of preparation were recognized within this type (table 8-4). Distinguishing between these forms was often a rigorous task of classification, therefore some transitional forms and some combinations of techniques were left undifferentiated. Some cores had flake scars covering their back and lateral surfaces, to the extent that the origins and pattern of the preparation blows were obliterated. Most of these were placed in the random category. Others had two or more forms of preparation and required a compromise of classification to avoid a cumbersome number of types. Thus, each of the six kinds of preparation form ideal categories, with combinations existing in some cases, and grading between techniques in others. The types are, in the majority of cases, consistent with the primary form of preparation, however, and variation is discussed for each form.

Bifacial

This technique appears to be of two general forms. The first exhibits quite extensive and fine bifacial retouch, forming two ridges comparable to a handax, with the crest along the planned axis of blade removal. These are the largest of all cores recovered and many show only initial removal of blades. Much of the bifacial trimming is of very fine quality (and probably was done with a soft hammer technique). This may account for the fairly equivalent percentages of lipped platforms on flakes and primary flakes (table 8-5). The second form (fig. 8-5e) consists of cores already quite well reduced, with the bifacial retouch occurring on the back of the core, usually in the form of a keel, but also sometimes on the distal extremity as well (fig. 8-4c). This latter form often appears simply to be cores with the remnants of bifacial retouch following considerable blade removal and probably reduction in core length (i.e., platform rejuvenation). The bifacially prepared cores are slightly larger than the other prepared types; they have a mean length of 70.60 mm, as opposed to a mean length of 65.80 mm for all other prepared forms (figures are for those on nodules only). This greater length is likely due to the first form of bifacially prepared cores, those in an early stage of reduction.

Keeled Back, Unilateral

This very characteristic form is similar in profile to the bifacial form illustrated in Fig. 8-5e, except the keel is formed by unifacial retouch. The keel, in all cases, gives the core a triangular cross section, with the blade removal surface forming the base of the triangle. It occurs quite commonly in connection with the next form of preparation, distal trimming, but when the keel is present, it was placed in this category. Many of the bifacial forms are identical to the keeled forms, the only difference being the type of retouch used to form the keel.

TABLE 8-4

Single Platform Core Preparation Techniques

Type of Preparation	Percent on Nodule	Percent on Flake	Total Number	Total Percent
Bifacial	95.24	4.76	84	15.53
Keeled Back, unilateral	92.55	7.45	94	17.38
Distal	66.26	33.74	163	30.13
Bilateral	93.94	6.06	66	12.20
Transverse Back	79.17	20.83	72	13.31
Random	96.77	3.23	62	11.46
Total	83.92	16.08	541	100.01

Distal

This is the most common form of preparation. It is utilized as a technique more than indicated by its frequency, however, owing to its use in coordination with other more distinct techniques, such as bifacial, keeled, or random (fig. 8-4e). This kind of preparation also "blends" into other forms, particularly the twisted core type. The keeled cores sometimes have unilateral retouch which extends down the entire length of the core to the distal end, with retouch there which is indistinguishable from the normal distal preparation. Distal preparation is evidenced on a large number of the blades. These were not considered core-trimming elements as the transverse retouch on their distal surfaces was far more restricted than that of the *lame à crête*.

Bilateral

This preparation technique is highly characteristic (and of the form in fig. 8-11i), except it is, of course, bilateral. The resulting shape of the core is rectangular, with the back of the core being flattened by either random or transverse flaking. This form of preparation seems to be used more for the removal of lateral cortex, as is probably the case with the bifacial, yet, the resulting core shape is very distinct from the keeled forms.

Transverse Back

This has been differentiated from the random on the basis of its very regular character, as in Fig. 8-11i. It sometimes occurs with unilateral preparation, as in the illustrated example. It always gives the core a rather flat, rectangular cross section.

Random

On these cores, the backs are flaked in a random fashion (fig. 8-5h). The final cross sections are quite variable.

Twisted

This highly characteristic core type has two platforms. The "main" platform, from which most of the blades are removed, is prepared with the tablet technique, and is similar in form to those of the single platform simple and prepared types. The secondary platform is opposite the main platform and has a very acute striking edge which is oriented perpendicularly to the striking edge of the main platform. The bifacial core shown in Fig. 8-4c shows how the secondary platform would be oriented with respect to the main platform. The right-hand view of that core shows moderate amounts of retouch parallel to the axis of the main platform. For the twisted cores, this blade removal would produce blades about equal in length to those produced from the main platform, and they would extend parallel to, and alongside the main face of the core, terminating at the lateral margin of the main platform.

It should be noted here, for emphasis, that the above "types" of cores account for just over 78% of all the cores from this site. The remaining types, while morphologically distinct, are all minor in occurrence relative to the three types previously described. Thus, while this type list may imply a highly variable nature for the cores from this assemblage, the contrary may as well be inferred from the standardization of general core *forms*. This classification has simply emphasized the differences for descriptive purposes. In terms of the types of debitage produced, the three main core types appear to be exceedingly similar. They vary in terms of the preparation required to produce that debitage, but in little else.

Opposed Platform

While low in frequency, this type is clearly a distinct technique from the other single platform core types. These cores often have faceted platforms and the core tablet technique is not evident (fig. 8-4a). Lateral or bilateral preparation is very common. The size range is similar to the main types.

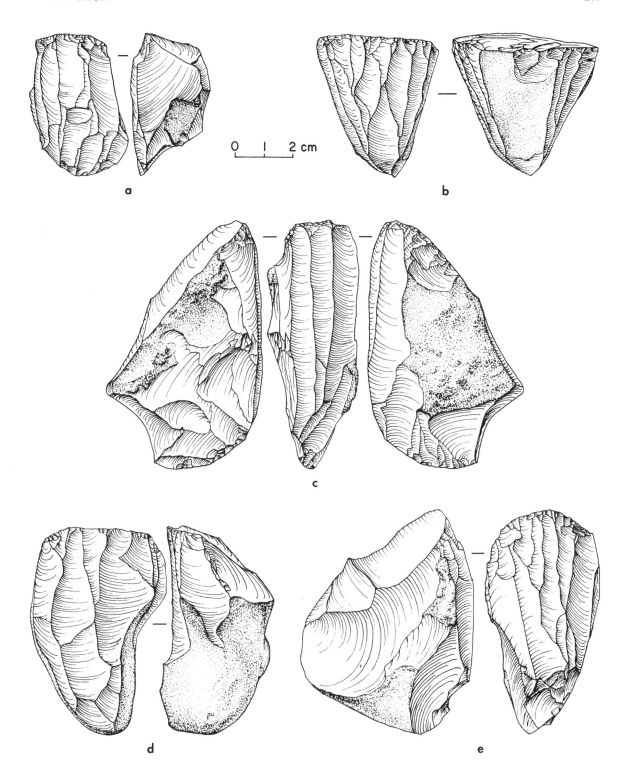

FIG. 8-4–Cores from Sde Divshon: *a*–opposed platform blade core; *b*–sub-pyramidal blade core; *c, e*–single platform, prepared blade cores (*e* with stepped platform); *d*–simple single platform blade core.

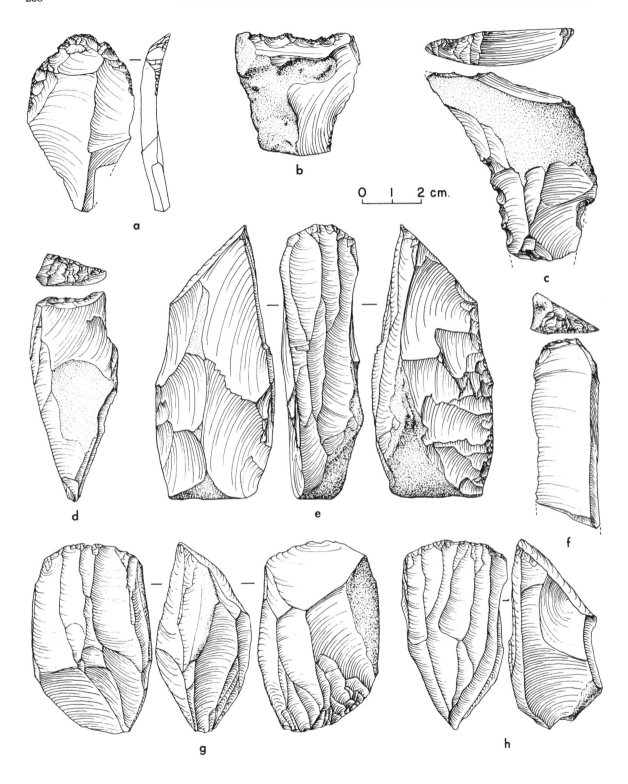

FIG. 8-5–Tools and cores from Sde Divshon: *a, f*–endscrapers; *b, c*–denticulates; *e, h*–single platform, prepared blade cores; *g*–opposed alternate platform blade core; *d*–concave distal truncation.

Alternate Platform

This type is also highly characteristic with the blades from each platform being terminated by the rear of the opposite platform. The core tablet technique is evidenced here, as shown in the illustrated example (fig. 8-5*g*). The size range is similar to the opposed platform types.

Pyramidal and Sub-pyramidal

This small group of cores includes typical pyramidal cores (8) and sub-pyramidal cores (6). The latter have platforms not completely encircling the circumference of the core, but have classic pyramidal shape (fig. 8-4*b*). Included within this group are six cores which have two platforms on opposite sides of a core, similar in shape to that illustrated. The blades removed from those platforms overlap at the apex of the core as in the pyramidal forms, but the retouched portions of the platform are restricted to either end of the nodule. All three varieties of this group are very similar in size, which is considerably smaller than all other types.

Carinated

A limited number of cores exhibit an overall morphology which is very similar to that of carinated scrapers of the nucleiform variety. In terms of size, as well as preparation techniques, this group is consistent with the other types described here.

Ninety Degree

Five cores, three of which are among the smallest from the entire assemblage, have two platforms oriented at 90° on the same plane.

Flake Cores

This category comprises the total range of identifiable cores which are not prepared and utilized for the production of blades. A higher percentage of these cores is made on flake blanks than can be recognized on other types. These do not have the appearance of crude blade cores, or of cores in initial stages of preparation, but are quite distinct, always single platform, flake-producing cores. The platforms are always more extensive than on the blade cores, and give the cores a circular to oval cross section, with a relatively short striking axis dimension. Owing to the broad area of the platform, faceted platforms are the most common form, except for those made on flakes, which generally have the ventral surface of the flake serving as the platform for the core. This latter form rarely shows evidence of platform preparation.

Globular

These cores are battered, completely or greatly reduced, and do not conform to any of the above classifications.

DEBITAGE

While the debitage in this assemblage is composed mainly of flakes (table 8-1), the core technology shows the overwhelming emphasis on the production of blades, and the selection of those blades for tools also is clearly evidenced. This trend is also seen in the very low frequency of flake cores. The length/width scattergram of the debitage from Sde Divshon shows a clear bimodal division between the blades and flakes (fig. 8-6). With such a division between flakes and blades in this assemblage, and the absence of a unimodal debitage scatter as seen at some other Upper Paleolithic sites in the area, this technology indeed takes on a specialized character. The flakes from this assemblage appear to be largely the by-products of the highly specific blade core technique which produces elongated, thin blades, many of which probably were intended to be blanks for the El Wad points. While the sample of complete points was small, the large number of fragmentary specimens (even most of the fragments were of blade proportions) indicate quite restricted ranges of blank width and thickness. The blade debitage and core meas-

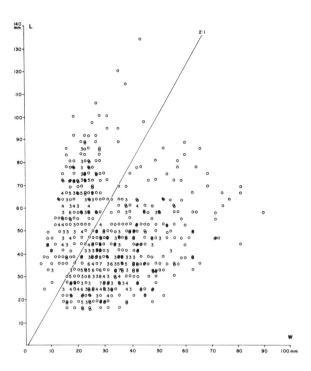

FIG. 8-6—Length/Width scattergram of debitage at Sde Divshon.

urements indicate a fairly consistent mean length for these blades of about 65 millimeters. Thus, with quite specific demands for the production of blade blanks, and techniques of core preparation and reduction which would produce numerous by-products of preparation and rejuvenation (i.e., flakes and primary flakes, in addition to core-trimming elements), we find rather simplified explanatory factors for the minority of blades in the assemblage.

The techniques of removal show that blades were struck the majority of the time with a technique producing a lipped platform (table 8-5). Whether this represents a soft-hammer technique or one of indirect percussion is a matter of debate. This author is not convinced of a means to distinguish clearly between the techniques on the basis of platform morphology. The blades from the assemblage do not appear to exhibit the striking consistency of those from an assemblage of known punched blades, however, and the

somewhat inefficient use of the cores hint at a direct soft-hammer technique. Both flakes and primary flakes are dominated by unfaceted platforms, with the lipped forms being much less frequent than on blades. The primary elements show a higher frequency of cortex platforms as expected, with the difference from flake platforms being within the multifaceted category. Faceting is quite rare throughout the assemblage.

Primary elements are rare, given the number of cores which were utilized (about two primary elements per core). Apparently this is not due to initial reduction of cores elsewhere, as no such concentrations of primary flakes were found anywhere in the vicinity of the site or the raw material source. This aspect can be explained in part by the method of analysis. Since 50% of the dorsal surface of any piece had to be covered with cortex for it to be classified as a primary element, the many blades and flakes which had less than that were placed into those respective categories. In many cases it was apparent that cortex was "peeled" gradually, from the face of the core toward the lateral portions, with a blade having a margin of cortex along one edge which did not cover half of its dorsal surface. In this manner, cortex was efficiently removed without substantial increase in the frequency of "primary elements."

The core-to-tool ratio is quite low (1:1.2). This could be interpreted as either low utilization of the available blanks, or as the production of an excessive amount of debitage to produce *suitable* blanks (i.e., blades with specific morphology and size). Both of these interpretations are felt to be applicable here and will be elaborated upon below.

The problems involved in dealing with debitage morphology are quite complex, requiring considerable recording of attributes and still more statistical handling of data. While it is felt that the only promising approach to the problem is on a multivariate level, this properly constitutes another study of the material

TABLE 8-5

Debitage Platform Type Frequencies from Sde Divshon

Platform Type	Blade Percent	Flake Percent	Primary Element Percent	Total Number	Total Percent
Unfaceted	18.51	46.86	42.61	3,185	40.27
Dihedral unfaceted	1.10	3.31	2.27	212	2.68
Multifaceted	2.68	10.24	4.09	605	7.65
Lipped	60.54	13.82	11.14	1,825	23.07
Crushed	15.90	15.30	16.91	1,241	15.69
Cortex	1.28	10.47	22.97	842	10.64
Number	1,642	4,949	1,319	7,910	100.00

beyond this descriptive account. In this analysis of the debitage, attributes were recorded independently for the most part, prohibiting any multivariate study. Even these preliminary results, however, show certain patterns in blade morphology which are useful in assessing the overall blade producing technology. A sample of 781 blades was examined for three attributes: distal morphology, dorsal shape, and lateral profile. Blunt distal ends were more common (61.3%) than pointed ones (38.7%). Dorsal shapes were 59.9% parallel, 23.2% convergent, and 16.8% expanding. The majority of the blades were flat (57.9%), those incurvate accounted for 32.2%, while blades which were twisted were relatively rare (9.9%).

In the selection of El Wad point blanks, several of these observations are important. No El Wad points were made on twisted or incurvate blades, indicating that the flat blades were being intentionally produced, as well as selected from the debitage. The dominance of blunt distal ends on blades is of interest, considering the distal retouch on points, and supports the contention that many of the broken distal ends should have had retouch. The abundance of parallel-sided blades is highly consistent with the well-shaped blade cores, and is evident on many of the tool blanks. El Wad points comprise 18.1% of all tools made on blades in this

assemblage. This leaves numerous other factors to consider in assessing the role of blade morphology in the production and selection of blanks in tool production. The point blanks are highly distinct in several attributes: width, thickness, edge configuration, etc. Thus, while it is easy to say that most blades produced had parallel edges, it cannot be directly inferred (however apparent intuitively) that the production of El Wad point blanks is the reason for this consistency. Many other blade tool blanks also have parallel edges, but have several attributes which preclude their being used in El Wad point production. A detailed analysis of tool blanks by tool class is required to explore this fully, and that is not feasible here. In relation to other sites in the area, however, blade production at Sde Divshon is a clearly distinct technological activity.

Selection of Blanks for Retouched Tools

Of the 18,634 pieces of debitage recovered from Sde Divshon, only 8.20% were utilized for retouched tools. The composition of the tool assemblage by debitage class shown in Table 8-1 illustrates the differential selection of the available debitage forms. Most obvious is the near doubling of the blade frequency over that of the debitage assemblage, making blades the dominant blank form in the tool assemblage. The selection coefficients for each debitage class illustrate that core tablets are the only other class of debitage showing positive selection (i.e., use in greater proportion than production), and it is quite minimal compared to the blade selection. The platforms on the pieces selected for tools illustrate several technological observations (table 8-6). Blade platforms are clearly dominated by lipped and crushed forms, indicating a similar blade morphology and most probably a similar removal technique for pieces with either type of platform. The slight increase in multifaceted platforms here is on those heavier blades used for the larger tools. Platforms on flake tools show a marked decrease in the frequency of lipped platforms from that in the debitage sample. This is accompanied by an increase in the frequency of multifaceted and dihedral forms. The higher frequency of lipped flake platforms in the debitage sample probably indicates mis-struck blades, or trimming pieces without the traditional dorsal scar pattern. Primary elements show almost no changes in their platform frequencies other than slight increases in faceted and cortex forms.

The size of the original tool blanks is obviously difficult to assess owing to their modification by retouch, and particularly for blade tools because of the high rate of broken pieces. The scattergram of measurable tools shows a considerable range of variation around a fairly dense central concentration of flake tools. The blade tools are grossly underrepresented in this scattergram, and would undoubtedly lend more of a *bicenter* appearance to the tool distribution (fig. 8-7). Individual tool class scattergrams are presented as Figs. 8-12 and 8-13.

From each core in this sample, 14.30 pieces of debitage were produced. Only 1.17 tools per core resulted from that debitage. This inefficiency of core use no doubt has some basis in the proximity to the large raw material source, but is felt that the specialization of

the technology in terms of blade production is also an integral factor. While considerably more detailed analysis of the debitage and cores is required to explore fully the specifics of debitage production, some of the observations presented here point the way toward the understanding of this technology and its differences from other Upper Paleolithic sites in the vicinity (see Marks and Ferring, this volume).

TOOL TYPOLOGY

The general character of the retouched tool assemblage from Sde Divshon is similar to several Upper Paleolithic habitations in northern Israel, which contain El Wad points in fair proportions. No detailed comparison with other assemblages is presented, however, in keeping with the descriptive format of this first volume, yet every effort has been made to present, either in the type list or in the notes, information sufficient to make general comparisons possible. It should be reemphasized that the sample reported here is the total assemblage recovered, and that the individual concentrations to be reported later will undoubtedly contain different proportions of the tools reported here. The very large surface area collected has provided, however, a sample which certainly is statistically representative for purely typological purposes.

The overall complexion of the tool assemblage is best represented by the following indices:

Scrapers	31.64	El Wad points	7.72
Burins	16.92	Denticulates	5.17
Truncations	6.27	Retouched pieces	16.94
Backed pieces	0.39	Notches	10.46

Particularly noticeable are the quite high indices of retouched and notched pieces, most of which are blade tools, and the meager representation of backed elements. No evidence whatsoever was found of the *chanfrein* tech-

TABLE 8-6
Tool Platform Type Frequencies

Platform Type	Blade Percent	Flake Percent	Primary Element Percent	Total Number	Total Percent
Unfaceted	14.24	44.50	33.84	223	30.88
Dihedral faceted	1.66	7.04	4.61	33	4.57
Multifaceted	5.96	17.14	7.69	85	11.77
Lipped	56.62	4.23	10.78	193	26.73
Crushed	20.20	13.80	16.92	121	16.76
Cortex	1.32	12.96	26.15	67	9.28
Number	302	355	65	722	99.99

nique. Scrapers are the dominant tool class; most of them are simple endscrapers, and the carinated scraper group is neither particularly common nor well made, as discussed below. The complete type list (table 8-7) provides considerable sub-class description, and the notes on the typology should be referred to for sub-type, or attribute description. Tool sizes have been given for most classes (table 8-8), and specifically for scraper sub-types (table 8-9) and burin sub-types (table 8-11).

NOTES ON TOOL TYPOLOGY

Scrapers

Scrapers are the most common tools, with an index of 31.64. The most frequent forms are flat scrapers, endscrapers on retouched pieces, etc. Thick forms, particularly the carinated scrapers, have lower frequencies than might be expected for an assemblage of this character. The size of all scrapers is very consistent, with only sidescrapers being somewhat larger than the other types (table 8-9). Short scrapers, particularly endscrapers, are very rare. Very few types have mean lengths lower than the 65 mm mean length of blades. The location and origin of the scraping edge retouch is quite similar for most types (table 8-10). Proximal and lateral scraping edges are quite rare, and are found mostly on the thick scrapers. Inverse retouch is very rare for all types except the endscraper on retouched piece. Lateral retouch, that

which originates on a very steep lateral edge and is struck obliquely or transversely toward the ventral surface, is also uncommon except on the thick scrapers. It is far less common here than at some other sites in the area, such as Ein Aqev (Marks, this volume).

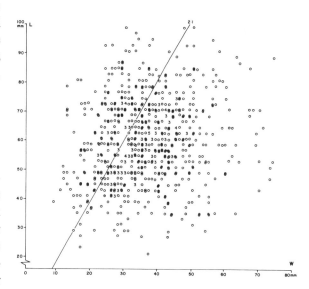

FIG. 8-7—Length/Width scattergram of tools at Sde Divshon.

Simple endscrapers are, by far, the most frequent scraper type. Almost all of these are "typical" (figs. 8-8a, c, h; 8-9d, e; 8-5f), as only ten could be considered "atypical" owing to roughness of retouch and irregularity of shape (figs. 8-10i; 8-8f; 8-5a). Retouch is generally very fine, with the wider examples having

TABLE 8-7
Sde Divshon Typology

Type	Blank Forms						Total	Percent
	Blade	Flake	Primary Element	Core Trimming Element	Core Tablet	Core		
Simple endscraper	71	66	30	2	11		180	11.77
Unilateral endscraper	3	6	1				10	0.65
Bilateral endscraper		9	2				11	0.72
Endscraper on retouched piece	28	24	6	1			59	3.86
Ogival endscraper	2	7	1	1			11	0.72
Thin nosed scraper	2	7	4				13	0.85
Thin shouldered scraper	3	3	1				7	0.46
Thick nosed scraper		7	4				11	0.72
Thick shouldered scraper		6		1			7	0.46
Carinated, typical	5	13	4	2	1	5	30	1.96
Carinated, atypical		17	3	4	2	5	31	2.02
Carinated, lateral	1	2					3	0.20
Double scraper	5	7	4	1		1	18	1.18
Endscraper/Burin	4	12	2			1	19	1.24
Endscraper/Truncation	6	1	1				8	0.46
Burin, dihedral	12	37	13	2	11	5	80	5.23
Burin, dihedral, multifaceted	3	16	3	1	7		30	1.96
Burin, dihedral, angle		8	2		2	1	13	0.85
Burin, dihedral, angle, multifaceted		1					1	0.07
Burin, on old surface	3	17	6	1	3		30	1.96
Burin, on old surface, multifaceted		7			2		9	0.58
Burin, busquoid	1				1		2	0.13
Burin, on snap	9	10	4	1	2		26	1.70
Burin, on snap, multifaceted		2					2	0.13
Burin, on straight truncation		3					3	0.20
Burin, on oblique truncation	2	9	1	1	7		20	1.30
Burin, on oblique truncation, multifaceted	2						2	0.13
Burin, transverse on lateral truncation	2	3	4		3		12	0.78
Burin, multiple dihedral	3	14	3	1	1	2	24	1.57
Burin, multiple on truncation			1		1		2	0.13
Burin, multiple mixed	1	2					3	0.20
Perforator	8	14	1	1			24	1.57
Truncation, straight	29	8	1	1			39	2.55
Truncation, oblique	41	9	1		2		53	3.46
Truncation, double	3	1					4	0.26
Backed piece	6						6	0.39
El Wad point	118						118	7.72
Retouched piece	141	98	11	7	2		259	16.94
Denticulate	21	51	6		1		79	5.17
Denticulate endscraper	15	18	13		3		49	3.20
Notched piece	100	51	6		3		160	10.46

Type							Total	Percent
Sidescraper		16	6		1		23	1.50
Core scraper		10	3			2	15	0.98
Massive scraper		4	2				6	0.39
Bec burin		4			1		5	0.33
Varia	5	6	1				12	0.78
Total	652	609	151	28	67	22	1,529	
Percent	42.64	39.83	9.88	1.83	4.38	1.44	100.00	99.99

TABLE 8-8

Observations on Tool Size (mm)

Type	Number	Length		Width	
		Mean	Range	Mean	Range
Retouched pieces	77	52.9	78-27	36.9	73-15
Notches	57	54.2	106-27	33.1	73-09
Denticulates	42	57.2	116-35	38.8	69-21
Denticulate scrapers	33	65.3	90-39	41.9	64-20
Truncations	47	57.0	116-27	24.5	55-11
Perforators	15	40.6	63-16	32.9	55-17
El Wad points, complete	8	64.1	81-46	13.0	16-12

TABLE 8-9

Scraper Size (mm)

Type	Number	Length		Width	
		Mean	Range	Mean	Range
Typical endscraper	86	67.6	102-28	35.5	58-18
Endscraper on retouched piece	40	64.7	99-43	37.0	68-14
Unilateral and bilateral endscraper	11	65.2	95-39	46.8	60-19
Thin shouldered scraper	4	57.0	75-42	29.0	47-19
Thin nosed scraper	6	66.3	83-48	41.8	56-26
Thick nosed scraper	10	61.3	82-34	40.1	70-28
Thick shouldered scraper	6	61.0	74-42	38.0	50-28
Ogival scraper	5	65.0	89-50	39.2	47-28
Double endscraper	17	66.5	108-48	35.8	49-18
Typical carinated scraper	28	62.0	93-40	34.8	70-24
Atypical carinated scraper	30	65.3	105-40	37.7	74-20
Lateral carinated scraper	3	67.3	80-59	36.3	49-26
Sidescraper	8	74.8	103-44	49.3	69-36
Transverse sidescraper	9	67.0	92-55	42.1	62-30
Massive scraper	6	121.5	153-96	90.2	118-76

wide overlapping retouch, followed by smaller nibbled retouch adding final shape to the scraping edge. Inverse retouch is very rare (fig. 8-9a). The scrapers made on thick blades often have lamellar retouch with additional fine nibbled retouch, with some forms approaching a semicarinated form. Scraping edge shapes are: 173 circular, 4 straight, and 3 oblique.

TABLE 8-10

Observations on Scraper Attributes

Type	Scraping Edge Location			Origin of Retouch		
	Distal	Proximal	Lateral	Ventral[1]	Dorsal[2]	Lateral
Simple endscraper	154	9	16	177	2	
Unilateral endscraper	6	1		7		
Bilateral endscraper	9		2	11		
Endscraper on retouched piece	54	1	4	48	11	
Ogival endscraper	10	1		10	1	
Thin nosed scraper	7		2	9		
Thick nosed scraper	3	6	2	7		4
Thin shouldered scraper	3	2		5		
Thick shouldered scraper	5	1		4		2
Typical carinated scraper	21	4	3	20	1	7
Atypical carinated scraper	23	3	3	25	1	4
Lateral carinated scraper	2	1		2		1
Sidescraper	9		10	19		
Denticulate endscraper	42	2	4	46	2	

[1] Obversely retouched.

[2] Inversely retouched.

The endscrapers on retouched pieces differ from the simple forms in the added lateral or bilateral retouch and in the higher incidence of inverse forms. Only three of these would be classed as "atypical," while all of the scraping edges are circular (fig. 8-10b). The retouch on the scraping edge is the same as that of the simple forms, and the retouch on the blank edges is predominately light and continuous (33 pieces). Invasive retouch is found on 6 pieces, denticulate retouch on 9, alternate retouch on 10, and "Aurignacian" retouch on one.

Unilateral and bilateral forms are quite distinct, with scraper retouch generally extending along the greater part of one or both edges. They are in many cases the larger scrapers (fig. 8-8i), but are not exceptionally thick. The retouch is similar to that on the simple endscraper forms. All of the bilateral scrapers are made on flakes or primary flakes, while a few of the unilateral scrapers are on blades.

Ogival scrapers are not very common, and in most cases do not present an accentuated ogival shape, but a rather slight convergence of the edges to a point

(fig. 8-10m). They are similar to the simple endscrapers in all other attributes.

Thin-nosed and shouldered scrapers are quite well made, but the scraping edges are more distinctly shouldered and nosed in the thick forms. The retouch on the thin forms is similar to that of the simple endscrapers, while the thick-nosed and shouldered scrapers are formed either by continuous lamellar retouch or by one or two deep blows which form the shoulder or nose, with lighter trimming on the scraping edge.

Carinated scrapers are mostly on quite thick blanks, with the length of retouch often as much as 4 centimeters. Most of this retouch is lamellar, with fine retouch trimming the edge (fig. 8-9e). Almost all of the scraping edges are circular, or slightly nosed. The lateral carinated forms are noticeably rare.

Double scrapers include twelve double flat endscrapers (fig. 8-9c), two carinated scrapers opposite flat endscrapers (fig. 8-9f), two double carinated scrapers (fig. 8-9b), and two double thick-nosed scrapers.

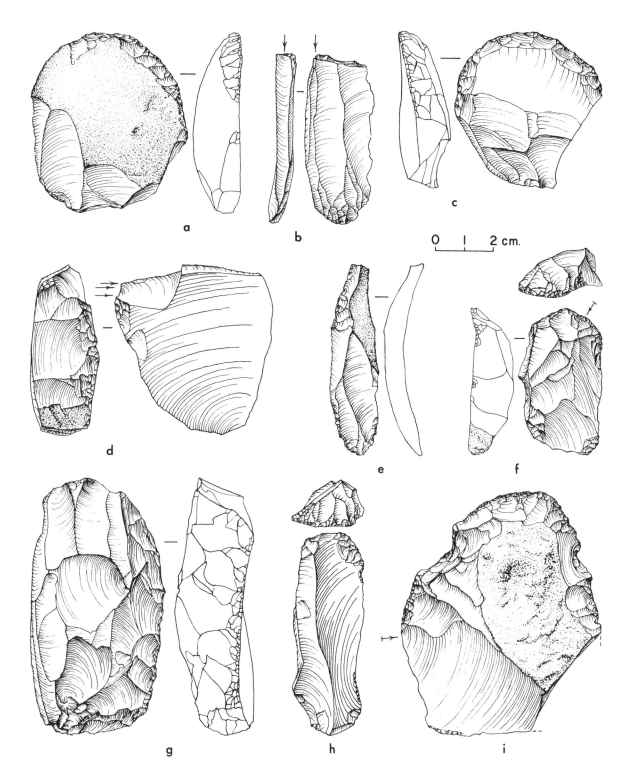

FIG. 8-8–Tools from Sde Divshon: *a, c, f, h, i*–various endscrapers; *b*–burin on truncation; *d*–transverse burin on lateral truncation (core tablet); *e*–retouched blade; *g*–core scraper.

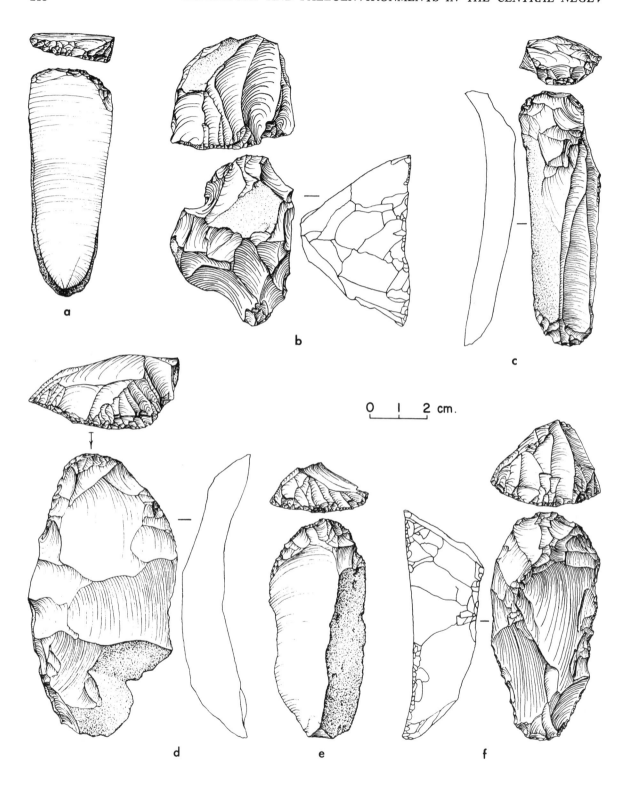

FIG. 8-9—Tools from Sde Divshon: *a*—inverse endscraper; *b*—double thick nosed scraper; *c*—double endscraper; *d*—endscraper; *e*—semicarinated endscraper; *f*—double carinated endscraper.

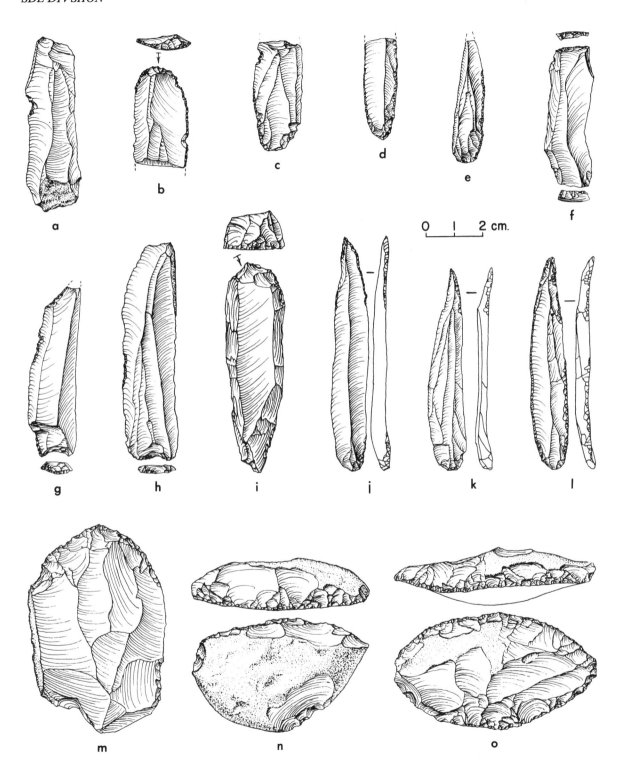

FIG. 8-10–Tools from Sde Divshon: *a*–notched blade; *b*–endscraper on broken blade; *c*–retouched blade; *d, e, j-l*–el Wad points; *f-h*–truncated blades; *i*–endscraper; *m*–ogival endscraper; *n*–transverse sidescraper; *o*–double transverse sidescraper.

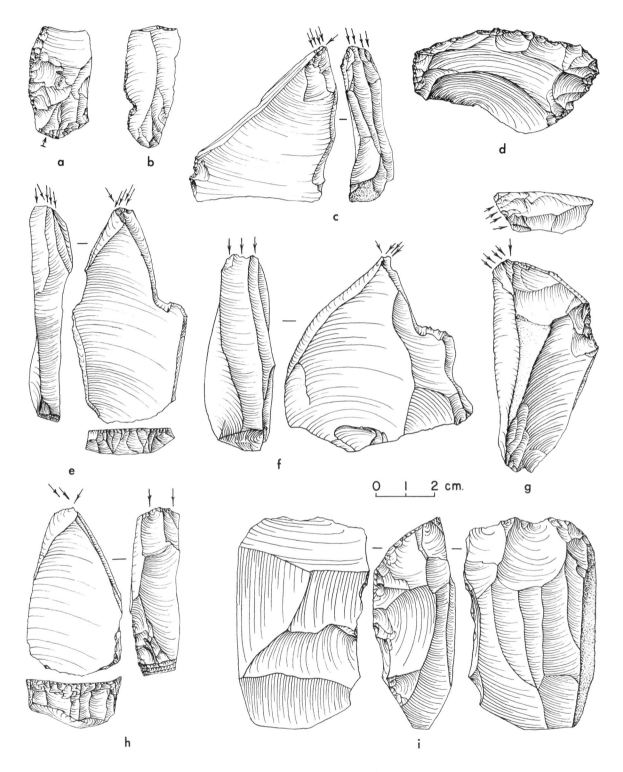

FIG. 8-11—Tools and cores from Sde Divshon: *a*—retouched piece; *b*—notched blade; *c*—burin on snap; *d*—transverse sidescraper; *e, f, h*—dihedral burins (*e* and *h* on core tablets); *g*—busquoid burin; *i*—single platform, prepared blade core.

TABLE 8-11
Observations on Burin Metrics and Attributes

	Dihedral, simple	Dihedral, multifaceted	Burin on snap, simple	Burin on old surface, simple	Burin on old surface, multifaceted	Dihedral, angle	On oblique truncation, simple	On straight truncation, simple	Transverse on lateral truncation	On oblique truncation, multifaceted	Multiple dihedral
N	70	25	20	26	10	10	18	3	9	3	19
Length											
Mean	60.6	62.0	51.7	63.5	63.1	50.4	66.2	60.3	60.7	53.6	57.5
Range	103-29	90-44	70-29	96-35	85-48	71-29	110-41	68-48	85-34	65-45	92-38
Width											
Mean	39.4	38.5	28.6	41.5	41.0	39.0	33.7	53.0	39.1	32.0	34.7
Range	106-21	51-30	61-15	59-23	54-32	67-21	51-19	67-33	54-16	36-30	40-26
Mean Bit											
Width	9.6	14.4	6.2	10.1	11.1	10.6	8.4	8.3	12.6	9.0	8.8
Mean Number											
Blows	1.5	3.3	1.2	1.4	3.5	1.8	1.2	1.3	1.7	3.3	1.8
Symmetric	21	10	2	6	1	2	4	1			7
Lateral	10	2	8	3		2		1			10
Déjeté	30	8	8	10	6	5	13	1	3	3	21
Transverse	9	5	2	7	3	1	1		6		1
Location											
Distal	50	18	13	16	8	6	11	3	9	2	18
Proximal	20	7	7	10	2	4	7			1	21
Mean Bit											
Angle	62.2	58.8	72.2	66.1	67.5	84.0	61.3	75.0	66.6	73.3	68.4

Sidescrapers include simple and double forms. The simple sidescrapers include three straight, six convex, one concave, and five convex transverse (fig. 8-10n). The double forms include one double convex, one double convex/concave, and six transverse double convex (fig. 8-10o). Several of the transverse convex forms approach double scrapers, with the retouch on one side not being continuous (fig. 8-11d). All of the sidescrapers have retouch which is quite invasive and overlapping. The double transverse scrapers, in some cases, approach *limace* form, with retouch that meets at the center of a quite thick piece.

Core scrapers are large and thicker than the other thick scraper forms, and have exceptionally heavy scraping retouch. These most often have a circular scraping edge on a very thick flake, but also occur on two reutilized cores (fig. 8-8*g*).

Massive Scrapers

As can be seen in Table 8-9, these are considerably larger than any other class of scraper. They are characterized by exceedingly heavy retouch, which is in three cases almost of Quina type and for the others is simply overlapping. While all are morphologically scrapers, in a true sense they are highly distinct and several might well represent initial reduction of large flakes into cores.

Burins

Burins are mostly simple, in that only 17.8% are multifaceted. Burins on truncations account for only 10.4% of all forms (fig. 8-8*b, d*), leaving the majority of all burins some simple dihedral form, i.e., simple dihedral (fig. 8-11*h*), on old surface, or on snap (fig. 8-11*c*). Asymmetric forms dominate all others, accounting for about half of the sample, with symmetric being the next most common. Lateral burin blows, those driven down the side of the piece, as in Fig. 8-8*b*, and transverse burin blows each account for about 12% of the sample (table 8-11). About two-thirds of the burins are located on the distal ends of the pieces. Considerable variability was found in the angles of the burin bits, yet the means for most forms fall between 60° and 70°. Size is not particularly variable between types, although the burins on snap, dihedral angle, and burins on oblique truncations are somewhat smaller than the others. Multifaceted burins do have somewhat wider bit widths than the simple types (fig. 8-11*e, f*), as do the transverse burins on lateral truncations (fig. 8-8*d*). While only two busquoid burins were noted, both are of classic form (fig. 8-11*g*).

There is greater selection of core tablets for burin manufacture than for any other tool class, and most of these are quite thick. In some cases a core tablet removed a portion of the keel of a core, which gave the piece the full appearance of a burin. Thus, only those pieces which had burin blow undercutting the ventral surface of the tablet were classified as burins, although they differ little from the "false" burins.

Perforators

Twenty-one of the perforators are simple borers, with fairly small tips made by convergent obverse retouch, while only a single example had alternate retouch. Two are double-backed perforators with elongated tips formed by quite steep backing. These are, in general, quite small tools, some of them having minor amounts of light retouch in addition to the perforator tip.

Truncations

While only straight and oblique truncations are listed, the presence of concave truncations was noted in classification. They have been lumped with straight truncations in the type list. The location of truncations by form is as follows:

	Straight	Oblique	Concave
Distal	11	45	6
Proximal	8	8	14

All of the truncations are made with quite abrupt retouch (fig. 8-10*f*). The angles on the oblique truncations range fully from only slightly to markedly oblique. Concave truncations are well made, and most are nearly as wide as the piece (fig. 8-10*g*), but a few are somewhat more limited (fig. 8-10*h*). The blanks for truncations are 76% blades, usually quite elongated and thin, although thicker flakes were sometimes used (fig. 8-5*d*).

Backed Pieces

Both in frequency and form, backed pieces are poorly represented. None have backing which extends the full length of the blade, making these all partially backed blades.

El Wad Points

The sample of El Wad points consists of 8 com-

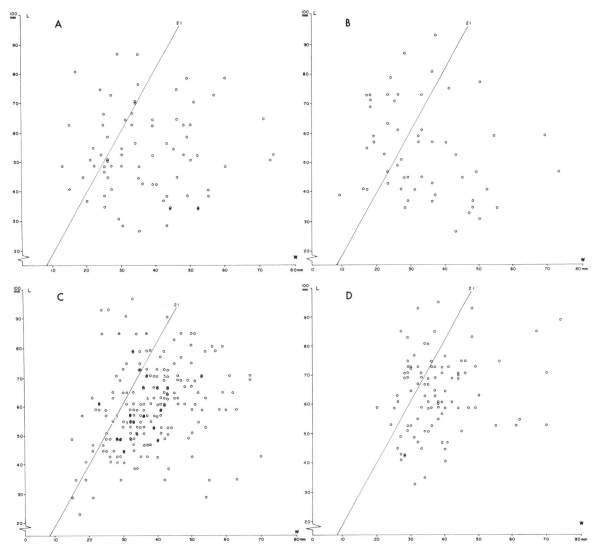

FIG. 8-12—Length/Width scattergrams of: *A*—retouched pieces; *B*—notched pieces; *C*—burins; *D*—thick scrapers.

plete pieces and 110 fragments (fig. 8-10*d*). All are made on blades with exceptionally consistent morphological and technological attributes. Platforms on 73 identifiable pieces exhibited 91.4% lipped and 8.6% crushed. Widths of the blades ranged between 9 and 17 mm (mean, 11.9), and all of them are thin and generally with numerous dorsal flake scars, but none have any cortex on their dorsal surface, and all are flat. Retouch is in almost all cases semisteep, but some of this grades into slightly flatter retouch, or thin backing. The location of this retouch is as follows:

FRAGMENTS

	Complete	Proximal	Medial	Distal	Percent
Unilateral, right	3	44	18	11	64.4
Unilateral, left	1	3	2	3	7.6
Bilateral	4	15	9	1	24.6
Alternate	–	3	1	–	3.3
TOTALS	8	65	30	15	

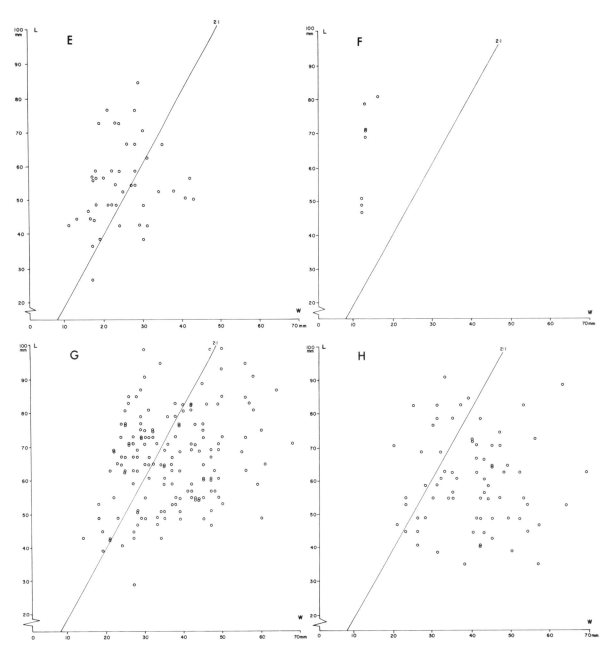

FIG. 8-13—Length/Width scattergrams of: *E*—truncations; *F*-el Wad points; *G*—thin scrapers; *H*—denticulates (including denticulate scrapers).

The high incidence of unilateral right retouch (fig. 8-10*e*) is viewed as having more stylistic than technological significance. In most cases, the retouch is apparently implemented to modify the piece to a rather consistent symmetrical profile. This often requires very little retouch (fig. 8-10*k*), but for some pieces the retouch is extensive (fig. 8-10*j, l*). Basal retouch obviously identified all of the proximal pieces, but one of the complete points lacked it (fig. 8-10*k*), indicating that some basal fragments may not have been identifiable. All of the complete points had retouch at their tips, however, and it is assumed that if a large number of points had retouch only at their distal extremities, a much larger number of those fragments would have been found. There was no paucity of suitably shaped distal portions of unretouched blades. The disproportionate ratio of proximal to distal fragments implies then either that there was a large number of points with no retouch on their tips, or that those distal portions were lost. Possible evidence for the former case exists in the unretouched blade tips mentioned. Another possible explanation is somewhat more interesting and proportionately difficult to test: that is that the El Wad points, in fact, were utilized as projectile points, and that, as is known from several new world ethnographic and archaeological examples, these points represented less effort in production than the shafts in which they were mounted. The result of this difference in value was that the shafts with broken points still attached were retrieved and carried back to a camp or workshop, where a new point was knapped to replace the old one. The archaeological result of this practice is a relative abundance of point bases compared to point tips. The analogy applied here would imply that similar activities were conducted at Sde Divshon.

Further investigation of this hypothesis will be taken up later, but the potential relevance to the technological specialization of this assemblage, as well as to the future exploration of functional hypotheses at the site level, provoked mention at this time. The care with which the blanks for these points were produced and selected is immediately apparent, however, and is considered as a primary focus of the core technology. The presence of these points is also of typological interest as well, owing to their well-known occurrence in the northern Levant.

Retouched Pieces

Retouched pieces are the most common tool type in this assemblage, and about 54% of them are on blades. Obverse retouch dominates, with only 19.3% being inverse. The most common form of retouch is fairly light and continuous (fig. 8-10c), with flat retouch being much less common (fig. 8-8e), and true Aurignacian retouch occurring on only a few pieces (fig. 8-11a). Notches sometimes occur with the retouch (fig. 8-10c), and those pieces were classified as retouched, not notched tools.

Denticulates

These are an exceptionally well-made group of tools, with either overlapping single-blow notches (fig. 8-5c) or more commonly, overlapping retouched notches (fig. 8-5b). In most cases the denticulation covers the greater part of the edge. The location of the retouch is 60.7% unilateral, 36.6% bilateral, and 12.6% distal.

Denticulate Endscrapers

This group of tools is similar to the simple endscrapers in all attributes, except that the scraping retouch is well denticulated. The denticulation in almost all cases is achieved with the fine secondary retouching which follows the initial preparation of the scraping edge. In some cases, however, broader and deeper denticulation is present, apparently indicating an incomplete scraper.

Notched Pieces

Notches are for the most part quite restricted in length, and rarely more than 2 mm in depth. Single-blow notches were not classed as tools, thus all listed are retouched, usually quite finely (fig. 8-10a), and sometimes with retouch extending slightly beyond the notch itself (fig. 8-11b). Multiple-notched pieces are quite rare, accounting for only 6.8% of the sample. Notched blades far outnumber the other debitage categories; the blade blanks are fairly wide, and are similar to those used as blanks for truncations and simple retouch.

Bec Burins

These have very heavy, opposed retouch on fairly thick edges of flakes, forming a sharp chisel edge. The retouch is confined to the immediate area of the bit, and is stepped, as if crushed.

Varia

Four of these have scaled retouch on their distal ends; one has heavy alternate retouch adjacent to the scaled retouch. Two other pieces have convergent bilateral retouch making them "points" of some form. One is wide and ogival in shape with quite flat retouch; the other is much narrower, on a blade with about half its surface cortex, and has steeper retouch forming a sharp point. The latter is not unlike some of the various points illustrated from unpublished plates from Ksar Akil. Six other pieces are irregularly shaped flakes and blades with eccentrically oriented and combined notches, partial backing, or retouch.

SUMMARY

Sde Divshon is an Upper Paleolithic habitation located on the northern edge of the Divshon Plain overlooking the Nahal Zin. Its location is marked by its proximity to a large source of flint nodules, and its position central to the perennial springs in the area. The site is 800 sq m in area, with lithic artifacts contained on and in a shallow soil covering bedrock, with little evidence of disturbance. Several concentrations, marked by differential densities and differential artifact class distributions were recorded, and the position of each artifact was mapped in order to permit locational analysis. This report is the result of technological and typological analysis of the total surface artifactual sample, irrespective of location.

Technologically, the assemblage is characterized by the production of blades. The sample of 1,303 cores indicates that over 90% are blade cores, mostly single platform and twisted types. The production of blades is marked by specialization of core preparatory techniques, including bifacial preparation, the core-tablet technique, and several other forms. The debitage is composed of a dominance of flakes and primary elements over blades, yet blades were selected more than the former classes of debitage for the production of retouched tools. Platforms indicate that indirect percussion, or more probably a soft-hammer technique, was employed for the removal of blades, and for certain forms of core preparation. Just over 8% of the debitage was selected for use as retouched tools. This was expressed as a core-to-tool ratio of 1:1.17, indicating very low efficiency in the use of the raw material.

Typologically the assemblage is dominated by scrapers, and also has relatively high proportions of burins, truncations, typical El Wad points, and denticulates, as well as retouched and notched pieces.

Distributional analysis of the artifacts is at an intermediate stage, but has defined specific areas of debitage production as well as differential distribution of certain tool classes. Upon completion it is hoped that it will allow fuller explanation of the present impression that Sde Divshon is a multiple habitation by a group or groups with the same technology and presumably of close cultural affiliation. The variation observed *within* the site is seen as a most promising avenue of research for a fuller interpretation of the Sde Divshon habitation.

EIN AQEV: A LATE LEVANTINE UPPER PALEOLITHIC SITE IN THE NAHAL AQEV

Anthony E. Marks

Southern Methodist University

INTRODUCTION

While numerous open-air Upper Paleolithic sites have been located in the Central Negev, site Ein Aqev (D31) represents one of the few which was still largely *in situ*, both geologically and archaeologically. This permitted not only the firm placement of the site into the geological sequence within the Nahal Aqev, but also resulted in the preservation of non-lithic artifacts: bone, charcoal, shell, and ocher. As a result, considerable time was spent excavating and plotting the specific position of all artifacts within the deposits.

The site of Ein Aqev is located within the Nahal Aqev, 2.3 km south of the Nahal Zin/Nahal Aqev junction and 250 m downstream from the present perennial spring of Ein Aqev (fig. 9-1). The site is situated within the top of the western side of the Upper Paleolithic terrace at an elevation of 390 m, some 15 m above the present nahal bed. The deposits of the Upper Paleolithic terrace in which the site is located abut against the northern end of the Ein Aqev box canyon, which forms a shoulder, flaring outward at this point (fig. 9-2). The nature and origin of these terrace sediments have already been described in detail (Goldberg, this volume), but from a purely archaeological point of view, their most significant aspect lies in their extremely soft composition. This had led to extensive deflation and much erosion from local runoff, resulting in a miniature badlands topography (fig. 9-3).

When the site was first located in 1970, about 5 m of the upper terrace deposits had already been deflated, exposing part of the site, while small channels had truncated a portion of some occupation layers. Both the deflation and erosion had brought many arti-facts to the surface, but their extremely fresh condition and the absence of patination suggested that they were only recently derived. Owing to the soft nature of the deposits and the apparent current rate of erosion, a surface collection and a small (2 sq m) test pit was excavated in order to place the material into geological context, in case it was not possible to return to the field in 1971.

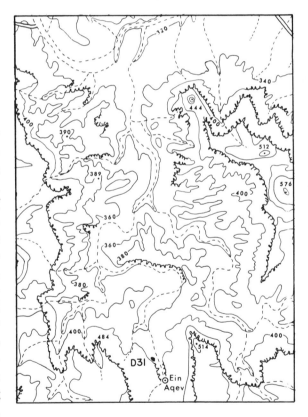

FIG. 9-1—Location of Site Ein Aqev (D31), within the Nahal Aqev.

In fact, the work did continue in 1971 when the full site was excavated, obviating the necessity of using the surface material as a

FIG. 9-2—View of Site Ein Aqev (D31) to south, showing Upper Paleolithic terrace.

sample. Upon close inspection, the *in situ* portion of the site was restricted to the northern half of a tongue-shaped terrace remnant of some 100 sq meters.

As the initial test excavation failed to indicate any clear microstratigraphy, excavations were carried out in horizontal 5 cm levels, within a framework of a one sq m grid. Within each 5 cm level, all recoverable artifacts were mapped in horizontal position and the removed fill was screened through 1/18 inch mesh. The mapping was done so that basic artifact classification took place during excavations. In this process, all debitage was mapped by its class (flake, blade, primary element, etc.), while each tool was given a specific number. This system proved to be quite workable, although a very small number of tools were not recognized during mapping or were recovered in the screen. While these could not be placed into their original, exact horizontal position, they could be placed

within the one sq m excavation unit, minimizing the loss of distributional information.

The use of 5 cm excavation levels, while not optimal, provided reasonably good vertical control and permitted the excavation of a much larger area than would have been possible if each artifact had been plotted in its exact three-dimensional position. The total depth of cultural deposit reached 60 cm, so that twelve 5 cm levels were excavated. As there was no indication of any significant slope to the terrace sediments, it is reasonable to assume that the artifacts across any 5 cm level were, in fact, contemporaneously deposited. This is reinforced by the presence of one fireplace and discrete clusters of artifacts which fall within these 5 cm levels. While it is clear that no group lives in 5 cm levels, these may be taken as reasonable approximations of occupation levels.

The excavation levels, numbered 1 through 12 from top to bottom, revealed a series of

FIG. 9-3—Topographic map of Site Ein Aqev (D31), showing recent erosional pattern and area of excavation. *A-A'*, *B-B'*, and *C-C'* refer to cross sections on Figs. 9-4 and 9-5.

areally differential artifact concentrations, tending to a shift in concentration area from north to south as the terrace built up (fig. 9-4). To some extent, this is the result of the more advanced deflation of the northern surface of the tongue, which removed at least part of the upper three levels and, perhaps, somewhat less of Level 8. On the other hand, the northern limit of most concentrations fell within the hill remnant.

At the opposite, southern, end of the site, the excavations did not fully expose the areal extent of the upper four levels, although the density of artifacts in Levels 2 through 4 was extremely low along the southern edge of the excavations, and it is unlikely that these concentrations continued for any appreciable distance. For the remaining levels, the original southern limits of their concentrations were fully defined (fig. 9-4).

The western edge of the tongue was recently cut by erosion, and this clearly removed portions of the concentrations of the upper five levels. Most erosion took place on the southern half of the site, with only minor damage on the northern half (fig. 9-5). The same situation was present along the eastern edge, where the top five excavation levels also had undergone some erosion. It is significant, however, that almost no erosion was seen for Levels 6 through 12.

DATING

The initial test excavation was made, among other reasons, to recover datable mate-

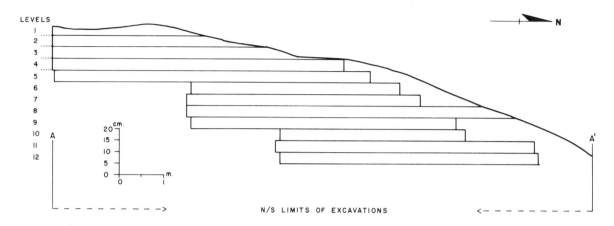

FIG. 9-4—Schematic north/south profile, showing extent of artifact concentrations within the excavated levels.

rials from what appeared to be an eroding firepit. During this excavation, two charcoal samples were obtained. The following season an additional three charcoal samples were recovered. Those from the initial pit cannot be placed exactly into the excavated levels, as the levels utilized for the test did not correspond with the latter levels. Therefore, only an approximation may be given. Those from the later excavations include one where the charcoal from two adjacent excavation levels were combined to achieve a reasonable sample size, while the other two came from single levels (table 9-1).

While these dates do not follow strict stratigraphic sequence, the first four overlap significantly at one sigma, while even the last date,

TABLE 9-1
Radiocarbon Dates from Ein Aqev

Level	Date B.P.		Date B.C.	Lab Number
Test c. 8-9	16,900 ±	250	14,950	I-5494
8 and 9	17,890 ±	600	15,940	SMU-6
Test c. 9-10	17,520 ±	790	15,560	I-5495
11	17,390 ±	560	15,440	SMU-8
12	19,980 ± 1,200		18,030	SMU-5

which is certainly too old, overlaps three others at two sigmas (fig. 9-6). Given the overlap, it seems reasonable to assign a date of between 16,000 B.C. and 15,000 B.C. as the total probable time of occupation. This is not to say that the site was occupied continuously for 1,000 years, but merely that the occupa-

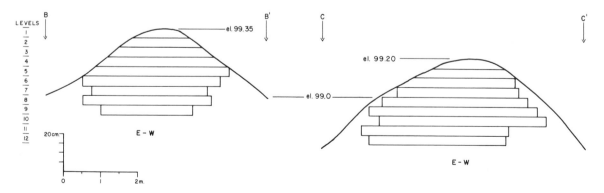

FIG. 9-5—Schematic east/west profiles showing extent of artifact concentrations within the excavated levels.

LEVELS

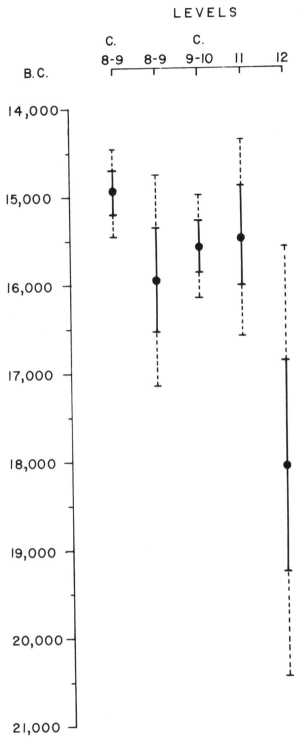

FIG. 9-6—Radiocarbon dates from Site Ein Aqev (D31).

tions should fall within the sixteenth millennium B.C.

INTRALEVEL STRUCTURE

Of the twelve excavation levels, detailed artifact mapping was carried out on the lower eleven. While the analysis of the artifact distributions are not yet complete, some aspects are of interest here. This includes not only chipped stone distributions but also the distributions of large numbers of burned and unburned limestone cobbles which occurred throughout the deposits.

These cobbles, ranging in size from 5 to 30 cm in maximum length, were apparently derived from the nahal bed or from the eroding conglomerate immediately to the south of the site. As they are not found on the surface of the terrace today and did not occur within artifactually sterile areas, it appears that they were brought to the site by its inhabitants. In at least one case, from Level 5, some functioned as liners for a firepit, but in most cases, their use is conjectural, although the high percentage which were burned is indicative of their association with fire.

Certain amorphous distributional patterns can be distinguished. If the distributions of limestone cobbles are considered separately from those of artifacts, four basic patterns occur: random distribution; more or less curved lines of cobbles in association with a firepit; a pattern which is suggestive of two to three curved lines of cobbles often associated with other randomly scattered cobbles; and a patterning with one or more dense concentrations of cobbles.

When combined with artifact distributions, these patterns are often accentuated (fig. 9-7). That is, those levels with cobble distributions suggestive of oval patterns often have the main artifact densities following the cobbles or even accentuating their oval aspect. This is not always the case, however, as a few with such a cobble distribution have the main den-

FIG. 9-7–Part of artifact concentration and burned rock from Level 11.

sities of artifacts following a different pattern (fig. 9-8). Level 5, with the firepit, exhibits a combination of these patterns (fig. 9-9).

FAUNA

MAMMALIAN FAUNA

While not found in abundance, mammalian faunal remains were recovered from all but Level 1. These tended to be in poor condi-tion–quite dry and friable. The total number of bones recovered did not exceed 250, of which less than 25 were identifiable as to species (Tchernov, this volume). Those identi-fiable bones represented the following spe-cies: *Equus hemionis*, *Capra* sp., *Gazella* sp., and *Lepus europaeus*. In addition, there were a few pieces of ostrich egg shell. The limited number of bones, however, makes any numer-ical manipulation useless.

With the exception of the *Equus* and os-

FIG. 9-8—Schematic map of artifact concentrations and burned rock from Level 7. (*Shaded areas* indicate dense concentration.)

trich, all these forms are still present in the area today. The gazelle is most likely found along the shallow nahals on the edges of the Divshon Plain above the Nahal Aqev, or farther down the nahal, where its width increases. The *Capra* are still present along the cliffs of the Nahal Aqev and other nearby cliffs. While no *Equus* has been known in the Central Negev since modern times, its most likely habitat would have been either the Divshon Plain or the Nahal Zin, both of which present large, open areas. The Divshon Plain, however, most probably would have had better grass cover than the nahal, and it is

perhaps there that the people from site Ein Aqev hunted *Equus*. Ostrich was common in the Central Negev until sometime after World War I. Its habitat was along the open ground, including both the Divshon Plain and the eastern hammada-covered extension of the plain.

The normal habitats for the recovered species suggest that the people at Ein Aqev exploited a wide range of forms which occurred in all the major areas of the survey zone, going somewhat far afield for the large forms.

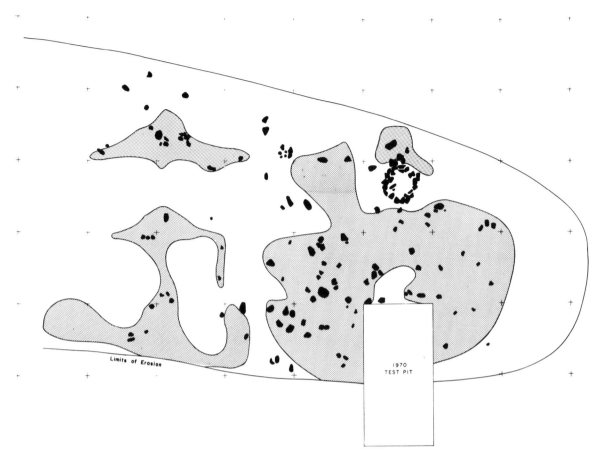

FIG. 9-9—Schematic map of artifact concentrations, burned rock, and the firepit from Level 5. (*Shaded areas* indicate dense concentrations.)

SHELLS

A number of shells were recovered throughout the excavations. Three species were represented, all of which inhabit the Mediterranean: *Dentalium dentale, Nassa gibberula*, and *Mitrella scripta*. Of the three, *Nassa gibberula* was most common, with twelve examples (two from the surface). *Dentalium dentale* accounted for only two small pieces, while only a single *Mitrella scripta* was recovered. Three of the *Nassa gibberula*, one each from Levels 5, 8, and 9, were covered with red ocher.

The presence of these shells in a late Levantine Upper Paleolithic site may not be unique, but their occurrence some 54 km from the nearest possible point on the Mediterranean shore, at Khan Yunis, indicates either some form of trade at this early date or, more likely, that the people who inhabited site Ein Aqev included the Mediterranean coast within their range of movement. If the latter is true, there is the indication that this group exploited at least two major environmental zones: the Negev highlands and the Mediterranean coastal zone. While a distance of 54 km is not great, this is the minimal map distance. Actual passage from Ein Aqev to the coast entails moving some 75 km along meandering nahal beds or minimal distance replete with numerous steep cliff ascents and descents.

NON-LITHIC ARTIFACTS

Red and yellow ocher pieces were recovered from all excavation levels. Often they occurred in small fragments weighing no more than 0.1 gm, although some pieces weighed as much as 2.0 grams. Distribution was not uniform throughout the deposits, as some levels produced almost none and others considerable amounts (table 9-2).

TABLE 9-2
Occurrence of Ocher by Weight and Level

Level	Red (gm)	Yellow (gm)
1	1.7	2.9
2	3.2	1.7
3	4.9	0.2
4	1.5	2.4
5	10.5	0.3
6	0.9	0.1
7	0.1	—
8	2.5	2.1
9	2.4	0.7
10	5.0	2.0
11	0.8	1.2
12	0.3	—

Ocher is available within the Nahal Aqev in large pockets within the greenish sediments of the Taqiye Formation. *In situ* occurrences are all yellow and the red ocher is formed by oxidation (burning).

The use to which the ocher was put can be partially seen as ritual, or at least decorative, in that three of the shells were covered with it. It is difficult to tell how the *Nassa gibberula* were used since, although they do not seem to have been purposely perforated, the natural breakage of the shell resulted in perforation which could easily be utilized for stringing.

LITHIC ARTIFACTS

During the 1971 excavations, a total of 8,981 lithic artifacts was recovered, exclusive of chips and chunks which numbered in the thousands. Of this number, all but three pieces (ground stone) were chipped stone artifacts. Excavation level samples ranged from 303 to 1,108, with levels exhibiting considerable variability in density, both on interlevel and intralevel bases (table 9-3).

The mean density for any excavation level is well separated from its extremes. In part, this reflects both the completeness of the levels and, partially, the type of concentrations present. Even those levels exhibiting some erosion of their concentrations were intact on the southern edge of the site, accounting for consistent low minimal densities, while those uneroded levels clearly exhibited tight central concentrations with marked drops in artifactual densities around their peripheries.

A striking feature is the small size of the concentrations even for the uneroded levels. It must be remembered, however, that the initial test pit did cut into these concentrations, but, for the vast majority of levels, no more than a single one sq m area should be added to arrive at an original concentration size. Thus, it appears that the normal size of the occupations, as seen by artifactual remains, varies from ca. 27.5 sq m to only 16.5 sq meters.

In spite of the differences noted above, the proportional occurrence of artifact classes shows only little variation from level to level, suggesting that a similar proportional range of production activities is represented in each level sample (table 9-4). The general pattern expressed is indicative of the full range of primary and secondary stages of tool production. This suggests that raw material was collected near the site and brought back before the core reduction process began. More specifically, excluding Level 1 which was badly deflated, all but three excavation Levels (2, 3, and 12) exhibit extremely uniform ratios between cores and other major artifact classes

TABLE 9-3
Basic Data for Excavation Levels

Level	Area in sq m[1]	Total Artifacts[2]	Mean Density per 0.05 cu m	Range in Density per 0.05 cu m
1	9.0	303	33.66	25- 79
2	10.5	829	78.95	8-157
3	15.5	1,108	71.48	8-119
4	18.5	1,014	54.81	8-122
5	26.5	1,037	39.13	6-110
6	15.5	818	52.77	7- 98
7	17.5	584	33.37	2- 93
8	21.0	931	44.33	4-202
9	21.0	627	29.86	2- 70
10	16.0	659	41.19	3-136
11	17.0	604	35.53	5-125
12	16.5	467	28.31	3- 96

[1] To nearest half square meter.
[2] Excluding chips and chunks.

(table 9-5). Levels 2 and 3 exhibit high core to primarily flake ratios, while Levels 3 and 12 are suggestive of more intensive flake and blade production than seen for other levels. The apparently nonintensive utilization of cores in most levels is reinforced by the cores themselves, which rarely exhibit complex preparation and which often have large amounts of cortex remaining on one or more surfaces.

There is a virtual absence of core tablets in these samples, contrasting sharply with most other Upper Paleolithic assemblages. This is suggestive of an absence of this form of core rejuvenation within the technological habits of the people who occupied Ein Aqev.

Both flakes and blades, excluding twisted microblades, were struck from cores with normally simple platforms. This is reflected in the high percentage of butts which are either unfaceted or have cortex surfaces (table 9-6). One noticeable trait is the sizable number of platforms where the "cortex" is nothing more than a patinated surface showing only surface discoloration.

Detachment appears to have been achieved mainly through the use of a hard hammer, as the vast majority of blanks of all classes exhibit pronounced bulbs of percussion with marked sympathetic (bulbar) scars. Only a small percentage exhibit lipped platforms with very diffuse bulbs or no bulbs at all, attributes often associated with the use of a soft hammer or indirect percussion. This latter type does occur on one out of five blades, particularly on the thinner examples, suggesting that not all blanks may have been removed by hard-hammer technique. This is reinforced by the high percentage of the twisted microblades which exhibit either lipped (43.5%) or crushed platforms (45.4%). Thus, the indirect evidence for the use of a soft hammer or indirect percussion is stronger for the secondary flaking of carinated tool forms (which resulted in the production of the twisted microblades) than it is for the production of blades from cores.

BLADES

Unlike blades from most Upper Paleolithic assemblages, these exhibit rather large plat-

TABLE 9-4
Occurrence of Artifact Classes by Excavation Level

Level	Cores Number	Percent	Core Trimming Elements Number	Percent	Primary Elements Number	Percent	Flakes Number	Percent	Blades Number	Percent	Microblades Number	Percent	Subtotals	Burin, Spalls/Cobbles	Totals
1	8	2.65	14	4.65	36	11.92	144	47.68	65	21.52	35	11.59	302	1/0	303
2	23	2.79	57	6.93	126	15.31	288	34.99	194	23.57	135	16.40	823	5/1	829
3	21	1.94	44	4.06	137	12.65	454	41.92	218	20.13	209	19.30	1,083	25/0	1,108
4	35	3.46	40	3.96	106	10.48	452	44.71	257	25.42	121	11.97	1,011	3/0	1,014
5	38	3.70	32	3.12	114	11.10	446	43.43	255	24.83	142	13.83	1,027	6/4	1,037
6	28	3.46	26	3.21	71	8.78	363	44.87	165	20.40	156	19.28	809	6/3	818
7	17	2.92	14	2.41	55	9.45	270	46.39	144	24.74	82	14.09	582	1/1	584
8	29	3.13	36	3.88	85	9.17	361	38.94	215	23.19	201	21.68	927	2/2	931
9	25	4.01	18	2.88	60	9.62	265	42.48	136	21.79	120	19.23	624	3/0	627
10	19	2.90	21	3.20	94	14.33	220	33.54	175	26.68	127	19.36	656	3/0	659
11	20	3.17	22	3.67	75	12.52	218	36.39	136	22.70	128	21.37	599	5/0	604
12	9	1.94	25	5.40	34	7.34	204	44.06	104	22.46	87	18.79	463	4/0	467

TABLE 9-5
Ratios of Artifact Classes to Cores

Levels	Primary Elements to Cores	Core Trimming Elements to Cores	Blades to Cores	Flakes to Cores	Total to Cores[1]
2	5.5	2.5	8.4	12.5	28.9
3	6.5	2.1	10.4	21.6	40.6
4	3.0	1.1	7.3	12.9	24.4
5	3.3	0.9	7.3	12.7	24.2
6	2.5	0.9	5.9	12.9	22.3
7	3.2	0.8	8.5	15.9	28.4
8	2.9	1.2	7.4	12.5	24.0
9	2.4	0.7	5.4	10.6	19.2
10	4.9	1.1	9.2	11.6	26.8
11	3.8	1.1	6.8	10.9	22.6
12	3.8	2.8	11.6	22.7	40.8

[1] Sum of previous observations. Excludes twisted microblades and burin spalls, as these are derived from blanks—not cores.

TABLE 9-6

Platform Characteristics
as Percentages

Platform Type	Primary Elements N=48	Flakes N=230	Blades N=140
Unfaceted	52.1	61.7	57.9
Dihedral faceted	6.2	6.1	3.6
Multiple faceted	4.2	3.9	1.4
Lipped	6.2	6.5	20.0
Cortex	25.0	18.7	7.9
Crushed	6.2	3.0	9.3
	99.9	99.9	100.1

forms with markedly obtuse angles, particularly on those blades measuring over 50 mm in length. These angles range from 91° to 131°, with a mean of 107.6° (n=75). These longer blades tend to be markedly incurvate. The smaller blades and bladelets have similar platform angles, but the size of the platform is greatly reduced and there is much less tendency for incurvature of the lateral profiles.

Blade length is extremely variable, from 18 to 138 mm, with a clear bimodal curve, showing modes between 30 to 40 mm and 60 to 70 mm, when only blade debitage is considered (see Appendix B for detailed metric observations).

FLAKES

Aside from the difference in length/width proportion, flakes parallel blades in most attributes; platforms are large and have obtuse angles, bulbs of percussion are marked, and the larger flakes tend to be incurvate. Flakes show lengths similar to the blades, although there are more within the smaller range than is true for blades (see Appendix B).

MICROBLADES

This group includes all bladelets which are markedly twisted in lateral profile. The normal form has a converging dorsal shape coming to a sharp point at the distal extremity. Platforms are rather evenly divided between those with crushed or lipped forms, although a small number may be considered unfaceted. These microblades do not derive from true cores but are the waste products of carinated tool manufacture. They range in length from 9 mm to a very few at 36 mm (mean length, 19.41 mm), and in width from 3 to 10 mm (mean width, 6.68 mm). They tend to be rather long in relation to their width, with length/width ratios from 2:1 to 6.75:1 (mean length/width ratio, 3.06:1). As blanks for tool production, they were only utilized for *lamelles Dufour* and an obversely retouched variant of that type.

RETOUCHED TOOLS

Excavations recovered 1,287 retouched tools and 3 ground stones. A striking aspect of the tools is the extreme range in size and tool type, from minute *lamelles Dufour* to large choppers made on limestone cobbles. In spite of this, there is relatively little variability in style of manufacture, in types present between excavation levels and in blanks utilized (table 9-7). As a general rule, the larger the tool sample, the larger the number of types present. Some variation is seen throughout the deposits, particularly in Levels 3, 4, and 8, but most levels are quite homogeneous. Greater differences between level samples are noticeable, however, in the proportional utilization of blanks by artifact class (table 9-8). Overall, proportional utilization of blanks is highest between Levels 4 through 10, levels which also have the highest absolute number of tools, although differences between these and other levels are only minor. While tools on core-trimming elements and cores are rare in absolute number, in many levels they show a high proportional utilization. For the core-trimming elements this is directly associated

TABLE 9-7
Occurrence of Tools by Artifact Class

Level	Cores/Chunks		Core Trimming Elements		Primary Elements		Flakes		Blades[1]		Microblades[2]		Total
	Number	Percent	Number	Percent	Number	Percent	Number	Percent	Number	Percent	Number	Percent	
1	1	4.00	0		6	24.00	9	36.00	9	36.00	0		25
2	5	6.49	7	9.09	8	10.39	21	27.27	25	32.47	11	14.29	77
3	5	4.63	6	5.56	16	14.81	41	37.96	23	21.30	17	15.74	108
4	4	2.63	5	3.29	23	15.13	78	51.32	24	15.79	18	11.84	152
5	7	4.00	4	2.29	28	16.00	66	37.77	53	30.29	17	9.71	175
6	9	6.62	5	3.68	17	12.50	50	36.76	39	28.68	16	11.76	136
7	4	3.77	1	0.94	11	10.38	42	39.62	30	28.30	18	16.98	106
8	8	4.82	2	1.20	16	9.64	64	38.55	39	23.49	37	22.29	166
9	3	3.49	2	2.33	11	12.79	27	31.40	26	30.23	17	19.77	86
10	6	5.00	0		15	12.50	48	40.00	36	30.00	15	12.50	120
11	2	2.47	1	1.23	7	8.64	28	34.57	27	33.33	16	19.75	81
12	3	5.56	1	1.85	3	5.56	18	33.33	21	38.98	8	14.81	54
Total	53	4.12	34	2.64	158	12.29	496	38.57	353	27.45	192	14.93	1,286

[1] Includes both blades, *sensu stricto*, and normal bladelets.
[2] Includes only twisted microblades.

TABLE 9-8

Percentage of Blanks Utilized in Tool Production by Artifact Class

Level	Cores/ Chunks	Core Trimming Elements	Primary Elements	Flakes	Blades[1]	Twisted Microblades	Overall Percentage
1	12.50	0.00	16.67	6.25	13.85	0.00	8.28
2	17.39	14.04	6.34	7.29	12.37	8.15	9.36
3	23.81	13.64	11.68	9.03	10.55	8.13	9.97
4	5.71	12.50	21.70	17.70	9.34	14.88	15.03
5	7.89	12.50	24.56	14.80	20.78	11.97	16.65
6	21.43	19.23	23.94	13.77	23.64	24.24	16.81
7	17.65	7.14	20.00	15.56	20.83	21.95	18.04
8	20.69	5.56	18.82	18.28	18.14	18.41	17.69
9	12.00	11.11	18.33	10.19	19.12	14.17	14.10
10	10.53	0.00	15.96	21.82	20.57	11.81	18.29
11	10.00	4.54	9.33	12.84	19.85	12.50	13.52
12	22.22	4.00	8.82	8.82	20.19	9.20	11.66

[1] Includes both blades, *sensu stricto*, and normal bladelets.

with the presence of *lames à crête*, which invariably are made into tools, either by retouch or through use, (e.g., battered pieces [*lames à mâchures*]). The high percentage of core utilization includes pieces not only on strict cores but also on chunks and cobbles, a fact which somewhat inflates the figures.

In order to give a very general view of the tool content, a very simplified typology is presented for both individual levels and for all the tools recovered, which might be taken as an expression of the mean proportional occurrence of each sub-class for the site as a whole (table 9-9). Complete type lists, by level, are presented in Appendix A.

Within the groups recognized in Table 9-9, where not obvious, the following types are important:

1. Flat endscrapers—typical endscrapers on blades and flakes, endscrapers on retouched pieces, and ogival endscrapers

2. Thick endscrapers—carinated and lateral carinated scrapers

3. Other scrapers—sidescrapers and core-scrapers, both of which are rare

4. Multiple tools—burin/endscrapers

5. Dihedral burins—burins on snap and dihedral burins, both simple and multifaceted

6. Burin on truncation—no type dominates, but includes some Corbiac burins

7. Burins, carinated and busquoid—only carinated burins occur with regularity

8. Burins multiple—burins multiple mixed

9. Backed blades—no type dominates

10. Notches and denticulates—retouched notches and lateral denticulates

11. Retouched pieces—the obversely retouched pieces dominate

12. *Lamelles Dufours*, etc.—both inversely and alternately retouched examples with a few only obverse retouch

13. Backed bladelets—no type dominates, but backed fragments are most common

14. Other tools—almost all fall within the varia class, except for a number of battered pieces (*pièces à mâchures*).

Notes on the Typology

The following notes utilize the detailed

TABLE 9-9
Simplified Typology by Excavation Level

Typology	Levels												Total
	1	2	3	4	5	6	7	8	9	10	11	12	
(Samples)	(25)	(77)	(108)	(152)	(175)	(136)	(107)	(166)	(86)	(120)	(81)	(54)	(1,286)
Flat endscrapers	24.0	16.9	12.0	19.7	24.0	20.6	14.2	18.1	20.9	19.2	22.2	11.1	18.8
Double, flat endscrapers		1.3	0.9	2.0	1.1	2.2		2.4		1.7	1.3		1.3
Thick scrapers	24.0	7.8	17.6	17.1	12.0	13.2	16.0	10.8	17.4	8.3	3.7	9.3	12.8
Double thick scrapers			0.9	0.7	1.7		0.9	1.2		0.8	1.2		0.8
Other scrapers			1.9		1.1	0.7	1.9	0.6		0.8	1.2		0.8
Multiple tools		2.6	2.8	2.6	2.9	1.5		5.4		0.8	2.5	1.9	2.3
Burins, dihedral	24.0	6.5	8.3	9.9	9.7	6.6	4.7	3.6	2.3	10.0	7.4	11.1	7.6
Burins, on truncation		5.2	3.7	2.0	6.3	4.4	0.9	1.8	7.0	0.8		3.7	3.2
Burins, carinated and busquoid		3.9	3.7	10.5	2.9	3.7	4.7	2.4	3.5	3.3	4.9	1.6	4.2
Burins, multiple		3.9	0.9		1.7	0.7	0.9	1.2	1.2				0.9
Perforators		1.3	1.9	2.0	1.7	1.5		0.6		1.7	1.2		1.2
Truncations			1.9	0.7	2.9	2.2	0.9	0.6	1.2	2.5	4.9	1.9	1.7
Backed blades		5.2	1.9		0.6		1.9			5.0	2.5	1.9	1.4
Notches and Denticulates	16.0	10.4	13.0	11.8	13.7	9.6	10.4	10.8	14.0	6.7	6.2	14.8	11.1
Retouched pieces	8.0	11.7	9.3	5.3	1.7	10.3	14.2	11.5	8.4	17.5	14.8	18.5	10.1
Lamelles Dufour, etc.		14.3	15.7	11.8	9.7	11.8	17.0	22.3	19.8	12.5	19.8	14.8	14.8
Backed bladelets	4.0	2.6			1.1	2.2	2.8	1.8	1.2	1.7	1.2	3.7	1.6
Choppers		1.3			2.3	2.2	0.9	1.2					0.9
Other tools		5.2	3.7	4.0	2.9	6.6	7.6	3.6	3.5	6.7	4.9	5.6	4.7

typologies presented as Appendix A of this chapter. As tools from all levels show the same range of stylistic variations and metric attributes (see Appendix B), types will be discussed for the site as a whole, although when idiosyncratic pieces occur, their level provenience will be noted.

Flat Endscrapers

These include all types which are noncarinated and are not on cores. They are the most prevalent tool sub-class and are also among the finest tools from the site.

Simple Endscrapers

These are the most numerous of the flat endscrapers and include complete and broken, typical and atypical, straight, normal, and oblique examples. Several attributes stand out (table 9-10): distal position, obverse retouch of the scraping edge, the use of blanks with one blunt edge (fig. 9-10b), the propensity for the use of flat to semisteep retouch, and the tendency for significant numbers with scraping edges which approach but do not achieve true ogival configuration (fig. 9-13h). A small number of simple endscrapers on flakes have the scraping edge laterally positioned, including one with a "basal" notch (fig. 9-13j).

TABLE 9-10
Attributes of Simple Endscrapers

Attributes		Subtypes				
		Typical	Typical Lateral	Typical Oblique	Typical Straight	Atypical
Blank Form	Blade	27	0	3	1	5
	Flake	29	8	6	2	14
	Primary Elements	11	1	1	1	4
	Core Trimming Elements	1				
Position	Distal	67	—*	10	4	23
	Proximal	1	—*			1
Type of Retouch	Marginal					3
	Flat	29	6	2		4
	Semisteep	33	3	7	4	18
	Steep	6		1		
Lateral Edge	Blunt	35	2	1		12
	Sharp	33	7	9	4	11
Shape of Scraper	Flattish	15		—*	—*	6
	Normal	29	4	—*	—*	14
	Converging	24	5	—*	—*	5

*Signifies observation does not apply.

Simple Endscrapers on Retouched Pieces

Each is an endscraper made by obverse retouch at the distal extremity of a blank; eighteen on blades, fourteen on flakes, three on primary elements, and one on an elongated crested blade (*lame à crête*). While all are carefully formed, three have straight and three have convex oblique scraping edges; the remaining examples have generally symmetric edges, with only a few tending toward ogival form. Those on blades include fourteen with flat to semisteep retouch, one with steep retouch, while on three the retouch approaches semicarination. Additional retouch normally occurs on a single lateral edge—thirteen examples—but five do show bilateral treatment. On the unilaterally retouched pieces, six have continuous marginal treatment, one has inverse re-touch (fig. 9-13*d*), three are microdenticulated, two have flat, invasive retouch (fig. 9-14*l*), and a single example has what approaches Aurignacian retouch. Of the bilaterally retouched examples, two are alternately retouched (one bilaterally marginal and one bilaterally denticulated). The remaining three include one bilaterally microdenticulated, one with an edge denticulated and the other heavily retouched (fig. 9-10*f*), and a third with simple continuous retouch opposed to a rough denticulation (fig. 9-10*g*).

All but four of those on flakes have semisteep scraping edges; the remainder include two with flat, one with steep, and three with somewhat semicari-nated edges. Nine of those on flakes have lateral treatment and five have bilateral. The former exhibit the following types of retouch: three semisteep, two flat, and one each denticulated and bifacially battered.

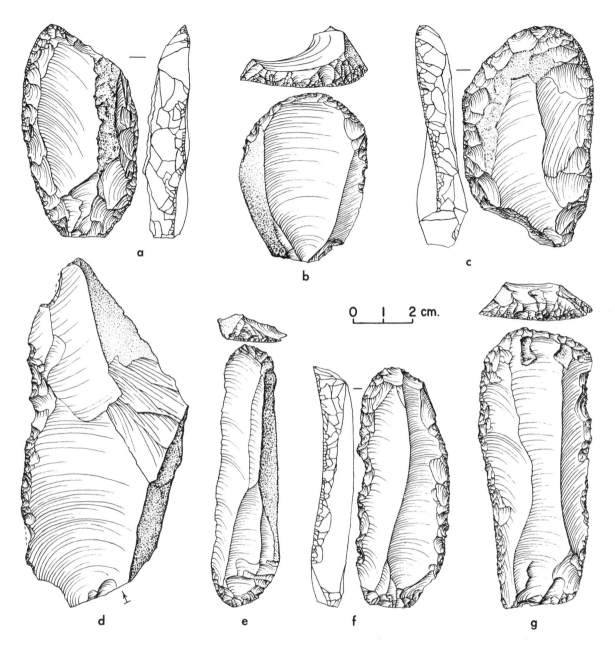

FIG. 9-10—Tools from Site Ein Aqev (D31): *a*—ogival endscraper; *b*—endscraper; *c*—bilateral endscraper; *d*—denticulate; *e*—double endscraper; *f, g*—endscrapers on retouched pieces.

The bilaterally treated pieces include one each of the following: semisteep retouch opposite bifacial battering, denticulation paired with bifacial battering, a combination of marginal retouch and microdenticulation, and bilateral semisteep retouch.

All those on primary elements have semisteep scraping edges. Two are laterally treated, one each with backing and flat microdenticulation, while the third example has bilateral marginal retouch.

The single piece on a core-trimming element has a semisteep scraping edge and a continuous unilateral marginal retouch.

While the type exhibits considerable size and proportional variability, the number of large blanks is striking when compared to simple scraper forms (fig. 9-11).

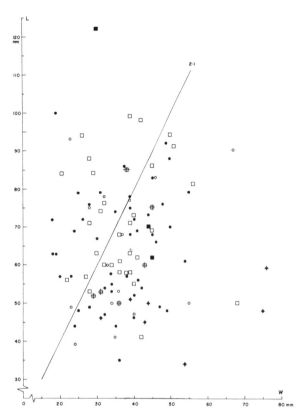

FIG. 9-11—Length/Width scattergram of endscrapers. Key: *square*—on retouched piece; *dot*—typical; *open circle*—atypical; *crossed circle*—lateral; *crossed square*—oblique.

Ogival Endscrapers

These are among the finest tools found (fig. 9-13e). They are rather evenly divided between those on blades (22) and those on flakes (19), with only rare occurrences on primary elements (4) and core fragments (1). All but two are distally positioned and, with the exception of one from Level 6, all are obversely retouched. This retouch varies from very flat to a few which might be considered semicarinated, with semisteep retouch most common. Of the 46 examples, only 12, evenly divided between flakes and blades, exhibit any collateral retouch. When present, it is restricted to a flat or flat to semisteep retouch,

resulting in microdenticulation. Only a single example, from Level 9, has strong bilateral retouch which approaches backing along one edge (fig. 9-10a), and almost falls into the varia class. These scrapers exhibit considerable range in the size and relative proportions, although they do tend to cluster with other scraper forms (fig. 9-12).

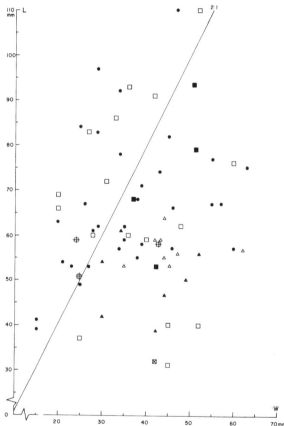

FIG. 9-12—Length/Width scattergram of scrapers. Key: *open triangle*—unilateral; *closed triangle*—bilateral; *open square*—double; *closed square*—side-scraper; *dot*—ogival; *crossed square*—thin nosed; *diagonally crossed square*—circular.

Unilateral and Bilateral Endscrapers

The unilateral examples occur only sporadically. They are on short, wide flakes and cluster strongly in size as compared to the bilateral examples (fig. 9-12). Retouch on both types is always continuous and carefully applied; on the unilateral examples eight have

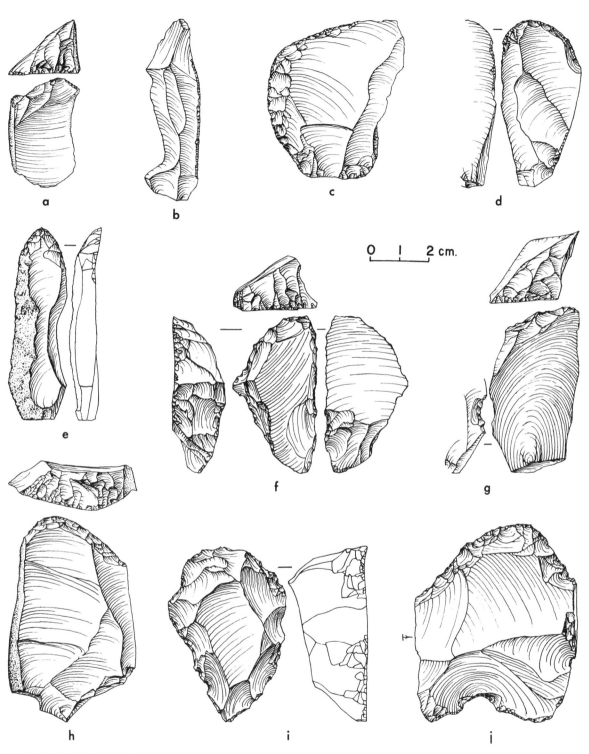

FIG. 9-13–Tools from Site Ein Aqev (D31): *a*–lateral carinated scraper with sheen on lateral edge; *b*–retouched blade; *c*–sidescraper; *d*–endscraper on retouched piece; *e*–ogival endscraper; *f*–double lateral carinated scraper; *g*–lateral carinated scraper with notch; *h*–endscraper approaching ogival form; *i*–thick scraper; *j*–lateral endscraper with opposed notch.

semisteep retouch and two flat retouch, while the bilateral are evenly divided between those with semi-steep and those with flat retouch. On all but two laterally positioned pieces, the main portion of the scraping edge is distally placed, with scraper retouch extending well down one or both lateral edges. On only a few examples, however, does the side treatment actually extend as far as the butt (fig. 9-10c), usually covering from one-third to two-thirds of the edges.

Circular Scraper

There is a single example from Level 8, which is more ovoid than circular. It is one of the smallest scrapers (fig. 9-12) and is well formed by semisteep retouch.

Endscrapers on Notch

This type refers only to those endscrapers where the scraping edge actually intersects with a notch. Each is a typical obverse, distal endscraper with a large, obversely retouched notch.

Thin-Nosed Scrapers

This is a rare type, which generally is morphologically atypical. All exhibit flat retouch, with the noses formed by very shallow indentations. While few are intact, two fall within the size range of the other flat-scraper types (fig. 9-12).

Double Flat Endscrapers

Of the 36 individual scraping edges, all are obverse; 22 semisteep and 12 flat. Only 2 forms of scrapers occur: 29 typical, with even-arched edges, and 5 ogival. While blanks are rather evenly divided between flakes (6) and blades (8), with 2 on primary elements and one on a crested blade (lame à crête), all those on blades have one blunt lateral edge, while this characteristic is absent on the other blank forms. The blunt edges are formed by cortex surfaces (fig. 9-10e) on all but one example, which has retouched backing. These double scrapers show considerable size range, with

those which are wider than they are long having laterally placed scraping edges (fig. 9-12).

Carinated and Thick Scrapers

These include only a small number of thick-shouldered pieces but a large number of various carinated forms. Many of the latter grade into carinated burins, and the exact line of demarcation between the two is rather arbitrary. There are two basic carinated forms, normal and lateral. The distinction between them rests on the shape and orientation of the scraping edge. On normal examples, the scraping edge may be from slightly convex to ogival, but is basically symmetric, with retouch occurring on both sides of the convexity. On lateral examples the scraping edge is asymmetric and it has a convex oblique form.

Typical Carinated Scrapers

These are mainly on flakes (66.7%), or primary elements (15.1%), with only low frequencies on other blank forms: blades (7.6%), core-trimming elements (3.0%), and cores/chunks (7.5%). They are mostly moderate in size and show rather strong clustering, with even those on blades closely approaching flake proportions (fig. 9-16).

While all scraping edges are formed by lamellar scars, there is some variation as to the origin of this retouch. On most examples, 62.9%, it originates from the dorsal surface of the blank (fig. 9-14j), making the scraper "inverse." This form is most clearly seen on the lateral carinated scraper shown in Fig. 9-14i. A fair percentage, 24.2%, has the retouch originating from a lateral edge which is perpendicular to the plane of the flake. It is particularly these which approach carinated burin form. Only a few, 12.9%, have the retouch originating from the ventral surface (fig. 9-14h). In this respect, these typical carinated scrapers are curious, although this pattern is consistent for all carinated scrapers and represents a marked stylistic characteristic.

The scraping edges range from quite straight (4.5%), wide and only slightly convex (16.7%),

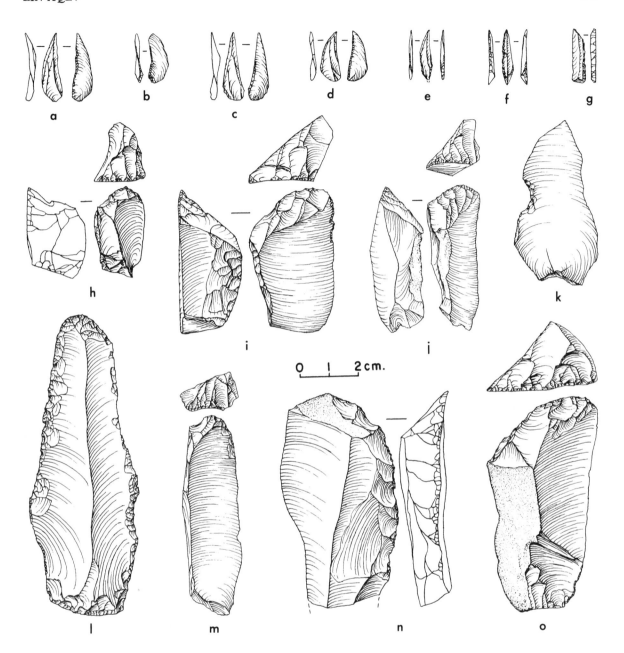

FIG. 9-14—Tools from Site Ein Aqev (D31): *a, b, d—lamelles Dufour* (inverse); *c—lamelles Dufour* (alternate); *e*—bilaterally retouched bladelet; *f*—microgravette; *g*—backed and truncated bladelet; *h*—microcarinated scraper; *i, j, o*—lateral carinated scrapers; *k*—notch; *l*—endscraper on bilaterally retouched blade; *m*—inverse, semicarinated scraper; *n*—backed blade.

through normally convex (56.1%) or ogival (9.1%), to those which approach lateral carinated form (13.6%). These edges range from only 10 mm in width on the smallest piece, perhaps microcarinated (fig. 9-14*h*), to 32 mm with a mean width of 19.6 mm—just under twice that of carinated burins. The position of the scraping edge is also quite variable; 42.7% are proximal, 46.9% are distal, while 10.6% are not clear. This variability appears to be directly related to the blank cross section, with the utilized extremity being that which provided the best "preformed" keel, although the cross section, too, shows variation. Those with retouch originating from a lateral face have symmetric cross sections with high keels (24.2%), while the others have markedly asymmetric keels. This lack of symmetry is caused by one steep edge, which is normally a cortex surface, but which, on a few examples, is produced by heavy retouch. This steep edge is situated overwhelmingly on the left side; 91.0% left vs. 4.5% right, with 4.5% bilaterally steep.

Atypical Carinated Scrapers

These are atypical mainly because the retouch is not truly lamellar, the edge is slightly denticulated, or the piece is unfinished. In many attributes, these parallel the typical examples, although ventral origin for the retouch is dominant (57.1%), as opposed to dorsal (19.1%), or lateral (23.8%), while distal placement is most common (61.9%). Other differences between these and the typical examples include a tendency toward a greater size range (fig. 9-16), elongation of the large examples, and a strong tendency for blanks to be core fragments or chunks (25.0%). A single example, classified here, might be considered a rough *grattoir eventail* (fig. 9-13i).

Typical Lateral Carinated Scrapers

These form part of the continuum which runs from multifaceted dihedral burins, through busquoid burins, typical carinated burins, to typical carinated scrapers. Even within the lateral carinated scrapers there is some morphological variation from those which approach burins to those where the scraping edge is very wide and formed by markedly transverse retouch. These latter approach what might be termed "planes" (fig. 9-15i).

Most of the blanks used for these tools have high, asymmetric, triangular cross sections (fig. 9-13g: note notch, as if a busquoid burin were intended), often with cortex along the thick lateral edge, although retouch is also used (fig. 9-14i). When these scrapers are oriented as shown in the illustrations (scraping edge toward the top of the page and the retouch scars showing), 98% have the thick edge along the left side,

resulting in a scraping edge which arcs upward from left to right. In this position the right lateral edge is sharp and longer than the left edge. This form is suggestive of a backed knife as well as of a scraper and, on at least one example (fig. 9-13a), there is actual sheen along the sharp edge and no microscopic evidence of use of the scraping edge. Many other examples, however, do exhibit clear microscopic wear of the scraping edge (fig. 9-14o), suggesting that while lateral carinated scrapers may form a morphologically homogeneous group, they undoubtedly served more than one function.

These scrapers also show a division between those with a proximal and those with a distal scraping edge; 52.3% to 47.7%, with six examples on core fragments or chunks not counted. A more consistent trait, also found on the typical carinated scrapers, is the utilization of the dorsal surface as the platform for retouch (86.4%), with only 13.6% with retouch originating from the ventral surface.

While morphologically transitional between the carinated burins and the typical carinated scrapers, the mean width of scraping edges, 23.08 mm, is even greater than that of the typical carinated scrapers, and the range is also higher—13 mm to 43 millimeters.

The lateral carinated scrapers show the same size pattern as that of the typical carinated scrapers (fig. 9-16). This apparent preference in both absolute size and in length/width proportions resulted in the utilization of mainly flakes (67.3%) as blanks, with primary elements and core fragments or chunks both accounting for 12.2%, and blades for only 8.2 percent.

Atypical Lateral Carinated Scrapers

There are five examples which are atypical because of their unfinished state. On each, the convex oblique scraping edge has been defined roughly, but it is irregular and lacks the typical twisted microblade scars.

Double Carinated Scrapers

These conform in all ways to the other carinated scrapers, except that there is one scraper present at

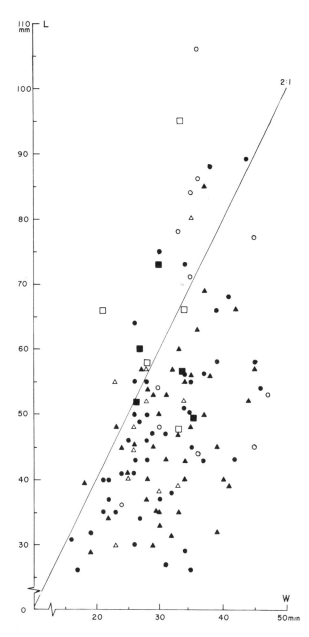

FIG. 9-16—Length/Width scattergram of thick scrapers at Site D31. Key: *open triangle*—double carinated; *closed triangle*—lateral carinated; *open circle*—atypical carinated; *closed circle*—typical carinated; *open square*—thick shouldered; *closed square*—thick nosed.

each extremity (fig. 9-13*f*). There are two atypical examples placed here; one where a typical carinated scraper is paired with a thick-nosed scraper and one where a lateral carinated scraper is found opposite a

flat ogival endscraper. Otherwise, there are eleven lateral carinated scrapers, two typical, and five atypical carinated scrapers in various paired combinations. Like the single carinated scrapers, these tend to be of moderate dimensions (fig. 9-16).

Thick-Nosed and Thick-Shouldered Scrapers

These are rare and tend to be atypical. The seven thick-shouldered examples might all be considered atypical carinated, as the shoulder is normally poorly defined. Seven of the eight scraping edges are distal but exhibit variability as the origin of retouch: four from the ventral surface; one from the dorsal surface, which is semicarinated (fig. 9-14*m*); and two from the lateral surfaces. All but one have a blunt lateral edge, three with cortex and three owing to natural surfaces. Three thick-nosed scrapers are on core fragments and would be considered carinated except for the nosed profile. Of the remainder, three are naturally backed and retouched distally. More in line with the carinated scrapers, all those not on core fragments have retouch originating from the dorsal surface.

Other Scrapers

Sidescrapers

These occur only in Levels 5 through 7. There is one biconvex and three simple convex examples (fig. 9-13*c*). Retouch is flat to semisteep, all are carefully made, and are of moderate size (fig. 9-12).

Core Scrapers

Generally, core scrapers are almost impossible to distinguish from bladelet cores. In this assemblage, however, the paucity of true bladelets, as opposed to twisted microblades, suggests that bladelet cores were, at best, rare. In any case, of the ten core scrapers, only four approach bladelet core morphology. The remaining examples are mostly core fragments with a scraping edge formed along one side, rather than by a modification of the original striking platform. There are two rather large examples which are, perhaps, best described as "planes."

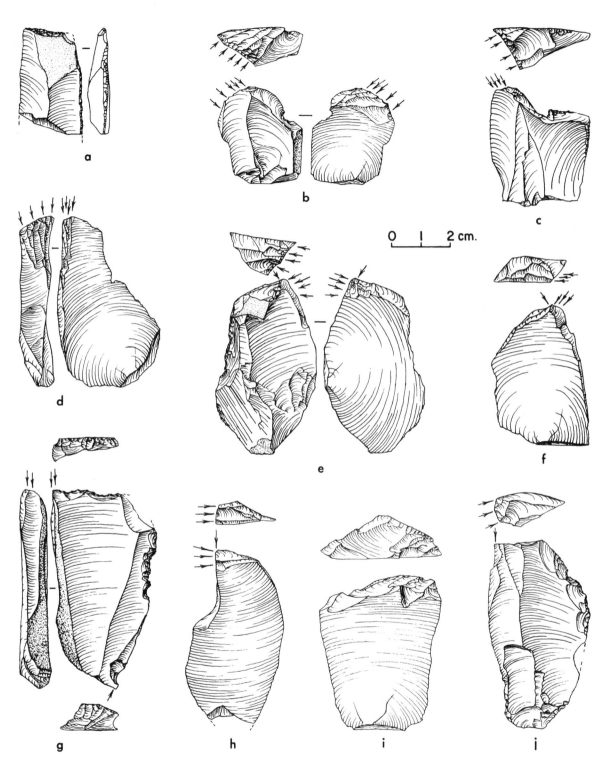

FIG. 9-15—Tools from Site Ein Aqev (D31): *a*—backed and truncated blade; *b, e, j*—busquoid burins (*b* approaches a scraper); *c*—carinated burin; *d*—burin on natural surface; *f*—dihedral burin; *g*—multiple burin on truncations; *h*—dihedral angle burin; *i*—lateral carinated scraper approaching a "plane."

Multiple Tools

Four combinations occur: burins and arch-tipped blades; burins and truncations; scrapers and truncations; and burins and endscrapers. The first three occur only as more or less isolated specimens, while burins in combination with endscrapers are quite common. Whatever the combination, however, all these pieces tend to be relatively average in size, with no differential clustering between those on blades and those on other blank forms (fig. 9-18).

Burins/Arch-Tipped Blades

While only two were found (one each from Levels 8 and 11), they are worth noting. Each is a naturally backed blade with a more or less carinated burin on the proximal extremity and a markedly convex backing at the distal extremity, which merges into the cortex backing. In this regard, it would be difficult to view this backing as a form of truncation. In both cases, the burin bits are fairly narrow, 5.9 and 8.2 mm, with the burin formed by the intersection of one straight facet with three convexly curved facets.

Burin/Truncation

Only one example was found, from Level 3. It is a flake with a straight oblique proximal truncation and a distal burin on a retouched notch. The burin bit is formed by the intersection of the notch and a single burin facet, but measures 11.6 mm across the bit.

Endscrapers/Truncations

Two occur, one each from Levels 5 and 8. The former is a distal ogival scraper formed by semisteep obverse retouch paired with a straight oblique proximal truncation, while the other is a typical carinated scraper paired with an atypical, inverse straight distal truncation.

Endscrapers/Burins

Only this type occurs with any frequency: 24 examples. These are found in small numbers in all but 3 levels (see Appendix A), except in Level 8, where seven were recovered.

The scraper elements include all normally occurring types: typical (4), atypical (3), ogival (5), carinated (4), lateral carinated (4), unilateral (2), simple oblique (1), and on retouched piece (1). The position of the scrapers is quite uniform; thin scrapers, with a single exception, occur at the distal extremity, while carinated forms always occur at the proximal extremity.

The burins also include almost all forms which occur separately: on truncation (6), transverse on lateral truncation (2), carinated (5), dihedral (3), on old surface (1), and dihedral angle (1). Burin bits parallel those on normal burins, with the carinated and multifaceted examples having wider bits (mean—8.9 mm and 11.7 mm, respectively) than those on truncations, on snap, or those of simple dihedral form (mean—5.4 mm, 7.9 mm, 7.3 mm, respectively).

Burins

While burins are not nearly as numerous as scrapers, there are a considerable number of types present, from the most simple to the most complex. In a general sense, they may be grouped into those on truncations and those where no retouched truncation is present. On this basis, the latter are, by far, dominant (80.2% vs. 19.8%). The types represented within each group are described below, selected attribute data are presented in Table 9-11, and the sizes of complete examples are shown in Fig. 9-17.

Dihedral Angle Burins

These include four which are multifaceted, two of which might be considered transverse, as on each there is a single burin facet parallel to the long axis of the blank and three to four facets transverse to that axis (fig. 9-15*h*).

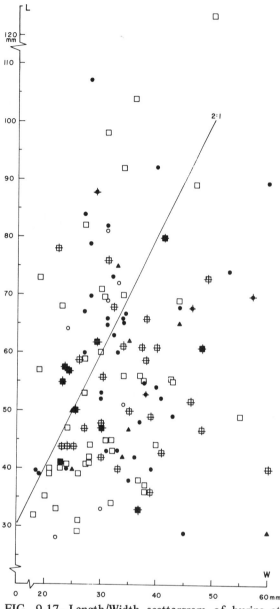

FIG. 9-17–Length/Width scattergram of burins at
Site D32. Key: *closed circle*–on truncation; *open
circle*–multiple mixed; *crossed closed circle*–
Corbiac; *open square*–dihedral; *closed square*–
multiple dihedral; *crossed open square*–on snap;
crossed closed square–on natural surface; *closed
triangle*–busquoid.

Simple Dihedral Burins

Most have asymmetric bits (78.6%) and, with few
exceptions, tend to be quite narrow and mostly

present on distal extremities (table 9-11). Of the fourteen found, only five exhibit any *plan* facets, but on
all of these the *plan* facets form marked shoulders,
which effectively thin the bit width.

Dihedral Burin, Multifaceted

The most common dihedral burin is multifaceted,
with twenty-nine examples. Of these, eleven have
generally straight facets, while on the remainder they
are somewhat curved (fig. 9-15*f*). Of the more classic
variety, there is always a strong tendency for a
marked imbalance in the number of facets present on
each side of the bit. In fact, only one with six facets
is evenly balanced with three on each side, while one
other has two facets opposed by three. All the rest
exhibit a single facet opposed by three or four facets.
These include six where one or two facets are *plan*.
Perhaps because of the facet imbalance, the vast
majority are asymmetric (81.8%), with some approaching transverse forms.

The most numerous multifaceted burin group is
that which approaches carinated burins. All eighteen
of these are asymmetric and all but two have bits
formed by the intersection of a single facet, which is
generally parallel to the long axis of the blank, with
three to five which show somewhat curved and somewhat transverse facets. Half have at least one *plan*
facet, but never more than two. Unlike the more
classic examples, a sizable majority are formed at the
proximal end of flakes. In spite of the tendency for
these to have more facets per burin than the classic
examples, there is little difference between the mean
bit widths (table 9-11).

Burins on Snap

These are typified by a minimal number of burin
facets per piece (table 9-11). They were produced on
a wide variety of snaps or breaks, with little concern
for standardization; only 40.6% exhibit snaps which
are perpendicular to the long axis of the blank, while
the remainder are markedly oblique. Only four, including one of the two multifaceted examples, have
one *plan* facet. When present, these tend to form
distinct shoulders.

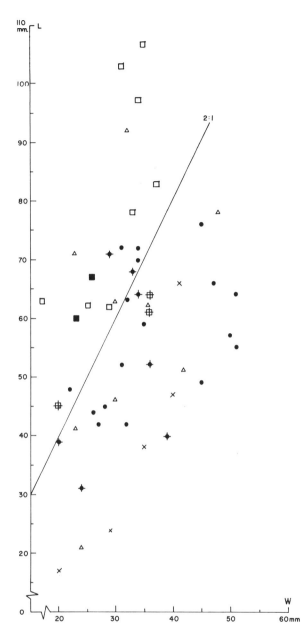

FIG. 9-18—Length/Width scattergram of various tools at Site D31. Key: *open square*—backed blades; *closed square*—burins plus arch tipped; *crossed square*—burin plus truncation; *dot*—burin plus endscraper; *crossed dot*—burin plus carinated scraper; *open triangle*—truncated piece; *cross*—perforator.

The burins on snaps tend to have very narrow bits, with the mean bit width among the lowest for all types (table 9-11). In addition to those noted above, there is a single transverse burin on a laterally snapped primary flake.

Burins on Natural Surface

These are mainly of very simple form with narrow bits (table 9-11). Eight have a single burin facet struck from the natural distal end of a blank. Only a single example is multifaceted, with four burin facets (fig. 9-15d). Three others are transverse, whereas the other simple examples are only rarely even oblique to the long axis of the blank.

Burins on Truncation

All normal forms are present but usually only in small numbers (table 9-11). Of particular interest are five typical Corbiac burins (Brézillon, 1968, p. 413), a type rarely described for the Levant. The most common truncation form is straight oblique, followed by concave, convex oblique, and lateral, with only rare examples of straight truncations. Almost all are simple burins with one or two burin facets, although there is considerable variability in bit width (table 9-11).

A few examples may be specially noted. Those on lateral truncation include two which approach Corbiac burins, while another is struck off inverse lateral retouch. The two on straight truncations are both *plan*, as are three of the twelve on straight oblique truncations. There is one example where the truncation merges into backing and it might well be classified as a burin on a backed flake.

Burins, Multiple Mixed

These combine a number of types, including busquoid, transverse on lateral truncation, and multifaceted dihedral examples. On all but two the truncated burin is at the distal extremity. Burin bits on these burins parallel those on the single varieties, with only two multifaceted examples exhibiting shouldering, owing to *plan* facets.

TABLE 9-11
Site D31—Selected Attributes by Type for Single Burins

Type	Blank Form				Position[1]		Number of Facets[2]							Bit Width (mm)	
	Blade	Flake	Primary Element	Core Trimming Element	Distal	Proximal	Simple 1	2	3	Multifaceted 4	5	6	7	Range	Mean
Dihedral, simple	5	5	4		9	5	6	8						3.0-16.7	6.94
Dihedral, multifaceted	5	17	6	1	13	13				15	11		3	3.6-15.3	8.64
Dihedral, angle, simple	1	4			5		3		2					4.0-10.2	6.14
Dihedral, angle, multifaceted		2	2		2	2				2	2			3.8-13.7	8.48
On snap	11	20	2		22	9	21	9	2					1.5-11.9	5.49
On transverse snap			1		1		1							5.1	5.10
On old surface, simple	4	2		2	8		7	1						4.5- 8.6	6.28
On old surface, multifaceted				1		1			1					7.0	7.00
Transverse on old surface	1	2			3		3							3.5- 5.7	4.67
Busquoid	2	6	2		7	3		3	2			5		4.3-15.1	8.73
Carinated	10	22	7	6	23	21		10		26	6	2	1	4.0-16.9	10.18
On straight oblique truncation, simple	5	3	1	1	5	4	7	3						4.1-12.8	7.61
On straight oblique truncation, multifaceted	1	1			2	2			2					6.6-13.6	10.10
On convex truncation	4	1	2		4	2	6	1						3.2- 7.3	4.46
On concave truncation, simple	1	4	2		4	2	4	3						4.1-17.7	10.10
On concave truncation, multifaceted	1	1			1	1			2					9.0-11.6	10.30
Corbiac	1	3	1		2	3	5							–	–

[1] When observations could not be accurately made, the piece was not counted.

[2] Refers only to major burin facets caused by burin blows. Snaps and retouched truncations not included. Multifaceted burins are those with a total of more than three facets, including snaps, retouched truncations, and natural surfaces when they are part of the bit formation.

Multiple Burins on Truncation

These always have the burins at opposite ends of the blanks (fig. 9-15*g*), while only a single multiple dihedral burin was recovered.

Busquoid Burins

None of these is highly typical, although each has a notch at the end of the burin facets. Three have facets which are clearly transverse, with little or no curvature (fig. 9-15*j*), while the others exhibit a curvature but are poorly made (fig. 9-15*e*). Two of the transverse examples and one other have the burin facets struck off an original dorsal scar, while on another they are struck from a natural fracture. The remaining examples have a single facet opposed by three or four curved, transverse facets, at times resulting in rather wide bits which approach scraping edges (fig. 9-15*b*) (table 9-11).

Carinated Burins

These run the gauntlet from typical, with narrow bits and markedly curved burin facets, to those which have rather wide bits and approach lateral or regular carinated scrapers (fig. 9-15*c*). The burin edges are normally markedly convex, often accentuated by the presence of one or more *plan* facets. There is considerable variability as to bit width, and a rather even distribution in positioning (table 9-11).

Perhaps the most characteristic element that this group shares with other carinated tool forms is the strong tendency to use an old or a purposely formed dorsal scar as the surface from which the burin facets are struck (fig. 9-15*c*); twenty utilize an old dorsal scar, while thirteen are struck off single facets perpendicular to the plane of the blank.

Other Tools

Perforators

These are mainly on flakes or flake fragments of generally small proportions (fig. 9-18). Of the fourteen recovered, eight are either at a distal extremity or at the junction between the distal extremity and a lateral edge. All exhibit rather short, straight, pointed tips, formed by converging, steep obverse retouch, except for a single example from Level 8, where the projection is pointed but quite thick.

Truncated Pieces

These range from typical examples to those which approach atypical endscrapers. They occur on a variety of blank forms, with wide metric parameters (fig. 9-18). They are a minor typological element, but they do show general consistency as to the position of the truncation and its specific form (table 9-12). It should be noted that some typological systems would have included the arch-tipped blades here, causing no siginficant increase in number, but reinforcing tendencies toward both distal placement and oblique form.

TABLE 9-12
Attributes of Truncated Pieces

	Blade	Flake	Primary Element	Core Trimming Element
Position				
Distal	5	7	1	1
Proximal	3	3		
Form				
Straight	1	2		
Concave		1		
Concave oblique	4	3		
Straight oblique	3	4	1	1

Backed Blades

These occur only sporadically. The most common are arch backed, followed by blades with arch tips and partially backed blades. The arch-backed blades show a marked convexity but rather rough backing, always along the right edge. Two are more or less pointed (fig. 9-19*a*), two are clearly blunt (fig. 9-14*n*), while one is a fragment. All complete examples are rather large (fig. 9-18). The arch-tipped

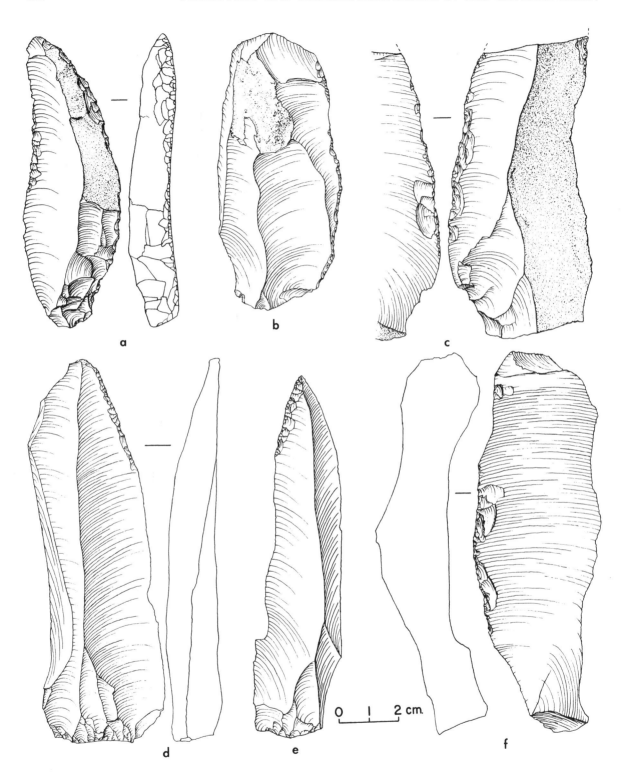

FIG. 9-19–Tools from Site Ein Aqev (D31): *a*–backed blade; *b*–retouched piece; *c*–bifacially battered piece; *d, e*–distally retouched blades; *f*–inversely battered piece.

blades include three which are rather small, but still well outside the range of bladelets (fig. 9-18). Of the four, two are arched proximally and two distally. On all but one, the arching merges into a naturally backed edge, making these more like backed blades than truncated pieces. The partially backed blades are mostly fragmentary, with rough backing present along either the distal or proximal sections of one lateral edge. There are single examples of a fragmentary blunt, straight-backed blade from Level 10 and a straight-backed and truncated blade from Level 7 (fig. 9-15*a*). Both exhibit a fine, regular backing along thin edges.

Notched Pieces

These are found on all blank types, except for cores and core-trimming elements, although notched bladelets and notched twisted microblades are very rare. Notches formed either by retouch or by a single blow are micronotches (less than 7 mm in width) or macronotches (greater than 7 mm in width). While it is recognized that this boundary line is essentially arbitrary, clustering suggests some reality. For all retouched notches, there are clear clusters between 4 and 7 mm, 10 and 12 mm, and 20 and 21 mm, although notches of other sizes occur sporadically. For single-blow notches, the clusters are between 4 and 6 mm, 8 and 11 mm, 15 and 16 mm, while individual notches reach all the way to 45 millimeters.

Of the ninety-six notches present in this class (counting each notch), 78.1% are obverse, with inverse notches occurring only rarely in each type (fig. 9-14*k*). The multiple notches are, with only three exceptions, two adjacent notches, and when single-blow multiple notches occur on flakes or primary elements, these are on large thick pieces. This tendency is not present for the multiple retouched notches, where the blanks tend to be rather thin.

Denticulates

These are on all blank forms, except for bladelets and twisted microblades, and tend to be quite large (fig. 9-20). Denticulates are defined as having at least three interesting notches, which may be formed by

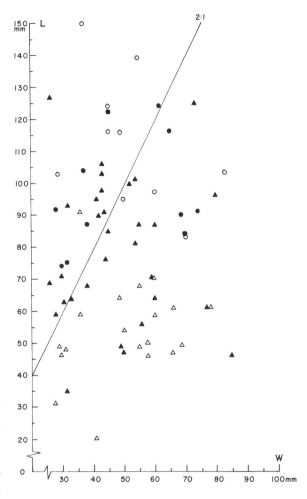

FIG. 9-20—Length/Width scattergram of various tools at Site D31. Key: *dot*—bifacially battered pieces; *open circle*—inversely battered pieces; *closed triangle*—lateral denticulates; *open triangle*—other denticulates.

retouch or by single blows. The size of the notches varies considerably, from 2 to 20 mm in width, and considerable size range is often present along a single denticulated edge (fig. 9-10*d*). There is, however, a rather high correlation between denticulates formed by retouch and small notches (between 2 and 7 mm in width), and a less clear but still noticeable correlation between those formed by single blows and large notches (greater than 7 mm). Almost all denticulates are obverse (92.2%), while side preference on lateral examples appears to be random (table 9-13).

A number of rare sub-types are noted in Table

TABLE 9-13
Characteristics of Denticulated Tools

Subtype	Blank	Number	Type of Retouch	Size Micro.	Macro.	Face Retouched Obverse	Inverse	Side Left	Right
Bilateral:	Blade	3	Single blow	1	1	1			
			Retouched	3	3	3			
	Flake	1	Retouched	1	1	1			
	Primary Element	1	Retouched	1	1	1			
Converging:	Flake	3	Single blow	3	3	3			
	Primary Element	3	Single blow	3	3	3			
End:	Flake	7	Single blow	4	4	4			
			Retouched	3	3	3			
	Primary Element	1	Single blow	1	1	1			
Transverse:	Flake	6	Single blow	2	2	2			
			Retouched	4	2	2	4		
	Primary Element	2	Retouched	2	1	1	2		
Lateral:	Blade	20	Single blow	11	5	6	11	5	6
			Retouched	9	8	1	8	1	4	5
	Flake	19	Single blow	10		10	9	1	3	7
			Retouched	9	7	2	8	1	6	3
	Primary Element	10	Single blow	4	1	3	4	1	3
			Retouched	6	6	6	3	3
	Core Trimming Element	2	Retouched	2	1	1	2	1	1

9-13. Of interest are the bilateral examples on blades, since the denticulations are normally extremely regular and approach "saws."

Retouched Pieces

These are blanks of all types which have one or more edges modified by various kinds of retouch but in which this retouch follows the natural limits of an edge or edges, without modifying them sufficiently to form any other recognizable tool type. Retouch tends to be one of four types: marginal (figs. 9-13*b*; 9-19*b*), strong semisteep, flat invasive, and steep. The latter might be considered backing, except that it always occurs opposite a cortex edge. Each type of retouch occurs both obversely and inversely, but only twenty pieces exhibit only inverse retouch, three are alter-nately retouched, while eighty-two (78.1%) have only obverse retouch. The amount of obverse retouch, its position along an edge, and its type are all variable (table 9-14).

Clearly, retouched blades tend to have larger portions of their edges retouched and to show stronger retouch (semisteep or flat) than do retouched flakes. Those few blades with less than 25% of an edge retouched have strong retouch by a normally pointed distal extremity, although some examples with more retouch have this form too (fig. 9-19*d, e*).

Seven blades and blade fragments exhibit bilateral obverse retouch, covering the total length of all extant lateral edges. This retouch is either marginal (2) or semisteep (5), although in most cases it is generally weak and somewhat uneven.

There is a group of three flakes and a primary

TABLE 9-14
Characteristics of Lateral, Obversely Retouched Pieces

Observation	Blade	Flake	Primary Element	Core Trimming Element
Percent of Edge				
a. 100-75	12	8		1
b. 75-50	9	16	2	
c. 50-25	9	6	2	2
d. 25	3			
Total	33	30	4	3
Position of Retouch				
a. Whole edge	3	1		
b. Distal portion	3	10	3	
c. Central portion	15	15		2
d. Proximal portion	8	2		1
e. Tip only	4			
f. Distal end		2	1	
Total	33	30	4	3
Type of Retouch				
a. Marginal	7	12	1	3
b. Flat, invasive	7	4	2	
c. Semisteep	18	9	1	
d. Steep	1	3		
e. Irregular		2		
Total	33	30	4	3

element which are wider than they are long and are retouched along the distal (transverse) end. These approach transverse sidescrapers, but the semisteep retouch is much too weak to classify the pieces as scrapers. For the class, there is a clear tendency toward blade proportions as the blanks increase in length (fig. 9-21).

Aurignacian Retouched Pieces

One each occurs in Levels 6 and 11. Both pieces are broken (a flake and a blade) and neither is typical, although the retouch is strong, clearly overlapping, and somewhat scaled.

Lamelles Dufour

Two types are present: those with inverse, semisteep retouch which normally originates at the base of one edge and becomes progressively lighter as it approaches the distal extremity (fig. 9-14*a, b, d*) and those which have additional, minor, obverse retouch on the opposed edge, which is also strongest by the base and usually only extends a short distance along

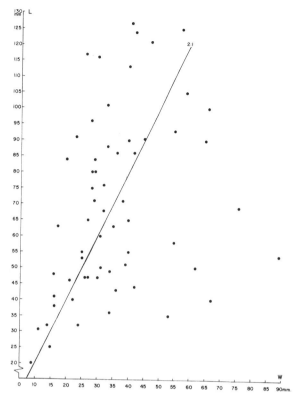

FIG. 9-21—Length/Width scattergram of retouched
   pieces at Site D31.

the edge (fig. 9-14*c*). Both forms are produced on
strongly twisted microblades derived from the manufacture of the various carinated tools. There is an
extremely high degree of uniformity in both placement of retouch and tool size. The 54 examples
which are alternately retouched always have the
inverse retouch along the left edge (ventral face up),
while this is also true on 86 of 91 (94.5%) of those
with simple inverse retouch. Size is highly standardized, with only a single inverse example and three
alternate examples falling outside a tight cluster (fig.
9-22).

Retouched Microblades

These are comparable both in blank type and in
the position of the retouch to the *lamelles Dufour*,
except that the retouch tends to be somewhat lighter.
Retouch does, however, most commonly originate at
the proximal end and only very rarely extends the

whole length of the edge. Unlike the *lamelles Dufour*,
there is no strict convention for the edge to be retouched, as 17 are treated on the left edge and 12 on
the right edge (dorsal face up), while 3 exhibit bilateral retouch (fig. 9-14*e*). Their lengths are comparable
to the *lamelles Dufour* (range 12 to 28 mm; mean,
17.12 mm), while their widths best match the alternately retouched examples (range, 4 to 8.5 mm;
mean, 5.15 mm). Given their form and the type of
blank utilized, these may be unfinished or atypical
lamelles Dufour.

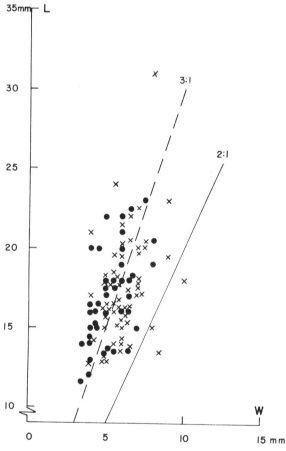

FIG. 9-22—Length/Width scattergram of *lamelles
   Dufour* at Site D31. Key: *dot*—alternately retouched; *cross*—inversely retouched.

Backed Bladelets

The most common is the backed bladelet fragment, but even these occur in only 6 of the 12 levels. In spite of their low number, backed bladelets of a number of varieties are found: arch backed, partially backed, and even one example may be considered a microgravette point (fig. 9-14*f*). Backing is abrupt and formed by obverse retouch, although a single example from Level 6 has Ouchtata retouch, and a single backed fragment from Level 8 shows clear backing by *sur enclume* technique. With the exception of two arch-backed and one partially concave-backed examples, all others are straight backed. The majority of these are fragmentary, with the four complete examples measuring 13 by 3 mm, 15.5 by 4.5 mm, 21 by 10.5 mm, and 24 by 6 millimeters. It should be noted that the bladelet blanks are all flat and well outside the morphological range of the twisted microblades used in the production of *lamelles Dufour*.

Backed and Truncated Bladelets

There is one each in Levels 5, 7, and 8. All are extremely fragmentary and have straight-backed edges, but each exhibits a different truncation form: straight oblique (fig. 9-14*g*), convex oblique, and concave oblique. The first of these is the second, and last, backed piece showing *sur enclume* technique.

Other Backed Bladelets

There is a single bladelet fragment with a rounded base from Level 10, and a pointed bladelet with a retouched tip from Level 2.

Microburins

A single classic proximal microburin was recovered from Level 11. While morphologically typical, its unique occurrence makes it of little significance.

Battered Pieces (Pieces à mâchures)

Two forms are recognized: those typical examples which exhibit variable amounts of bifacial scarring from apparent heavy use and those where the battering scars are only on the ventral surface. While the

latter are not too common, they form a highly homogeneous group, of which all but four are on extremely large incurvate blades (fig. 9-19*f*), while the others are on large incurvate flakes (fig. 9-20). The area of battering is invariably strongest along the central and most incurvate portion of each piece. The length of the battered surface falls either between 20 and 28.6 mm (6 examples), or between 35.1 and 49.5 mm (5 examples), and on all but a single piece the battering occurs along the right edge (dorsal face up).

The bifacially battered examples are not so uniform either in size or in blank form. All, however, tend to be quite large (fig. 9-19*c*), with examples over 100 mm in length common (fig. 9-20). The typological attributes of this group are shown in Table 9-15.

On blades there is a strong correlation between incurvature and inverse battering and lack of incurvature and bifacial battering. This, however, breaks down when other blank forms are considered. Again, the strict side preference seen for the inversely battered blades is not present for the bifacially battered pieces, where it is random. These differences might suggest that the large, incurvate blades with inverse battering had a very specific function, somewhat different from the bifacially battered pieces.

Choppers

All but two are on rather large limestone cobbles, the others being on large flint chunks. Most exhibit minimal bifacial or unifacial flaking perpendicular to the long axis of the cobbles, but none exhibit the edge-crushing which is characteristic of hammerstones or fabricators. There is, however, a single transverse, bifacial example (fig. 9-23), and a few pieces are either bifacially or unifacially flaked almost around their circumference (fig. 9-24*a, b*). It is probable that the low number of these pieces is partially the result of the effects of thermal damage. Large numbers of limestone cobbles occurred at the site, but most were heavily burned, obscuring whatever evidence of flaking might have been present originally.

Varia

These represent only ca. 2% of all tools. Nine are

TABLE 9-15
Characteristics of Bifacially Battered Pieces

Blank	Profile		Length of Battering	Position of Battering[1]	Side of Battering[2]
	Flat	Incurvate			
Blade	8	1	19.5 mm-44.5 mm	C=4 D=2 P=2	L=3 R=4 B=2
Flake	3	3	29.7 mm-49.5 mm	C=4 P=2	L=1 R=4 B=1
Primary Element	2	3	31.5 mm-49.5 mm	C=3 P=1 ?=1	L=2 R=2 B=1

[1] Position: C–central; D–distal; P–proximal; ?–unidentifiable.
[2] Side (dorsal surface up): L–left; R–right; B–bilateral.

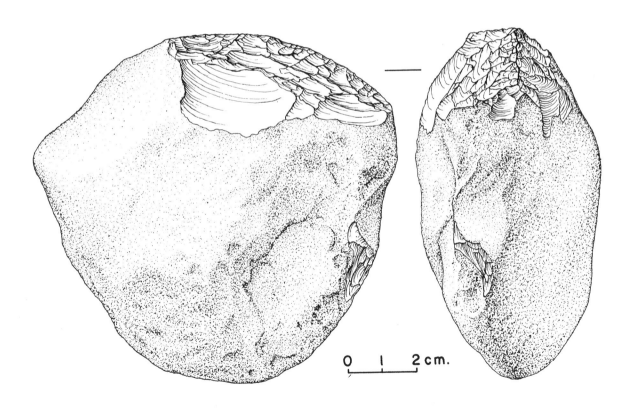

FIG. 9-23–Bifacial chopper from Site Ein Aqev (D31).

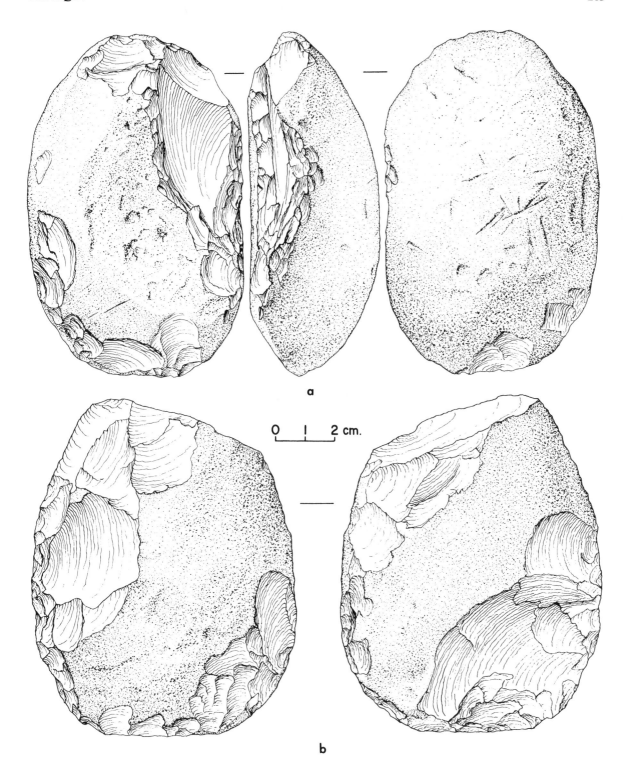

FIG. 9-24—Tools from Site Ein Aqev (D31): *a*—unifacial chopper; *b*—bifacial chopper.

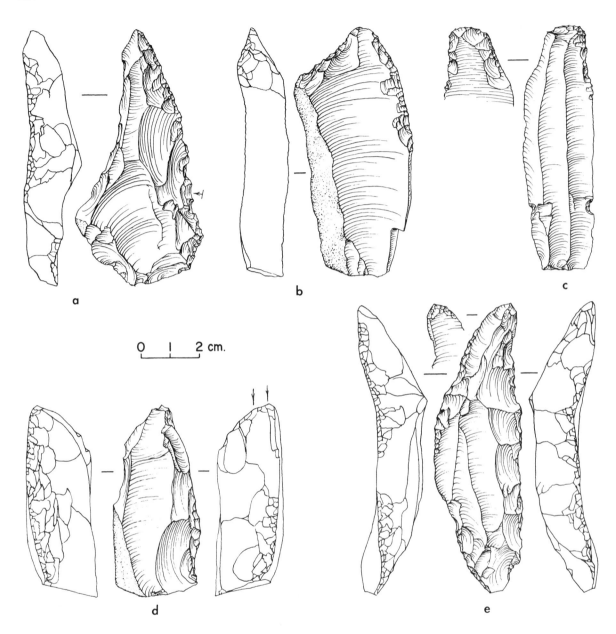

0   1   2 cm.

FIG. 9-25—Tools from Site Ein Aqev (D31): *a-e*—varia.

probably no more than highly atypical, incomplete, and unsuccessful attempts to produce various carinated scraper forms.

There are a number of tools which are quite well formed but are either unique in the collection or do not conform to types normally encountered. Included is a side-raclette from Level 5 and two distally scaled pieces from Levels 6 and 11. In addition, there are two rough picklike objects, one each from Levels 8 and 9. One, on a large flake, 83 by 45 mm, has heavily retouched converging sides, one convex and one concave, and the tip shows some minor battering (fig. 9-25a). The other is a chunk or core fragment, 77 by 35 mm, with rough bilateral retouch which converges toward one end, although no battering is present at the tip.

Among the unique forms is a large blade from Level 9 which has a plano-convex, bifacially retouched, bottle-shaped distal extremity (fig. 9-25c). Another blade, from Level 11, 83 by 37 mm, has an oblique concave truncation which merges into a cortex back, while the opposite edge has heavy, flat retouch. This retouch almost meets the truncation, forming a more or less ogival-shaped distal extremity (fig. 9-25b).

Three pieces, one each from Levels 3, 10, and 12, have three *plan* blows which originate from the distal extremity and cover the whole width of each ventral surface.

Three artifacts have backing as a dominant element: one from Level 4 and two from Level 6. The first is a blade bilaterally backed to a distal point and with inverse retouch at its tip (fig. 9-25e). The two from Level 6 include one squat, double-backed piece with two burin facets (fig. 9-25d) and another piece which is similar but without the facets.

CORES

A striking aspect of the assemblages from Ein Aqev is the poverty of cores, both in number and quality. Only 163 classifiable cores were recovered; there were 69 unidentifiable examples and fragments. Generally, the cores display a wide range in size and shape. Raw material was almost exclusively derived from either *in situ* or very recently eroded flint deposits, as the cortex is always fresh. This material included small pebbles, irregular large nodules, and even some tabular flint slabs. On almost all cores, bulb scars are pronounced, little or no regularization of the striking platform is present. Abandonment owing to extensive hinge-fracturing is common. There is a wide variety of types present (table 9-16), but few approach typical examples seen at other Upper Paleolithic sites in the area.

Notes on the Core Typology

Unlike all other Upper Paleolithic sites in the Avdat/Aqev area, the cores here are dominated by those which produced flakes rather than blades. The blade cores are mostly of single-platform type, with less than one-third exhibiting any complicated preparation (fig. 9-26a). About half are formed so that only a single thin edge was utilized as the flaked surface in blade production, another 10% utilized one edge along with a single face, while the remainder utilized only a single rather flat face (fig. 9-27b) or were flaked in an arch covering about one-half of the core periphery (fig. 9-27a). Single-platform blade cores are relatively large (mean length, 64.95 mm) and have only somewhat acute platforms (mean platform angle, 71.9°). The range in length, however, is marked—from 29 to 123 mm—with about one-third having produced blades under 50 mm in length. The platform angles do not show this type of range (58° to 86°).

Multiple-platform blade cores appear to have had only one platform utilized at a time (fig. 9-26b), rather than being alternately flaked. These, also, are large (mean length, 62.40 mm) and have platform angles comparable to the single-platform blade cores (mean platform angle, 69.8°). Only the ninety-degree blade cores exhibit a smaller size (mean length, 51.22 mm), although their platform angles are similar (mean platform angle, 71.5°).

If all blade cores are considered in a group, they have a mean length of 63.06 mm and a mean platform angle of 74.3 degrees. Only 7.94% are devoid of cortex, while 70.43% have considerable amounts. Some 52% have been flaked along only one thin edge, 11.27% have been flaked along one edge and a single face, while only 36.62% have been flaked on one or more faces. Only a small percentage of the blade cores, 9.52%, are made on flakes or primary elements. Of some note is the very minor occurrence of stepped platforms, somewhat less than one in ten.

Of the flake cores, those with simple single platforms are the most common. These approach simple single-platform blade cores in size (mean length, 64.0 mm), although plat-

TABLE 9-16
D31 Cores

Types	1	2	3	4	5	6	7	8	9	10	11	12	Total	Percent
A. Blade Cores														
Single Platform														
a. Simple		1	5	5	6	4	2	5	2	6	5	1	42	25.77
b. Prepared		2		1	2			2	2		2	1	12	7.36
c. Carinated		1				1							2	1.23
Subtotal		4	5	6	8	5	2	7	4	6	7	2	56	34.36
Multiple Platform														
a. Opposed, simple				1	2			1	1		1		6	3.68
b. Opposed, opposite side					1	2			1				4	2.45
c. Ninety-degree			1	1	2	1							5	3.07
Subtotal			1	2	5	3		1	2		1		15	9.20
Total Blade Cores		4	6	8	13	8	2	8	6	6	8	2	71	43.56
B. Flake Cores														
Single Platform														
a. Simple	1	5	4	6	5	4	1	5	4	5		2	42	25.77
b. Isolated flake				1			1	1		1			4	2.45
Subtotal	1	5	4	7	5	4	2	6	4	6		2	46	28.22
Multiple Platform														
a. Opposed, simple	1	2		3	1		1		2				10	6.13
b. Opposed, opposite side		1				1	1					1	4	2.45
c. Ninety-degree		3	2	2	1	3	2	1	1	1	1		17	10.43
d. Globular		1		1	1			1		1	1	1	7	4.29
e. Discoidal					2	1		1	2		2		8	4.91
Subtotal	1	7	2	6	5	5	4	3	5	2	4	2	46	28.22
Total Flake Cores	2	12	6	13	10	9	6	9	9	8	4	4	92	56.44
Totals	2	16	12	21	23	17	8	17	15	14	12	6	163	100.00
Unidentifiable and Fragments	5	3	4	13	12	5	6	6	5	3	6	1	69	

form angles are less acute (mean platform angle, 78.4°).

While few in number, opposed-platform cores are the largest in the flake category (mean length, 70.0 mm), with platform angles comparable to those above. Other flake-core

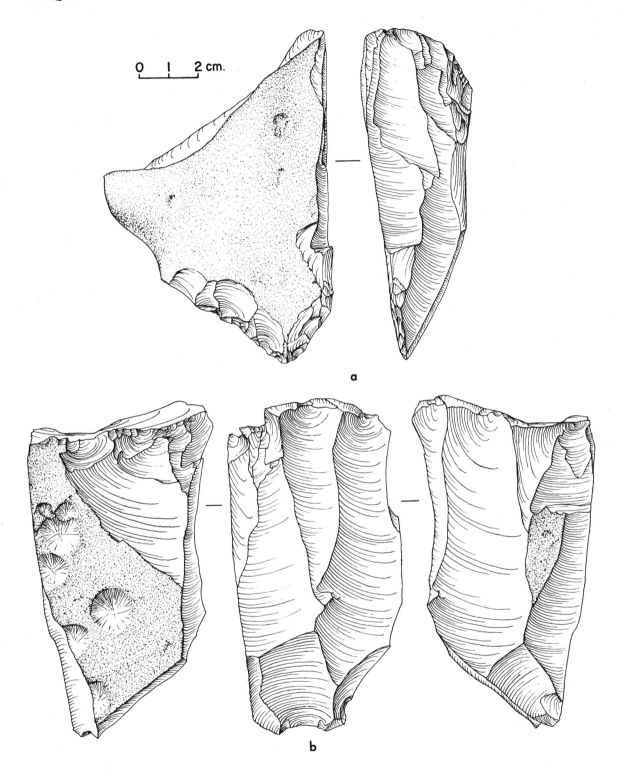

FIG. 9-26—Cores from Site Ein Aqev (D31): *a*—unifacially prepared blade core; *b*—opposed platform blade core.

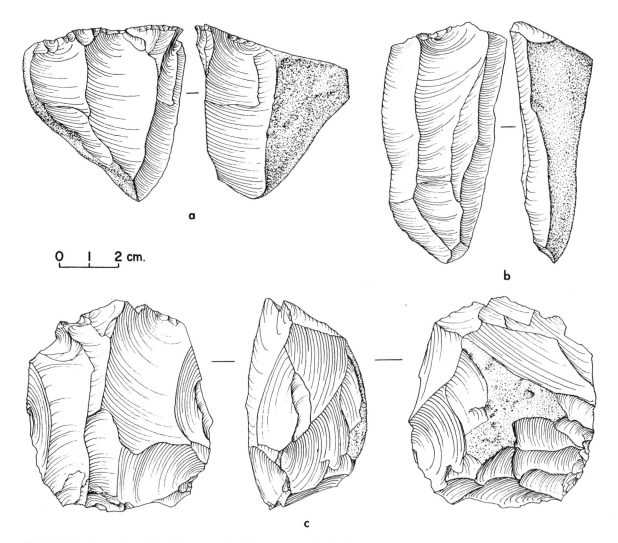

FIG. 9-27—Cores from Site Ein Aqev (D31): *a, b*—single platform blade cores; *c*—core approaching Levallois form.

types occur only in small numbers and show only a minimum of morphological consistency, but at least one approaches Levallois morphology (fig. 9-27*c*).

GROUND STONE

Three pieces of ground stone were recovered—a basalt handstone and a basalt fragmentary quern, both from Level 3, and a fragmentary, burned limestone handstone from Level 12. Those from Level 3 occurred together in a concentration of artifacts and, in

spite of being relatively close to the surface, all evidence indicates that they were in primary context. The one from Level 12 was clearly *in situ*, some 60 cm below the surface of the site.

The most complete is the basalt handstone (fig. 9-28*a*), which exhibits both pecking and extensive grinding on both surfaces and around its edges. The marked concavity of its dorsal surface suggests that it may have been formed from an exhausted quern. The larger basalt piece, measuring ca. 164 mm in diameter and ca. 50 mm in thickness, is quite

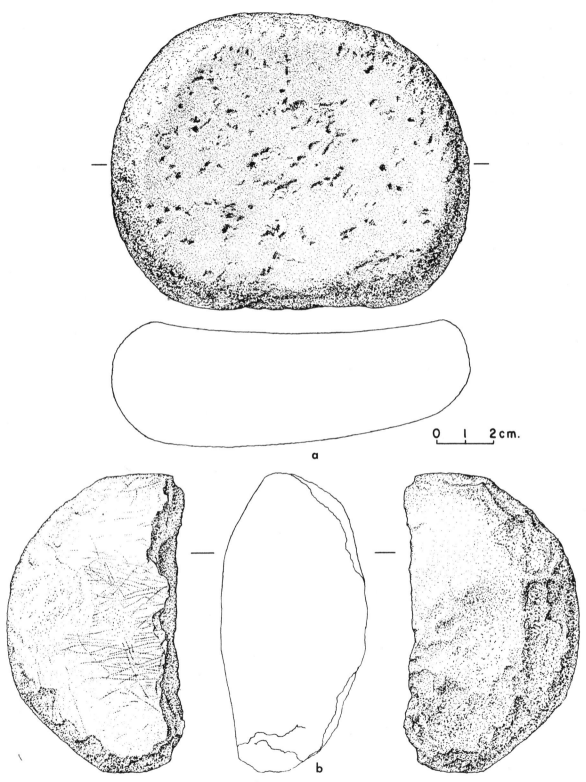

FIG. 9-28—Groundstone from Site Ein Aqev (D31): *a*—basalt handstone; *b*—limestone cobble showing use striations.

poorly shaped. While there is a well-utilized concave dorsal surface extending across the whole of the piece, the edges are not regular and there is some obvious wear extending over the edges of the concave basin onto the convex-shaped sides. Originally, the piece must have been roughly circular in shape, but about one-third of it is missing. These two basalt pieces articulate well with each other and seem to be meant to be used together.

The limestone handstone is in poor condition, but both polish and use striations are visible on its utilized surface (fig. 9-28b). Unlike the basalt examples, there are minimal signs of shaping by circumferential battering, although this is somewhat obscured by thermal damage.

SUMMARY

Because of the exceptional condition of Ein Aqev, more descriptive material has been presented for it than the other Upper Paleolithic sites. Out of this myriad of detail, a number of observations stand out which warrant emphasis.

GENERAL CONSIDERATIONS

The site of Ein Aqev has been firmly dated to the sixteenth millennium B.C. by multiple radiocarbon determinations. It represents a highly traditional site locality, occupied on a number of occasions for short periods of time. As there is no significant variability in the technological, typological, or stylistic parameters within the various occupation levels, it may be assumed that each occupation was by the same cultural group, and even, perhaps, the same ongoing residential unit. The assemblages are typologically and stylistically unique in the survey zone, indicating that this specific locality was the only one in the area occupied by this group.

While the faunal sample is poor, it does indicate that a number of microenvironments were exploited. This was perhaps necessary given the pollen data which tends to suggest rather dry steppe conditions.

The presence of basalt grinding stones and Mediterranean shells indicates either considerable movement during yearly travels or the existence of some form of trade network.

TYPOLOGY AND TECHNOLOGY

The assemblages from Ein Aqev exhibit a rather crude blade technology accompanied by a complex and varied typological inventory. While this inventory remains rather constant throughout the deposits, there are statistically significant differences in tool samples between some excavation levels and others. Given the present data, however, these differences cannot be correlated with different activities or exploitative practices.

Typologically, two elements stand out: *lamelles Dufour* and various carinated tool forms. Along with these elements, there is a wide range of other tool forms and size, from nongeometric microliths to large cobble choppers, and the tendency toward blade tools, *sensu stricto*, is only moderate. When combined with microliths, however, usually half or more of all tools were produced on blades (*sensu lato*). It should be emphasized that there is a typological gradation between the various carinated tool forms, and it is unlikely that truly discrete types exist within this group.

Stylistically, tools show some characteristic patterns: *lamelles Dufour* are almost always inversely retouched along the left edge, a high percentage of carinated tools have an unmodified dorsal surface as the platform for secondary retouch, and thin scrapers exhibit flat, invasive to semisteep retouch, with inverse treatment extremely rare.

Technologically, typologically, and stylistically, these assemblages are fully within the Levantine Upper Paleolithic tradition and show little tendency toward true Epipaleolithic patterns. Even the microliths, for the most part, are derived from Upper Paleolithic secondary retouch technique, rather than from bladelet core technology.

BIBLIOGRAPHY

BREZILLON, M., 1968. *La dénomination des objets de pierre taillée*. Paris: CNRS.

Appendix A
Detailed Typology by Excavation Levels

Level 1

Type	Bladelet	Blade	Primary Element	Flake	Core Trimming Element	Core	Total	Percent
Simple endscraper, typical		1					1	4.00
Simple endscraper, atypical				1			1	4.00
Simple endscraper, lateral				1			1	4.00
Endscraper on retouched piece			1				1	4.00
Ogival endscraper		1		1			2	8.00
Carinated scraper, typical		1		1			2	8.00
Lateral carinated scraper, typical				1		1	2	8.00
Double carinated scraper			1				1	4.00
Burin, dihedral, angle				1			1	4.00
Burin, dihedral, angle, multifaceted			1				1	4.00
Burin, dihedral		2	1				3	12.00
Burin, dihedral, multifaceted				1			1	4.00
Burin, carinated				1			1	4.00
Notch, retouched		1					1	4.00
Multiple notch, retouched			1				1	4.00
Denticulate, lateral		1					1	4.00
Denticulate, converging			1				1	4.00
Retouched piece, lateral, obverse				1			1	4.00
Retouched piece, lateral, inverse		1					1	4.00
Backed bladelet fragment	1						1	4.00
Total	1	8	6	9		1	25	
Percent	4.0	32.0	24.0	36.0		4.0		100.00

Level 2

Type	Bladelet	Blade	Primary Element	Flake	Core Trim- ming Element	Core	Total	Percent
Simple endscraper, typical		1	1				2	2.60
Simple endscraper, atypical			1	3			4	5.19
Simple endscraper, oblique		1					1	1.30
Endscraper on retouched piece		1		1			2	2.60
Endscraper on retouched piece, oblique			1				1	1.30
Ogival endscraper		1		1			2	2.60
Thin nosed scraper		1					1	1.30
Double flat endscraper					1		1	1.30
Carinated scraper, typical			1	1		2	4	5.19
Carinated scraper, atypical					1	1	2	2.60
Core scraper						1	1	1.30
Endscraper/Burin			1	1			2	2.60
Burin, dihedral, multifaceted		1		2			3	3.89
Burin, on snap		1		1			2	2.60
Burin, on straight truncation			1				1	1.30
Burin, transverse on lateral truncation					2		2	2.60
Burin, Corbiac		1					1	1.30
Burin, carinated		1		2			3	3.89
Burin, multiple on truncation			1				1	1.30
Burin, multiple mixed		2					2	2.60
Perforator				1			1	1.30
Arch-tipped blade		2					2	2.60
Arch-backed blade		1					1	1.30
Blade with rounded base		1					1	1.30
Notch, single blow			1	2			3	3.89
Denticulate, lateral		2		2			4	5.19
Denticulate, converging				1			1	1.30
Retouched piece, lateral, obverse		2		1	2		5	6.49
Retouched piece, lateral, inverse		1					1	1.30
Retouched piece, distal, inverse				2			2	2.60
Retouched piece, alternate		1					1	1.30
Lamelle Dufour, alternate	3						3	3.89
Lamelle Dufour, inverse	8						8	10.39
Partially backed bladelet	1						1	1.30
Pointed bladelet with retouched tip	1						1	1.30
Battered piece		2			1		3	3.89
Chopper						1	1	1.30
Total	13	23	8	21	7	5	77	
Percent	16.88	29.87	10.39	27.27	9.09	6.49		100.00

Level 3

Type	Bladelet	Blade	Primary Element	Flake	Core Trimming Element	Core	Total	Percent
Simple endscraper, typical		2	1	3			6	5.56
Simple endscraper, atypical				1			1	0.93
Simple endscraper, straight			1				1	0.93
Endscraper on retouched piece				2			2	1.85
Ogival endscraper			1				1	0.93
Unilateral endscraper				1			1	0.93
Bilateral endscraper				1			1	0.93
Double flat endscraper		1					1	0.93
Carinated scraper, typical			3	4	1		8	7.41
Carinated scraper, atypical		1		2	1	1	5	4.63
Lateral carinated scraper, typical				2		1	3	2.78
Double carinated scraper						1	1	0.93
Thick shouldered scraper				1			1	0.93
Thick nosed scraper		1	1				2	1.85
Core scraper						2	2	1.85
Endscraper/Burin				2			2	1.85
Burin/Truncation				1			1	0.93
Burin, dihedral, multifaceted		2	1				3	2.78
Burin, on snap			1	1			2	1.85
Burin, on natural surface		2		2			4	3.70
Burin, on convex truncation		1		1			2	1.85
Burin, on concave truncation				1			1	0.93
Burin, on concave truncation, multifaceted				1			1	0.93
Burin, carinated		1		2	1		4	3.47
Burin, multiple mixed			1				1	0.93
Perforator				2			2	1.85
Truncated piece			1	1			2	1.85
Arch-tipped blade		1					1	0.93
Partially backed blade		1					1	0.93
Notch, retouched		1					1	0.93
Notch, single blow				1			1	0.93
Multiple notch, retouched		2					2	1.85
Multiple notch, single blow		1	1	1			3	2.78
Denticulate, end				1			1	0.93
Denticulate, lateral			3	1	2		6	5.56
Retouched piece, lateral, obverse		2		3			5	4.63
Retouched piece, lateral, inverse		2					2	1.85
Retouched piece, bilateral		1					1	0.93
Retouched piece, transverse				1			1	0.93
Retouched piece, alternate				1			1	0.93
Lamelle Dufour, alternate	4						4	3.47
Lamelle Dufour, inverse	7						7	6.48
Retouched microblade	6						6	5.56

PREHISTORY AND PALEOENVIRONMENTS IN THE CENTRAL NEGEV

Type	Bladelet	Blade	Primary Element	Flake	Core Trimming Element	Core	Total	Percent
Battered piece		1	1				2	1.85
Varia				1	1		2	1.85
Total	17	23	16	41	6	5	108	
Percent	15.74	21.30	14.81	37.96	5.56	4.63		99.61

Level 4

Type	Bladelet	Blade	Primary Element	Flake	Core Trimming Element	Core	Total	Percent
Simple endscraper, typical		1	1	5			7	4.61
Simple endscraper, atypical			2	2			4	2.63
Simple endscraper, lateral				2			2	1.32
Endscraper on retouched piece		1	1	2			4	2.63
Ogival endscraper			1	3			4	2.63
Unilateral endscraper			1				1	0.66
Bilateral endscraper				3			3	1.97
Endscraper on notch		1					1	0.66
Thin nosed scraper			1				1	0.66
Double flat endscraper		3					3	1.97
Carinated scraper, typical		1		13	1	1	16	10.53
Carinated scraper, atypical				1	2		3	1.97
Lateral carinated scraper, typical		2		5			7	4.61
Double carinated scraper				1			1	0.66
Core scraper						2	2	1.32
Endscraper/Burin			1	3			4	2.63
Burin, dihedral		1		3			4	2.63
Burin, dihedral, multifaceted			1	4			5	3.29
Burin, on snap		2		3			5	3.29
Burin, transverse on natural surface				1			1	0.66
Burin, on straight oblique truncation			1				1	0.66
Burin, on convex truncation		1					1	0.66
Burin, Corbiac				1			1	0.66
Burin, busquoid		1	1	2			4	2.63
Burin, carinated		2	6	2	2		12	7.89
Perforator	1			2			3	1.97
Truncated piece				1			1	0.66
Notch, retouched			2	4			6	3.95
Multiple notch, retouched			1	1			2	1.32
Multiple notch, single blow			1	1			2	1.32
Denticulate, end				2			2	1.32
Denticulate, lateral		2		2			4	2.63
Denticulate, bilateral				1			1	0.66
Denticulate core scraper						1	1	0.66
Retouched piece, lateral, obverse		1	1	2			4	2.63

Retouched piece, lateral, inverse				1		1	0.66
Retouched piece, bilateral		1				1	0.66
Retouched piece, alternate		1				1	0.66
Retouched piece, transverse				1		1	0.66
Lamelle Dufour, alternate	5					5	3.29
Lamelle Dufour, inverse	9					9	5.92
Retouched microblade	4					4	2.63
Battered piece		2	1	2		5	3.29
Varia				2		2	1.32
Total	19	23	23	78	5	4	152
Percent	12.50	15.13	15.13	51.32	3.29	2.63	100.04

Level 5

Type	Bladelet	Blade	Primary Element	Flake	Core Trimming Element	Core	Total	Percent
Simple endscraper, typical		6	4	2			12	6.86
Simple endscraper, atypical			1	6			7	4.00
Simple endscraper, lateral				2			2	1.14
Simple endscraper, oblique		1					1	0.57
Endscraper on retouched piece		4		2			6	3.43
Endscraper on retouched piece, straight				1			1	0.57
Ogival endscraper		6	1	3			10	5.71
Unilateral endscraper				1			1	0.57
Bilateral endscraper				1			1	0.57
Endscraper on notch				1			1	0.57
Double flat endscraper		1	1				2	1.14
Carinated scraper, typical		1		6			7	4.00
Carinated scraper, atypical		1	1	2		1	5	2.86
Lateral carinated scraper, typical			1	6			7	4.00
Double carinated scraper			2	1			3	1.71
Thick nosed scraper				1		1	2	1.14
Sidescraper					1		1	0.57
Core scraper						1	1	0.57
Endscraper/Burin		2	1	1			4	2.29
Burin/Truncation			1				1	0.57
Burin, dihedral		1	2	1			4	2.29
Burin, dihedral, multifaceted		1	1	2	1		5	2.86
Burin, on snap				4			4	2.29
Burin, on snap, multifaceted				1			1	0.57
Burin, on natural surface					1		1	0.57
Burin, transverse on natural surface		1		1			2	1.14
Burin, on straight oblique truncation		3		2			5	2.86

Burin, on straight oblique truncation, multifaceted		1		1			2	1.14
Burin, on concave truncation		1		1			2	1.14
Burin, on concave truncation, multifaceted		1					1	0.57
Burin, Corbiac			1				1	0.57
Burin, busquoid				1			1	0.57
Burin, carinated		1		3			4	2.29
Burin, multiple on truncation		2					2	1.14
Burin, multiple mixed				1			1	0.57
Perforator			2	1			3	1.71
Truncated piece		2		2	1		5	2.86
Arch-tipped blade		1					1	0.57
Notch, retouched		2	3				5	2.86
Notch, single blow		1	3	1			5	2.86
Denticulate, end			1				1	0.57
Denticulate, lateral		2		1			3	1.71
Denticulate, bilateral		1					1	0.57
Denticulate, converging			1				1	0.57
Denticulate, transverse		4	1	3			8	4.57
Retouched piece, lateral, obverse		1		1			2	1.14
Retouched piece, bilateral		1					1	0.57
Lamelle Dufour, alternate	6						6	3.43
Lamelle Dufour, inverse	7						7	4.00
Retouched microblade	4						4	2.29
Partially backed bladelet	1						1	0.57
Backed and truncated bladelet	1						1	0.57
Battered piece		2		2			4	2.29
Chopper						4	4	2.29
Varia				1			1	0.57
Total	19	51	28	66	4	7	175	
Percent	12.00	29.71	14.29	37.71	2.29	4.00		99.98

Level 6

Type	Bladelet	Blade	Primary Element	Flake	Core Trimming Element	Core	Total	Percent
Simple endscraper, typical		3		1			4	2.94
Simple endscraper, atypical				2			2	1.47
Simple endscraper, lateral				2			2	1.47
Simple endscraper, oblique				1			1	0.74
Simple endscraper, straight		1		1			2	1.47
Endscraper on retouched piece		4		4	1		9	6.62
Endscraper on retouched piece, straight				1			1	0.74
Ogival endscraper			1	1			2	1.47
Bilateral endscraper			1	1			2	1.47
Endscraper on notch				1			1	0.74

Thin nosed scraper		1			1		2	1.47
Double flat endscraper		1	2				3	2.21
Carinated scraper, typical			2	4			6	4.41
Carinated scraper, atypical				1			1	0.74
Lateral carinated scraper, typical			1	4		3	8	5.88
Lateral carinated scraper, atypical				1		1	2	1.47
Thick shouldered scraper						1	1	0.74
Sidescraper				1			1	0.74
Endscraper/Burin			1	1			2	1.47
Burin, dihedral, angle		1					1	0.74
Burin, dihedral			1				1	0.74
Burin, dihedral, multifaceted		1		2			3	2.21
Burin, on snap		1					1	0.74
Burin, transverse on snap			1				1	0.74
Burin, on natural surface		1					1	0.74
Burin, on natural surface, multifaceted					1		1	0.74
Burin, on straight oblique truncation				1			1	0.74
Burin, on concave truncation			1	1			2	1.47
Burin, on convex truncation		1	1				2	1.47
Burin, transverse on lateral truncation		1					1	0.74
Burin, carinated				3	2		5	3.68
Burin, multiple mixed		1					1	0.74
Perforator				2			2	1.47
Truncated piece		3					3	2.21
Notch, retouched		1		1			2	1.47
Notch, single blow		1	1				2	1.47
Multiple notch, single blow		1	2	1			4	2.94
Denticulate, end				1			1	0.74
Denticulate, lateral				1			1	0.74
Denticulate, bilateral		1					1	0.74
Denticulate, converging			1				1	0.74
Denticulate core scraper						1	1	0.74
Retouched piece, lateral, obverse		6		5			11	8.09
Retouched piece, lateral, inverse		2		1			3	2.21
Lamelle Dufour, alternate	6						6	4.41
Lamelle Dufour, inverse	7						7	5.15
Retouched microblade	3						3	2.21
Backed bladelet fragment	1						1	0.74
Partially backed bladelet	1						1	0.74
Microgravette point	1						1	0.74
Battered piece		2	3	1			6	4.41
Chopper						3	3	2.21
Varia		2		1			3	2.21

	Bladelet	Blade	Primary Element	Flake	Core Trimming Element	Core	Total	Percent
Total	19	36	17	50	5	9	136	
Percent	13.97	26.47	12.50	36.76	3.68	6.62		100.13

Level 7

Type	Bladelet	Blade	Primary Element	Flake	Core Trimming Element	Core	Total	Percent
Simple endscraper, typical		1	1	1			3	2.83
Simple endscraper, atypical		2					2	1.89
Endscraper on retouched piece		1		1			2	1.89
Endscraper on retouched piece, straight				1			1	0.94
Ogival endscraper		2		2			4	3.77
Unilateral endscraper			1	1			2	1.89
Bilateral endscraper				1			1	0.94
Carinated scraper, typical		1	1	1		1	4	3.77
Carinated scraper, atypical			1	2		1	4	3.77
Lateral carinated scraper, typical			1	4		1	6	5.66
Lateral carinated scraper, atypical			1	2			3	2.83
Double carinated scraper				1			1	0.94
Sidescraper				2			2	1.89
Burin, dihedral, multifaceted			2	1			3	2.83
Burin, on snap		1		1			2	1.89
Burin, Corbiac				1			1	0.94
Burin, busquoid				2			2	1.89
Burin, carinated		2		1			3	2.83
Burin, multiple on truncation					1		1	0.94
Truncated piece				1			1	0.94
Arch-backed blade		1					1	0.94
Backed and truncated blade		1					1	0.94
Notch, retouched				1			1	0.94
Notch, single blow				1			1	0.94
Multiple notch, single blow		1					1	0.94
Denticulate, end				1			1	0.94
Denticulate, lateral		2		3			5	4.72
Denticulate, transverse			1	1			2	1.89
Retouched piece, lateral, obverse		4	1	5			10	9.43
Retouched piece, lateral, inverse		1					1	0.94
Retouched piece, alternate		1					1	0.94
Retouched piece, bilateral		2					2	1.89
Aurignacian retouched piece				1			1	0.94
Lamelle Dufour, alternate	3						3	2.83
Lamelle Dufour, inverse	12						12	11.32
Retouched microblade	3						3	2.83
Arch-backed bladelet	1						1	0.94
Backed bladelet fragment	1						1	0.94

Type	Bladelet	Blade	Primary Element	Flake	Core Trimming Element	Core	Total	Percent
Backed and truncated bladelet	1						1	0.94
Battered piece		3		1			4	3.77
Chopper						1	1	0.94
Varia		1	1	2			4	3.77
Total	21	27	11	42	1	4	106	
Percent	19.81	25.47	10.37	39.62	0.94	3.77		99.94

Level 8

Type	Bladelet	Blade	Primary Element	Flake	Core Trimming Element	Core	Total	Percent
Simple endscraper, typical		4		4			8	4.82
Simple endscraper, atypical		2		3			5	3.01
Simple endscraper, lateral			1	1			2	1.20
Simple endscraper, oblique				2			2	1.20
Endscraper on retouched piece		3	1	1			5	3.01
Endscraper on retouched piece, oblique		1					1	0.60
Ogival endscraper		3		1			4	2.41
Unilateral endscraper				1			1	0.60
Circular scraper				1			1	0.60
Thin nosed scraper		1		2			3	1.81
Double flat endscraper			1	3			4	2.41
Carinated scraper, typical				8			8	4.82
Carinated scraper, atypical				1		1	2	1.20
Lateral carinated scraper, typical		1	2	4			7	4.22
Double carinated scraper						2	2	1.20
Thick shouldered scraper		1					1	0.60
Core scraper						1	1	0.60
Endscraper/Burin		1	3	2		1	7	4.22
Endscraper/Truncation		1					1	0.60
Burin/Arch-tipped blade		1					1	0.60
Burin, dihedral				1			1	0.60
Burin, dihedral, multifaceted			1	2			3	1.81
Burin, on snap		2					2	1.20
Burin, on straight oblique truncation					1		1	0.60
Burin, transverse on lateral truncation				1		1	2	1.20
Burin, busquoid				1			1	0.60
Burin, carinated		1		2			3	1.81
Burin, multiple dihedral, multifaceted			1				1	0.60
Burin, multiple mixed		1					1	0.60
Perforator			1				1	0.60
Truncated piece		1					1	0.60

Type							Total	Percent
Notch, retouched		1	1				2	1.20
Notch, single blow		1		1			2	1.20
Multiple notch, retouched		1	1				2	1.20
Multiple notch, single blow				2			2	1.20
Denticulate, end				1			1	0.60
Denticulate, lateral			2		1		3	1.81
Denticulate, converging				1			1	0.60
Denticulate, transverse				3			3	1.81
Retouched piece, lateral, obverse		4	2	8			14	8.43
Retouched piece, lateral, inverse	1	2		2			5	3.01
Lamelle Dufour, alternate	16						16	9.64
Lamelle Dufour, inverse	15						15	9.04
Retouched microblade	6						6	3.61
Backed bladelet fragment	2						2	1.20
Backed and truncated bladelet	1						1	0.60
Battered piece				1			1	0.60
Chopper						2	2	1.20
Varia		1		4			5	3.01
Total	41	35	16	64	2	8	166	
Percent	24.70	21.08	9.64	38.55	1.20	4.82		99.91

Level 9

Type	Bladelet	Blade	Primary Element	Flake	Core Trimming Element	Core	Total	Percent
Simple endscraper, typical		2	1	1	2		6	6.98
Simple endscraper, oblique		1		1			2	2.33
Endscraper on retouched piece		3	1	1			5	5.81
Ogival endscraper		3		1			4	4.65
Bilateral endscraper				1			1	1.16
Carinated scraper, typical		1		3			4	4.65
Carinated scraper, atypical			3	3		2	8	9.30
Lateral carinated scraper, typical			1	2			3	3.49
Burin, dihedral, angle				1			1	1.16
Burin, on natural surface						1	1	1.16
Burin, on straight truncation		1					1	1.16
Burin, on straight oblique truncation		2					2	2.33
Burin, on concave truncation			1				1	1.16
Burin, on convex truncation				1			1	1.16
Burin, transverse on lateral truncation				1			1	1.16
Burin, carinated				3			3	3.49
Burin, multiple mixed				1			1	1.16
Truncated piece	1			1			2	2.33
Notch, retouched			1				1	1.16

Type	Bladelet	Blade	Primary Element	Flake	Core Trimming Element	Core	Total	Percent
Notch, single blow		2					2	2.33
Multiple notch, retouched				1			1	1.16
Multiple notch, single blow		1		2			3	3.49
Denticulate, lateral		3	1				4	4.65
Denticulate, bilateral		1					1	1.16
Retouched piece, lateral, obverse		4	1	2			7	8.14
Lamelle Dufour, alternate	7						7	8.14
Lamelle Dufour, inverse	8						8	9.30
Retouched microblade	2						2	2.33
Battered piece		1	1	1			3	3.49
Total	18	25	11	27	2	3	86	
Percent	20.93	29.07	12.79	31.40	2.33	3.49		99.99

Level 10

Type	Bladelet	Blade	Primary Element	Flake	Core Trimming Element	Core	Total	Percent
Simple endscraper, typical		1	2	8			11	9.17
Simple endscraper, atypical				1			1	0.83
Simple endscraper, oblique			1	1			2	1.67
Endscraper on retouched piece		1		1			2	1.67
Endscraper on retouched piece, oblique				1			1	0.83
Ogival endscraper		2		3			5	4.17
Unilateral endscraper				1			1	0.83
Double flat endscraper		1		1			2	1.67
Carinated scraper, typical			1	2		1	4	3.33
Carinated scraper, atypical	1						1	0.83
Lateral carinated scraper, typical				3			3	2.50
Double carinated scraper						1	1	0.83
Thick nosed scraper	1					1	2	1.67
Core scraper						2	2	1.67
Endscraper/Burin			1				1	0.83
Burin, dihedral, angle, multifaceted			1	1			2	1.67
Burin, dihedral, multifaceted				2			2	1.67
Burin, on snap		2		4			6	5.00
Burin, on snap, multifaceted				1			1	0.83
Burin, on natural surface		1					1	0.83
Burin, on convex truncation			1				1	0.83
Burin, busquoid		1	1				2	1.67
Burin, carinated		1		1			2	1.67
Perforator				2			2	1.67
Truncated piece			1	2			3	2.50
Arch-backed blade		3					3	2.50
Blunt-backed blade		1					1	0.83
Partially backed blade		2					2	1.67

Notch, retouched		3		1		4	3.33
Notch, single blow		2		1		3	2.50
Multiple notch, single blow			2			2	1.67
Denticulate, end				1		1	0.83
Denticulate, lateral		2	2	5		9	7.50
Denticulate, bilateral		1				1	0.83
Denticulate, converging				1		1	0.83
Retouched piece, lateral, obverse	1	2				3	2.50
Retouched piece, lateral, inverse		2	1			3	2.50
Retouched piece, bilateral		2				2	1.67
Lamelle Dufour, alternate	4					4	3.33
Lamelle Dufour, inverse	7					7	5.83
Retouched microblade	4					4	3.33
Partially backed bladelet	1					1	0.83
Bladelet with rounded base	1					1	0.83
Battered piece				1		1	0.83
Varia		1	1	3	1	6	5.00
Total	18	33	15	48	6	120	
Percent	15.00	27.50	12.50	40.00	5.00		99.98

Level 11

Type	Bladelet	Blade	Primary Element	Flake	Core Trim- ming Element	Core	Total	Percent
Simple endscraper, typical		5		2			7	8.64
Simple endscraper, atypical		1		1			2	2.47
Simple endscraper, oblique				1			1	1.23
Simple endscraper, straight				1			1	1.23
Endscraper on retouched piece		1					1	1.23
Ogival endscraper		1		3		1	5	6.17
Unilateral endscraper				1			1	1.23
Double flat endscraper		1					1	1.23
Carinated scraper, typical			1				1	1.23
Lateral carinated scraper, typical				1			1	1.23
Double carinated scraper			1				1	1.23
Thick shouldered scraper				1			1	1.23
Core scraper						1	1	1.23
Endscraper/Burin		1					1	1.23
Burin/Arch-tipped blade		1					1	1.23
Burin, dihedral, angle				1			1	1.23
Burin, on snap		1		3			4	4.94
Burin, on natural surface				1			1	1.23
Burin, carinated		1	1	1	1		4	4.94
Perforator				1			1	1.23
Truncated piece	1	1		2			4	4.94
Arch-tipped blade		1					1	1.23

Type	Bladelet	Blade	Primary Element	Flake	Core Trimming Element	Core	Total	Percent
Partially backed blade		1					1	1.23
Notch, retouched			1				1	1.23
Denticulate, lateral		1	1				2	2.47
Denticulate, bilateral			1				1	1.23
Denticulate, transverse				1			1	1.23
Retouched piece, lateral, obverse		4		4			8	9.88
Retouched piece, lateral, inverse		1		1			2	2.47
Retouched piece, transverse			1	1			2	2.47
Lamelle Dufour, alternate	6						6	7.41
Lamelle Dufour, inverse	8						8	9.88
Retouched microblade	2						2	2.47
Backed bladelet fragment	1						1	1.23
Microburin	1						1	1.23
Battered piece		1					1	1.23
Varia		1		1			2	2.47
Total	19	24	7	28	1	2	81	
Percent	23.46	29.63	8.64	34.57	1.23	2.37		99.91

Level 12

Type	Bladelet	Blade	Primary Element	Flake	Core Trimming Element	Core	Total	Percent
Simple endscraper, typical				1			1	1.85
Simple endscraper, atypical				1			1	1.85
Ogival endscraper		3					3	5.56
Bilateral endscraper				1			1	1.85
Carinated scraper, typical			1	1			2	3.70
Lateral carinated scraper, typical				2		1	3	5.56
Endscraper/Burin		1					1	1.85
Burin, dihedral, angle				1			1	1.85
Burin, dihedral, angle, multifaceted				1			1	1.85
Burin, dihedral		1					1	1.85
Burin, dihedral, multifaceted				1			1	1.85
Burin, on snap		1		1			2	3.70
Burin, on convex truncation		1					1	1.85
Burin, Corbiac				1			1	1.85
Burin, carinated				1			1	1.85
Truncated piece		1					1	1.85
Arch-backed blade		1					1	1.85
Notch, retouched	1			1			2	3.70
Notch, single blow				1			1	1.85
Multiple notch, retouched		1					1	1.85
Denticulate, lateral		1		2			3	5.56
Denticulate core scraper						1	1	1.85
Retouched piece, lateral, obverse		3		2	1		6	11.11

Retouched piece, lateral, inverse	3						3	5.56
Aurignacian retouched piece	1						1	1.85
Lamelle Dufour, alternate	4						4	7.41
Lamelle Dufour, inverse	3						3	5.56
Retouched microblade	1						1	1.85
Arch-backed bladelet	1						1	1.85
Partially backed bladelet	1						1	1.85
Chopper						1	1	1.85
Battered piece			1				1	1.85
Varia			1				1	1.85
Total	11	18	3	18	1	3	54	
Percent	20.37	33.33	5.56	33.33	1.85	5.56		99.97

Appendix B

DESCRIPTIVE STATISTICS

J. Anne Attebury

Southern Methodist University

INTRODUCTION

This study will present some descriptive statistics of the lithic artifacts from Site Ein Aqev. The definition of terms utilized are those provided in the Glossary to this volume.

From the debitage, only blades and flakes were selected for statistical description. Primary flakes were rejected because of the small sample size, and microblades were rejected because they do not meet all the conditions of the definition of "debitage," since they were derived from something other than a true core. From the subset of blade and flake debitage, all broken pieces were excluded, because this served as an effective method for limiting the rather large sample size. The resulting debitage sample totals 2,588 pieces.

For the tools, all pieces were considered except for the varia, with incomplete pieces included if even one measurement could be taken. The resulting tool sample totals 789 pieces. Cores were excluded from the analysis because the sample size was small.

STATISTICAL DESCRIPTION OF THE DATA

During the initial stages of the analysis, the debitage was divided into flakes and blades. The plotted values of the debitage as a body (fig. 9-29), however, did not reveal that any natural clustering exists within this particular site. A comparable procedure for the tools also failed to reveal any distinct clustering in terms of length and width, with the exception of the *lamelles Dufour* blanks (fig. 9-30). This is significant in a consideration of the debitage, since the definitions used to separate "blades" from "flakes" are based solely on arbitrary cutoff points determined by these two measurements. After it became apparent that a separation of the data into groups based on blank type within the respective classes was not statistically demonstrable, the procedure was discontinued. The results obtained in this manner, however, are presented for communicative purposes, although the debitage is also treated as a single unit.

Blades and flakes are considerably different in the mean values associated with the groups of debitage

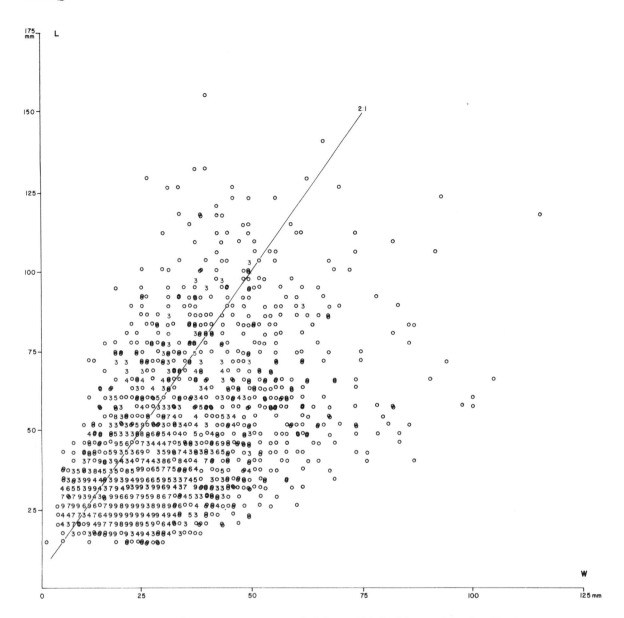

FIG. 9-29—Length/Width scattergram of all flake and blade debitage from Site Ein Aqev.

(table 9-17). The blades are very narrow in relation to their lengths, and width appears to be better controlled in this group than in the flake category, as illustrated by the lower standard deviations. Conversely, flakes exhibit less deviation in length and are considerably wider. The relationship between length and width is extremely high in the blade category with high linear correlation coefficients across all twelve levels. Although the relationship in the flake category is lower, it is still meaningful. For compara-

tive purposes, histograms for length, width, and length/width ratio of both the debitage and tools, divided into two groups on the basis of blade and flake blank types, have been provided (fig. 9-31).

One problem which arose during the course of this description was the assignment of appropriate intervals for a histogram of length/width ratio. Although interval size is an arbitrary decision, the intervals should be equal spatially, so that the probability that a piece will fall within one interval is equal to the

TABLE 9-17
Descriptive Statistics: Debitage Blades and Flakes

A. Blades

Level	Number	Mean Length	S.D.	Mean Width	S.D.	Mean L/W Ratio	S.D.	Pearson
1	24	49.5417	26.8376	19.0000	10.5666	2.7639	0.7031	.8839
2	45	55.4444	27.2643	22.4444	11.3969	2.5197	0.4399	.9294
3	74	45.0676	24.6645	18.3108	10.7409	2.5729	0.6368	.9270
4	163	54.8528	22.9802	21.2025	9.5692	2.6790	0.5863	.8638
5	79	59.2152	29.9477	24.1013	11.5577	2.4937	0.5417	.8487
6	50	58.3600	31.5658	23.2200	13.9493	2.6381	0.6948	.9343
7	71	57.4507	23.7148	22.4648	10.5056	2.6452	0.5551	.8921
8	62	57.9194	30.0084	22.0000	11.9329	2.7555	0.6626	.9051
9	41	56.5610	26.4698	22.1220	11.2477	2.6327	0.4419	.8865
10	57	54.7544	32.0954	20.1579	10.7118	2.7267	0.6052	.8532
11	40	47.5000	27.4703	18.1250	10.7111	2.6650	0.5718	.9334
12	32	48.7500	28.7671	19.7813	13.3023	2.6187	0.7049	.8891
Total	738	54.3713	27.2525	21.2940	11.1551	2.6396	0.5953	.8879

B. Flakes

Level	Number	Mean Length	S.D.	Mean Width	S.D.	Mean L/W Ratio	S.D.	Pearson
1	63	34.2742	15.7773	30.4032	13.3471	1.1720	0.3296	.7056
2	123	40.2439	19.0948	34.5691	14.2139	1.1818	0.3349	.7724
3	213	33.7136	15.4201	30.8169	12.4024	1.1275	0.3573	.6340
4	283	38.4382	15.5374	32.0601	11.6889	1.2511	0.3608	.6302
5	202	40.0792	18.7824	33.7673	14.3086	1.2229	0.3538	.7358
6	181	34.3094	18.5039	33.0663	16.2787	1.0812	0.3569	.7715
7	171	41.8363	20.4231	35.7427	13.8311	1.2021	0.4144	.6032
8	184	38.6576	19.5148	35.1141	15.2101	1.1285	0.3467	.7747
9	142	40.7324	22.3797	34.2746	14.5423	1.2000	0.3978	.7423
10	125	37.1280	20.4048	33.2720	16.8936	1.1607	0.3736	.7110
11	90	33.8889	16.7113	32.3111	15.4888	1.0900	0.3235	.7337
12	74	32.7973	15.3248	33.4189	15.9021	1.0271	0.3191	.6804
Total	1,850	37.6265	18.4784	33.2757	14.3312	1.1663	0.3697	.7040

probability that the same piece will fall within any other interval. Initially, the variable was assigned intervals which varied by 0.5, however, this did not yield intervals that were equal (fig. 9-32a). To correct this, a new set of intervals was assigned, based on the tangents of multiples of six-degree angles (fig. 9-32b).

The choice of the angle is, of course, arbitrary, depending on the size of the intervals desired.

As a class, the debitage from D31 represents a sample with a wide range of variability, as exhibited by the high standard deviations associated with each variable. The total sample yields a mean length of

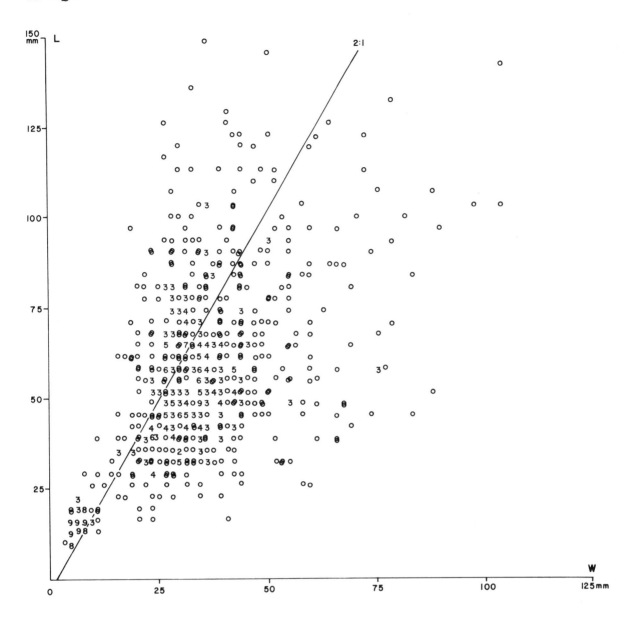

FIG. 9-30—Length/Width scattergram of tool blanks from Site Ein Aqev. Note cluster of small bladelets.

42.40 mm, a mean width of 29.86 mm, and a length/width ratio of 1.5865 (table 9-18). Even though there is considerable variability in terms of what is produced, the majority of pieces fall within more limited ranges. In terms of length, 48.4% of the pieces fall within a range of 20 to 40 mm (fig. 9-33), while 47.2% of the total fall within 15 to 30 mm in width (fig. 9-33). In terms of length/width ratio, 71.4% of the pieces have a ratio less than or equal to 1.9626

(table 9-19), with 46% of the pieces falling within a range of 0.9004 to 1.7321 (fig. 9-33).

The distribution of length/width ratios increases slightly (0.8%) between the intervals 1.3764 to 1.7321 and 1.7321 to 2.2460. The lengths of the pieces represented in the debitage seem to be relatively independent of their widths, with a correlation coefficient (r) of 0.51818 and an associated r^2 of 0.26851. It is improbable, however, that in reality,

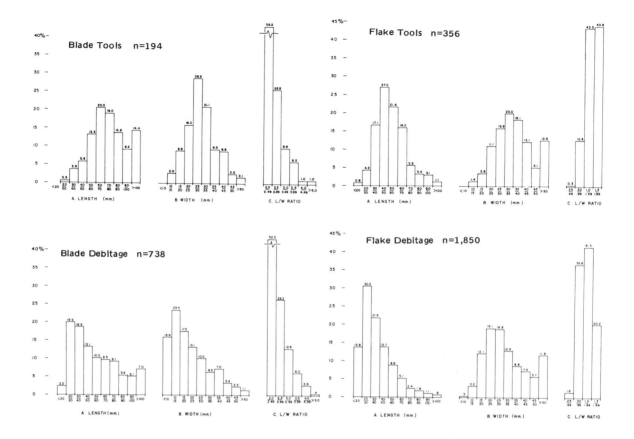

FIG. 9-31—Histograms of length, width, and length/width ratio for debitage and tools at Site Ein Aqev.

even 27% of the variability in length can be explained by the width, because of the heteroscedasticity of the sample, which biases the relationship between two variables upward.

The tool sample, as it once represented a portion of the debitage, illustrates a selection of larger and slightly longer pieces on the part of the makers. This must be taken as a minimal difference, since many pieces were shortened by retouch during the production of tools such as endscrapers and burins. Proportionally, the length/width ratio increases within the tool sample, indicating that less variability was considered desirable in tool production. The overall mean values show a marked increase in larger pieces with a mean length of 60.39 mm, a mean width of 34.68 mm, and a mean length/width ratio of 1.8567 (table 9-18). The standard deviations of the variables generally decrease within this class, indicating that desired blank attributes were more limited in vari-

ability than was the potential blank universe. Of the total observations, 53.5% of the pieces fall within a range of 30 to 60 mm in length (fig. 9-33), and 52.7% fall in a range of 25 to 40 mm in width (fig. 9-33). The distribution of length/width ratios is essentially normal, with 63.9% of the ratios less than or equal to 1.9626 (table 9-19), and 47.9% of the observations falling in a range of 1.3764 to 2.2460 (fig. 9-33). The correlation between length and width increases slightly in this class, with a correlation coefficient (r) of 0.63109, and an associated r^2 of 0.39827. Again, however, these figures are probably biased upward.

The basis on which tools were selected from the debitage seems to be unrelated to length or width in particular; however, selection on the basis of length/width ratio does occur. The relative frequency distribution of debitage for length/width ratio shows a slight bimodality, with the differentiation occurring at approximately the 2:1 line. The total distribution

TABLE 9-18
Descriptive Statistics: Total Sample

A. Debitage

Level	Number	Mean Length	S.D.	Mean Width	S.D.	Mean L/W Ratio	S.D.	Pearson
1	86	38.5439	20.5178	27.2209	13.5841	1.6168	0.8530	—
2	168	44.3155	22.5344	31.3214	14.5196	1.5402	0.6472	—
3	287	36.6411	18.8756	27.5923	13.1720	1.4999	0.7738	—
4	446	44.4372	20.1954	28.0919	12.1375	1.7729	0.8342	—
5	281	45.4591	24.0282	31.0498	14.2525	1.5802	0.7065	—
6	231	39.5152	24.0575	30.9351	16.2898	1.4182	0.7845	—
7	242	46.4174	22.5461	31.8471	14.2723	1.6255	0.8026	—
8	246	43.5122	24.0601	31.8089	15.5180	1.5385	0.8367	—
9	183	44.2787	24.2039	31.5519	14.7464	1.5210	0.7241	—
10	182	42.6484	25.9065	29.1648	16.3773	1.6511	0.8599	—
11	130	38.0769	21.4612	27.9462	15.6013	1.5746	0.8388	—
12	106	37.6132	21.4882	29.3019	16.3592	1.5076	0.8697	—
Total	2,588	42.4015	22.6452	29.8590	14.5436	1.5865	0.8009	.51818

B. Tools

Level	L	W	R	Mean Length	S.D.	Mean Width	S.D.	Mean L/W Ratio	S.D.	Pearson
1	19	19	19	53.8947	23.4115	33.4737	15.2875	1.8077	0.7931	—
2	41	46	41	65.2439	27.0488	29.8478	11.6923	2.3120	0.9248	—
3	59	67	59	60.7119	24.2587	31.8806	11.6743	1.8812	0.7323	—
4	93	99	93	54.3871	16.2180	35.6667	13.6195	1.7131	0.7548	—
5	104	117	104	60.6346	23.3845	34.0427	13.1250	1.8879	0.7849	—
6	77	82	77	60.5584	21.5342	35.3659	13.3088	1.8753	0.8005	—
7	54	59	54	65.2407	24.6477	38.6102	14.4473	1.7802	0.7016	—
8	82	91	81	56.9024	21.5977	34.7582	12.6477	1.7607	0.7908	—
9	50	54	50	59.2000	22.2564	32.4630	20.6695	1.9054	0.6845	—
10	68	70	67	60.2059	24.0190	36.6857	14.7349	1.7374	0.6628	—
11	46	54	46	66.8261	24.4770	35.6296	14.0287	1.8911	0.7953	—
12	31	31	31	67.5806	27.1953	36.0000	15.1658	2.0297	0.6784	—
Total	724	789	722	60.3867	22.9879	34.6781	13.3329	1.8567	0.7680	.63109

does not exhibit this tendency, nor does the distribution of tools, suggesting that the bimodality present in the debitage is due to the selection of pieces from this range for tool production (fig. 9-34).

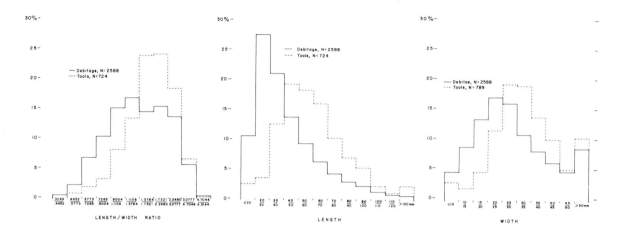

FIG. 9-33—Histograms of length/width ratio, length, and width for all tools and debitage at Site Ein Aqev.

TABLE 9-19
Frequency Distribution of Length/Width Ratios: 9° Angles

Angle Categories	Debitage		Tools		Total	
	Number	Percent	Number	Percent	Number	Percent
.3249 to .5095	31	1.2	4	0.5	35	1.1
.5095 to .7265	206	8.0	15	2.1	221	6.7
.7265 to 1.0000	470	18.2	47	6.5	517	15.6
1.0000 to 1.3764	610	23.6	129	17.9	739	22.4
1.3764 to 1.9626	526	20.4	266	36.9	792	24.0
1.9626 to 3.0777	590	22.8	212	29.4	802	24.3
3.0777 to 6.3138	150	5.8	48	6.7	198	5.9
	2,583	100.0	721	100.0	3,304	100.0

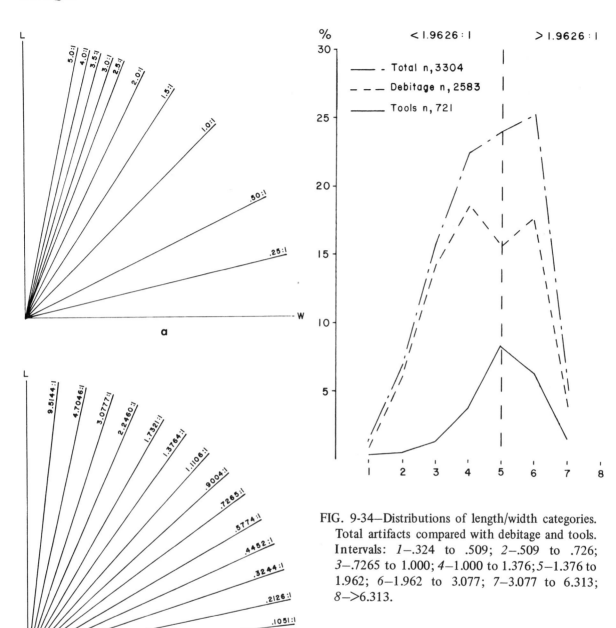

FIG. 9-34—Distributions of length/width categories. Total artifacts compared with debitage and tools. Intervals: *1*—.324 to .509; *2*—.509 to .726; *3*—.7265 to 1.000; *4*—1.000 to 1.376; *5*—1.376 to 1.962; *6*—1.962 to 3.077; *7*—3.077 to 6.313; *8*—>6.313.

FIG. 9-32—Possible length/width intervals: *a*—intervals of 0.5; and *b*—intervals of 6°.

SITE D5: A GEOMETRIC KEBARAN "A" OCCUPATION IN THE NAHAL ZIN

Anthony E. Marks
Southern Methodist University

INTRODUCTION

There are more known Epipaleolithic occurrences in the Levant than in any other major period of Levantine prehistory. Their distribution is extremely widespread: from Jaita II on the northern fringe of the Levant, to well south into Sinai (Bar-Yosef, 1975), and from the Mediterranean coast to the high plateau of Transjordan. Within the Negev, Epipaleolithic sites are numerous, particularly on the broad coastal plain (Bar-Yosef, 1970) and on the high ground of the Har Harif in the Central Negev (Marks, et al., 1972; Marks, in press). Therefore, it was somewhat surprising that the survey of the Avdat/Aqev area recorded only two such sites—D5 and Rosh Zin (D16). The latter site is clearly within the later, Natufian, phase of the Epipaleolithic (Henry, 1973; Henry, this volume), while the former, reported here, is within the earlier Kebaran Complex.

While there is considerable typological variability within the Kebaran Complex, two major phases have been defined: a Kebaran and a Geometric Kebaran "A" (Bar-Yosef, 1970, 1975). The assemblage from D5 appears to fall within the broad typological parameters of the Geometric Kebaran "A" and, as such, is the only assemblage clearly of this type within the whole of the surveyed areas of the Central Negev.

Site D5 is located within the Nahal Zin, at an absolute elevation of 360 m (fig. 10-1). It is situated on a limestone platform, along the northern edge of the present nahal streambed. This platform is ca. 20 m above the present nahal floor and, from the streambed, the site may be reached only by climbing a steep rise.

The platform is part of the larger remnant which forms the western divide between the main northward flowing streambed of the Nahal Zin and the less-developed eastward flowing drainage of the western extension of the East/West Nahal Zin. The site is situated 400 m upstream from this contact point, just before the entrance of the box canyon of the Nahal Mor. Its position provides a spectacular view eastward, down the main portion of the Nahal Zin, and southward into the Nahal Mor. Considering the high cliffs which enclose the main Nahal Zin Complex, the site is positioned so as to maximize visibility and still make the viewed area of quick and simple access. Owing to the narrow entrance into the Nahal Mor, in which are located the only perennial springs in the immediate area, and the position of the site just before its entrance, most megafauna going to the spring would have been seen easily and would have been within quick reach of hunters. The only exception to this would have been *Capra ibex*, which even today approach the springs by going straight down the cliffs of the Nahal Mor.

While it is doubtful that the streambed provided constantly running water during the Epipaleolithic period, the site is located only 850 m downstream from the perennial spring of Ein Mor. Also, a small area of cemented pebbles on the steep northern slope just below the site is suggestive of a small fossil spring. Unfortunately, the area of cementation is minor and no artifacts were found within it.

Flint sources in the area occur in two major zones: along the top and bottom of the cliffs, and low in the cliff within the Nahal Mor (fig.

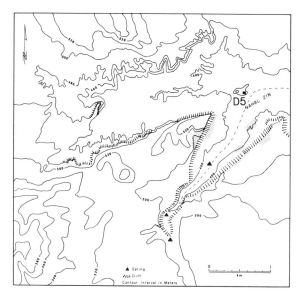

FIG. 10-1—Location of Site D5, within the Nahal
Zin. Shaded areas show flint sources.

10-1). The former source is the major one,
containing large cobbles of a fine-grained,
light-colored flint, while that *in situ* near the
floor of the nahal contains black flint, which
occurs in thin irregular bands, producing small
blocks of rather brittle material. The closest
source of the better flint occurs only 1.2 km
south of the site, both at the base and at the
top of the western cliff of Nahal Mor. Owing
to the cliff height, 150 m, it is most likely
that the flint at the base of the cliff, which is
derived from the top, was that most utilized.
The absence of the black flint at D5 indicates
that the Nahal Mor exposures were not exploited.

Thus, within a little more than 1 km of the
site both a constant source of water and a
major supply of flint were available, while the
topographic configuration of the immediate
area would have highly favored hunters
camped at D5.

The site was located early in the initial
survey (Marks, et al., 1971), by the presence
of a dense surface concentration of artifacts.
This concentration covered the whole of a
small finger which was defined on three sides

by very steep slopes (fig. 10-2). The configuration of the finger spatially limited the
potential site size to ca. 80 sq m, although it
originally may have been a bit larger, owing to
some clear erosion of the northern edge of the
site, seen by a scatter of artifacts down that
slope.

The surface artifacts appear to have been
uncovered for quite some time, as all have a
dark brown patination. The fact that so little
of the site seems to have been washed down
the steep slopes probably is due to the presence of derived conglomerate boulders which
are located around the tip of the finger, preventing the movement of sediments and artifacts over that edge.

During work carried out in 1970, a total of
14 sq m, in one sq m units, was systematically
collected and excavated either to bedrock or
to sterile deposits. Of these, the artifacts from
11 sq m were used as the study sample and
provided the basis for this report.[1]

Owing to the small size of the site and
some surface indications of possible features,
the one sq m units were not randomly placed.
The surface condition suggested that the
northern edge of the site had undergone some
erosion, but this did not seem to be the case
along the southern edge. Thus, it was thought
that the latter area would provide the best
opportunity to recover *in situ* material. In
addition, a small portion of this area showed
ash just below the surface, and the possibility
of acquiring charcoal had to be taken into
account. For these reasons, two areas were
chosen for testing: the extreme eastern portion of 7 sq m which had a very heavy surface
concentration, and a southcentral area of 7 sq
m, with the indications of burning. A single
one sq m unit somewhat to the west of the
burned area was included in this group.

These excavations confirmed that the site
was in the very last stages of deflation. The
present slope of the surface, from west to
east, was reflected in the depth of the artifact-bearing deposits, which were minimal at

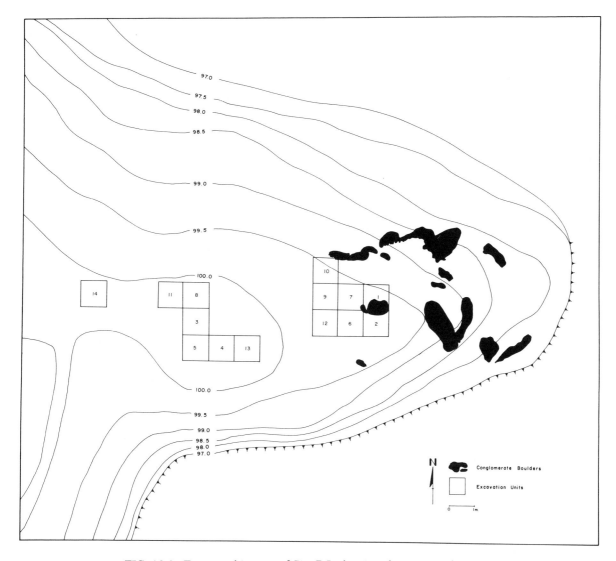

FIG. 10-2—Topographic map of Site D5, showing the excavated units.

best. At the extreme eastern end of the site, Unit 2, the depth of artifactual deposit was only 11 cm, while at the western end, in Unit 14, sterile soil was reached at 22 centimeters. Unfortunately, the artifact recovery from Unit 14 was poor, with few artifacts occurring at depths greater than 14 centimeters. In fact, so few artifacts were recovered *in situ* that no distinction will be made between them and the surface sample.

In the eastern area, excavations revealed a level of variable thickness, consisting of fine deposits of eolian and colluvial origin, which contained artifacts and a few large cobbles. This deposit rested on a thin layer of gravels which were sterile. The upper portion of the gravel layer was a fine matrix of very small pebbles and sand, but became coarser with depth and was mixed with large water-worn cobbles at its base. These lower gravels rested on the limestone bedrock (fig. 10-3). The stratigraphy at this end of the site closely parallels that of the present streambed just below the site. It appears as if this portion of the site represented a small section of a much higher streambed, which subsequently cut to a lower

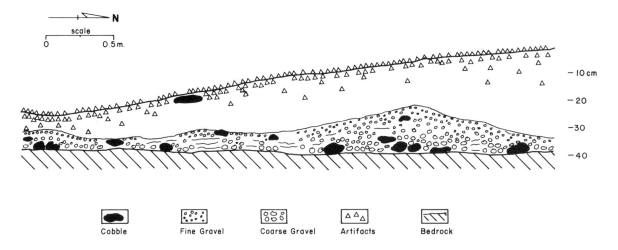

FIG. 10-3—Stratigraphic profile of the eastern end of Site D5.

level, leaving this remnant on the limestone bedrock. The absence of artifacts both on and in the gravels clearly indicates that the site was occupied well after the streambed had cut below the present site level.

The stratigraphic configuration of the southcentral portion of the site was somewhat different from that described above. The upper 15 cm or so consisted of the same fine-grained deposits with artifacts as was encountered in the eastern section. This deposit, however, rested on a somewhat coarser matrix devoid of pebbles. It appears to be a slope-wash, derived from the higher elevations directly to the west. No evidence was found for a streambed in this area, although the contact point between the slopewash deposits and the streambed was not encountered.

The stratigraphy indicates that both the streambed and the slopewash deposits accumulated well prior to the occupation of the site. The fine-grained deposits containing the artifacts, therefore, are little more than surficial deposits, which cannot be related to any others in the area.

DATING

An additional element was encountered in the southcentral area—rodent holes. These often reached a depth of 35 cm below the surface and contained artifacts and charcoal. These rodent holes, particularly in Unit 8, supplied the charcoal used for two of the dated samples, while the third sample was obtained from bits of charcoal found scattered throughout what appeared to be the base of two firepits in Units 4 and 5 (fig. 10-2). It was hoped that these samples would provide a reasonable radiometric dating of the site. Unfortunately, this was not to be the case. All samples were minimal in size and all three produced considerably different readings (table 10-1).

The extremely high sigma on the first date makes it useless: lack of overlap between the first and second dates makes it impossible to judge an even probable date for the occupation of the site, although the earliest date does appear to be aberrant. This leaves the dating essentially where it was before the samples were run. If Bar-Yosef (1970) is correct in viewing the Geometric Kebaran "A" as being at the end of the Kebaran development, then the 11,220 B.C. date would be reasonable. On the other hand, the acceptance of this date would be based purely on data external to that from D5.

TABLE 10-1
Radiocarbon Dates from Site D5

Sample Location	Date B.P.	Date B.C.	Lab Number
From bottom of fire pits, Units 4 and 5	15,820 ± 1,730	13,870	Tx-1121
From rodent hole, Unit 8	13,170 ± 230	11,220	I-5497
From rodent hole, Unit 8	18,840 ± 680	16,890	SMU-7

NON-LITHIC ARTIFACTS AND FAUNA

Because of the extremely shallow *in situ* zone across the site, only one non-lithic artifact was recovered: a small piece of yellow ocher (0.2 gms). Within the Nahal Zin and the subsidiary Nahal Aqev, there are a number of localities where yellow ocher occurs naturally. Therefore, this material must be considered locally available.

Identifiable faunal remains were minimal, although a fair number of minute splinters of bone were encountered throughout the *in situ* deposits, particularly in the burned areas of Units 3 through 5. A single identifiable fragment of megafauna was recovered: a tooth of a *Capra* cf. *ibex*. In addition, five pieces of *Dentalium* of Mediterranean origin were found, pointing to connections to the West.

LITHIC ARTIFACTS

The two main areas tested by excavation were chosen because of specific surface indications which were suggestive of possibly different activity areas. The eastern zone, with its heavy surface concentration, might have represented a workshop area, while the south-central zone, with the burned materials, was suggestive of a hearth area. Thus, the lithic analyses were carried out treating these two areas separately. Within each area, however, initial studies were done by the original one square meter excavation units. Owing to the small size of these units and their close proximity, the variability which was seen between individual excavation units in the same area

could not be considered to have potential cultural significance. On the other hand, the major test areas were felt to be sufficiently isolated spatially so that the difference between the lithic structure of the two areas could be amenable to cultural interpretation. When the excavation units were combined into the major areas, however, it was found that no significant differences were present. This can be seen partially in the consideration of the proportional occurrences of artifact classes within each area (table 10-2). The only real apparent difference lies in the greater density of artifacts in the eastern area, which also was the lowest and, thus, the most likely to receive artifacts moved from the slightly higher portions of the site. The extremely high density of artifacts per square meter indicates either very intense occupation or considerable deflation, as noted elsewhere.

This homogeneity strongly indicates that there was no difference in the basic manufacturing processes which took place in each area. The very low percentage of cores, core-trimming elements, and primary elements makes it necessary to reject the proposition that either area constituted a primary workshop zone. In fact, the extremely low occurrence of cores as compared with flakes and blades in both areas, and the sizeable percentage of the site sampled (17.5%), indicates that primary workshop activities most probably took place outside the present site area. Given the distance to the supply of raw material, this is not surprising. It must be noted, however, that no primary workshop for this site was located near the raw material source.

TABLE 10-2
Occurrences of Artifact Classes

Artifact Class	Eastern Area		Southcentral Area		Combined	
	Number	Percent	Number	Percent	Number	Percent
Cores	30	1.19	35	1.13	65	1.16
Core Trimming Elements	56	2.23	39	1.26	95	1.69
Primary Elements	140	5.57	203	6.54	343	6.11
Flakes[1]	1,009	40.14	1,402	45.17	2,411	42.92
Blades[1]	1,279	50.88	1,425	45.91	2,704	48.13
Total	2,514	100.01	3,104	100.01	5,618	100.01
Microburin Technique	11		14		25	
Chips and Chunks[2]	4,836		4,096		8,932	
	7,361		7,214		14,575	
Density per sq m[3]	1,840.25		1,030.57		1,325.00	

[1] This includes both blades, *sensu stricto*, and bladelets.
[2] These are not considered to have potential use for tool modification.
[3] While some depth was present, only a very small percentage of artifacts were recovered *in situ*; no more than 10% in any one square. The eastern area covered 4 sq m, the southcentral, 7 sq meters.

It is possible that cores were roughed out near the source of raw material, leaving no diagnostic debris, and then were carried to the site for exploitation. This interpretation is consistent with the high flake and blade to core ratio—85.43 pieces of debitage for each core—and the low ratio between primary elements and cores—5.3 primary elements for each core.

The production of tools from the totally available pieces again shows marked homogeneity between the two areas (table 10-3), so that even secondary workshop activities do not appear to have been dominant in one area as opposed to the other.

The foregoing observations have been presented for both areas in order to document their high degree of homogeneity. As this homogeneity extends to all technological and typological observations made during the study, it would be redundant to present separate sets of observations for each area. Therefore, the remaining technological and typological characteristics will be presented for the assemblage as a whole, utilizing samples combined from both areas.

The removal of flakes and blades from cores may be achieved through a number of basic techniques: with a hard hammer, a soft hammer (billet or punch), or by pressure. Each technique leaves more or less diagnostic characteristics on the removed pieces. At D5, there is clear evidence for the use of both a hard hammer and a billet or punch technique for debitage manufacture. This is seen by the types of bulbs of percussion and their associated platforms as they occur on both flakes and blades. In this assemblage, there is a marked increase in the proportional occurrence of both lipped and crushed platforms in

TABLE 10-3
Proportional Occurrence of Blank Utilization
in Tool Production by Artifact Class

Artifact Class	Eastern Area	Southcentral Area
All Debitage[1]	21.11%	18.04%
Blades/Bladelets	32.35%	31.93%
Flakes	6.74%	5.28%
Primary Elements	0.64%	0.79%
Cores	6.67%	5.71%
Core Trimming Elements	7.14%	5.13%

[1] This does not include chips or chunks.

the blade class, as opposed to the flake class (table 10-4), indicating a greater use of a billet or punch technique for blades than for flakes.

TABLE 10-4
Platform Types on Flakes
and Blades as Percentages

Platform Type	Flakes N=383	Blades N=180
Unfaceted, bulb present	42.04	21.67
Dihedral faceted, bulb present	10.18	7.78
Multifaceted, bulb present	8.09	1.11
Lipped unfaceted, bulb absent	10.79	35.00
Crushed, bulb often absent	20.10	32.78
Cortex, bulb present	8.62	1.67

While the total number of flakes recovered is somewhat less than the number of blades, this is probably due to the tendency of flakes to break into fewer sections than blades. In spite of this possible bias, it is clear that flakes were not used extensively in tool production, as noted in Tables 10-3 and 10-6. There is considerable variability in size and proportion of the flake debitage. Flakes range in length from 11 to 58 mm, of which slightly under half (47.80%) ranged between 20.0 and 30.0 mm, while only 4.40% measured over 50.0

millimeters. The remaining flakes for the most part fall between 30.0 and 50.0 mm, with a reduction in proportional occurrence as length increases (fig. 10-4). A similar pattern occurs for flake widths: 51.14% are between 20.0 and 30.0 mm, while only 1.07% exceed 50.0 millimeters. On the other hand, over a quarter of all flakes measured had widths of less than 20.0 mm (fig. 10-4). This has resulted in a mean flake width of 24.43 mm, somewhat lower than the mean flake length of 29.30 millimeters.

In terms of proportions (length/width ratio), there is a relatively low percentage of flakes which approach blade shape; only 23.95% fall between 2:1 and 1.5:1. On the other hand, 46.10% are between 1.5:1 and 1:1 and almost one-third (29.94%) are wider than they are long. This proportional distribution suggests that there was a sharp manufactural distinction between flake and blade production, and that blades from this assemblage cannot be considered merely as part of an unbroken length/width ratio continuum.

Blades appear to have been the predominantly desired tool blank form, as clearly seen in the high percentage of those actually used in tool production (table 10-3), as well as by the types of cores utilized (table 10-8).

As with the flakes, there is considerable variability in blade length—from 16.0 mm to a high of 60.0 mm (mean length, 36.70 mm). In spite of this range, almost nine out of ten (87.82%) fall into the "bladelet" category, at least when length (< 50 mm) is used as the sole criterion (fig. 10-5). Blade widths show both a rather tight cluster, 68.61% being between 10.0 mm and 20.0 mm, and a relatively low percentage of pieces (30.94) which have widths under 12 mm, that being another criterion for the recognition of "bladelets" (Tixier, 1963). This discrepancy between the length and width criteria for "bladelet" classification means that this assemblage has either a considerable number of wide bladelets or, if one prefers, of short blades. This can be seen

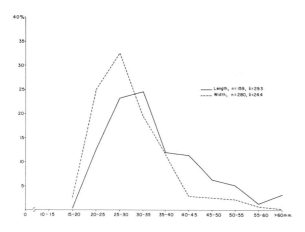

FIG. 10-4—Length and width distributions of flakes from Site D5.

as well in terms of the blade length/width ratios, where almost half of the blades (49.15%) fall between 2:1 and 2.5:1. The remaining half also tends toward the proportionately wide side: 28.81% fall between 2.5:1 and 3.0:1; 16.10% between 3.5:1 and 3:1; while only 5.93% have a length/width ratio in excess of 3.5:1.

Blade shapes are, within limits, rather variable, indicating a lack of a high degree of standardization during manufacture (table 10-5). It must be remembered that these observations are taken from those blades *not* chosen for additional modification. This sug-

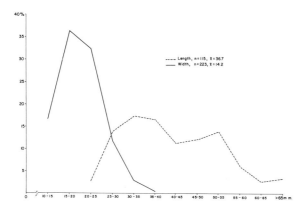

FIG. 10-5—Length and width distributions of blades from Site D5.

gests that incurvate pieces were not considered suitable for tool production, but that other attributes, particularly the distal shape, were of no particular significance. This is reasonable when it is considered that the vast majority of blade tools, *sensu lato*, are backed microliths, made from blade or bladelet fragments, and that most of these forms have retouched modification of their extremities.

In short, the production of flakes and blades resulted in a fairly wide range of available blanks for modification into tools. Flakes tend to be small and rather squat and the same may be said for the blades, where the production of "bladelets" with widths under 12 mm is clearly in the minority, and the number of proportionately long, narrow blades or bladelets is very low.

While 25 microburins (fig. 10-9*i*) were recovered, resulting in a Microburin Index of 2.34, the extremely small number suggests that they were produced fortuitously (table 10-2).

RETOUCHED TOOLS

Technology

Retouched tools are made on blanks selected from the totality of available pieces which resulted from the flaking of cores. In this assemblage, tools were produced not only on flakes, blades, and primary elements, but also occasionally on exhausted cores and even core-trimming elements (table 10-6). As many of the tools are backed and on fragmentary blanks, it is not usually possible to tell whether blades (width greater than 12 mm) or "bladelets" (width less than 12 mm) were utilized. On the other hand, over 200 unbacked tools occurred on blades or bladelets. From this sample it was possible to note that bladelets were utilized in unbacked tool production only one-half as frequently as bladelets occurred in the debitage; of 242 unbacked blade tools, *sensu lato*, only 15.71% were on blade-

TABLE 10-5
Blade Shape Attributes Seen in the Blade Debitage

Attribute	Number	Percent
Dorsal Shape		
Parallel	255	58.22
Converging	98	22.37
Expanding	85	19.41
	438	100.00
Distal Shape		
Pointed	55	41.05
Blunt	79	58.95
	134	100.00
Lateral Profile		
Flat	153	39.53
Incurvate	234	60.17
	387	100.00

lets. The choice of what width blade would be utilized in tool production appears to reflect a general preference toward the wider end of the range seen in the debitage. While 64.47% of the unbacked blade tools fall between 10.0 and 20.0 mm in width (fully comparable with the debitage sample), 25.62% have widths greater than 20.0 mm, as opposed to only 14.80% for the same width range in the debitage.

Little can be said of blade length, as tools are mostly on fragments, either through choice or through breakage during use. It is noticeable, however, that there are some rather large blade tools—most of which are endscrapers—which fall outside the measured parameters of the blade debitage (fig. 10-6).

While tools on flakes and primary elements also occur mainly on fragments, those on complete pieces show considerable size vari-

ation. The overall impression for nongeometric tools is that there is little absolute size or proportional standardization. It is possible to see, however, a marked tendency toward increased width associated with increased length for nongeometric tools, but a totally different pattern for geometric and proto-geometric forms (fig. 10-6). Both geometrics and proto-geometrics clearly show that for the vast majority of the examples the one significant size parameter was the width of the piece, which was tightly controlled.

It must be noted that in discussing metric attributes for retouched tools, only those on complete blanks were considered. By far the greatest number of nongeometric tools were on fragments of blanks.

Typology

The typology utilized in this study does not correspond directly with any specific published or circulated type list.[2] Types recognized here normally follow those already defined for the Levant and North Africa, but modifications were made occasionally when groups of artifacts did not conform to the published types. In these cases, a detailed description of the group will be given. There has been a tendency to use broad type designations in order to prevent the type list from becoming excessively long. In these cases, the minor typological variations will be noted in the discussion of the typology, which follows the listing of the types present (table 10-6).

As a considerable portion of the retouched tools were recovered from the surface of the site, their physical condition was taken into account during classification. Those recovered *in situ* were absolutely fresh, devoid of both patination and any crushing of their edges. Those from the surface were normally heavily patinated a dark red brown and, as often as not, the larger pieces showed some minor edge crushing. This difference between the surface and *in situ* material has been taken

TABLE 10-6
Type List of Retouched Tools from Site D5

Type	Blade	Bladelet	Flake	Primary Element	Core Trimming Element	Core	Total	Restricted Percent	Percent
a) Tools without backing									
Simple endscraper	31	2	2	6			41	9.51	3.93
Endscraper on retouched piece	15	2	2				17	3.94	1.63
Ogival endscraper	11		2		1		14	3.25	1.34
Thin nosed or shouldered scraper	2		8	3			13	3.02	1.25
Thumbnail scraper			2				2	0.46	0.19
Double endscraper	4			1			5	1.16	0.48
Carinated scraper	4			1		1	6	1.39	0.57
Core scraper						3	3	0.70	0.29
End-*raclette*	6	1					7	1.62	0.67
Simple endscraper + truncation	1						1	0.23	0.10
Simple endscraper + bilateral sheen	2						2	0.46	0.19
Burin, angle on snap	1		4		1		6	1.39	0.57
Burin, dihedral			2	1			3	0.70	0.29
Burin, on truncation			3				3	0.70	0.29
Perforator	6	1	13	2	1		23	5.34	2.20
Multiple perforator	1						1	0.23	0.10
Denticulate endscraper	2		5	1	1		9	2.09	0.86
Denticulated piece	10		10	3			23	5.34	2.20
Laterally notched piece	29	5	33	3			70	16.24	6.70
End-notched piece	7	2	3	2			14	3.25	1.34
Multiple notched piece	15	1	9		2		27	6.27	2.59
Straight truncated piece	12	8	3	1			24	5.57	2.30
Straight oblique truncated piece	15	14	7				36	8.35	3.45
Concave truncated piece	5		2				7	1.62	0.67
Concave oblique truncated piece	12	2	5				19	4.41	1.82
Double truncated piece		3					3	0.70	0.29
Retouched piece, lateral	17		16				33	7.66	3.16
Retouched piece, bilateral	5		2				7	1.62	0.67
Retouched piece, alternate	3	1	1				5	1.16	0.48
Bec burin	3		1				4	0.93	0.38
Scaled piece			3				3	0.70	0.29

Type	Blank Forms						Total	Restricted Percent	Percent
	Blade	Bladelet	Flake	Primary Element	Core Trimming Element	Core			
Subtotal	220	39	138	24	6	4	431		
Percent	51.04	9.05	32.02	5.57	1.39	0.93	100.00	100.00	
b) Backed tools and geometrics									
Rectangles, backed		11					11	1.79	1.05
Trapeze, symmetric, backed		10					10	1.63	0.96
Trapeze, asymmetric, backed		20					20	3.26	1.92
Trapeze, asymmetric		6					6	0.98	0.57
Trapeze, atypical	3		1	1			5	0.82	0.48
Backed and double truncated bladelet		57					57	9.30	5.46
Backed fragment with oblique truncation		217					217	35.41	20.79
Backed fragment with perpendicular truncation		73					73	11.91	6.99
Scalene bladelet		4					4	0.65	0.38
Pointed straight backed piece	1	3	2				6	0.98	0.57
Pointed arch-backed bladelet		6					6	0.98	0.57
Pointed arch-backed bladelet with oblique truncation		8					8	1.31	0.77
Pointed arch-backed bladelet with straight truncation		2					2	0.33	0.19
Arch-tipped bladelet		2					2	0.33	0.19
Blunt straight backed piece	1	5					6	0.98	0.57
Blunt partially backed piece		2	1				3	0.49	0.29
Partially backed fragment		1					1	0.16	0.10
Backed fragment, medial	2	155					157	25.61	15.04
Backed fragment, proximal	1	2					3	0.49	0.29
Straight backed fragment with rounded base		3					3	0.49	0.29
Straight backed fragment with acute truncation		1					1	0.16	0.10
Fragment with Ouchtata retouch, medial		12					12	1.96	1.15
Subtotal	8	602	4	1			618		
Percent	0.98	98.21	0.65	0.16			100.00	100.00	
Total Tools	228	639	142	25	6	4	1,044		
Percent	21.84	61.21	13.60	2.40	0.58	0.38	100.01		100.01

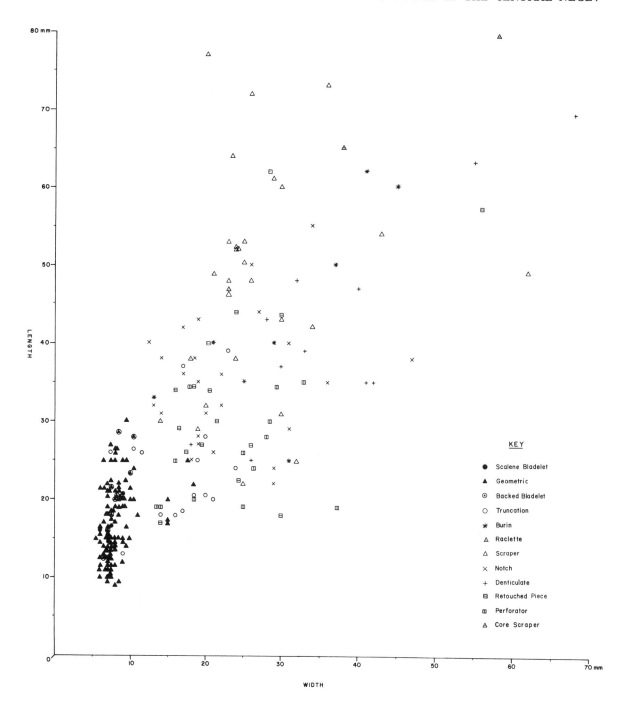

FIG. 10-6—Length/Width scattergram of retouched tools from Site D5.

into account, so that small, irregular "retouch" on surface artifacts was not considered a valid criterion for tool designation.

The type list has been presented in a somewhat complex form. Because of the large number of tools in the sample and the heavy dominance of a few specific types, which results in a massive reduction in the proportional occurrence of other tool types, the type list has been subdivided into two sections: one of unbacked tools and the other of backed tools and geometrics (only a few of which are unbacked). For each type, two percentages are given: a restricted percentage which refers only to the subsection in which the type is placed (unbacked or backed); and a normal percentage which refers to that type's proportional occurrence within the total tool sample. Using both of these, it is possible to get a more realistic view of the proportional occurrence of any type or class of tools in both the total samples and in that sample of related types or classes of tools.

Notes on the Typology

Almost 60% of the recovered tools include backing as a major attribute, although the vast number of these belong to relatively few specific types. This is not true for the unbacked tools, where there is a relatively sizeable number of artifacts in a number of tool types. Endscrapers are most common as a class, but notched pieces, truncated pieces, and simple retouched pieces are also very well represented (table 10-7).

While certain information is implicit in the type list itself, some typological observations should be made, and these are included in this section.

Endscrapers

By far the dominant form is a simple endscraper on either an unretouched or retouched blade fragment (figs. 10-7*c, d*; 10-9*ii*); those on complete blades are rare but are usually quite large (fig. 10-8*b*). Retouch on all simple endscrapers tends to be well formed and the working edges are normally even, lacking irregularities. Those on retouched pieces show a considerable variety in the lateral retouch, from light marginal treatment to quite heavy serration.

Ogival scrapers are similar to the simple varieties and include a number which have additional lateral

TABLE 10-7
Selected Typological Indices

A. Inclusive

Scraper	10.6	Burin	1.2
Perforator	2.2	Notch and Denticulate	11.7
Truncation	14.6	Retouched piece	4.3
Geometric[1]	5.0	Geometric[2]	38.2
Backed tool	58.7	Backed bladelet	20.5

B. Restricted (to class)

Endscraper on blade	71.2	Multiple notch	37.0
Burin on truncation	25.0	Geometric	8.5
Geometric and Proto-geometric[3]	17.8	Geometric, Proto- and Broken Geometric	65.1

[1] Includes only trapezes and rectangles.

[2] Includes trapezes, rectangles, double truncated backed bladelets, and backed and truncated fragments.

[3] Includes trapezes, rectangles, and double truncated backed bladelets.

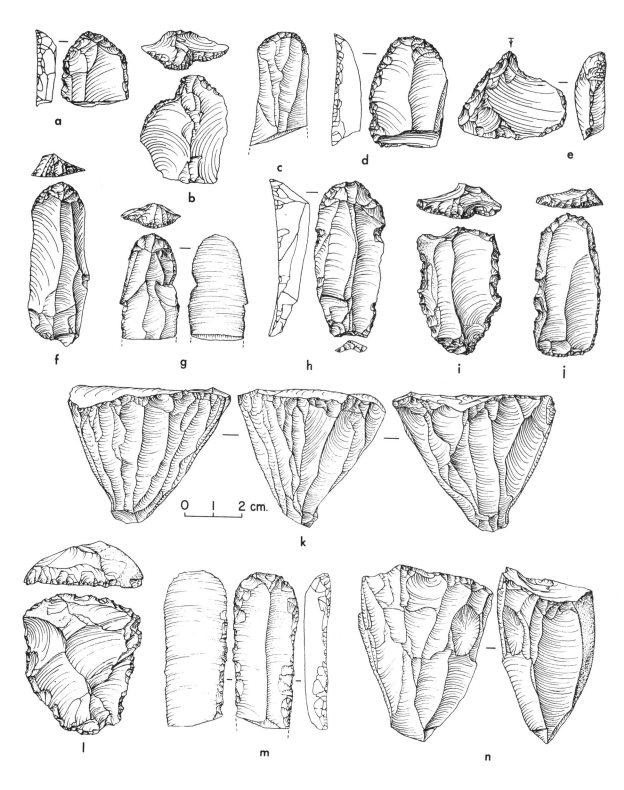

FIG. 10-7–Tools from Site D5: *a-d, f-j, m*–scrapers (*g* and *m* show bilateral sheen); *e*–perforator; *k, n*–cores; *l*–denticulate.

retouch (fig. 10-7*a*). There are, however, a few made on complete blades where the tool is relatively short and almost semicarinated (fig. 10-7*f*). As a group, the ogival forms are extremely well made. This cannot be said for the thin-nosed and shouldered group, many of which tend to be atypical, because of minimal or somewhat irregular retouch (fig. 10-7*b*). Here, too, are examples with lateral retouch, including heavy serration (fig. 10-7*i*).

Both core (fig. 10-8*a*) and carinated scrapers occur only sporadically, and the carinated examples are, for the most part, only semicarinated (fig. 10-7*h*).

Of particular note are two fine simple endscrapers on blades, both of which exhibit some bilateral "sheen" (fig. 10-7*g, m*). In one case, this "sheen" has been removed to a large extent by an irregular, flat bilateral retouch, which may well have served to re-sharpen the edges. The presence of these pieces cannot be taken as evidence for the systematic cutting of plants, but they indicate that the prerequisite technological base probably was present to some extent.

Other endscraper types are rare and generally atyp-

ical, with the exception of the double endscrapers which are well formed on rather wide blades (fig. 10-7*j*).

Burins

These are at best atypical, and a number may well be accidental, particularly those on snap. Given the sample size for all tools, it is clear that burins were a very marginal element within the tool kit.

Perforators

While occurring in moderate numbers, perforators show little internal morphological consistency beyond that necessary for them to be called perforators. They range from very small, sharp lateral protrusions made by fine retouched notches (fig. 10-9*gg*) to rather large, wide tips formed by heavy bilateral retouch (fig. 10-7*e*). A number of atypical examples are present, as well, where the protrusion is formed by the intersection of a natural broken edge and a shallow retouched notch.

Denticulates

While the type list only recognizes two forms—denticulate endscrapers and others—there is considerable variability within this group. The denticulate endscrapers are generally poor, closer to transverse denticulates than to true serrated endscrapers (fig. 10-7*l*). Other forms include seventeen where the denticulation is along one lateral edge (fig. 10-9*qq*), four where it is transverse (fig. 10-9*pp*), and two where it is bilateral (fig. 10-9*oo*) or converging.

Notched Pieces

The most common are single lateral notches on pieces with or without additional retouch (fig. 10-9*tt*). The majority of these notches are formed by fine retouch: 33 obverse and 19 inverse. The remaining pieces have notches initially formed by a single blow, but all also show additional fine crushing or retouch within the notch itself. Of these, 6 are inverse and 12 obverse. The most striking characteristics of the notches are their shape and size. Of 124 notches

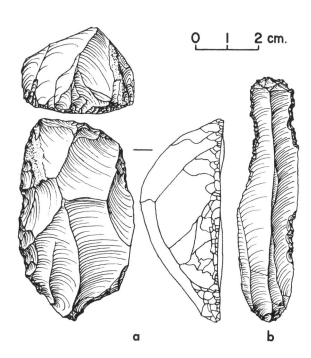

FIG. 10-8—Tools from Site D5: *a*—core scraper; *b*—endscraper on retouched blade.

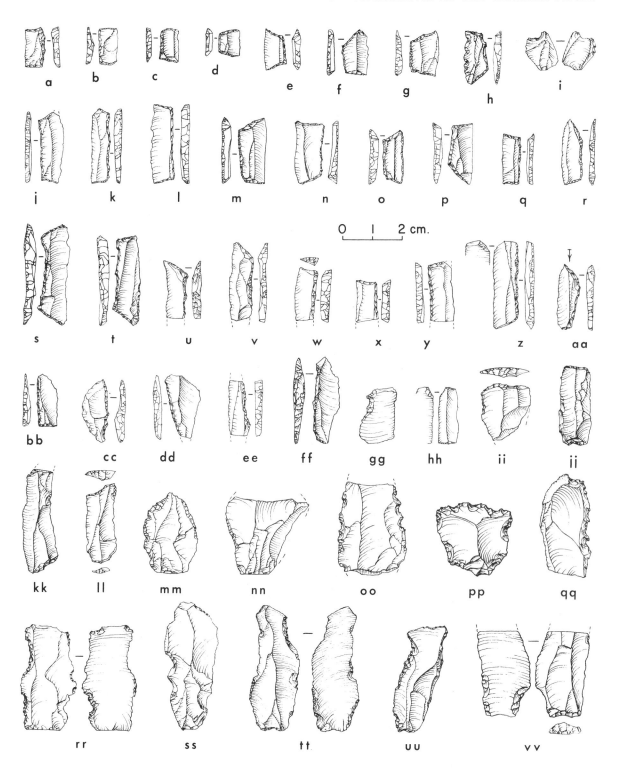

FIG. 10-9—Tools from Site D5: *a-h, j-bb*—geometrics, broken geometrics, and proto-geometrics and other forms; *i*—microburin; *cc-ee*—backed pieces; *ff*—La Mouillah point; *gg*—perforator; *hh, jj, ll*—truncated pieces; *ii*—endscraper; *mm, nn, uu*—retouched pieces; *oo-qq*—denticulates; *rr-tt*—notched pieces; *vv*—bec burin.

which were complete, 62.09% were between 5 and 10 mm wide, while an additional 34.28% were between 10 and 15 mm in width. In fact, only two exceeded 15 millimeters. While over 95% had widths between 5 and 15 mm, the same percentage (95.16) were less than 3 mm deep. Thus, many notches, particularly those 10 to 15 mm wide were little more than very shallow concavities, although their limits were always well defined.

Endnotched pieces, excluded from the above observations, are all obverse, and a majority, 11, are formed by single blows. These may merely represent a minimal technique of truncation, as most occur on blades or bladelets.

Multiple notched pieces, while not very common, show considerable variation. Most, 22, have retouched notches which are unopposed: three formed by inverse notching, four by alternate (fig. 10-9*rr*) and fifteen by obverse blows (fig. 10-9*ss*). The few opposed notched pieces show the notches adjacent to the proximal extremity, but none can be considered fragments of the "Natufian" double-notched points. On these examples, one pair is inverse, one obverse, while three are formed by alternate notches.

Truncations

Straight truncations, either perpendicular or oblique to the axis of the piece, are by far the most common. Of the straight oblique variety, 23 are distal and 11 are proximal (fig. 10-9*kk*), and two could not be identified as to which extremity was utilized. A similar pattern is present for the straight truncations: 16 are distal (fig. 10-9*hh*), four are proximal, while four could not be identified. For the concave oblique examples, however, proximal truncations outnumber distal ones—11 to 8—as is also true for those which are perpendicular, where all are proximal.

Unlike the other unbacked tool types, a significant percentage of these are on bladelets. In this, they most probably belong within the whole complex of geometric and proto-geometric forms. The three double truncated pieces would, in fact, have been included within the geometrics if they had not been of blade proportions (fig. 10-9*hh, jj, ll*).

Retouched Pieces

A piece was considered retouched if at least one-third of one edge had regular, continuous retouch, but the piece, as a whole, could not be classified as any other tool type. Of the laterally retouched pieces, all but six are obversely retouched (fig. 10-9*nn, uu*); of those six, five are inverse, while one has both inverse and obverse retouch along one edge. Of the bilaterally retouched examples (fig. 10-9*mm*), only one is inverse. Retouch shows considerable range, from marginal examples to fragments with heavy, flat retouch, although marginal retouch is most common.

Other Unbacked Tool Types

While bec burins are uncommon, they are quite typical (fig. 10-9*vv*). Scaled pieces are poor, only lightly scaled along a single edge, and occur on relatively large flakes.

Geometrics and Backed and Double-Truncated Bladelets

While three major "types" have been recognized in the type list—rectangles, trapezes, and backed and double-truncated bladelets—the distinctions between them are less important than their similarities. The geometrics have been separated from the backed and double-truncated bladelets (proto-geometric of Bar-Yosef, 1970) by a simple difference in their length/width ratios: geometrics having length/width ratios of less than 2:1, and backed and double-truncated bladelets having ratios which exceed 2:1. As can be clearly seen in Fig. 10-6, this dichotomy does not describe two discrete clusters, but merely draws a rather arbitrary line through a single cluster.[3] This total group seems to share one metric characteristic: a minimal variation in width, from 5.5 to 10.0 millimeters. In this regard, it is true that some of these fall above 9 mm, the "magic" width which turns a backed bladelet into a backed blade. On the other hand, as there is a clear unimodal distribution of widths, with those over 9 mm representing one segment of the continuum, all have been listed as being "bladelets" rather than blades.

The distinction between rectangles and trapezes is

merely one of degree; the truncations on the rectangles closely approach 90° to the backed edge (fig. 10-9a, b), while on trapezes at least one angle is clearly oblique to that edge (fig. 10-9c–g). For this assemblage, this distinction probably has little value, as it does not separate two readily identifiable groups. The vast majority of truncations are only slightly oblique, and there are numerous examples where one truncated trapeze edge is perpendicular to the backing, or very nearly so. This strong tendency toward perpendicular truncations can be seen in the extremely low mean truncation angle of all typical geometrics, of which only one-third can be called rectangles, and in the paucity of truncation angles which exceed 125° (fig. 10-10). Of 78 angle measurements, 58—or 74.26%—are 100° or less.

The backed and double-truncated bladelets (fig. 10-9h, j, t) do show a difference in truncation angle from the true geometrics, although there is a considerable overlap (fig. 10-10). In these, the mean truncation angle is somewhat higher and the number of examples with angles over 100° is considerably greater. In short, those pieces with length/width ratios of more than 2:1 have significantly lower angles between the backed and truncated edges.

Both the geometrics and the backed and double-truncated bladelets show a preponderance of simple steep backing. A small proportion of them, however,

were formed by other types of retouch: of the geometrics, 7.23% have a semisteep backing, while of the bladelets, 8.77% have semisteep retouch, 5.26% are backed by a *sur enclume* technique, and a single example, 1.75%, has an inversely backed edge.

In addition to the backing techniques, a small number of both the geometrics and the backed and double-truncated bladelets have additional retouch along the unbacked edge. This varies from simple light retouch (fig. 10-9o) to somewhat irregular serration (fig. 10-9h), but is so rare as to be of only esoteric note.

Backed and Truncated Bladelets and Fragments

The fragmentary pieces, divided into two types, with or without oblique truncation, represent by far the largest single group of tools from the assemblage. Oblique truncations (fig. 10-9u, v, x, y) outnumber perpendicular ones (fig. 10-9w) by two to one, exactly the same ratio as that which occurs for true trapezes in relation to rectangles. These fragments, if such they are, show a considerable length variation, from 6.0 to 28.5 millimeters. It is possible that the vast majority actually represent finished tools in which the simple break provided an acceptable blunt unretouched truncation, so that additional retouch was not necessary.

On these pieces, truncation angles (mean = 106.35, S.D. 13.29) fit well with those of the backed and double-truncated bladelets (fig. 10-10). If both the true geometrics and the backed and double-truncated bladelets are considered as a group, then a comparison between the length of these "fragments" and the former groups shows significant overlap (fig. 10-11), although 27 fragments are shorter than any of the complete pieces. That is not to say that *all* of the fragments are finished tools. Of 290 examples, 8 have irregular, highly acute angles between the breaks and the backed edges, while another 74 have breaks with angles of less than 90 degrees. That is, only 20.82% have an angle of the broken edge which falls outside the range of those pieces with two truncations. While this might constitute reason for excluding those particular pieces from consideration as finished tools, in reality, a large percentage of them, 65.85%, have angles above 80° but less than 90 degrees. These

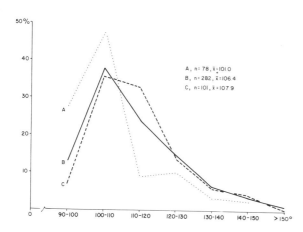

FIG. 10-10—Distribution of truncation angles measured on: *a*—backed and double truncated bladelets; *b*—backed and truncated bladelet fragments; and *c*—geometrics.

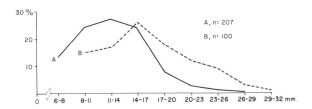

FIG. 10-11—Distribution of lengths displayed by: *a—* backed and truncated bladelet fragments; and *b—*geometrics and backed and double truncated bladelets (proto-geometrics).

latter might well have fit within an acceptable range for the tool type. Thus, we are left with only 30 pieces, a mere 10%, which are clearly not finished tools as judged by the double-truncated pieces.

As with the other backed tools, these mainly have steep backing formed by normal obverse retouch. Semisteep backing does occur, however, on 11.72% of the pieces, while *sur enclume* technique was used on only 1.38 percent. A single example shows a portion of an inverse truncation (fig. 10-9*z*). In addition, there are four typical scalene bladelets, a small number considering the number of truncated and backed fragments.

Pointed Backed Pieces

These are poorly represented, are mostly distal fragments, although a single backed flake is present (fig. 10-9*cc*). Within this group are ten pieces which approach the backed and double-truncated bladelets. These have a clear straight or oblique truncation on one extremity, while the other is either pointed by straight backing, in two cases, or is pointed by an arched backing, in eight others (fig. 10-9*aa*). While these latter eight certainly approach backed and double-truncated bladelets, the mere curvature at the tip is not sufficient to be classified a true truncation. In addition to the above, there are two arch-tipped bladelet fragments which also approach truncations, and two straight-backed bladelets with straight proximal truncations (fig. 10-9*bb*).

Blunt-Backed Bladelets

As for all untruncated bladelet distal extremities,

these are rare (fig. 10-9*dd*). They seem to be more idiosyncratic than significant as a typological element. Included here is a single La Mouillah point (fig. 10-9*ff*).

Backed-Bladelet Fragments

This constitutes a very strange group, in that while it represents a very significant percentage of the backed pieces, it is almost exclusively made up of medial fragments. Of 161 pieces, only 7 are proximal. As with all the backed pieces, a vast majority of the medial fragments are steeply backed by obverse retouch, but as with the others, both *sur enclume* technique and semisteep backing are present. A single example shows only partial backing (fig. 10-9*ee*). In spite of the very small number of proximal fragments in the assemblage, four of the seven have been basally modified.

Bladelets with Ouchtata Retouch

While Ouchtata retouch does occur on some geometrics and truncated fragments, it is not common. All are medial fragments and the blanks are clearly at the small end of the range in terms of both width and thickness.

General Comments on Backed Microliths

The foregoing description makes it clear that the assemblage is strongly oriented toward backed and truncated pieces of various types. While considerable variation exists in the specific forms these took, a number of traits may be noted which help to define their stylistic parameters (table 10-8). Most significant is the apparent lack of preference for both the position of the truncated element in relation to the original blank (distal or proximal) and the equal lack of consistency in the placement of the truncated element in relation to the backing. These both appear to be random. On the other hand, there are clear stylistic preferences in the shape of both truncations and backing, as well as in the type of

TABLE 10-8
General Stylistic Attributes of Backed Microliths

			Number	Percent
1. Position of truncation on backed and truncated fragments	(a)	Proximal	65	60.53
	(b)	Distal	45	39.47
2. Position of backing on backed and truncated fragments (truncation up)	(a)	Right side	64	56.14
	(b)	Left side	50	43.86
3. Shape of truncation on backed and truncated fragments	(a)	Straight	171	75.33
	(b)	Convex	20	8.81
	(c)	Concave	36	15.86
4. Shape of backed edge on backed and truncated fragments	(a)	Straight	144	80.45
	(b)	Convex	15	8.38
	(c)	Concave	20	11.17
5. Shape of backed edge on backed medial fragments	(a)	Straight	301	87.25
	(b)	Convex	11	3.19
	(c)	Concave	33	9.56
6. Forms of retouch for backing on microliths	(a)	Abrupt	460	86.14
	(b)	*Sur enclume*	9	1.69
	(c)	Semisteep	65	12.17

retouch employed for backing. Most striking is the rarity of both convex backing and truncations, and, when they occur, the convexity is very slight. Concave elements are somewhat more numerous and, in this case, the shape is normally more pronounced. It is not surprising that abrupt retouch is the most common technique used to produce backing, but the very low occurrence of *sur enclume* technique is noticeable, as is the relatively high occurrence of semisteep retouch.

The significance of these observations rests in their potential utilization in interassemblage comparison. Through these, certain stylistic alternatives may be compared, which are not directly related to function. Unfortunately, other Geometric Kebaran "A" assemblages have not been sufficiently described to make this possible.

A final consideration is needed. How can the very large number of medial-backed frag-

ments be accounted for in light of the paucity of untruncated distal and proximal fragments? The answer clearly relates to the high proportional occurrence of backed and truncated fragments, and to the rather even occurrence of both distal and proximal types. Their large number suggests extensive production. It would seem that the presence of truncations was integral to the production of most microlithic tools and that the double-truncated geometric or double-truncated backed bladelet were normally the only forms produced. If either of these forms broke in half, either through purposeful snapping or by accident, both sections would have a truncation present. Only if such a piece broke into three or more parts would a nontruncated backed fragment be present, and this, of course, would always be medial. Given the short length of the double-truncated geometrics, it is unlikely that many broke into two, much less three sections. Therefore, it is only the backed and double-truncated bladelets which are a reasonable original form from which the many fragmentary pieces must have come. This is reinforced by the paucity of untruncated distal and proximal-backed fragments, as well as by the extremely limited number of such types as scalene bladelets, pointed straight-backed bladelets, etc. When the widths of the backed fragments are compared with those of the backed and truncated fragments, it is clear that no significant difference can be seen (fig. 10-12). It is also noticeable in this case that the 9 mm line between backed "bladelets" and "blades" is totally arbitrary and without diagnostic reality for the sample. In light of these observations, the backed medial fragments should *not* be grouped with the untruncated microliths in any measure of the proportional occurrence of truncated forms, but rather should be excluded from consideration, as they are most probably no more than fragments of the truncated forms, or at best unfinished geometrics.

Cores

While the recovery of cores from D5 was extremely limited, those found show considerable homogeneity and, for the most part, a high standard of manufacture. Only three types occur with any frequency (table 10-9).

The most impressive cores are pyramidal; they are not only the largest but also the most utilized (fig. 10-7*k*). On the other hand, the single platform, bladelet cores often approach the latter in quality. In this type there is a range of platform utilization from a single, slightly convex-flaked surface, to one which approaches the pyramidal form (fig. 10-7*n*).

The opposed platform bladelet cores are comparable to the single platform types. In fact, they are rather poor opposed platform examples in that one platform rarely indicates the removal of more than a very small number of bladelets, while the other always shows extensive utilization.

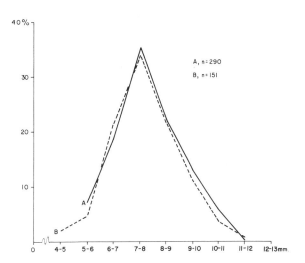

FIG. 10-12—Distribution of the widths of: *a*—backed and truncated fragments; and *b*—backed fragments.

Those cores characterized as flake cores appear to have been bladelet cores originally, but had been utilized for flake production after their size became too small to produce the desired bladelet size.

A striking element is the absence of any cores which could have produced the large, wide blades which were utilized in unbacked tool production. Either these blade cores were reutilized to produce the bladelet cores of the types found, or blades were struck away from the site. The low number of core-trimming elements suggests that the latter is most likely.

SUMMARY AND DISCUSSION

The assemblage described in the previous sections has a number of traits which are useful for general characterization. It is recognized that they are those which the author perceives to be significant, and in his listing of them there is necessarily a simplifying tendency which must blur some fine observations and variations within the assemblage.

It is hoped, however, that the typological and technological descriptions have been suf-

TABLE 10-9
Core Typology from D5

Type	Bladelet	Flake	Total	Percent
Single Platform				
a. Simple	14	6	20	47.62
b. Pyramidal	4		4	9.52
Subtotal	18	6	24	57.14
Multiple Platform				
a. Opposed, simple	10	1	11	26.19
b. Ninety-degree	2	3	5	11.90
Subtotal	12	4	16	38.10
Discoidal		2	2	4.76
Subtotal		2	2	4.76
Total	30	12	42	100.00
Percent	71.43	28.57		
Unidentifiable and Fragments	16	3	19	

ficiently extensive so that anyone may choose his own significant observations.

SITE CONSIDERATIONS

Site D5 appears to contain an assemblage unique to the Avdat/Aqev area. While faunal remains are almost nil, presence of *Capra*, the dominance of backed microliths, and the site situation all suggest that hunting was a main occupation of the people inhabiting the site. The naturally restricted area chosen for the site implies it was occupied by a small group of people. The density of artifacts, however, suggests intensive occupation, or a number of repeated occupations, since deflated.

The extremely low occurrence of cores and primary elements indicates that much primary flaking took place outside the site area, while the overall high percentage of retouched tools at the site suggests that actual tool manufacture took place there, and that a high degree of efficiency was realized, particularly in the utilization of blades and bladelets.

TECHNOLOGICAL CONSIDERATIONS

From both the core types and the debitage, it is clear that blades, *sensu lato*, were primarily desired as tool blanks. This is also obvious from the high percentage of tools made on both blades, *sensu stricto*, and bladelets. The production of bladelets appears to have been dominant, but large blades were not only produced but also utilized to a great extent. The production of blades and bladelets was primarily carried out through the use of a soft hammer or punch. This contrasts with the production of flakes and primary elements where the use of a hard hammer appears to have been dominant. The techniques used for backing are heavily weighted toward simple, abrupt retouch, but semisteep retouch was also used and *sur enclume* technique, while rarely seen, was known. While some microburins are present, their low number is suggestive of fortuitious occurrence (Microburin Index—2.34).

TYPOLOGICAL CONSIDERATIONS

The assemblage has a strong microlithic element which is almost exclusively formed by the combination of backing and truncations, resulting in the presence of a series of morphologically related types—rectangles, trapezes, backed and truncated bladelets, etc. Backing is almost always straight, as are truncations. When convex shapes occur, they are only minimally convex, although concave forms are more pronounced.

Of the unbacked tools, endscrapers, notched pieces, and truncated pieces are most common. Endscrapers are primarily made on blades (68.46%), the vast majority of which are fragmentary. Whether this means that blade fragments were the normally desired blank form or that most were broken during use cannot be ascertained. Endscrapers are dominated by simple convex pieces, but ogival and thin-nosed forms occur with some frequency. All other types, particularly thick scrapers, are rare and generally atypical.

As noted at the beginning of this report, this assemblage has been assigned to what has been called Geometric Kebaran "A" (Bar-Yosef, 1970). It is not the intention of the author to make extensive comparisons between the D5 assemblage and other Geometric Kebaran "A" assemblages. However, the assemblage from D5 exhibits the following defined Geometric Kebaran "A" traits: more scrapers on blades than on flakes; few burins; more geometric and proto-geometric microliths than non-geometric microliths; and trapezes and rectangles dominant in the geometric class.

The archaeological significance of the Geometric Kebaran "A" is still obscure. While clearly within the Kebaran Complex both typologically and technologically, it does show some typological and technological traits which are suggestive of at least a separate facies or phase. It is Bar-Yosef's contention (1970) that a phase difference is involved, although there is a paucity of stratigraphic or radiometric confirmation. Unfortunately, the excavation of D5 was unable to date the assemblage successfully, and it must be noted that the Kebaran is among the most poorly dated archaeological complexes in the Near East. Stratigraphically, the Kebaran can be placed, at least in part, between the Levantine Aurignacian and the Natufian, neither of which is itself well dated. Only when the temporal parameters of these groups are fully revealed will it be possible to focus on intra-Complex relationships. At the moment, it is equally possible that the Geometric Kebaran "A" is merely one industry within a generally synchronous Industrial Complex or that it is a late phase of the Kebaran, evolving toward the Natufian (as suggested by Bar-Yosef, 1970).

NOTES

[1] The additional 3 sq m units were given to the Department of Antiquities, without detailed study.

[2] For example, J. Tixier, 1963; de Sonneville-Bordes and Perrot, 1954-1956; Bar-Yosef, 1970; or the unpublished type list put together during the Wenner-Gren Conference on Levantine Typology, held in London, 1970.

[3] Five atypical trapezes fall way outside the cluster. These are only trapezes in the grossest sense.

BIBLIOGRAPHY

BAR-YOSEF, O., 1970. "The Epi-Paleolithic Cultures of Palestine." Ph.D. dissertation, The Hebrew University.

————, 1975. "The Epipaleolithic of Palestine and Sinai." In *Problems in Prehistory: North Africa and the Levant*, edited by F. Wendorf and A. E. Marks, pp. 363-78. Dallas: Southern Methodist University Press.

HENRY, D., 1973. "The Natufian Site of Rosh Zin: A Preliminary Report." *Palestine Exploration Quarterly* 105:129-40.

MARKS, A. E., in press. "The Epipaleolithic of the Central Negev: Current Status." *Eretz Israel* 13.

————; CREW, H.; FERRING, R.; and PHILLIPS, J., 1972. "Prehistoric Sites near Har Harif." *Israel Exploration Journal* 22(2-3):73-85.

————; PHILLIPS, J.; CREW, H.; and FERRING, R., 1971. "Prehistoric Sites near En-Avdat in the Negev." *Israel Exploration Journal* 21(1):13-24.

de SONNEVILLE-BORDES, D., and PERROT, J., 1954. "Lexique typologie du paléolithique supérieur: Outillage lithique—I, Grattoirs—II, Outils solutréens." *Bulletin de la Société Préhistorique Française* 51(7):327-35.

————, and PERROT, J., 1956*a*. "Lexique typologie du paléolithique supérieur: Outillage lithique—IV, Burins." *Bulletin de la Société Préhistorique Française* 53(7-8):408-12.

————, and PERROT, J., 1956*b*. "Lexique typologie du paléolithique supérieur: Outillage lithique—V, Outillage à bord abattu—VI, Pieces tronquées—VII' Lames retouchées—VIII, Pieces variés—IX, Outillage Lamellaire, Pointe Azilienne." *Bulletin de la Société Préhistorique Française* 53(9):547-59.

TIXIER, J., 1963. *Typologie de l'epipaléolithique du Maghreb*. Mémoires du Centre de Recherches Anthropologiques, Préhistoriques et Ethnographiques. Paris: Arts et Métiers Graphiques.

ROSH ZIN: A NATUFIAN SETTLEMENT NEAR EIN AVDAT

Don O. Henry

The University of Tulsa

INTRODUCTION

During the archaeological survey of the Avdat area in 1969, the Natufian site of Rosh Zin, covering approximately 900 sq m, was discovered (Marks, 1969; Marks, et al., 1971; Henry, 1973a). Initial testing of the site was begun in 1969, with excavations beginning in 1970 and continuing in 1971 and 1972.

The site of Rosh Zin, elevation 520 m, is situated on the crest of a finger of the North Divshon Ridge which forms a partial northern border of the Divshon Plain. The site overlooks the plain and is about 1.5 km north of the perennial spring of Ein Avdat (fig. 11-1).

Although the region around Avdat normally receives under 200 mm of precipitation annually and exhibits an Irano-Turanian floral community (Zohary, 1952), the broken topography and the presence of perennial springs in the immediate area of Rosh Zin result in considerable variation in microenvironments (see Munday, this volume).

EXCAVATIONS

METHODOLOGY

The site was initially excavated in 7 randomly placed one sq m units in order to determine its subsurface area and depth. The lack of observable geologic stratigraphy necessitated the use of 5 cm arbitrary levels for vertical control which followed from ground contour. Mapping of individual artifacts was impossible because of the richness of the site in terms of artifact density. Horizontal provenience, however, was maintained by one sq m units, which were subdivided by features, such as walls or pavement, if the situation demanded it. All units were screened through 2 mm wire mesh in an attempt to recover the smallest of artifacts and microfauna.

In excavating the randomly placed units, an area containing a midden deposit and architectural evidence was encountered (fig. 11-2). The delimitation of this midden area and its associated structures became the main focus of excavations.

RESULTS

Nine units located outside the midden/structure area varied in depth from 40 cm to as little as 5 cm because of the undulating bedrock. The matrix of the deposits consisted of a yellow desert loess and occasional nodules or fragments of limestone derived from the locally weathered bedrock. Flint artifacts constituted most of the cultural material, although isolated pieces of *Dentalium* shell were also recovered. Some faunal remains were found, but they were generally unidentifiable because of termite activity.

The excavated midden/structure area consisted of 62 sq m, ranging in depth from 50 cm to 5 centimeters. Like the outside units, the depth of deposit was controlled by the underlying bedrock. The bedrock in this area formed a shallow basin about 8 m in diameter, outcropping on the surface at the edge of the basin and sloping downward until it reached a depth of about 50 cm near the basin's center (fig. 11-3). The deposit in the midden/structure area was a gray to dark gray fine-grained sand and loess containing large quantities of splintered and burned bone.

The midden/structure area displayed a high

317

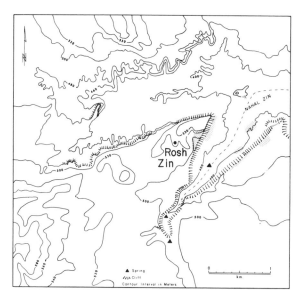

FIG. 11-1–Location of Site Rosh Zin (D16) on the North Divshon ridge.

density of flint artifacts in addition to containing ground stone and ornamental objects (decorated ostrich eggshells, perforated discs, and *Dentalium* shells). Although faunal material was prevalent throughout the area, bone preservation was rarely good.

While there was no observable geologic stratigraphy within the occupation deposits at Rosh Zin, it was possible to distinguish three phases of occupation within the midden/structure area on the basis of architectural constructions.

The earliest occupation appeared as a deposit 6 to 10 cm thick directly overlying the limestone bedrock. A bedrock mortar at a depth of 40 cm below the surface was associated with this occupation (fig. 11-4).

The next occupational phase was recognized by the construction of a pavement of undressed limestone slabs covering an area of a little more than 6 sq m (fig. 11-5). Construction of the pavement acted to form a flat, level surface over much of the southwestern part of the midden/structure area, extending an area of naturally flat bedrock. This pavement and other associated stones defined

an occupational surface at a depth of 15 to 20 cm below the present surface. There was approximately 10 cm of artifact-bearing deposit overlying the pavement which was considered to be associated with the pavement occupation.

The final phase of occupation occurred with the construction of at least four oval structures (2.5 to 3.0 m in diameter) made of undressed limestone cobbles[1] (fig. 11-6). The walls of the structures were, for the most part, defined by a single course of stones of varying dimensions, with the lowest parts of the stones appearing at about 10 cm below the present surface. Although only a few segments of the walls displayed two courses of stones, with a maximum wall height of 35 cm, many areas exhibited considerable wall collapse, implying that three to four courses existed at the time of occupation.

An interesting feature appears in the last phase of occupation, contemporary with the wall construction. During the first season of excavation, a monolithic limestone column (1 m by 40 cm in diameter) was observed partially buried at the same depth as the structure. During the last season of excavation, it was discovered that the monolith, broken at one end, articulated nicely with another *in situ* limestone column fragment set into the ground in an upright position to a depth of 30 cm (fig. 11-4).

The monolith was situated directly inside the northwestern wall section of the largest of the four structures: Locus 4 (figs. 11-4 and 11-6). In erecting the monolithic column the prehistoric occupants of Rosh Zin had dug through the pavement level and had packed a cobble fill about the base of the column for support. Some of the disturbed pavement slabs were utilized to form the northwesternmost section of the wall. The material for the monolith was obtained on or near the site from natural columnar limestone. Although it appears to have been shaped into a phallic form, it is difficult to ascertain the degree of

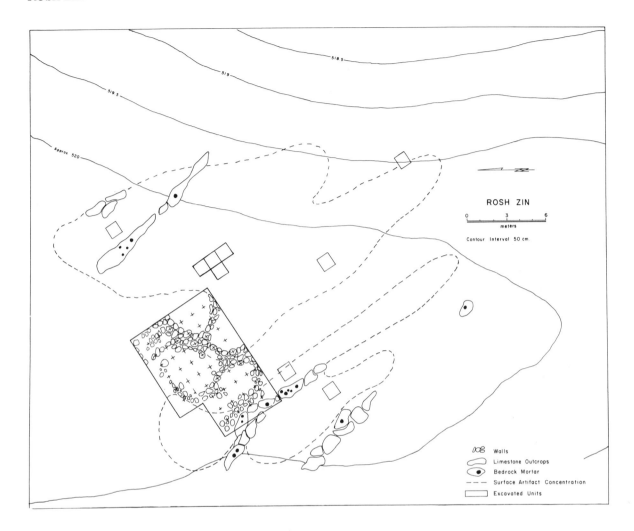

FIG. 11-2—Topographic map of Site Rosh Zin, showing areas of excavation. *Small squares* indicate initial test excavations.

modification resulting from natural weathering of the exposed limestone.

Near the base of the column in the cobble fill, and below the wall, a cache containing a matched pair of grooved stones (placed with their grooves together), a shaped limestone disc, and five unusually large pyramidal cores were recovered (fig. 11-7). The grooved stones are morphologically similar to other grooved stones found at the site, but the manner in which they were arranged and their association with the column and the other artifacts in the cache are suggestive of ritualistic placement, as opposed to utilitarian storage. The cores, while exhibiting a shape similar to other pyramidal cores at Rosh Zin, are unique in their size and symmetry. The mean maximum core facet lengths of the cores from the cache register 70.5 mm, thus exceeding mean maximum core facet lengths from elsewhere on the site by 42.3 mm and mean maximum lengths of primary elements by 36.3 millimeters. These metric observations imply that the cores from the cache were not merely unworked cores, but were specially manufactured. In addition to these items, it should be noted that several fragments of decorated ostrich eggshell were found in the occupation

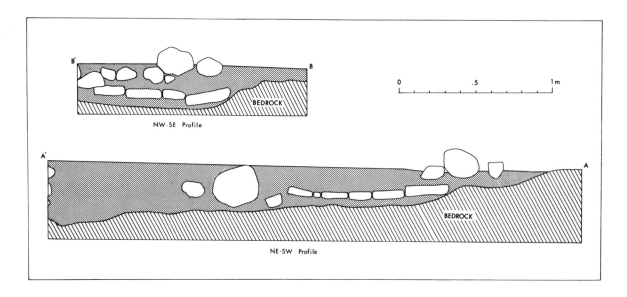

FIG. 11-3—Schematic profiles through structure/midden area. See Fig. 11-6 for transects.

deposit of the structure containing the column (Locus 4), but no where else on the site. The flint assemblage, however, does not display significant differences from other loci in the midden/structure area (to be discussed later).

While it is difficult to explain the specific significance of the limestone column and the cache buried adjacent to its base, it does appear that the feature and associated artifacts represent some form of ritual activity, which is not uncommon to Natufian settlements.

The site appears to have been deflated some 10 to 15 cm since the final phase of occupation. The extremely dense artifact concentration on the surface of the site (ca. 400 per sq m) would tend to support this proposal. In addition, examination of the weathering on bedrock outcrops in the site reveals three zones of patination: (1) an unpatinated zone corresponding with the buried surface of the rock; (2) a lightly patinated zone beginning at the present ground surface and extending 10 to 15 cm up the outcrops; and (3) a highly weathered zone over the remainder of the outcrops. Because it is in the

highly patinated zone that the bedrock mortars appear (excluding the buried mortar in Locus 4), it would seem that this zone has been exposed since the occupation of the site. It is also probable that the lightly patinated zone was buried during the final phases of occupation and was later exposed to weathering when the site was deflated.

FAUNA AND POLLEN

Faunal preservation, as mentioned earlier, was poor because of extensive termite activity. Due to the paucity of identifiable bones, intrasite distributions and other specifically faunal related studies could not be undertaken. It was possible, however, to identify a number of species, including *Gazella dorcus*, *Capra ibex*, and *Dama* sp. among the megafauna; and starred gecko, chucker partridge, and mole rat among the smaller forms (Tchernov, this volume). It is not surprising that gazelle and wild goat were found, as gazelle are common in all Natufian faunal assemblages, while the proximity of the Nahal Zin cliffs would have made the exploitation of wild goat a simple matter. The recovery of

FIG. 11-4—Photograph of Locus 4 showing part of pavement, walls, and base of pillar. Note bedrock mortar in lower right corner and displaced top of pillar at top center.

Dama remains indicates some arboreal vegetation in the area, which is now lacking. The presence of smaller forms, with the probable exclusion of the mole rat, suggests that Natufian exploitation included at least two small animals which are still common in the area and which provide reasonable amounts of edible meat.

Palynological information reinforces the faunal data, indicating a more humid environment during Natufian occupation than is the case today. The pollen samples clearly document a Mediterranean floral community with *Quercus calliprinos*, *Olea europaea*, and *Pistacia* sp., while the dominance of *Chenopodiaceae* among the N.A.P., combined with

the presence of A.P., reinforces an interpretation calling for a higher level of humidity than is present in the area today (Horowitz, this volume). The overall picture obtained for both the fauna and the pollen is of a somewhat dry Mediterranean biotope, but still much richer than the current Irano-Turanian biotope.

LITHIC ARTIFACTS

Detailed analyses of 18 sq m have furnished information on 3,994 flint tools and 59,162 pieces of debitage and debris. Because of the huge sample excavated, the studied samples were taken as follows: Locus 1–2 sq m, with

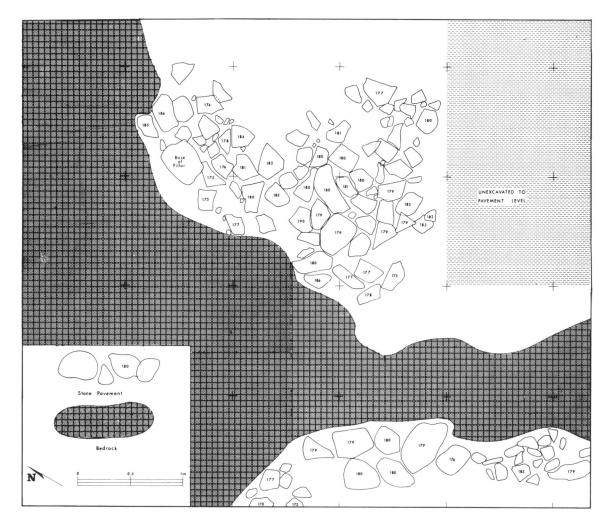

FIG. 11-5—Plan of pavement level, showing position and height of paving stones in relation to bedrock.

an average depth of 25 cm; Locus 2—2 sq m with an average depth of 25 cm; Locus 3—2 sq m with an average depth of 30 cm; Locus 4—4 sq m with an average depth of 35 cm; and within the outside area a total of 8 sq m was excavated, to an average depth of 20 centimeters. Samples were taken from each locus and from the outside area in order that studies of intrasite variability would be possible. Technological, stylistic, functional, and mechanical analyses were undertaken so that varying categories of information might be utilized in intrasite comparisons.

TECHNOLOGICAL ANALYSIS

Configurations of the debris and debitage inventories exhibit insignificant variability between the pavement and structure levels; however, the level below pavement displays a higher frequency of chips and cores (table 11-1). The greater number of chips and cores might indicate that this prepavement occupation was one of generalized activity, where flint tools were initially processed, fabricated, and used. Beginning with the pavement occupation, the midden/structure area seems to have been used less for the initial stages of

FIG. 11-6–Plan of structure level, showing position and height of building stones. Considerable rock fall is shown between Loci 1 and 4.

FIG. 11-7—Artifacts from cache: *a*—limestone disc; *b*—paired grooved stones; *c-g*—large blade cores.

TABLE 11-1
Comparison of Debitage and Debris Configurations by Occupation*
(as Percents)

	Structure (.3m^3)		Pavement (.4m^3)		Below Pavement (.3m^3)		Outside (.8m^3)	
		r†		r		r		r
Flakes	28.2	67.7	25.0	63.1	9.3	49.1	15.9	55.6
Blades	11.5	27.5	12.5	31.4	7.4	39.0	9.9	34.6
Primary Elements	1.1	2.6	1.3	3.2	1.1	5.8	1.2	4.2
Core Trimming Elements	0.6	1.4	0.5	1.4	0.6	3.1	1.1	3.8
Cores	0.3	0.8	0.4	0.9	0.6	3.0	0.5	1.7
Microburins	3.8	—	4.2	—	3.1	—	5.9	—
Burin Spalls	0.3	—	0.3	—	0.3	—	0.1	—
Chips	50.7	—	53.0	—	75.0	—	63.9	—
Chunks	3.5	—	2.8	—	2.6	—	1.5	—
Total	100.0	100.0	100.0	100.0	100.0	100.0	100.0	100.0
Sample	13,100	5,458	11,152	4,436	9,882	1,872	13,262	3,790

*Structure, Pavement, and Below Pavement samples were taken from Locus 4.

†Restricted to flakes, blades, primary elements, core trimming elements, and cores.

stone tool production. The frequencies of primary and core-trimming elements also are higher beneath the pavement, which would be expected if greater initial processing were being carried out during that occupation.

In addition to the vertical variability in debris and debitage configurations, there also appears significant horizontal variability. Comparison of the structure and pavement levels of Locus 4 with three contiguous units outside the midden/structure area reveals that chips, cores, primary elements, and core-trimming elements are more numerous in the latter (table 11-1). This, again, is believed to represent a greater emphasis on initial stone tool processing than is found in the later phases of occupation of the midden/structure area. Unfortunately, because of the absence of observable geologic stratigraphy, it is impossible to correlate the outside area with a specific level in the midden/structure area, although clear parallels may be seen between the below pavement and outside area.

The dimensional characteristics exhibited by blade and flake samples evidence considerable homogeneity between levels and areas of the site (table 11-2). The absence of dimensional variation would imply that similar technological processes were employed in stone tool production in the various phases of the occupation and in the different areas of occupation.

In examining the distrubution of tools according to the artifact class on which they were manufactured, it is notable that primary elements and cores were seldom utilized (table 11-3). Core tools are often in the form of hammerstones, although scrapers on cores occasionally appear. The infrequent use of primary elements is no doubt a result of the

TABLE 11-2
Mean Dimensional Characteristics of
Blades and Flakes (mm)

	Structure Level	Pavement Level	Below Pavement	Outside Area
Blades				
Length	30.5	30.0	31.9	28.3
Width	11.7	11.3	11.7	10.8
Sample	99	105	117	112
Flakes				
Length	25.9	24.0	23.6	26.5
Width	20.1	21.2	20.9	21.5
Sample	104	126	118	110

TABLE 11-3
Distribution of Tool Sample
by Artifact Class
N = 1.225

	Percent
Blade	60.1
Flake	38.5
Primary Element	1.1
Core	.3
	100.0

paucity of this artifact class at Rosh Zin (table 11-3). This low frequency of primary elements might indicate that much of the raw material utilized at the site was being initially trimmed at its source or at least outside the site's confines.

Blade platform and bulb attributes tend to confirm that there is little variation in the techniques of stone tool fabrication (table 11-4). Perhaps the only significant variability occurs in the number of cortex platforms with the level below pavement and the outside area displaying a somewhat higher frequency than those of the structure and pavement levels. This, of course, does not indicate

a different technique of production, but merely more initial processing during these occupations. An examination of other blade attributes, including lateral profile, alignment of lateral edges (dorsal shape), and distal shape, shows considerable consistency between the various occupations (table 11-5). Some exceptions may be seen, however. The outside area appears to be somewhat aberrant in the higher proportional occurrence of parallel-sided blades and in the lower occurrence of those with oblique distal extremities. The significance of these differences remains obscure.

The cores recovered at Rosh Zin (fig. 11-8*a-i*) are predominantly multiple-platform varieties of which opposed-platform cores are the most common (table 11-6). The platforms are normally unfaceted, being formed by a single blow. The mean maximum core facet length observed on Rosh Zin core samples was 28.2 millimeters. In comparing this measurement to the dimensions of debitage, particularly blades (table 11-2), it would seem that there was little difference in the initial size of cores and their exhausted dimensions.

Examination of the microburin technique at Rosh Zin reveals significant variation in its utilization during the various occupations (table 11-7). In using the conventional Microburin Index, the structure level and the outside area indicate greater utilization of this technique than do the pavement and below pavement levels. The conventional Microburin Index is not restricted to only those tools that are associated with microburin production; therefore, as a computational method designed to indicate the amount of utilization of the microburin technique, it is often misleading (Henry, 1973*b*). Restricted Microburin Indices imply that the microburin technique was least used in the outside area (table 11-7). The structure level displays the highest Restricted Microburin Index and the highest microburin to tool ratio. This would suggest that the fabrication of geometrics and trunca-

TABLE 11-4
Platform and Bulb Attributes
on Blade Samples as Percents

	Structure Level	Pavement Level	Below Pavement	Outside Area
Platforms				
a. Unfaceted	55	60	61	64
b. Multifaceted	10	8	9	7
c. Cortex	1	1	7	4
d. Crushed	34	31	23	25
Total	100	100	100	100
Sample	99	110	86	174
Bulbs				
Lipped	11	6	7	6
Pointed	–	3	7	1
Unlipped	56	64	60	69
Crushed	33	27	26	24
Total	100	100	100	100
Sample	99	110	78	181

tions was emphasized in this occupation. This proposed final fabrication of tools agrees with the other debitage information, which indicates final processing, use, and maintenance of tools during this occupation phase, within the midden/structure area.

Examination of the position of the microburin scar in relation to the truncated piece reveals that of a sample of 793 microburins, 54.5% are on proximal pieces (fig. 11-11*ee, ii, jj*), 38.3% are on distal pieces (fig. 11-11*ff, gg*), 0.3% are double, while the remaining 6.9% are indeterminate. *Piquant trièdres* consistently appear, but always in very low numbers (fig. 11-11*hh*).

In summary, the technological analysis of Rosh Zin artifacts demonstrates that the variability between occupations is a result of emphasis being placed on different stages of stone tool production, rather than differences in technological methods.

FUNCTIONAL ANALYSIS

In comparing tool classes from the various areas and levels across the site, major variability exists between the midden/structure and the outside area (table 11-8). The tool class configuration of the outside area (upper 10 cm) does not fall within the range of variation displayed by the four loci of the midden/structure in several tool classes. Geometrics are much less common in the outside area than in the midden/structure loci. This paucity of geometrics corresponds to the lack of emphasis placed on the microburin technique in that area. On the other hand, backed pieces, retouched pieces, denticulates, and notches are more abundant in the outside area. Although the functions of these tool classes are unknown, they tend to covary directly in the Rosh Zin assemblage (table 11-8). Thus, it would seem that the midden/

TABLE 11-5
Blade Attributes by Areas and Levels shown as Percents of Samples

Attribute	Structure Level	Pavement Level	Below Pavement	Outside Area
Lateral Profile				
a. Incurvate	66	60	62	57
b. Flat	32	37	29	40
c. Twisted	2	3	9	3
Total	100	100	100	100
Sample	99	90	84	120
Dorsal Shape				
a. Parallel	15	24	26	35
b. Expanding	31	26	23	13
c. Converging	54	50	51	52
Total	100	100	100	100
Sample	99	90	84	494
Distal Shape				
a. Pointed	32	31	29	38
b. Blunt	61	59	54	61
c. Oblique	7	10	17	1
Total	100	100	100	100
Sample	99	90	82	270

TABLE 11-6
Core Varieties from
Locus 4, All Levels

Core Varieties	Percent
Single Platform, Unfaceted	10.6
Single Platform, Faceted	7.3
Opposed Platform, Opposite Side	6.9
Opposed Platform, Same Side	23.3
Opposed Platform, Combination	4.2
Ninety-Degree Opposed Platform	42.0
Irregular	.0
Ninety-Degree	6.2
TOTAL	100.0
Sample	74

structure area, a place of intensive habitation, would have been a location where a variety of tasks were performed with a wide range of tools that were, for the most part, initially processed elsewhere. The high frequency of geometrics would indicate that the manufacture of composite tools was carried out in this area.

STYLISTIC ANALYSIS

This analysis views the following three particular attributes which most probably do not effect the function of the types on which they occur and, therefore, may be considered stylistic: the types of retouch used on geo-

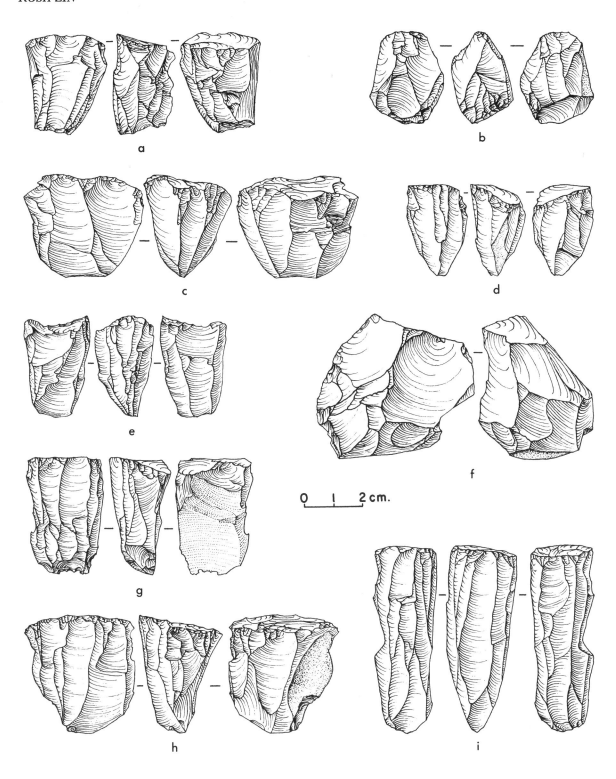

FIG. 11-8—Cores from Site Rosh Zin: *a, b*—opposed platform types; *c-e, g-i*—single platform (*i* is quite atypical for the assemblage); *f*—flake core.

TABLE 11-7

Microburin Indices and Microburin to Tool Ratios

	Structure Level	Pavement Level	Below Pavement	Outside Area
Microburin Index	54.7	42.6	46.3	52.1
Restricted Microburin Index	84.8	78.9	79.1	73.8
Ratio of Microburins to Tools[1]	5.5:1	3.8:1	3.8:1	2.8:1
Sample	908	1,097	660	650

[1] Includes geometrics, backed and truncated pieces, and truncations.

TABLE 11-8

Tool Kit Configurations by Loci, Level, and Area as Percents

Level[1]	Locus 1			Locus 2			Locus 3			Locus 4			Outside Area
	S	P	BP	S	P	BP	S	P	BP	S	P	BP	
Tool Class													
Scrapers	6.1	5.4	7.2	5.6	5.8	8.3	6.2	7.4	2.5	9.2	5.1	6.5	9.8
Burins	6.1	3.9	8.7	2.1	7.0	15.3	12.4	7.6	5.1	11.9	11.0	11.5	2.1
Geometrics	33.5	39.8	36.2	42.6	39.9	29.0	38.9	43.1	63.3	40.5	43.8	47.3	4.9
Backed pieces	6.1	8.1	8.7	11.3	5.8	4.2	8.8	7.8	3.8	11.3	10.2	10.5	13.7
Perforators	1.7	1.2	2.9	1.0	3.1	0.0	1.8	0.2	0.0	0.7	1.4	2.0	1.9
Truncations	8.4	10.4	8.7	9.2	8.5	4.2	7.1	8.5	3.8	10.7	6.7	4.3	11.5
Multiple tools	0.0	0.8	0.0	0.0	1.2	0.0	0.9	0.9	0.0	1.0	0.5	0.4	0.0
Denticulates	2.8	2.3	4.4	2.6	1.9	9.8	1.8	1.9	3.8	4.4	1.4	0.4	9.4
Notches	17.3	13.9	10.1	12.8	12.4	11.1	11.5	11.6	6.3	15.1	11.3	8.5	21.7
Retouched pieces	16.2	11.6	8.7	12.8	13.2	11.1	4.4	6.8	6.3	9.7	8.3	5.7	23.4
Massive pieces	1.7	2.3	2.9	0.0	1.2	5.6	4.4	3.0	1.3	0.5	1.6	1.3	0.0
Sickle blades	0.0	0.4	0.0	0.0	0.0	0.0	0.9	0.6	0.0	0.5	0.6	0.7	0.0
Varia	0.0	0.0	1.5	0.0	0.0	1.4	0.9	0.6	3.8	0.5	0.3	0.0	2.6
Sample	179	259	69	195	258	72	113	527	79	411	629	459	286

[1] S—Structure level; P—Pavement level; BP—Below Pavement or equivalent depth.

metrics, the specific form of truncations, and some varieties of burins.

The type of retouch used in the manufacture of geometrics is quite variable, but the proportional occurrence of each is virtually the same within both the midden/structure and outside areas (table 11-9). It should be noted that while Helwan retouch occurs, its incidence is so low that it has no diagnostic value. There is a total absence of inverse, semisteep retouch, which is usually associated with a true Helwan technology.

The internal consistency of burin forms is quite high between occupation levels within the midden/structure area. Considering only simple burins on snap or on truncation, in

TABLE 11-9
Varieties of Retouch on Geometrics

Form	Midden/Structure Area		Outside Area	
	Number	Percent	Number	Percent
Abrupt	188	72.03	170	66.14
Semisteep	9	3.45	13	5.06
Bipolar (*sur enclume*)	46	17.63	54	21.01
Alternate	16	6.13	15	5.84
Bifacial (Helwan)	1	0.38	5	1.95
Inverse, semisteep	0	0.00	0	0.00
Abrupt/Bipolar	1	0.38	0	0.00
TOTALS	261	100.00	257	100.00

each level burins on snap account for between 50% and 52% of the sample, and those on straight truncation for another 25% to 28 percent. The only significant variation occurs for oblique and concave truncations in the structure level. In the lower two levels the former accounts for between 12% and 14% and the latter for between 8% and 9 percent. In the structure level, however, obliquely truncated burins reach 22%, while those on concave truncations are rare, only 3 percent. In spite of this variability, the degree of similarity between occupation levels is striking.

It is only within the forms of simple truncations that variability reaches significant proportions, although the general preferential patterns remain the same in each level and area, with oblique truncations followed by straight truncations in every case (table 11-10).

MECHANICAL ANALYSIS

The raw material at Rosh Zin consists of a gray chert, a dark brown flint, and a gray, translucent chalcedony. The flint and chert are available as large outcrops ca. 300 m from the site. The chalcedony appears in limestone deposits on the cliff east of the site and forms the bulk of the utilized raw material.

A differential utilization of the raw material is reflected in the change from chalcedony to flint or chert as the size of the tools increases. Few tools over 70 mm in length are made on chalcedony, and none of the microliths are fashioned on flint or chert. It is possible that the different uses of the raw material are results of the chalcedony being more amenable to the fine retouch required in the manufacture of microliths, particularly geometrics, than are the chert or flint. The chalcedony tends to occur in thin veins, and its small size would tend to discourage the manufacture of the larger pieces.

MORPHOLOGICAL TYPOLOGY

A morphological typology on a tool sample from the midden/structure area furnished considerable information on the tool types exhibited at Rosh Zin (table 11-11). This sample is generally similar to other Natufian assemblages on the class level and, therefore, should be representative of the Natufian on the type level. The tool sample, consisting of about one-third of the tools analyzed at Rosh Zin, was recovered from 8 m² (representing all the loci) in the midden/structure area.

TABLE 11-10
Varieties of Truncations, as Percents

Form of Truncation	Structure Level	Pavement Level	Below Pavement	Outside Area
Straight	26	31	24	34
Oblique	51	57	67	42
Concave	13	8	6	8
Convex	10	4	3	15
TOTALS	100	100	100	100
Samples	39	26	33	52

Notes on the Retouched Tools

The *scraper class* is made up primarily of simple endscrapers, with those on blades occurring only somewhat more frequently than those on flakes. Although the majority of endscrapers occur on pieces under 50 mm in length, there seems to be a fairly wide range in the width of their working bits (fig. 11-9*d, e, i*). The carinated scrapers are considerably smaller than those associated with the local Upper Paleolithic, but they are typologically the same, including some semicarinated examples (fig. 11-9*f, g*).

The *multiple tool class* displays the endscraper/burin as the most common variety (fig. 11-9*a-c*). Various other tool combinations appear, but not consistently enough to establish them as separate types.

The *burin class* is nearly evenly divided between burins on truncations (fig. 11-10*k-m*) and burins on snaps and old surfaces (fig. 11-10*g-i, n*). The majority of the truncated varieties appear as straight and oblique forms on blades with well-formed truncations. The burins on snaps and old surfaces do not consistently appear on any specific kind of blank, and most of the burins are formed with single blows. Multiple burins are mostly on truncations (fig. 11-10*o-q*), although a very few are on snaps (fig. 11-10*j*).

The *perforator class* is characterized by the bilaterally converging backed bladelet (a variety of *mèche de foret*) which is consistent in form and fine workmanship (fig. 11-11*oo, pp*).

In the *notch class*, single notches, the most common type, represent about one-third of the sample (fig. 11-10*e*). Multiple notches occur less fre-quently and appear primarily on blades (fig. 11-10*d, f*). Micro-notches (< 5 mm across) form a major part of the class (fig. 11-10*b, c*), and are possibly associated with the microburin technique. Notches on retouched pieces are also well represented (fig. 11-10*a*).

Within the *denticulate class* two out of three occur on continuously retouched pieces. As a group, they are generally poor, except when very large. These latter, however, have been classed as massive tools.

The *truncation class* mainly includes oblique truncations (fig. 11-11*dd*). The retouch is normally abrupt, but it often lacks the regularity exhibited on backed pieces. Truncations are found on a wide range of sizes of blanks, but appear about equally on blades (46%) and flakes (54%).

The *geometric class* is dominated by lunates, varying in length from less than 10 mm to over 30 mm (mean, 18 mm) (fig. 11-11*h-t, v, w*). A number of pieces were recovered which exhibit the various stages of geometric manufacture, normally utilizing the microburin technique (fig. 11-11*x-z*). Triangles are the second most common geometric and they display about the same size range as do the lunates (fig. 11-11*b-g*). There is considerable morphological variation and some might be considered atypical.

In the *abrupt retouch class*, straight-backed bladelets, pointed straight-backed bladelets, and arch-backed bladelets are most common (fig. 11-11*kk-mm*), although a number of irregularly and partially backed pieces were also recovered. Backed and truncated pieces are rare (fig. 11-11*cc*), as are backed bladelets with variously modified bases (fig. 11-11*u, aa, bb, nn*).

TABLE 11-11
Typology of Tool Sample from Midden/Structure Area

Type	Number	Percent
Scraper Class		7.3
Endscraper on flake	28	2.3
Endscraper on retouched flake	4	0.3
Endscraper on blade	33	2.7
Endscraper on retouched blade	5	0.4
Circular scraper	1	0.1
Core scraper	1	0.1
Denticulated endscraper	5	0.4
Carinated endscraper	7	0.6
Shouldered or nosed scraper	4	0.3
Endscraper with lateral notch	1	0.1
Multiple Tool Class		0.6
Endscraper/burin	2	0.2
Other multiple tool	5	0.4
Burin Class		10.3
Dihedral burin	6	0.5
Burin on snap or old surface	52	4.2
Burin on straight truncation	26	2.1
Burin on oblique truncation	19	1.6
Burin on concave truncation	4	0.3
Burin on convex truncation	3	0.2
Transverse burin on lateral retouch	4	0.3
Transverse burin on lateral notch	3	0.2
Multiple burin on truncation	3	0.2
Multiple mixed burin	8	0.7
Perforator Class		1.9
Perforator	9	0.7
Double backed perforator	15	1.2
Notch Class		12.2
Single notch	79	6.4
Single notch with retouch	16	1.3
Multiple notch	18	1.5
Multiple notch with retouch	2	0.2
Micronotch	34	2.8
Denticulate Class		2.7

Denticulated piece	10	0.8
Denticulated piece with retouch	23	1.9
Truncation Class		8.0
Straight truncation	26	2.1
Oblique truncation	56	4.6
Concave truncation	10	0.8
Convex truncation	6	0.5
Geometric Class		37.1
Lunate	264	21.4
Lunate with bifacial retouch	3	0.2
Lunate, atypical or incomplete	82	6.7
Isosceles triangle	49	4.0
Isosceles triangle, atypical or incomplete	5	0.4
Scalene triangle	3	0.2
Trapeze	10	0.8
Trapeze, atypical or incomplete	1	0.1
Fragment of geometric	41	3.3
Abrupt Retouch Class		8.8
Straight backed blade	3	0.2
Bifacially retouched blade (Helwan)	1	0.1
Arched backed bladelet	13	1.1
Straight backed bladelet with basal truncation	2	0.2
Straight backed bladelet with distal truncation	1	0.1
Straight backed bladelet	19	1.6
Double straight backed bladelet	5	0.4
Bifacially retouched bladelet (Helwan)	1	0.1
Pointed, straight backed bladelet	10	0.8
Pointed, straight backed bladelet with basal truncation	1	0.1
Various backed piece	16	1.3
Partially backed piece	18	1.5
Fragment of backed piece	16	1.3
Retouch Class		6.7
Retouched piece, unilateral-obverse	61	5.0
Retouched piece, unilateral-inverse	16	1.3
Retouched piece, bilateral-obverse	1	0.1
Retouched piece, bilateral-inverse	1	0.1
Pointed, straight retouched piece	2	.2
Massive Piece Class		1.6
Endscraper on massive piece	4	0.3

Denticulate on massive piece	5	0.4
Notch on massive piece	2	0.2
Bifacially worked massive piece	8	0.7
Utilized Piece Class		2.3
Sickle blade	6	0.5
Lame à mâchures	13	1.1
Hammerstone	9	0.7
Varia Class		.5
Varia	6	0.5
TOTAL	1,225	100.0

Pieces in the *retouch class* were primarily treated obversely along one edge, exhibiting a regular, fine retouch which resulted from intentional modification rather than from use. The retouched pieces appear about equally on blades (47%) and flakes (53%).

The *massive piece class* includes a number of types similar to those described in other classes (e.g., scrapers, notches, and denticulates); however, the pieces included in this class fall well above the size range exhibited by morphologically similar pieces, normally in excess of 80 mm in length, 50 mm in width, and often more than 30 mm thick (fig. 11-9*h*, *j*). Although these tools never appear in high frequencies, they are consistently displayed in Natufian assemblages (Garrod and Bate, 1937; Cauvin, 1966). The most common type at Rosh Zin is the bifacially worked massive piece, including two which appear to be rough axes (fig. 11-13*g*, *h*), but massive scrapers, denticulates, and notches also appear (figs. 11-12*a-c*, *e*, *f*; 10-13*d*). A large scraper was also found (fig. 11-14).

The *utilized piece class* includes those artifacts which have been unintentionally modified through use. *Lames à mâchures*, pieces with heavy use retouch, form the' majority of this class. Although pieces exhibiting sheen are rare, they do appear consistently in the assemblage. Of these, four appeared as backed bladelets and two as unbacked bladelets (fig. 10-11*a*). Hammerstones display considerable size variation, with the larger pieces being of flint (figs.

11-13*e*, *f*; 11-15) or chert and the smaller pieces fashioned of chalcedony (fig. 11-13*a-c*).

The *varia class* is comprised of artifacts that could not be classified within the other categories. Backed elements exhibiting unusual morphologies (e.g., concave backed bladelet with truncation on microburin scar) constituted the majority of the class.

Ground Stone Artifacts

The ground stone consists of bedrock mortars, pestles, handstones, querns, grooved stones, and pieces exhibiting wear striations.

Near the midden/structure area, limestone outcrops contain two clusters of bedrock mortars, a total of 17 individual examples, while another single mortar was discovered underlying the earliest occupation level in Locus 4. These cone-shaped mortars range in top diameter from 16 to 9.5 cm and converge to a bottom diameter of between 10 and 7 cm (table 11-12). The mortars range in depth from 46 to 12 cm, with an average depth of 24 centimeters. The mortars appeared in four stages of utilization: (1) those having been started but probably not used, with depths of 2.0 to 3.0 cm; (2) those being utilized at the time of occupation, with depths generally around 10 cm, but ranging to 30 cm (table 11-12, nos. 2-4, 7, 10, and 13); (3) those

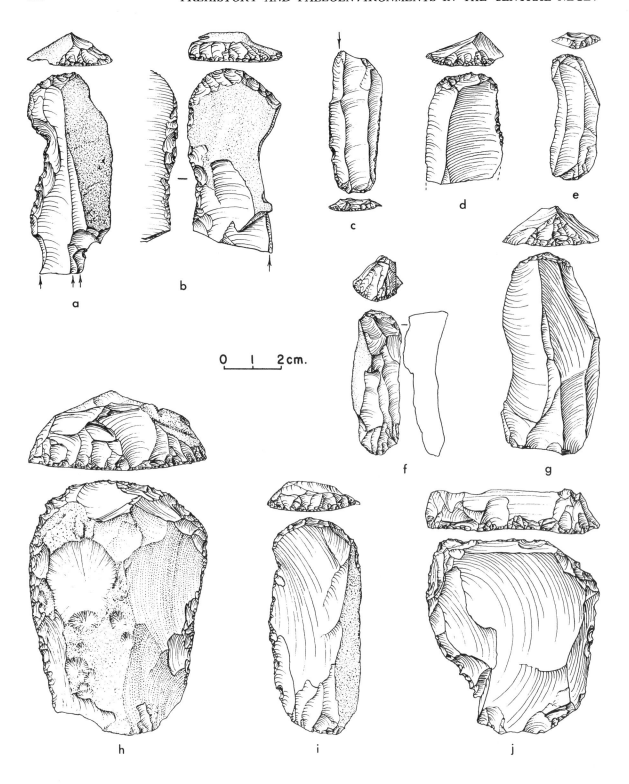

0   1   2cm.

FIG. 11-9—Tools from Site Rosh Zin: *a-c*—endscraper/burins; *d, e, i*—endscrapers; *f, g*—carinated scrapers; *h, j*—massive scrapers.

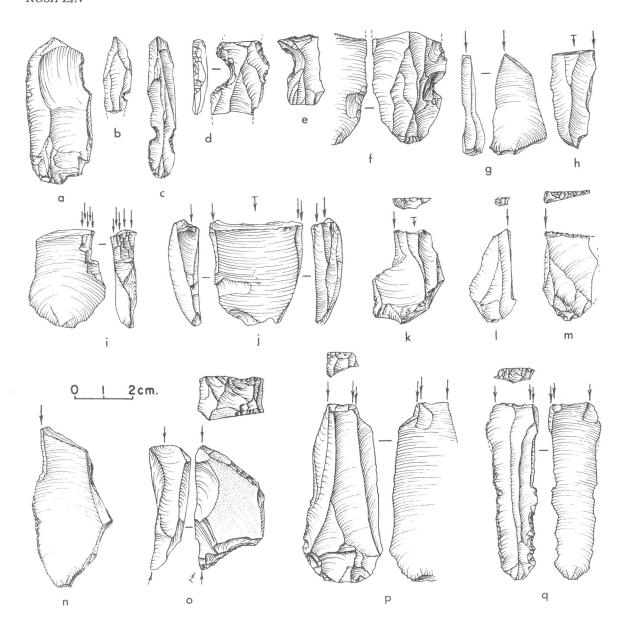

FIG. 11-10—Tools from Site Rosh Zin: *a-f*—notched pieces; *g-q*—various burins.

having been used to the point of penetrating the limestone stratum and exposing a softer, nonlithic substratum and, therefore, exhausting their utility (table 11-12, nos. 1, 11, 12, 14-16); and (4) those mortars that had been exhausted and rejuvenated by the positioning of a quartzite cobble (table 11-12, no. 9) or a flint core (table 11-12, no. 17) in the shaft to seal again the bottom of the mortar.

The striations on the internal walls of these mortars tend to run horizontally around the shaft, suggesting that the pestles were rotated in a circular manner, as opposed to being moved up and down.

A small saddle quern (fig. 11-16*c*) was recovered from the pavement level of Locus 4, along with a handstone which articulated perfectly with the ground surface of the quern

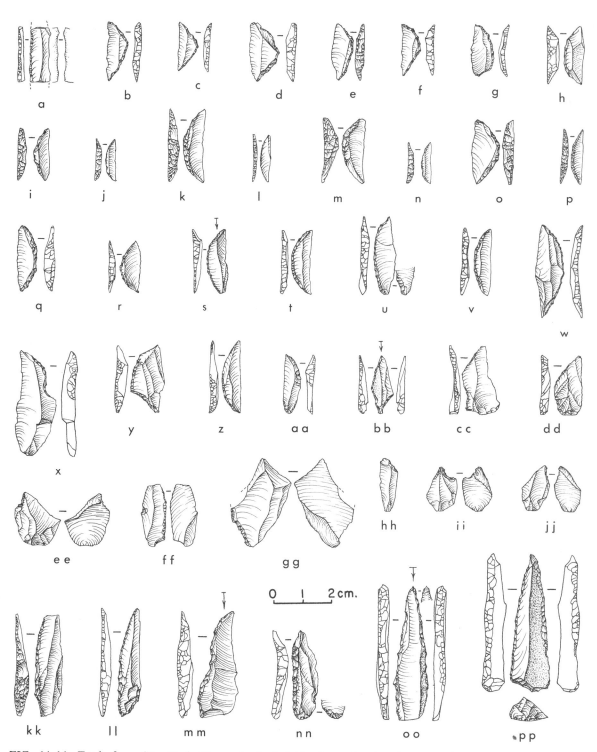

FIG. 11-11—Tools from Site Rosh Zin: *a*—backed sickle; *b-g*—triangles; *h-t, v, w*—lunates; *u*—pointed arch-backed bladelet with truncated base; *x-z*—unfinished geometrics; *aa*—arch tipped bladelet; *bb*—backed varia; *cc*—backed and truncated bladelet; *dd*—truncated bladelet; *ee-jj*—microburin products; *kk-nn*—various backed bladelets; *oo, pp*—double backed perforators.

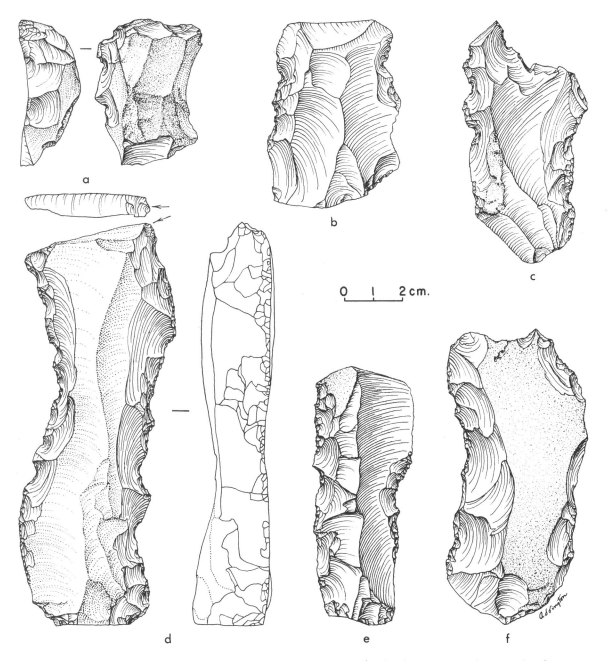

FIG. 11-12–Tools from Site Rosh Zin: *a-f*–massive denticulates (*d* also has transverse burin at distal extremity).

(fig. 11-16*b*). Two ovoid handstones were recovered from the pavement level of Loci 3 and 4, the larger of which is on an unshaped cobble (fig. 11-16*a, d*). A shaped "plug" or pestle was also recovered from below pavement in Locus 4 (fig. 11-18*f*). In addition, a fragmentary limestone block from the structure level of Locus 4 showed clear wear striations (fig. 11-16*e*).

Two small ground pieces, circular in shape with lenticular cross sections and flat sides were also found. One was recovered in the

FIG. 11-13—Tools from Site Rosh Zin: *a-c, e, f*—hammerstones; *d*—denticulate; *g, h*—massive axes, both of which have bifacially flaked bits.

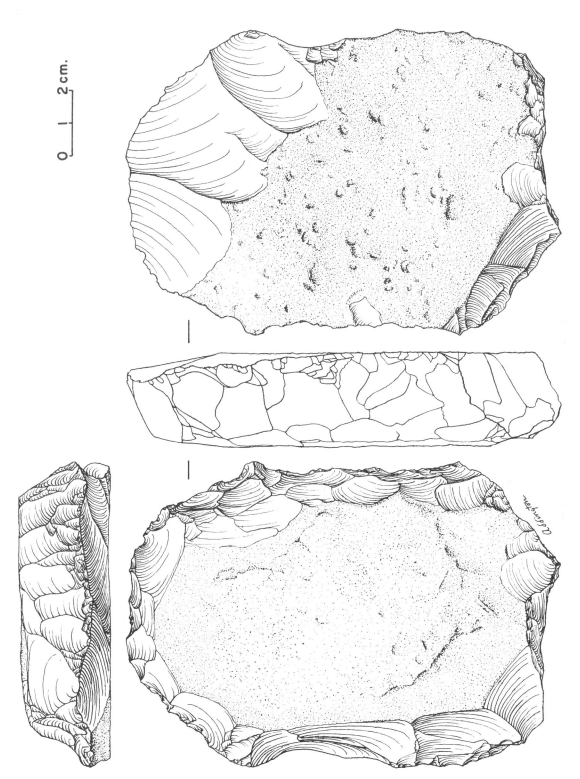

FIG. 11-14—Massive scraper from Site Rosh Zin.

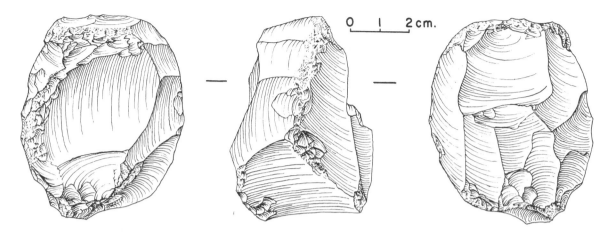

FIG. 11-15—Hammerstone on core from Site Rosh Zin.

cache next to the pillar base, while the other came from an outside test square. A somewhat similar artifact made of quartzite, with one highly polished surface bearing "Z"-shaped striations, was also recovered, but from the structure level of Locus 4 (fig. 11-18a).

TABLE 11-12
Dimensional Characteristics of
Bedrock Mortars (cm)

Mortar Number	Top Diameter of Shaft	Bottom Diameter of Shaft	Depth of Shaft
1	17.0	9.5	21.5
2	15.0	5.5	30.5
3	9.5	8.0	8.5
4	12.0	8.0	5.0
5	9.0	n.d.	2.5
6	8.5	n.d.	3.0
7	14.0	8.0	25.0
8	6.0	n.d.	2.0
9	10.0	n.d.	5.0
10	9.0	5.0	9.0
11	16.0	9.0	34.0
12	16.0	8.0	45.0
13	11.0	n.d.	11.0
14	12.0	7.0	46.0
15	8.0	6.0	17.0
16	16.0	7.0	26.0
17	8.0	7.0	n.d.
18	16.0	n.d.	12.0

Ten grooved stones were found. These occur in two forms; the first, represented by a single example from just above bedrock in Locus 3, is a pecked, egg-shaped piece with a large "V"-shaped groove running its whole length (fig. 11-18e). The others, mostly fragmentary (fig. 11-17d, f, g), consist of thin, elongated, plano-convex pieces of sandstone, each of which has a shallow, rounded groove down the long axis on the flat face. In two cases, in the pavement level of Locus 3 and the other in the cache in Locus 4, pairs of complete examples were recovered. Both pairs were found with the flat sides together, and in both cases the grooves matched. Both the differences in the groove shape and the overall configuration of the pieces suggest that these two basic forms were utilized in different manners.

ORNAMENTAL AND OTHER OBJECTS

Most of the ornamental objects were sections of unmodified *Dentalium* shell. Several hundred of these were recovered, mostly from the midden/structure area (table 11-13). Of those identifiable to species, the vast majority came from the Red Sea, although Mediterranean forms were present.

In fact, there is no significant difference between the proportional occurrence of these

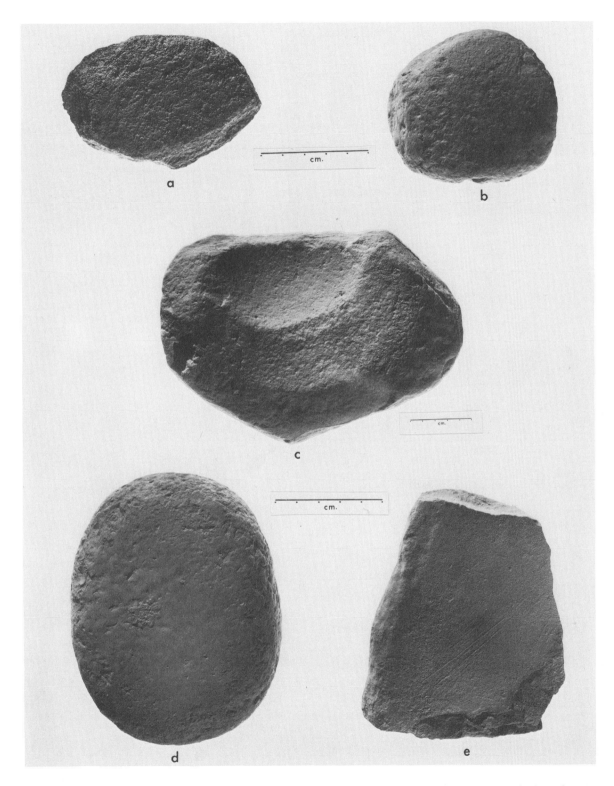

FIG. 11-16—Groundstone from Site Rosh Zin: *a, b, d*—handstones; *c*—quern; *e*—limestone block with striations.

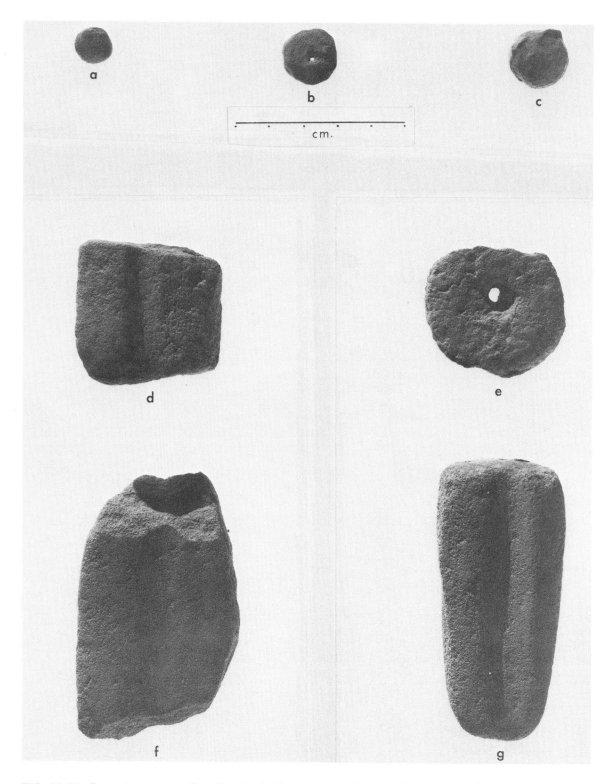

FIG. 11-17—Groundstone, etc., from Site Rosh Zin: *a, c*—round concretions; *b, e*—perforated limestone; *d, f, g*—grooved stones.

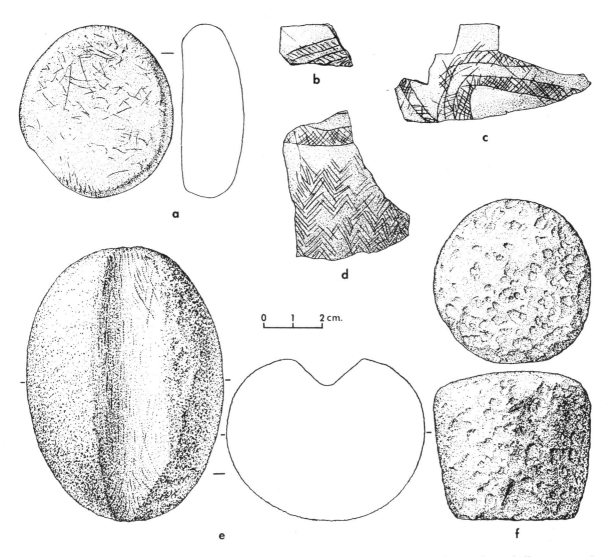

FIG. 11-18–Various objects from Site Rosh Zin: *a*–polished disc; *b-d*–incised ostrich eggshell; *e*–grooved stone; *f*–pestle.

two forms between the two lowest levels; Mediterranean examples account for 19.6% below pavement and 19.6% on the pavement, but this jumps to 26.3% for the structure level.

Four *Dentalium* beads were recovered from the pavement level: two from Locus 4 and two from Locus 3. These are very small, ca. 1.4 mm in thickness, but only one has been lightly ground along the cut faces.

A single true shell pendant was recovered from the pavement level of Locus 4 (fig. 11-19). While other shells were recovered, this was the only one which clearly showed an artificial perforation.

The most common decorated material was ostrich eggshell fragments, of which 19 were recovered, 17 from the pavement level of Locus 4. Three motifs were apparent: parallel lines filled with short diagonal slashes, similar parallel lines filled with rough cross-hatching, and a rough herringbone pattern which covers the majority of a large fragment (fig. 11-8*b-d*).

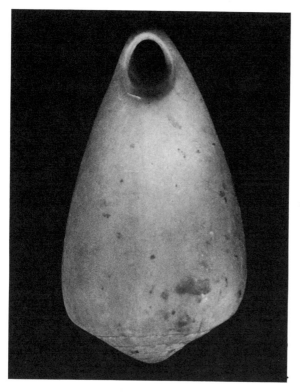

FIG. 11-19—Perforated shell from Site Rosh Zin 3.2 cm long.

Other apparently ornamental objects included two perforated limestone discs (fig. 10-17*b, e*), several small marble-shaped stones (fig. 10-17*a, c*), and 16 small pieces of red ocher. All of these came from around the site, rather than being concentrated in Loci 3 and 4.

CONCLUSIONS

Rosh Zin offers clear documentation for a Natufian base camp within the Central Negev, with only the absence of burials making it different from base camps in the north. Given the paleoclimatic data, however, this does not mean that these Natufians were desert adapted, but merely that the Avdat environment was of marginal Mediterranean type during the Natufian occupation.

Rosh Zin provides some information on intrasite artifactual variability. The earliest occupation, below pavement, seems to represent activities associated with initial processing of lithic tools, as well as a wide range of tasks performed in a habitation area. The next occupation phase, the pavement level, lacks evidence for intensive processing of tools, while retaining the same general tool kit configuration as in the earlier phase. The final phase of occupation, structure level, is similar to that of the pavement level.

In addition to the variability between levels, the outside area exhibits a markedly different tool kit than any locus or level within the midden/structure area. Unfortunately, it is impossible to correlate the outside area with any specific occupational level within the midden/structure area. It can be assumed, however, that the outside area was utilized as a specialized activity zone, periph-

TABLE 11-13

Distrubution of *Dentalium* Shells by Area and Level*

	Locus 1	Locus 2[†]	Locus 3	Locus 4	Outside Area
Structure	22	3	8	53	—
Pavement	14	29	20	65	—
Below Pavement	9	16	—	69	30[+]
Number per cubic meter	11.3	6.4	19.6	9.5	1.9

[*]Recovered during the 1970 and 1971 field seasons.

[†]Only part of the sample counted.

[+]Assumes outside area corresponds with earliest occupation.

eral to the midden/structure area during one   or more of the occupational phases.

NOTE

[1] Each structure was considered a separate "locus" for analysis (fig. 10-6).

BIBLIOGRAPHY

CAUVIN, M. C., 1966. "L'industrie Natoufien de Mallaha (Eynan), Israel. Note préliminaire." *L'Anthropologie*:485-94.

GARROD, D. A. E., and BATE, D. M. A., 1937. *The Stone Age of Mount Carmel* vol. 1. Oxford: Clarendon Press.

HENRY, D. O., 1973*a*. "The Natufian Site of Rosh Zin: A Preliminary Report." *Palestine Exploration Quarterly* 105:129-40.

————, 1973*b*. "The Natufian of Palestine: Its Material Culture and Ecology." Ph.D. dissertation, Southern Methodist University.

MARKS, A. E., 1969. "Prehistoric Sites in the Central Negev." *Israel Exploration Journal* 19(2):118-20.

————; PHILLIPS, J.; CREW, H.; and FERRING, R., 1971. "Prehistoric Sites near En-Avdat in the Negev." *Israel Exploration Journal* 21(1):13-24.

ZOHARY, M., 1952. "Ecological Studies in the Vegetation of Near Eastern Deserts." *Israel Exploration Journal* 2(4):201-15.

NAHAL DIVSHON: A PRE-POTTERY NEOLITHIC B HUNTING CAMP

A. Frank Servello
Southern Methodist University

INTRODUCTION

The site of Nahal Divshon, lying within the floor of the Nahal Zin, is located 980 m southeast of the Midrasha Sde Boker and 2.98 km east northeast of the spring of Ein Avdat. At this point, the nahal floor is 1.3 km wide, flanked by steep hillslopes which bank against the Nahal Zin cliffs (fig. 12-1). The site is situated on a low knoll along the southern side of the present stream bed at an elevation of 355 m, ca. 6 m above the normal flood level. The site was discovered several years ago by members of the Midrasha staff and was subsequently visited by T. Yisraeli, who named the site and made a small selective surface collection. The site was shown to members of the present project in 1968 by R. Cohen, Archaeologist for the Negev. Test excavations were undertaken in 1969 and more extensive excavations were carried out in 1970, resulting in a total of 13 sq m of excavations.

The site consisted of a dense surface concentration of ca. 90 sq m in its northwestern corner, with a large, thin surface scatter of artifacts to the south and east covering some 2,500 sq meters. The condition of the larger part of the site, compared to the northwestern corner, suggested that more than one occupation had initially existed at the locality. The 90 sq m area (fig. 12-2) had apparently undergone relatively little deflation or erosion; it is judged to be in the order of 5 to 10 centimeters. This was partially the result of a large historic rock tomb which was located just upslope from this portion of the site. After considerable examination, it was decided to work only the 90 sq m area, and to treat it as distinct from the large area of sparse artifact scatter, thus limiting the site of Nahal Divshon to that 90 sq m area.

During the 1969 season the site was tested to determine whether *in situ* material was present. Two 1 by 2 m units (Units 2 and 3, fig. 12-2) and two 1 m squares (Units 4 and 5) were excavated. While sterile deposits were reached at 18 cm below surface along the western boundary of the site in Units 4 and 5, and at 15 cm along the eastern boundaries of Units 2 and 3, a firepit 66 cm deep was encountered in the southwest quadrant of Unit 3. The firepit contained numerous flint artifacts, burned and unburned bone, charcoal, and firecracked rocks.

Excavations were continued during the 1970 season to obtain larger samples of chipped stone and faunal materials, as well as charcoal, soil, and pollen samples. The extent of the firepit and limits of artifact concentration were also examined by the excavation of the intervening units between 2-3 and 4-5 (fig. 12-2). This was carried out in 10 cm levels following ground contour, after all surface material had been discarded. Because of the relatively high density of artifacts, scatter patterns by level were not attempted. A single 1 sq m unit, 12, was excavated to the south at a distance of 2 m from the major excavation to test the density and depth of artifacts in this area (fig. 12-2). Below ca. 35 cm, Unit 12 consisted almost entirely of the large firepit, reaching a depth of 68 cm below the cleared surface—the deepest excavated portion of the site.

The major profile drawn is that of the east-west axis of the excavations, where the limits of artifact concentration were nearly reached

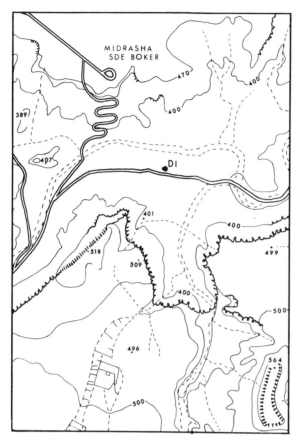

FIG. 12-1—Location of Site Nahal Divshon (D1)
within the Nahal Zin.

at both ends (fig. 12-3). Approximately 50%
of the large firepit was excavated, and judging
from the configuration of the stones near and
at its base, it was nearly 1 m in diameter. Two
smaller hearths not shown on the profile and
belonging to subsequent occupations of the
site were located in Units 8-9 at 20 to 32 cm
depth, and in Unit 12 between 24 and 34 cm
depth. Multiple occupation of the site may be
inferred from profile analysis, artifact density,
and the presence and position of the hearths.
From the profile of the firepit above, it is
possible to see at least three separate events
where it was used. The first entailed the basal
charcoal and ash with the lower layer of
stones. The firepit was then cleaned and new
stones placed some 20 cm higher. This second
event was followed, after the firepit was

allowed to fill considerably, by dense artifact
concentrations near and within the firepit
between 20 and 30 cm depth. Elsewhere in
the site, this layer shows markedly lower artifact densities than the levels above it, and
may represent material which had been
"walked in" or had resulted from sporadic
occupations. A poorly defined lamination of
finer particles in the gray sand at ca. 23 cm,
conforming to the contours of the firepit
below, represents a fine wash in the slight
depression, denoting definite termination of
occupation in this area. The small hearths
represent subsequent occupations that took
place after this wash. These hearths were excavated into the then existing site at ca. 20 to
25 cm below present surface, and correspond
stratigraphically to the dense artifact concentration across the site. It is possible, therefore,
to view this area of the site as occupied not
less than four times.

DATING

During the first season, a small charcoal
sample was taken from the large firepit from
ca. 50 cm depth. Larger samples were later
taken from this firepit, as well as the two
smaller hearths. The two initial dates were in
obvious conflict and required that a third date
be obtained, and a second large sample, also
from the firepit, was processed. The results
and position of these samples are:

Level 5/6   Scattered charcoal from firepit—
            6220 B.C. ± 120 years (Tx-1125)
Level 6   Charcoal from firepit—
            6670 B.C. ± 140 years (I-5501)
Level 6   Charcoal from firepit—
            6950 B.C. ± 180 years (SMU-3)

The initial determination falls within the
range acquired for the later Pre-Pottery Neolithic phases known from the Levant, while
the other determinations fall within the
middle Pre-Pottery Neolithic phase for the

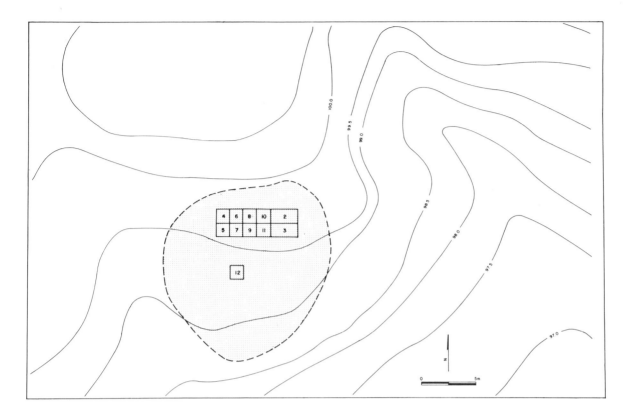

FIG. 12-2—Topographic map of Site Nahal Divshon and the immediate surrounding area showing excavation features.

southern Levant. The two older determinations, virtually identical, are felt to be representative of the actual date of occupation at Nahal Divshon on the basis of confidence in sample size and similarities in artifactual material with other Pre-Pottery Neolithic sites. These dates also correlate with dates obtained for the Pre-Pottery Neolithic B levels at Jericho, Beidha, and Munhatta, all dated to the first half of the seventh millennium B.C. (Henry and Servello, 1975).

FAUNA AND POLLEN

The non-lithic artifactual material recovered at Nahal Divshon consisted of vertebrate fauna and pollen. Although the vertebrate faunal remains were plentiful, their splintered condition and poor state of preservation per-

mitted only a small sample to be identified to species.

Four species of megafauna have been identified (Tchernov, this volume): *Capra ibex*, *Bos primigenius*, *Dama mesopotamica*, and *Gazella* sp. Three of these are generalized parkland or corbeled parkland dwellers, i.e., *Gazella*, *Capra*, and *Bos*, the last requiring some stands of trees (Churcher, 1972; Freeman, 1973), but otherwise having broad environmental parameters. *Gazella* and *Capra* are also known to inhabit semiarid areas of the Levant today, the latter requiring a permanent water source, presumably the perennial springs of Ein Avdat and Ein Mor (Harrison, 1968). *Bos primigenius* is somewhat more restricted, requiring short grasses and a permanent water source where water is available almost daily (Freeman, 1973). *Dama mesopotamica* is restricted in its natural habitat,

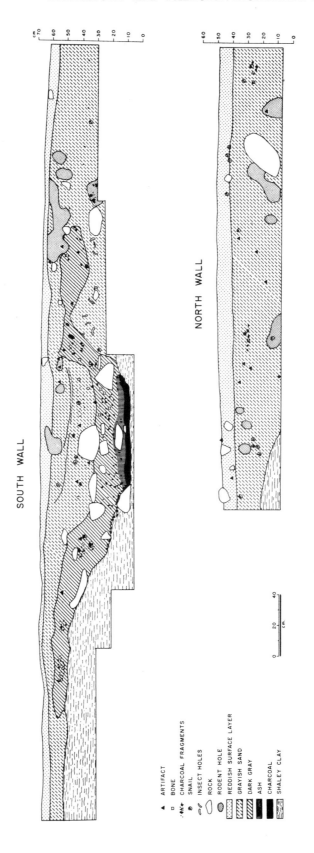

FIG. 12-3—Major profile of Site Nahal Divshon. Main profile taken along south wall of Features 3 through 5. Small profile taken along north wall of Features 4 through 10.

NAHAL DIVSHON   353

requiring forest cover of riverine variety, as
well as a running stream (Fisher et al., 1969;
Reed, 1965). The *Bos* and *Dama*, therefore,
offer reliable evidence that the Nahal Zin
floor was covered by much denser growth
than is probable under modern climatic conditions, even without the damage to the environment caused by historic overgrazing.
Under more favorable conditions of a medi-
mediterranean climatic regime, with early
spring and winter rainfall of 200 mm annually
(Biel, 1951), the nearly desertic highlands
around the Nahal Zin could sustain a short
grass parkland with sporadic stands of trees.

The pollen spectrum, while inconclusive
because of the small sample size, contained
some Mediterranean varieties of trees and
grasses (Horowitz, this volume). The presence
of Gramineae pollen larger than 60 microns
suggests that cultivation of the grain may have
been practiced in the vicinity, presumably
above the Nahal Zin basin.

LITHIC ARTIFACTS

A total of 16,637 chipped stone artifacts
was recovered from the excavations. Of this
number, 675 were retouched tools, 130 pieces
were cores or core fragments, while the remainder was debitage or debris (table 12-1).
Two pieces of ground stone and four hammerstones were also recovered. The term debitage
here refers to all pieces not secondarily retouched which fall within the size range used
by the manufacturers to produce tools by
secondary modification. All pieces placed
under this rubric are considered as possible
tools or "blanks." Debris refers to chippage
which falls outside this category, in all cases
material which falls below the minimal size
range of tool blanks. The total number of
pieces of debitage recovered, less cores, is
5,975 or 37.43% of all waste material. The
blade to flake ratio was 1:1.21, indicating
that the production of both forms as "tool
blanks" was of major concern, although the

blanks used favored blades over flakes by
2.21:1. This indicates a preference for blade
use and suggests that flake production was, in
part, incidental in initial stages of blade core
manufacture. From a measured blade sample
of 501 blades the mean length was 42.68 mm
and mean width 14.78 mm, with a mean
length/width index of 2.89:1.[1] In contrast,
from a flake sample of 611 flakes, the mean
length was 29.31 mm and mean width 26.03
mm, a length/width index of 1:0.89.[1] This is
in marked contrast to the majority of flake
tools. The mean length of 133 flake tools was
49.44 mm and the mean width of 186 flake
tools was 36.01 mm, with a length/width
index of 1:1.37, and the selection of large
flakes for tools is evident. Of the total
number of blades and flakes, 3,032 had complete bases with observable platform characteristics (table 12-2). Although intentional
removal of the bulb by snapping was present
at Abou Gosh (personal observation), a Pre-
Pottery Neolithic B site in the central Judean
Hills, this method was not utilized at Nahal
Divshon. It should be noted that 16.93% of
the unfaceted blades and 9.29% of the unfaceted flakes were of the lipped variety. The
platforms on all pieces showing this profile
are unfaceted.

CORES

The cores from Nahal Divshon, while
showing considerable variability in morphology (table 12-3) and technique of manufacture between classes, exhibit a high degree of
homogeneity within classes. The cores tend to
be exhausted, with large numbers of scars
which are considerably smaller than the majority of tools found at the site. Although
flakes were produced in greater quantity than
blades, blade cores exceed flake cores by a
ratio of 2.24:1 (fig. 12-4g), suggesting that
flakes were a by-product of initial blade core
manufacture, spent blade cores, and mis-
struck blade cores.

TABLE 12-1
Number and Frequency of Artifact Classes, Tool Blanks,
and Their Proportional Utilization by Class

| Debitage Class | Total | | Tools | | Percent of |
	Number	Percent	Number	Percent	Class Utilization
Cores	131	1.95	1	.16	.77
Core Trimming Elements	227	3.38	19	3.08	8.37
Primary Elements	634	9.45	32	5.18	5.05
Flakes	3,022	45.02	193	31.23	6.39
Blades	2,698	40.20	362	58.57	13.42
Total	6,712	100.00	607		
Chunks	719		11	1.78	1.55
Burin Spalls	17				
Chips	9,132				
Unidentifiable	57		57		
Total	16,637		675	100.00	

TABLE 12-2
Number and Frequency of Observable Platform Types
on Blade and Flake Debitage and Tools[1]

| Platforms | Blades | | | | Flakes | | | |
| | Debitage | | Tools | | Debitage | | Tools | |
	Number	Percent	Number	Percent	Number	Percent	Number	Percent
Unfaceted	744	69.17	107	81.06	968	67.41	86	75.44
Dihedral faceted	214	19.12	18	13.64	266	18.52	26	20.18
Multiple faceted	96	8.58	3	2.27	82	5.71	2	1.75
Cortex	35	3.13	4	3.03	120	8.36	3	2.63
Total	1,119	100.00	132	100.00	1,436	100.00	114	100.00
Indeterminant	216		20		261		4	
Total	1,335		152		1,697		118	

[1] Does not include 64 blades used as point blanks.

The proportional occurrence of blade cores remains constant for both complete specimens and total numbers (64.63% and 63.85%, respectively). Flake cores are generally not as well made as blade cores, tending to be more variable in form. Single platform flake cores are the dominant type (52% of all whole flake cores), followed by change of orientation flake, sub-discoidal, and amorphous varieties. Opposed platform cores are rare (16%), which contrasts with their blade core counterparts. Both the single and opposed platform flake

TABLE 12-3
Core Typology

Class	Number	Percent Unrestricted	Percent Restricted
Opposed Platform, blade	30	23.08	36.58
Single Platform, blade	19	14.61	23.17
Opposed Platform, flake	4	3.08	4.88
Single Platform, flake	13	10.00	15.85
Change Orientation, blade	2	1.54	2.44
Change Orientation, blade, opposed opposite side	2	1.54	2.44
Change Orientation, flake	3	2.31	3.66
Multiple Change Orientation	2	1.54	2.44
Subdiscoidal, flake	4	3.08	4.88
Globular or Amorphous, flake	1	.77	1.22
Varia	2	1.54	2.44
Subtotal	82		100.00
Blade Core Fragments	30	23.08	
Flake Core Fragments	12	9.23	
Unidentifiable Fragments	6	4.61	
Total	130	100.01	

cores are manufactured in the same manner as their blade counterparts, with correspondingly similar forms.

Platform angle variability was greatest on opposed platform blade cores (fig. 12-4*h*) and on single platform blade cores (table 12-4), and it is obvious that opposed platform blade cores fall significantly outside the mean range of other types. Over 36% of these have platform angles under 65 degrees.

Opposed and single platform blade cores and change of orientation with opposite side blade cores show the greatest range in length/width ratios. The greatest mean length/width ratios were for opposed platform blade (1.67:1) and the change of orientation blade cores (1.64:1). The range in length and width of all blade cores is shown in Table 12-5. Single and opposed platform flake cores are much larger than the blade cores (table 12-5). These also tend to be less regularized and have forms that are poorly defined, sub-rectangu-lar, sub-square, and sub-pyramidal. Other flake cores (i.e., sub-discoidal, globular) are generally rounded with length/width ratios approaching 1:1.

BLANKS

The full range of debitage was utilized as blanks in the manufacture of tools, as were occasional chunks and cores. Blades and flakes make up 89.80% of all tools, with the frequency of all other categories following (table 12-1). The debitage category most often used in point manufacture was blades (92.75%), followed by core-trimming blades (7.25%). Axes and picks were always produced on cores or chunks. Pieces which could not be placed into a specific debitage category numbered 57, including 16 point fragments, or 8.44% of the total 675 tools. Although the blade length from the restricted tool list falls within the range of blade debitage, the mean

TABLE 12-4
Selected Core Attributes: Length, Width, Platform Angle

Class	Platform Angle		Length (mm)		Width (mm)	
	Average (Degrees)	Range (Degrees)	Average	Range	Average	Range
Opposed Platform Blade	70	60-80	57.37	74-42	35.63	52-19
Single Platform Blade	75	60-85	57.68	99-40	41.89	56-30
Opposed Platform Flake	80	75-80	57.00	66-48	46.50	54-39
Single Platform Flake	80	70-85	46.08	62-30	46.23	56-35
Change Orientation Blade	80	75-85	53.00	64-42	50.00	57-43
Change Orientation Opposed Opposite Sides	75	70-75	50.00	55-45	35.50	45-22
Change Orientation Flake	80	70-85	60.67	82-48	56.00	75-42
Multiple Change Orientation	85	75-90	46.00	53-39	51.00	67-35
Subdiscoidal (Inform) Flake	75	65-85	44.50	53-35	47.50	54-41
Globular or Amorphous Flake	85	80-90	56.00	–	61.00	–
Varia	75	–	*			
Blade Core Fragments	75	70-85				
Flake Core Fragments	80	65-85				
Unidentifiable Fragments	75	70-85				

*No orientation.

of 57.50 mm is considerably greater than the 42.68 mm for the debitage. Overall selection for larger pieces as tool blanks is even more obvious for flake tools which have mean lengths of 49.44 mm and mean widths of 36.01 mm, as compared to flake debitage with mean lengths of 29.31 mm and mean widths of 26.03 millimeters. These also show a marked selection of flakes which are much longer than they are wide.

While the mean length of 50.42 mm and the mean width of 13.23 mm of points are considerably smaller than for other blade tools, this may be the result of greater reduction during manufacture, the small sample of 19 unbroken points, or the tendency for longer point forms to break. Consideration must also be given to the possibility that the recovered points are mostly discards.

Large amounts of small debitage were being produced, while only little debitage of this size was utilized in tool production. One possible explanation is that some small debitage may be the manufacturing debris of picks, axes, or chisels carried from the site. These implements often have blades and flakes removed which fall within the parameters of debitage from Nahal Divshon. This has been noted at numerous Pre-Pottery Neolithic B sites in the southern Levant, i.e., Abou Gosh (Perrot, 1952; Dollfus and LeChevallier, 1969) and Beidha (Kirkbride, 1966; Mortensen, 1970).

Dorsal shape of blades shows that, with the exception of irregular pieces, blanks were selected in the same frequency as they were available in the blade population (table 12-5).

When considering lateral profile and axial cross section, chi-square tests indicated that nonrandom selection of specific attributes is probable for both. Although the most commonly manufactured and utilized blade was flat, those with incurvate profiles were also proportionately favored (table 12-6).

TABLE 12-5
Dorsal Shape on Blade Tools and Debitage

Profile Type	Tools		Debitage	
	Number	Percent	Number	Percent
Convergent	28	28.93	280	32.44
Expanding	47	16.79	121	14.02
Parallel	97	34.64	294	34.07
Lozenge	50	17.86	102	11.82
Irregular	5	1.78	66	7.65
Subtotal	280	100.00	863	100.00
Broken	18		230	
Total	298		1093	

TABLE 12-6
Lateral Profile (Curvature on Blade and Flake Tools and Debitage)

Lateral Profile	Tools		Debitage	
	Number	Percent	Number	Percent
Incurvate, Medial	70	24.06	149	15.11
Incurvate, Distal	9	3.09	37	3.75
Twisted, Proximal	11	3.78	69	7.00
Twisted, Medial	61	20.96	218	22.11
Twisted, Distal	2	.69	20	2.03
Flat	132	45.36	464	47.06
Concave	3	1.03	9	.91
Irregular	3	1.03	20	2.03
Subtotal	291	100.00	986	100.00
Broken	7		107	
Total	298		1093	

Selection is even more obvious for blade axial cross sections. Trapezoidal forms were selected for tools (over 60%), as compared with their occurrence of only 40% in the blade debitage. This is at the expense of tri-angular forms, which are clearly selected against in tool manufacture. The reverse is true for points, however, as the most frequent blank used is triangular in cross section.

RETOUCHED TOOLS

The chipped stone tool kit appears to reflect a hunting and butchering specialization (table 12-7), which may be viewed a number of ways. The restricted list is without bi-facially or unifacially worked points, as well as axes and picks. It is felt that this is important for comparing sites, and the inclusion of points and/or heavy tools misrepresents and skews many similarities and differences. The diagnostic list demonstrates the specialization of tool classes in the more traditional analyses, which are masked when retouched pieces are included.

The types recognized here reflect previous work on the Pre-Pottery Neolithic industries in the Levant (table 12-8). Exceptions to this are points, where types per se have not as yet been defined.

While multiple occupation of the site was noted from the profile analysis, variability in frequency of types was not significant, and as sample sizes in some levels were very small, all tools will be considered together.

Notes on the Tool Typology

Burins

Of the 127 burins, 85.83% are dihedral, followed by transverse, 6.3%, on truncation, 4.72% (fig. 12-4a), with all others equally 3.15%. Simple dihedral forms dominate, i.e., single blow, angle on snap (fig. 12-4b), dihedral angle, and multiple dihedral, and are normally formed by less than three burin facets. The more complex dihedral types (fig. 12-5g) have more than three facets (table 12-9). The most common burin edge is oblique to the cross section of the piece, offering a flat or nearly flat surface (table 12-9). This shape, which is found on 38.58% of the burins, can

TABLE 12-7

Number and Frequency of Tool Classes at Nahal Divshon

Class	Number	Percent	Percent Restricted	Percent Diagnostic
Burins	127	18.82	21.64	28.29
Scrapers	46	6.81	7.84	10.24
Notches	97	14.37	16.53	21.60
Denticulates	45	6.67	7.66	10.02
Perforators	6	.89	1.02	1.34
Backed Pieces	13	1.93	2.21	2.90
Truncations	22	3.26	3.75	4.90
Multiple Tools	5	.74	.85	1.11
Retouched Pieces	226	33.48	38.50	—
Points	85	12.59	—	18.93
Picks, Axes	3	.44	—	.67
Total	675	100.00	100.00	100.00

TABLE 12-8

Type List from Nahal Divshon

Burins	Uniden-tifiable	Blade	Flake	Primary Flake	Core Trim-ming Element	Core Tablet	Core/ Chunk	Percent Class	Percent Total
Single Blow, on old surface	—	—	2	—	—	—	—	1.57	.34
Dihedral angle	1	5	8	—	2	—	1	13.39	2.90
Dihedral angle, on snap	2	15	5	5	1	2	2	25.20	5.45
Multiple dihedral	2	9	3	1	1	—	1	13.39	2.90
Dihedral, symmetric	—	4	1	1	—	—	—	4.72	1.02
Dihedral, asymmetric	3	8	2	—	—	—	—	10.24	2.23
Dihedral, Multifaceted (MF)	—	5	7	—	—	—	4	12.60	2.73
Transverse, on old surface	1	2	4	1	—	—	—	6.30	1.36
Multiple Dihedral, MF	—	—	—	1	—	—	—	.79	.17
Angle on snap, MF	1	1	3	—	—	—	—	3.94	.85
Multiple mixed	—	1	—	—	—	—	—	.79	.17
On oblique straight truncation	—	1	—	—	—	—	—	.79	.17
On oblique concave truncation	—	1	—	—	—	—	—	.79	.17

Table 12-8 (Cont.)

	Uniden-tifiable	Blade	Flake	Primary Flake	Core Trim-ming Element	Core Tablet	Core/ Chunk	Percent Class	Percent Total
On oblique convex truncation	–	–	–	–	1	–	–	.79	.17
On normal convex truncation	–	–	2	–	–	–	–	1.57	.34
Carinated	–	1	1	–	–	–	1	2.36	.51
Multiple, on truncation	–	1	–	–	–	–	–	.79	.17
Subtotal	10	54	38	9	5	2	9	100.00	21.65
Scrapers									
Simple endscraper, symmetric	1	5	2	–	–	–	–	17.39	1.36
Simple endscraper, asymmetric	1	2	8	–	–	–	–	23.91	1.88
Ogival endscraper	–	–	1	–	–	–	–	2.17	.17
Thick nosed	–	–	1	–	–	–	–	2.17	.17
Thin shouldered	–	2	1	–	–	–	–	6.52	.51
Thick shouldered	–	1	–	–	–	–	–	2.17	.17
Denticulated endscraper	–	–	3	1	–	–	–	8.70	.68
Sidescraper	–	2	8	2	1	1	–	30.43	2.38
Carinated	–	1	2	–	–	–	–	6.52	.51
Subtotal	2	13	26	3	1	1	–	100.00	7.83
Notches									
Single, retouched	6	25	29	1	1	1	–	64.95	10.73
Multiple, retouched	–	1	3	–	1	–	–	5.15	.85
Opposed	1	2	–	–	–	–	–	3.09	.51
Single, single-blow	3	6	14	2	1	–	–	26.81	4.43
Subtotal	10	34	46	3	3	1	–	100.00	16.52
Denticulates									
Normal	1	4	10	5	–	–	–	44.44	3.41
Serrated	1	21	1	2	–	–	–	55.56	4.26
Subtotal	2	25	11	7	–	–	–	100.00	7.67
Perforators									
Simple	–	3	2	–	–	–	–	83.33	.85

Table 12-8 (Cont.)

	Uniden-tifiable	Blade	Flake	Primary Flake	Core Trim-ming Element	Core Tablet	Core/ Chunk	Percent Class	Percent Total
Mèche de foret	–	1	–	–	–	–	–	16.67	.17
Subtotal	–	4	2	–	–	–	–	100.00	1.02
Backed									
Blunt, straight backed	–	4	–	–	–	–	–	30.77	.68
Pointed, arch-backed	–	1	–	–	–	–	–	7.69	.17
Blunt, arch-backed	–	1	–	–	–	–	–	7.69	.17
Pointed backed fragment	–	1	–	–	–	–	–	7.69	.17
Straight backed fragment	–	4	1	–	–	–	–	38.46	.85
Arch-backed fragment	–	1	–	–	–	–	–	7.69	.17
Subtotal	–	12	1	–	–	–	–	100.00	2.21
Truncations									
Perpendicular	–	3	3	1	–	–	–	31.82	1.19
Oblique	1	8	4	1	1	–	–	68.18	2.55
Subtotal	1	11	7	2	1	–	–	100.00	3.74
Multiple Tools									
Burin/Endscraper	–	1	2	1	–	–	–	80.00	.68
Burin/Sidescraper	–	–	1	–	–	–	–	20.00	.17
Subtotal	–	1	3	1	–	–	–	100.00	.85
Retouched									
Laterally retouched, obverse	3	81	31	3	–	–	–	52.44	20.10
Laterally retouched, inverse	1	30	12	2	–	–	–	20.00	7.67
Laterally retouched, bifacial	1	2	2	–	–	–	–	2.22	.85
Bilaterally retouched	–	25	14	1	–	–	–	17.78	6.81
Uni- and Bilateral alternating retouch	–	6	–	–	–	–	–	2.67	1.02

Table 12-8 (Cont.)

Retouched	Uniden-tifiable	Blade	Flake	Primary Flake	Core Trim-ming Element	Core Tablet	Core/Chunk	Percent Class	Percent Total
Retouched fragments	10	—	—	1	—	—	—	4.89	1.87
Subtotal	15	144	59	7	—	—	—	100.00	38.32
Scaled									
Scaled fragment	1	—	—	—	—	—	—	100.00	.17
Subtotal	1	—	—	—	—	—	—	100.00	.17
Total	41	298	193	32	10	4	9	99.98	
Points	16	64	—	—	5	—	—		
Axes, Picks							3		
TOTAL	57	362	193	32	15	4	12		

be further subdivided into oblique to the obverse or inverse (bulbar) surface. The high occurrence of the latter sub-type, 85.71%, gives the impression that the ventral face was toward the worker when the burin was formed. The broad range of burin angles attests to the considerable variability which exists within types (table 12-9). Three definite clusters can be discerned; 81.25% of burins on snap fall within a range of 75° to 88°, 94.12% of multiple dihedrals within 70° to 85°, and 69.23% of dihedral asymmetrical burins (fig. 12-5h) within 62° and 75 degrees. A more definite cluster can be seen for all burins, as 60% have angles that fall between 75° and 80°, indicating that the manufacturers were intent on producing a rather blunted edge. Burins with acute angles were produced only in low numbers, the most acute being a dihedral symmetric burin with an angle of 47° (fig. 12-5a).

Scrapers

Simple forms dominate the scraper class, with endscraper varieties (fig. 12-6d, e) composing the vast majority (table 12-8). Transverse forms, present in high numbers at such sites at Tell Eli (Prausnitz, 1970) and Sefunim (Ronen, 1968), were not significant in the assemblage. The most commonly used retouch was overlapping (65.21%), followed by flat lamellar with 17.39%, while the remaining 8.69% show regular or flat retouch. The majority of sidescrapers have heavy or light overlapping retouch. Five endscrapers (fig. 12-6a, b) are on unilaterally retouched pieces and another five show bilateral retouch. Most sidescrapers, including denticulated forms (fig. 12-6c), are simple convex (10), with other forms rare: two straight and one each of double mixed and transverse. Nosed or shouldered scrapers (fig. 12-5b) are rare. While considerable variability exists in the angle of the scraper edges, 73.92% of all scrapers have edge angles between 70° and 80 degrees. The working edge, measured to the top of the retouch through the cross section, shows 52.17% falling between 5 and 7 mm (mode, 6 mm), but with some carinated and thick-nosed examples as much as 16 mm thick.

TABLE 12-9
Major Burin Attributes

Burin Type	Number of Facets[1]									Form of Burin Edge[3]					Angle of Burin Edge, in degrees	
	1	2	3	4	5	6	7	8	9	St.	Ob.	P.	Tr.	C.	Range	Mean
Single Blow	2									1	1				74-85	79.5
Dihedral angle		8	9							5	9	3			66-97	78.9
Angle on snap	21	9	1	1						9	17	5			73-99	84.0
Multiple dihedral	3	14								3	7	3	2	1	59-89	78.6
Dihedral, symmetric		1	3	2						4	1	1			47-87	72.5
Dihedral, asymmetric		4	8	1						4	3	6			54-83	67.5
Dihedral, Multifaceted (MF)				7	5	2	1	1				4	9	3	55-92	77.1
Transverse	4	1	1	2						1	5		1	1	61-99	80.6
Multiple dihedral, MF[2]								1							—	81.0
Angle on snap, MF				1	4						1	1	3		64-83	77.0
Multiple mixed			1								1				—	81.0
On oblique straight truncation	1										1				—	87.0
On oblique concave truncation		1											1		—	61.0
On oblique convex truncation		1									1				—	85.0
On normal convex truncation	1	1								1	1				73-89	81.0
Carinated					2			1					1	2	67-86	75.3
Multiple, on truncation	1										1				—	78.0
Total	34	40	24	14	11	2	1	2	1	28	49	24	16	7		

[1] Includes only struck burin facets.

[2] Refers to multifaceted, more than three burin blows on a single burin.

[3] St—Straight, perpendicular; Ob—Oblique; P—Peaked; Tr—Trapezoidal; C—Circular.

Notched Pieces

Notches include lateral, end (proximal and distal), and multiple varieties. All may be formed by single blows with subsequent retouch or by simple retouch. Retouched notches account for 70.10% of the total, of which 72.06% are lateral (figs. 12-5*d*; 12-4*c*), followed by distal (17.65%) and proximal (2.94%). Multiple retouched notches of all types make up the remaining 7.35%. Of the single blow notches, the most common is lateral (fig. 12-4*d*) (69.23%), followed by distal end (23.07%) and proximal end (7.69%). Opposed notches are in low frequency, accounting for only 3.09%.

The majority of notches, especially retouched types, are shallow and poorly formed, giving the impression that they were manufactured for immediate use and then discarded. This would seem reasonable if production and refinement of shafts were of major concern. Considerable variability exists in the average notch width within types, although mean widths tend to be similar, ranging between 7.17 and 12.17 mm, with most falling between 7.50 and 9.00 millimeters.

Denticulates

The denticulates have been divided into two subclasses: normal varieties formed by a succession of adjoining notches, produced either by retouch or single blows, and serrated varieties formed by a series of very small single blow notches from regular, pressure or squamous retouch, resulting in a sawlike edge.

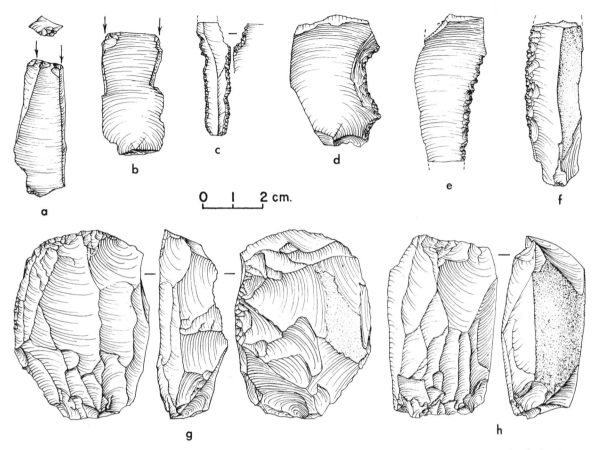

FIG. 12-4—Tools and cores from Site Nahal Divshon: *a*—multiple burin on truncation; *b*—multiple burin on snap; *c*—bilaterally retouched bladelet with multiple notches; *d*—single blow notch with secondary retouch; *e*—serrated blade; *f*—pressure serrated blade; *g*—change of orientation core; *h*—opposed platform blade core.

These latter have been referred to often as sickle blades (Crowfoot, 1936) and saw blades (Prausnitz, 1970). Sickle sheen was not located on any piece at Nahal Divshon, indicating that a serrated blade or flake was not necessarily used as a sickle.

The most common normal type is laterally denticulated, accounting for 80.0%, followed by transverse and bilateral types with 10.0% each. Considerable variability exists in the method of normal denticulate manufacture, although none is made by pressure flaking. The average notch width on denticulates is 7.65 mm, with a range from 7.44 to 9.50 millimeters. While the normal denticulates show very close affinity to the notched tools, as might be expected, serrated pieces are quite distinct.

Serrated pieces (fig. 12-4*e, f*) are either unilaterally or bilaterally retouched and 84% are on blades.

Retouch with one exception is either marginal or pressure, with the former accounting for 64% of the pieces. The average notch width for serrated pieces is 1.48 mm, considerably below that for normal denticulates. Nearly half of all serrated pieces had bifacial or alternating retouch.

Perforators

Only six were recovered; five are simple straight perforators formed by one or two notches, while the other is a double-backed and pointed bladelet, common at numerous other sites such as Beidha (Mortensen, 1970) and Abou Gosh. Epine or thornlike forms, common in sites in the central Levantine area, such as Tell Eli and Tell Ramad (de Contensen, 1971), are not found at Nahal Divshon.

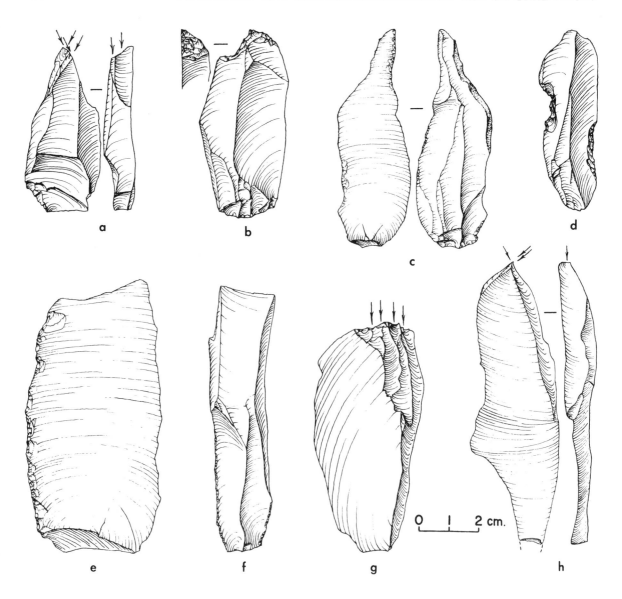

FIG. 12-5—Tools from Site Nahal Divshon: *a, h*—dihedral burin; *b*—thin shouldered scraper; *c*—bilaterally alternating retouched blade; *d*—multiple notched blade; *e*—retouched flake; *f*—marginally retouched blade; *g*—multifaceted burin on snap.

Backed Pieces

The backed element is not as important at Nahal Divshon as at other Pre-Pottery Neolithic B sites, notably Tell Eli where it accounts for 6.7% or El Khiam Ia-b where it is 18 percent. The most common type is the blunt, straight-backed bladelet, followed by pointed, arch-backed and blunt, arch-backed bladelets (table 12-8). Five of the seven backed frag-ments are straight backed with arched and pointed forms accounting for one each.

Truncated Pieces

Truncations are poorly represented. The most common type is the straight oblique truncation, with 9 examples. Backed and truncated forms were not encountered, although they are plentiful at other

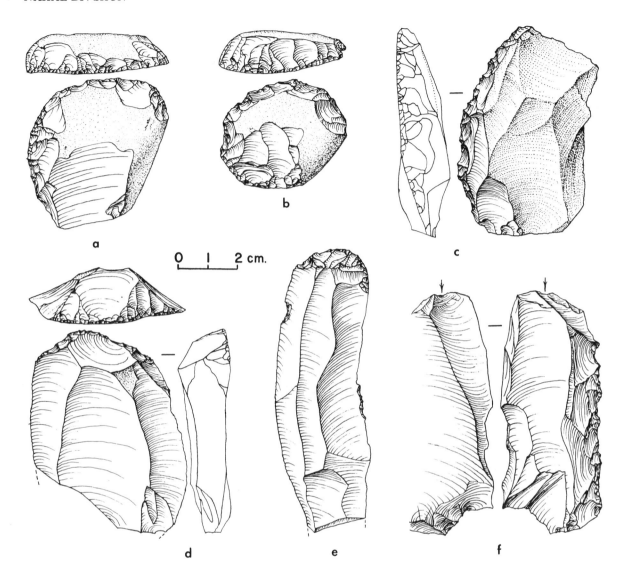

FIG. 12-6—Tools from Site Nahal Divshon: *a, b*—endscrapers on retouched flake; *c*—denticulated sidescraper on old flake; *d*—endscraper on flake; *e*—endscraper on blade; *f*—sidescraper plus burin.

Pre-Pottery Neolithic B sites, the most notable ones being Tell Eli and Tekufath (18N) (Burian and Friedmann, personal communication).

Multiple Tools

Each is a burin combined with a scraper. Four are burins/endscrapers, while the fifth is a burin/sidescraper. The scrapers are formed by regular retouch, which is characteristic of the scraper class at Nahal Divshon. Three of the four endscrapers were asymmetrical. The burins follow the same pattern in the burin class, with dihedral angle (fig. 12-6*f*), dihedral asymmetrical, and angle on snap present.

Retouched Pieces

A total of 226 retouched pieces were recovered: 63.72% on blades of various types (figs. 12-4*c*; 12-5*f*; 12-7*h, i*) and 26.11% on flakes. The remainder were either primary flakes (fig. 12-5*e*) or indeterminate. Only 6 of the 203 lateral and bilateral retouched

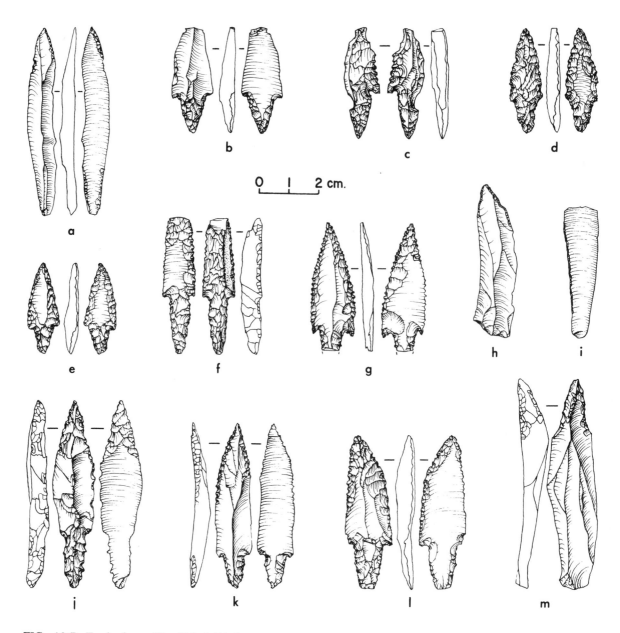

FIG. 12-7—Tools from Site Nahal Divshon: *a*—untanged, minimally worked point; *b-g, j-l*—tanged points; *h*—bilaterally retouched bladelet; *i*—inversely retouched bladelet; *m*—unfinished projectile point.

pieces were retouched by pressure flaking, four of these being bilaterally worked. The most common retouch is the light and regular. Of the 40 bilaterally retouched pieces, six were inversely worked. Alternating retouched pieces, distinguished by obverse and inverse work along one or both edges, but not in the same location, were predominantly bilateral (5 of 6 pieces) (fig. 12-5c). Bifacial retouch and pressure

flaking occur in only low frequency. They do, however, play an important role in point manufacture. The incidence of bifacial work outside of point manufacture was too low to define types readily. Six bifacial retouched pieces, one a fragment and six pressure flaked blades (one bifacial and four bilateral) were recovered. Serration, which normally accompanies pressure flaking, was not present. The removal of the barbs was accomplished by light retouch rather than by grinding. In addition, ten regular retouched fragments were recovered from the excavations.

Scaled Pieces

One scaled fragment was recovered, which has been initially placed into the retouched category. Although this piece is only fragmentary and cannot be seen as a diagnostic tool, numerous heavily scaled pieces were noted by Mortensen (1970) for Beidha. These were interpreted, through direct analogy to pieces in Northern Europe, as being flintstones.

Points

A total of 85 points and point fragments were recovered. Of these, twenty-three (27.06%) were proximal fragments, twenty (23.54%) were either medial or distal fragments, ten (11.76%) were unfinished, and 32 were complete or nearly complete (37.65%).

Of the 32 whole points, twenty-five (78.74%) were tanged (fig. 12-7*b-g, j-l*), four (12.50%) had bases formed by major reduction without tang formation, and three (9.38%) had bilaterally retouched butts (fig. 12-7*a*). Point blades were subdivided into elongated and short forms, elongated being defined as a blade measuring more than two-thirds of the total length of the point. Conversely, a tang was considered elongated when it was more than one-third of the total length. Elongated point blades were found to be slightly more common, at 61.54% (fig. 12-7*b, d, e, j, k, l*). All points with bases formed by reduction and without tangs were measured from where the reduction began. These pieces all had elongated blades.

The most characteristic blade shape was biconvex (60.65%) (fig. 12-7*d, e, g, j*), followed by straight (24.59%), with all others being irregular (fig. 12-7*l*). Almost all tangs and bases were triangular (79.70%), but 9.38% were parallel, and the remainder were either irregular, bi-concave, or expanding. Triangular-shaped tangs may be straight (fig. 12-7*b, e*) or bi-convex (fig. 12-7*c, f, j*), each having a frequency of ca. 40 percent. The proportion of short to elongated triangular straight and triangular bi-convex tangs was 1.6:1 and 1.4:1, respectively.

Only 21 points were measurable for total length, including one unfinished piece (fig. 12-7*m*) (table 12-10). Both central blade and tang thicknesses have means of ca. 3.5 mm and ranges between 2 and 7 millimeters.

TABLE 12-10
Total Length and Length/Width of Point Blades and Tangs (mm)

Attribute	Mean (mm)	Range (mm)
Total Length	50.42	30-89
Blade Length	40.44	20-89
Blade Width	11.23	6-17
Tang Length	13.97	8-21
Tang Width	8.00	5-16

The basic methods used in tang or base formation were notching and/or reduction of the lower lateral edges. Notch formation and lateral reduction to produce a tang or base was found on a majority of points (59.37%), followed by reduction only (28.13%) and mixed (12.50%).

The dominant retouch employed in point manufacture was pressure-flaking (63.29%), followed by light regular retouch (30.38%) and backing (6.33%). In most cases the reduction during tang formation was accomplished through pressure retouch, while all backed edges were limited to the tang. The use of pressure retouch in forming the blade edge was less (53.71%) than for tangs, with light regular and indirect percussion becoming more important (46.29%). The result of the pressure retouch and the indirect percussion technique is that 40.32% of all blades have serrated edges, with another 20.96% having their edges ground (table 12-11).

The most common blade cross section is triangular (54.10%) rather than trapezoidal (31.15%). This is the result of positive selection of "blanks" that have triangular cross sections, a factor which contrasts sharply with other blade tools from the site.

The majority (58.93%) of the tangs and bases were pointed or semipointed by regular or pressure retouch along the lower lateral edge (fig. 12-7*j, k*). Unmodified tips (12.50%) were characteristic of minimally worked points (fig. 12-7*a*) or unfinished points (fig.

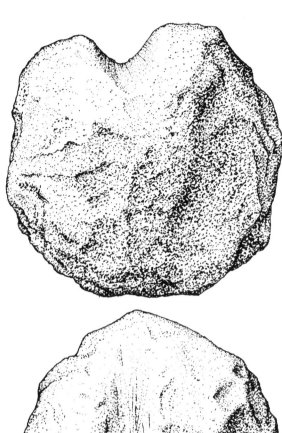

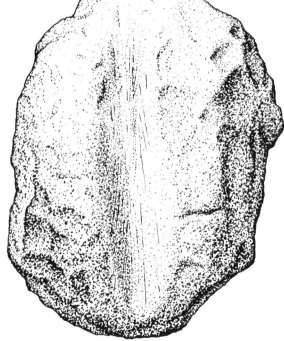

TABLE 12-11
Characteristic Point Blade Lateral Edges

Morphology	Number	Percent
Single Blow Notch	1	1.61
Serrated Regular[1]	8	12.90
Serrated Pressure	17	27.42
Straight Regular	23	37.10
Straight Ground	13	20.96
	62	99.99

[1] Indicates the technique of indirect percussion used in production.

than blades is further evident when considering obverse and inverse retouch. Bifacial retouch was present on 78.46% of all tangs and bases, but on only 53.45% of all blade portions (table 12-12). The non-tanged points tended to show less intensive modification, and the retouch was, in most cases, unifacial on both blade and base.

TABLE 12-12
Frequency of Bifacial Work
on Point Blades and Tangs

Retouch	Blades		Tangs	
	Number	Percent	Number	Percent
Bifacial	31	53.45	51	78.46
Obverse	19	32.76	9	13.85
Inverse	8	13.79	5	7.69
	58	100.00	65	100.00

Picks and Axes

FIG. 12-8–Grooved stone from Site Nahal Divshon, showing nonparallel striations.

12-7*m*). Regular or pressure retouch was used in 10.71% of the cases to produce a blunt (fig. 12-7*l*) or rounded tip, with all pressure thinning used in this manner being bifacial. The emphasis on tangs rather

Two pick fragments and one small biface were recovered. The pick fragments were semitrihedral in cross section and were formed by heavy overlapping and flat retouch, with some finer edge refinement by light or pressure retouch. The small square bifacial ax was bi-convex in cross section and had a flat base formed by an initial single blow. The retouch along the lateral edges and distal end was bifacial and flat, with some later regularization. This form falls within the range found at other Pre-Pottery Neolithic B sites, such as Beidha (Mortensen, 1970) and Abou Gosh.

GROUND STONE

Only two pieces of grooved stones were recovered (fig. 12-8). It has been suggested recently (Crabtree, 1974) that grooved stones were used to sharpen and manufacture bone implements for chipping. The interpretation was noted as especially true for bone pressure-flaking tools. This interpretation may be plausible for Nahal Divshon because of the rather high incidence of pressure flaking at the site and the seemingly nonparallel striations found along the grooves. An alternative interpretation is that the grooved stones were used to finish arrow shafts after initial formation by notches, the latter being plentiful at

Nahal Divshon. Whichever the case, they are both in keeping with the specialized aspect of the tool kit.

CONCLUSIONS

The tool kit from Nahal Divshon is viewed as representative of a specialized hunting type. The site represents a seasonally occupied hunters' camp for the following reasons: the apparent emphasis on point and shaft manufacturing, the remains of four wild forms of megafauna, open firepits, and the presumed hide-working implements, such as burins and denticulates. The complete absence of blades with sickle sheen, ground handstones and querns, and permanent or semipermanent structures all point to the ephemeral nature of the occupation and the absence of agricultural endeavors.

NOTES

[1] The index, although indicative of mean length/width ratio for blades and flakes, is not a true mean. It was calculated by taking mean length and dividing by mean width, rather than taking a mean of all length/width ratios for each piece.

BIBLIOGRAPHY

BIEL, E. R., 1951. *Climatology of the Mediterranean Area*, Department of Meteorology, Miscellaneous Report 13. Chicago: University of Chicago Press.

CHURCHER, C. S., 1972. *Late Pleistocene Vertebrates from Archaeological Sites in the Plain of Kom Ombo, Upper Egypt*. Toronto: Royal Ontario Museum Life Sciences Contributions 82.

CRABTREE, D., 1974. *Ancient Projectile Points*. Film by Norm Holve and Idaho State University, directed by E. H. Swanson, Jr. Burbank: Informational Materials, Inc. Distributors.

CROWFOOT, J., 1936. "Notes on the Flint Implements of Jericho; 1935." *Liverpool Annals of Art and Archaeology* 23:174-84.

de CONTENSON, H., 1971. "Tell Ramad, a Village in Syria of the Seventh and Sixth Millennia B.C." *Archaeology* 24:278-85.

DOLLFUS, G., and LE CHEVALLIER, M., 1969. "Les deux premières campagnes de fouilles à Abou Gosh (1967-1968)." *Syria* 46:277-87.

FISHER, J.; SIMON, N.; and VINCENT, J., 1969. *Wildlife in Danger*. New York: The Viking Press.

FREEMAN, L. G., 1973. "The Significance of Mammalian Faunas from Paleolithic Occupations in Cantabrian Spain." *American Antiquity* 38(1):3-44.

HARRISON, D. L., 1968. *The Mammals of Arabia* 2. London: Ernest Benn.

HENRY, D. O., and SERVELLO, A. F., 1975. "Compendium of Carbon-14 Determinations derived from Near Eastern Prehistoric Deposits." *Paleorient* 2(1):19-44.

KIRKBRIDE, D., 1966. "Five Seasons at the Pre-Pottery Neolithic Village of Beidha in Jordan." *Palestine Exploration Quarterly* 98:8-72.

MORTENSEN, P., 1970. "A Preliminary Study of the Chipped Stone Industry from Beidha." *Acta Archaeologica* 41:1-54.

PERROT, J., 1952. "Le néolithique d'Abou Gosh." *Syria* 29:119-45.

PRAUSNITZ, M. W., 1970. *From Hunter to Farmer and Trader*. Jerusalem: Sivan Press.

REED, C. A., 1965. "Imperial Sassanian Hunting of Pig and Fallow Deer, and Problems of Survival of These Animals Today in Iran." *Postilla* 92:1-23.

RONEN, A., 1968. "Excavations at the Cave of Sefunim (Iraq-el-Barud), Mount Carmel, Preliminary Report." *Quartar* 19:275-88.

GLOSSARY

Anthony E. Marks

Southern Methodist University

The following glossary provides a limited number of definitions used throughout the papers of this volume. These terms include those relating to basic artifact description and measurement, technological observations, and a few definitions of specific tool types. However, this section is not a complete and integrated list of terminology used in prehistoric lithic studies, as a number of such lists already exist (e.g., Bordes, 1961; Tixier, 1963; Brézillon, 1971). This section is divided into two parts—(1) technological terms and measurements and (2) tool types.

TECHNOLOGICAL TERMS AND MEASUREMENTS

Since these may be organized in any number of ways, for simplicity they are presented in alphabetical order by major topic. The only significant group of technological observations not covered here are those pertaining specifically to the Mousterian, since Crew (this volume) extensively cites references for each observation and discusses whatever deviations occur from the standard definitions.

ARTIFACT CLASSES. Groupings of artifacts which share similar gross morphology and are commonly recognized as being distinct. They are used here to help describe the assemblages and to point out the types of blanks chosen for tool manufacture. In addition, the proportional occurrence of these classes gives some insight into manufactural processes and site functions, as a number are derived from specific processes of raw material reduction. The following classes have been recognized: cores, primary elements, core-trimming elements, core tablets, flakes, and blades. All of these include artifacts which are used in final tool production, and each tool belongs in one of these classes on the basis of the blank utilized to make that tool. In addition, burin spalls and chips and chunks might be considered artifact classes. These, however, were not used as blanks in tool manufacture and are not included in the consideration of the proportional occurrence of major artifact classes in each assemblage.

ARTIFACT ORIENTATION. Basic artifact description is based upon a standard orientation of each piece. For those artifacts struck from cores, the following orientation is used—the artifact is placed with the bulbar side down against a flat surface; the platform is placed facing the viewer. Therefore, the left lateral edge is on the viewer's left-hand side, and the right lateral edge is on the viewer's right-hand side. In order to simplify description, the following terms are used with this orientation in mind:

Proximal Extremity. The end of the artifact with the bulb of percussion and the platform.

Distal Extremity. The end opposite the proximal end.

Ventral Surface. The surface of the artifact upon which the bulb of percussion occurs and which was toward the center of the core prior to removal.

371

Dorsal Surface. The surface of the artifact opposite the ventral surface. It was part of the face of the core prior to the artifact removal from the core. It is characterized by either cortex or negative scars from previous artifact removals from the same core face.

Plane of an Artifact. The plane parallel to the lines of force which removed it from the core. That is, it is a plane which runs between the left and right lateral edges, approximately along the ventral surface.

Long Axis. The direction of force which removed an artifact from a core. It begins at the point of percussion on the platform and passes through the center of the bulb of percussion toward the distal end. It may not, however, be in line with the distal extremity.

Lateral Surface. The surface of an artifact having a lateral side which is markedly oblique or even perpendicular to its plane (e.g., the cortex back on a naturally backed knife).

BLADES. This term is used in two senses. *Sensu lato*: any artifact which has a maximum length equal to or exceeding twice its maximum width and having no other attribute which places it in another artifact class. *Sensu stricto*: any artifact, as defined above, which has a maximum length equal to or greater than 50 mm and a maximum width equal to or greater than 12 mm (Tixier, 1963, p. 38). As noted in a number of papers, there are blades (*sensu lato*) which have lengths less than 50 mm but widths exceeding 12 millimeters. This problem is discussed when appropriate.

BLADE ATTRIBUTES. These are qualitative observations which describe the basic configuration of the blade.

Distal Shape. Refers to the distal extremity and the immediately adjoining lateral edges.

Blunt. The distal extremity ends in a blunt shape: straight, convex, irregular, etc.

Pointed. The distal extremity tapers to a point. This may be along the axis of removal or may be off axis. Henry (this volume) refers to the off-axis pointed extremities as oblique.

Dorsal Shape. Refers to the relationship between the lateral edges of a blade.

Parallel. The lateral edges are parallel to each other, although they may converge or expand at the distal extremity.

Converging. The lateral edges converge toward the distal extremity. In this case the lateral edges adjacent to the platform represent the maximum width of the blade.

Expanding. The lateral edges expand toward the distal extremity. In this case the distal extremity represents the maximum width of the piece.

Lateral Profile. Refers to the presence or absence of curvature and its form, when a blade is placed dorsal face up on a flat surface.

Flat. The ventral surface rests on the flat surface, discounting the effects of the bulb of percussion.

Incurvate. The ventral surface touches the flat surface only at both extremities.

Twisted. An incurvate blade where there is a bending of the blade both along the axis of removal and perpendicular to that axis. The twist may be in either direction. Normally, it is most pronounced near the distal extremity.

BLADELETS. This term applies to a subset of blades, *sensu lato*, which have a maximum length of less than 50 mm and a maximum width of less than 12 mm (Tixier, 1963, p. 38). Again, there are those pieces with lengths considerably less than 50 mm and with widths greater than 12 millimeters. Since the definitions for blade (*sensu stricto*) and bladelet are essentially arbitrary, their utility is recognized as being somewhat limited. A backed tool is considered to be on a bladelet blank when its maximum width is less than 9 mm (Tixier, 1963, p. 39). Again, this is quite arbitrary, particularly for the Negev Epipaleolithic, as can be seen in the figure showing backed tool widths for site D5.

BLANKS. This term is used in two senses throughout these papers. In most cases, it is used to describe an artifact chosen for additional retouch modification during tool manufacture (e.g., *the blanks chosen for endscraper manufacture were normally large*). The second usage is more general—to describe a subset of a class of artifacts which includes all those pieces which could have been utilized in tool manufacture, but were not, as well as those which were utilized (e.g., *of the total available blade blanks, only a small percentage were actually retouched*).

BURIN ATTRIBUTES. A number of terms which have special meaning are used in the description of burins.

Bit. The point of intersection of the burin facets.

Bit Width. The maximum width of one or more burin facets at the point of their intersection.

Burin Angle. The angle formed by the intersection of the burin facets.

Burin Facet. The scar produced by the removal of a burin spall.

Burin Spall. The piece removed from a blank to form a burin facet. It is normally elongated, triangular to rectangular in cross section, and is struck so that its scar is perpendicular or highly oblique to the plane of the blank. An exception is the *plan* facet, but the spalls derived from these cannot be separated from normal, small debitage.

Multifaceted. Burins with more than three burin facets forming a single bit. This includes snaps, truncations, or old surfaces when these function as facets.

Plan. A burin facet which is parallel or almost parallel to the plane of the blank.

Simple Burin. A burin formed by three or less burin facets, including snaps, truncations, or old surfaces when these function as facets.

Symmetric and Asymmetric. The relationship between the bit and the axis of the blank. When the bit is formed by burin facets of equal angle off the axis of the blank, the burin is referred to as symmetric. When one facet or group of facets is more oblique than the opposed facet or group of facets, the burin is referred to as asymmetric.

CHIPS AND CHUNKS. These are debris from flaking. They are too small, too irregular, or too fragmentary to have been utilized in tool production. Chips include small fragments from all artifact classes, and those complete pieces which measure less than 15 mm in greatest dimension. Chunks are very small fragments of cores or raw material which could not be otherwise classified.

CORES. Cores are the remnants of blocks of raw material (flint cobbles, slabs, chunks, etc.) which have been intentionally flaked to produce any other class of artifact (flake, blade, primary element, etc.). A number of terms specifically refer to core description:

Back. The back of a core is opposite the flaked surface. This occurs in cores which have limited flaked surfaces. In the case of pyramidal and opposite side cores, there is no back.

Distal Extremity. The distal extremity of a core is the end of the core opposite the platform. In the case of opposed platform cores or multiple platform cores, there is no distal extremity.

Flaked Surface. The flaked surface of a core is that which is utilized for the removal of the desired debitage or blanks, after the formation of the platform. A core may have one or more flaked surfaces. However, those scars on the core resulting from initial core preparation are not considered part of the flaked surface.

Platform. A core platform is that surface which is struck in order to remove a piece of debitage.

Platform Angle. The angle of intersection between the platform and the flaked surface. This angle can never exceed 90 degrees. On many cores with extensively flaked surfaces, the platform angle tends to vary around the platform periphery. Measurements are taken, therefore, in the center of the flaked surface, which gives only an approximation of the platform angles which may be present on the core.

Proximal Extremity. The platform, in the case of single platform cores. Other types of cores do not have proximal extremities.

Sides. The surfaces of the core which connect the flaked surface with the back of the core. In the case of pyramidal cores there are no sides, as is also true for globular and discoidal cores.

Stepped Platform. Stepped platforms, occurring on a significant number of blade cores in the Upper Paleolithic, exhibit the partial scar from the removal of a core tablet which has hinge-fractured. This leaves a stepped appearance, with that portion of the platform adjacent to the flaked surface lower than the remaining portion of the original platform.

CORE TABLETS. Byproducts of core rejuvenation, occuring when the striking platform needs major modification. A core tablet is formed by striking off the platform of a core with a blow perpendicular to the axis of major flake or blade removal (parallel to the old platform), a centimeter or so below the intersection of the flaked surface and the platform. This removes the old platform and those portions of the scars on the flaked surface just below the platform. Normally, in the Negev assemblages, the blow is delivered on the flaked surface of the core, so that the tablet platform consists of the upper *scar fragments* from the flaked surface of the core. This gives the impression of a massive convex faceted platform.

CORE-TRIMMING ELEMENTS. All artifacts which exhibit evidence of previous core preparation, except for core tablets. In the Negev assemblages, most are varieties of crested flakes or blades (*lames à crête*) and include those types described in Brézillon (1971, pp. 96-97).

DEBITAGE. All artifacts other than cores, burin spalls, chips, and chunks which have not been utilized in retouched tool manufacture. This is a general category, comparable to retouched tools and debris.

HINGE-FRACTURE. The negative scar, present on a core, when the force of a blow has bent sharply outward instead of continuing the length of the core. The resulting scar has a hollow, rounded distal extremity which makes additional removals difficult. Cores with such hinge-fractures are often abandoned. Flakes which have hinge-fractured exhibit a ventral surface which is markedly convex at the point of hinge-fracture, curving over onto the dorsal surface.

MEASUREMENTS. All artifact measurements were taken in the metric system to the nearest millimeter. The most common measurements are of length, width, and thickness (see definition of measurements for burin bits under "Burin Attributes").

Length. The length of an artifact is defined as the maximum distance between the platform and the distal extremity. In most cases, this is along, or parallel to, the axis of the blow which removed the artifact from the core, although it is not necessarily along that line. In the case of cores, the length is measured along the maximum flaked surface, from the platform either to the distal extremity or, in the case of opposed platform cores, to the other platform.

Width. The maximum width, measured perpendicular to the maximum length.

Thickness. The maximum distance between the dorsal and ventral faces at a point near the center of the artifact along the maximum length. An exception to this occurs in Munday (this volume), where the maximum thickness measurement may lie anywhere along the length of the artifact, excluding the bulbar area.

MICROBLADES, TWISTED. These have only been found at site Ein Aqev (D31). In that report they have been given the status of an artifact class, since they were used as blanks in *lamelle Dufour* manufacture. However, the twisted microblade is a byproduct of carinated tool manufacture and, therefore, is not strictly a major class of artifact. These twisted microblades are normally less than 30 mm in maximum length and are very narrow. They have a converging dorsal shape, a markedly twisted lateral profile, and their platforms are normally of crushed or lipped type, although a few exhibit minute unfaceted surfaces.

PLATFORM TYPES. Those types recognized for all but the Mousterian reports are as follows:

Unfaceted. A single plane, a remnant of a larger single scar which was part of the platform of the core from which the blank was struck.

Dihedral Faceted. Two intersecting planes, remnants of larger scars which were part of the platform of the core from which the blank was struck. The planes may intersect at any angle, but on most blanks with dihedral platforms the angle is very obtuse.

Multifaceted. The intersection of more than two planes, remnants of larger scars on the platform of the core from which the blank was struck.

Lipped. This type is defined by more complex criteria, including attributes which are not strictly related to platform morphology. The platform itself may be unfaceted, faceted, or cortex, but for the material in the Negev, it is almost always unfaceted. The diagnostic features are a marked flange between the platform and the ventral surface of the blank, the absence of a bulb of percussion, and the absence of a bulbar scar—*esquille* of Bordes (1961, p. 7, fig. 1,1). All other platform types are associated with recognizable bulbs of percussion and normally exhibit bulbar scars.

Cortex. A portion of the unmodified raw material. Normally it will display cortex, but may exhibit a patinated surface older than that present on the rest of the blank.

Crushed. A series of crushed ridges from previous blows which did not detach the blank, or a series of ridges formed upon impact when the point of percussion was very close to the intersection of the core platform and the flaked surface. The proximal end of the blank is unbroken, however, as the bulb of percussion is always intact. This type of platform, having no recognizable shape, is usually found on blades and bladelets, although it does occur on both thin flakes and thin primary elements.

PRIMARY ELEMENTS. All artifacts intentionally struck from a core which have one-half or more of their dorsal surface covered by cortex. Since there are no size or shape criteria, other than that of exceeding 15 mm in greatest dimension, these may be of blade or flake proportions. They are normally the first artifacts struck from a cobble or other piece of raw material.

RETOUCH All purposeful modification of a blank, excluding snapping and the removal of burin spalls.
Placement of Retouch. The face or faces of the blank on which the retouch scars lay.

Obverse (Normal). The ventral surface of a blank is utilized as the platform from which normally minute flakes or blades are struck. The scars of these removals are present on the dorsal surface of the blank or, occasionally, on a perpendicular edge (as in the case of normal backing).

Inverse. The dorsal surface of a blank is utilized as the platform from which normally minute flakes or blades are struck. The scars of these removals are present on the ventral surface of the blank or, occasionally, on a perpendicular edge (as in the case of inverse backing).

Alternate. A blank which has inverse retouch along one edge and obverse retouch along another. Usually these are lateral edges but may be one lateral edge and the distal end.

Alternating. A blank with both inverse and obverse retouch appearing on the same edge or edges and placed so that at no point along them do they occur together (which would form bifacial retouch).

Bifacial. This is a combination of obverse and inverse retouch along the same edge or edges. The scars of the removals are present on both the ventral and dorsal surfaces along the same portions of the edge or edges.

Position of Retouch. The position of the retouch on the blank in relation to the traditional blank orientation—dorsal face up, with the platform facing the viewer.

Unilateral (or Lateral). Retouch occurs only along a single lateral edge.

Bilateral. Retouch occurs along both lateral edges.

Proximal. Retouch occurs at the platform end of the blank. This only occurs when the platform is missing.

Distal. Retouch occurs at the distal end of the blank, such that the retouch is markedly oblique or transverse to the axis of blank removal.

Transverse. This may be distal or proximal but includes only those blanks where the width of the blank exceeds its length.

Types of Retouch. Refers to the form which the retouch takes. The main criteria include the angle which the retouch forms in relation to the plane of the blank, and even occasionally the technique of flaking used. Since these definitions follow common usage, built up over many years, there is no necessary consistency in the criteria from one type to another, although all are mutually exclusive. While many more types appear in the literature, particularly for the Mousterian, the following types are those most often referred to in this volume:

Marginal Retouch. May be inverse or obverse. It refers to any retouch with angles of less than ca. 80° which is extremely fine and barely modifies the shape of the retouch edge. It has also been referred to as "nibbling retouch" (Garrod and Bate, 1937, p. 48).

Flat Invasive Retouch. Retouch which has a very low angle off the plane of the blank, less than about 55°, and where the retouch scars extend well onto the surface of the blank. It may be inverse or obverse.

Semisteep Retouch. May be inverse or obverse. The sole criterion is that the retouch forms a semisteep angle with the plane of the flake. While normally not measured, owing to the difficulty of measuring such small areas, semisteep retouch has angles which may range from about 80° to about 55 degrees.

Ouchtata Retouch. This term is taken from Tixier (1963, p. 40). It refers to very fine, semisteep to steep retouch, usually obverse, which occurs only along very thin edges. It is probably a form of backing, although it is not typical backing. It is similar to marginal retouch in that little modification of the edge takes place, but it is almost always strongest adjacent to the proximal end.

Backing. All retouch, except Ouchtata, which has an angle of greater than ca. 85° to the plane of the blank. Normally, the angle is 90 degrees. Within this category a number of subdivisions are recognized: (1) *abrupt or steep retouch*—simple backing which may originate from either the dorsal (inverse backing) or ventral surface (obverse backing) of a blank, but which in the vast majority of cases originates from the ventral surface (obverse backing); (2) *bipolar or "sur enclume"*—backing which exhibits evidence of steep retouch originating from both the ventral and dorsal surfaces along the majority of a backed edge (the term *sur enclume* makes the assumption that this type of retouch is achieved using an anvil technique, although this is open to question; the backed edge is always ca. 90° to the plane of the blank); (3) *alternate backing*—a portion of the backed edge is formed by obverse backing and the remainder by inverse backing; (4) *Helwan*—a very specialized form of backing which occurs only in some Epipaleolithic industries in the Levant (the "backing" is formed by bifacial retouch such that the backed edge forms a ridge, rather than a 90° surface to the plane of the blank; Helwan retouch may have a rather blunt ridge, or it may be very sharp if the bifacial retouch is flat and invasive); (5) *irregular*—a general qualitative term (when a backed edge does not conform to an even shape—straight, convex, concave, etc.—or when it is inconsistently applied, it is referred to as irregular); (6) *partial backing*—may be of any form and refers to the fact that only a portion of an edge has been backed, as opposed to a completely backed edge; and (7) *semisteep backing*—while this is a seeming contradiction in terms, a small percentage of various backed tool forms, including geometrics, have semisteep rather than abrupt retouch (in such cases, the pieces have been placed in the normal backed tool class).

SCRAPER TABLETS. Morphologically similar to core tablets but much smaller. They occur only at the Upper Paleolithic site of D18 where carinated scrapers are common. They appear to be carinated and thick scraper resharpening flakes.

TOOLS, RETOUCHED. All blanks of any artifact class which have been modified to any great extent by purposeful secondary retouch. The only exception to this is the battered piece (*pièce à mâchures*) which exhibits heavy use retouch. Artifacts with very limited retouch, exhibiting no more than two or three secondary flake scars, are not included in tools, since the possibility is great for this "retouch" to have been caused by natural agencies.

TYPOLOGY

This section provides definitions for two kinds of tool types—those which rarely occur in the literature of Levantine prehistory but have been defined elsewhere, and those which are used here for the first time in print or for which some modification in meaning has been made of a previously published type definition. The vast majority of types recognized in this volume, however, need no new definition, as well-established definitions may be found in a number of publications (Garrod and Bate, 1937; de Sonneville-Bordes and Perrot, 1954-56; Brézillon, 1971). In addition to the available published definitions and those which follow, each paper which presents a type list also provides detailed typological notes on specific types and numerous illustrations. Combined, these sources should provide sufficient information so that the morphology of each listed type is understood. Again, this section will not include specific Mousterian types, since Crew (this volume) has extensively referenced and discussed the definitions used.

Of the more common Levantine Upper Paleolithic tools, the complex of carinated tool forms poses the greatest problem in classification. A detailed discussion of this problem may be found in Pradel (1962) and will not be repeated here. Only a single carinated type, not mentioned by Pradel, will be included here and in the report on Ein Aqev (Marks, this volume).

The following definitions are organized by tool class, when the class warrants comment and specific type definitions. Otherwise, they are listed alphabetically under "Other Tools."

BACKED TOOL CLASS. These follow the principles of classification used by Tixier (1963). Most are already published in the literature of Levantine prehistory. Only the following are rarely used or have been modified in definition:

Arch-tipped Blade or Bladelet. This term is taken from the term *lame ou lamelle à tête arguée* used by Tixier (1963, pp. 87, 103). It is defined here in its original meaning as a blade or bladelet which has one extremity exhibiting a convex oblique shape, formed by more or less abrupt retouch, and which does not form a sharp angle with the lateral edge from where it originates.

La Mouillah Point. This term is taken from Tixier (1963, p. 106), where it is defined as a bladelet backed by abrupt retouch, which terminates with a distal or proximal *piquant-trièdre*.

Proto-geometrics. This is a general term taken from Bar-Yosef (1970). In the D5 report (Marks, this volume), the only place where the term is used, it applies only to double truncated backed bladelets which have lengths equal to, or greater than, twice their widths. Only two types occur at D5: those where one or both truncations are oblique to the backed edge (proto-trapezes) and those where both truncations are perpendicular to the backed edge (proto-rectangle). This definition is at variance with Bar-Yosef's proto-rectangle, as he includes the latter type under true rectangles in spite of their blade proportions (1970, p. 218).

Scalene Bladelet. This term has been borrowed, with some modification, from Tixier (1963, p. 113) where it is defined as a straight-backed bladelet with a more or less oblique truncation, forming a well-marked angle between it and the backing. The backing and truncation are formed by abrupt retouch or, more frequently, by Ouchtata retouch, and part of the platform is always left intact. The only modification used here is that in the Negev these pieces rarely, if ever, exhibit Ouchtata retouch, although some have semisteep retouch along the backed edge. This type corresponds to a subset of Bar-Yosef's proto-triangle (1970, p. 217).

Shouldered Blade or Bladelet. This term is defined by Tixier (1963, p. 110) under the term *lamelle à cran*; it is a bladelet with one edge partially backed by abrupt retouch which extends from one extremity and stops before the other, forming a notch (*cran*). In the Negev, almost all those found to date are fragmentary, lacking the backed tip.

BURIN CLASS. These follow traditional types with a few exceptions. The type burin *plan* is not recognized. Instead, a *plan* facet is viewed only as one attribute of other burin types. Also, the term polyhedric, as a type, has been rejected, although when a burin has more than three facets, it is referred to by its type with "multifaceted" as an added notation. This, of course, is not done when the type definition includes a multifaceted state (e.g., carinated burin). Only a single type warrants definition, as it is not well known in the Levant:

Corbiac Burin. This term was introduced by Bordes (1970, p. 105). The corbiac burins found in the Negev are more morphologically limited than those which Bordes defines. They are characterized by a very fine lateral retouch from which a transverse or highly oblique burin spall has been struck. The resulting burin facet has a triangular shape, with no measurable bit at the intersection of the fine retouch and the facet. These are not chamfered pieces, however, since the burin facet is always perpendicular to the plane of the blank.

MICROBURIN TECHNIQUE. Microburins are classified following Tixier (1963), as is the case for most new studies from the Levant. Only the two following types may need specific attention, as they tend to be rare in the Levant:

Microburin Krukowski. The definition is taken from Tixier (1963, p. 142), where it is defined as an extremity of a backed blade or bladelet detached by the microburin technique along the backed edge.

Piquant-trièdre. The definition is taken from Tixier's *lame ou lamelle à piquant-trièdre* (1963, p. 137), where it is defined as a small blade or bladelet which shows the negative scar of a microburin at one extremity. For these papers, the definition is somewhat expanded to include flakes with negative microburin scars.

SCRAPER CLASS. The organization of the scraper typology in most papers of this volume is slightly different than that usually found in publications. This difference is merely one of form, however. Since all tool types are also shown by blank type, such specific terms as *endscraper on a blade* have not been used in the lists, although they may be easily determined from the tables. Most types used here are quite traditional; only the following warrant definition:

Bilateral Endscraper. An endscraper on a blank with flake proportions which has uniform scraper retouch extending beyond the normal scraping edge of a simple endscraper to a point at least one-third the way along both lateral edges. However, the retouch never removes the platform. This type is a subset of the *grattoir sur éclat* (de Sonneville-Bordes and Perrot, 1954, p. 330).

Endscraper, Lateral. An endscraper on a blank other than a blade where the scraping edge has typical endscraper shape—markedly convex, ogival, nosed, etc.—but is formed along a lateral edge, rather than at the distal or proximal extremity.

Endscraper, Oblique. An endscraper on any form of blank where the scraping edge is convex but positioned obliquely to the long axis of the blank. In form, it is similar to a truncation or arch-tipped piece, but the retouch is typically that found on endscrapers.

Endscraper, Straight. An endscraper where the distal or proximal extremity has typical endscraper retouch—flat and invasive to semisteep—but with the scraping edge straight rather than conforming to normal endscraper shapes. The angle of retouch prohibits these pieces from being considered truncations.

Lateral Carinated Scraper. While this type is now recognized widely in Levantine prehistoric studies, it has not been defined in publication. For the Negev material, the following definition was used: a scraper conforming in all ways to carinated form but having a scraper edge which is either totally oblique to the long axis of the blank (as in an oblique truncation), or largely so, with only a small part of the scraping edge bending onto the other edge of the blank.

Thumbnail Scraper. A small, short endscraper in the form of a thumbnail (*de l'ongle du ponce*), as defined by de Sonneville-Bordes and Perrot (1954, p. 330). The inclusion by Bar-Yosef (1970, p. 203) of scrapers on short blade fragments is rejected, however. These latter are classified under simple endscrapers, since it is never possible to tell whether the blade was purposefully snapped prior to retouch or was broken accidentally during use.

Unilateral Endscraper. An endscraper on a blank with flake proportions which has uniform scraper retouch extending beyond the normal scraping edge of a simple endscraper to a point at least one-third the way along one lateral edge. This type is a subset of the *grattoir sur éclat* of de Sonneville-Bordes and Perrot (1954, p. 330).

OTHER TOOLS. The following definitions cover a wide range of types and, therefore, have been organized in alphabetical order without regard to tool class:

Battered Piece (pièce à mâchures). These are large blanks of any type, although usually flakes or blades, which exhibit heavy signs of use on one or both lateral edges. This takes the form of heavy irregular "retouch" which may be present on both the ventral and dorsal surfaces, appearing as rough bifacial "retouch," or on only one face, as occurs on many markedly incurvate blades at site Ein Aqev (Marks, this volume). While not purposefully retouched, the heavy signs of use make it clearly a type of tool. The term was introduced by Bordes (1967).

El Wad Point. This term was introduced by the Symposium on Levantine Typology held in London in 1969 and is to replace the term Font Yves point (reported in Brézillon, 1971, p. 418). The Symposium suggested the following definition: "a small blade or bladelet pointed by fine obverse retouch." While this definition has the virtue of simplicity, it has the problem of leaving much undefined. This contradiction merely reflects the paucity of detailed study of those pieces from the Levant originally called Font Yves points. Another definition (Bar-Yosef, 1970, p. 211) adds more detail: "blade or bladelet retouched on both sides of the tip, frequently with complete or partial retouch on one or both edges." All illustrated el Wad points, however, do not have bilateral retouch of the distal extremity (e.g., Garrod and Bate, 1937, p. 48). For the purposes of this volume, a tentative definition is suggested: a narrow blade or bladelet with a pointed distal extremity formed by fine semisteep to steep retouch. In addition, there may be variable amounts of retouch along one or both lateral edges, which may be obverse, inverse, alternate, or alternating. It is altogether possible, however, that within this broad definition quite discrete types exist which have temporal and/or spatial limits.

Lamelle Dufour. The definition of de Sonneville-Bordes and Perrot (1956b, p. 554) serves as a basis for this tool. They define it as a bladelet, frequently with incurvate profile, which has fine continuous, semisteep retouch along its margins, either on only one face, dorsal or ventral, or on both faces; it may also be on alternate faces. The *lamelles Dufour*, thus far found in the Negev at site Ein Aqev (Marks, this volume), exhibit very limited morphological parameters. All are on very small bladelets which have twisted lateral profiles, and all exhibit either inverse or alternate semisteep retouch which begins most often at the proximal extremity. It becomes weaker as it passes toward the distal extremity and normally does not reach the distal tip. A distinction is made between those with alternate and those with only inverse retouch in the type lists, but this is considered to be of the sub-type significance only. There are also identical small bladelets, referred to as twisted microblades, which have only obverse retouch. This retouch is never semisteep, however, so they have been called retouched microblades.

Massive Tools. The concept of the massive tool is taken from Garrod and Bate (1937), where massive scrapers are listed for both the Natufian and the Atlitian. In the context of this volume, massive tools are those which are considerably larger than the vast majority of the examples of their type within a given assemblage. Normally, only scrapers, notches, and denticulates fall into the massive tool category.

Mèche de Foret. This follows the definition of Tixier (1963, p. 66), which calls for a piece with a lance-like shape, a trapezoidal or rectangular cross section, with both parallel lateral edges entirely or partially backed by abrupt retouch, and with one or both extremities more or less pointed but never sharply pointed.

Raclette. This is defined by Bar Yosef (1970, p. 222) as a flake with either partial or complete abrupt retouch, and by de Sonneville-Bordes and Perrot (1956, p. 552) as a flake or, more rarely, a blade fragment of variable shape—generally small and thin with subparallel faces—which has very thin and abrupt continuous retouch, usually on all edges. In the papers of this volume, the de Sonneville-Bordes and Perrot definition is followed generally, although some *raclettes* do not have retouch on all edges (see *end-raclette*).

Raclette, End. This type, under the name *raclette en bout*, is defined by de Heinzelin (1962, p. 27) as very regular and small retouch located at the end of an elongated flake. Here, it is used with slight modification. Following de Sonneville-Bordes and Perrot (1956, p. 552), the retouch is always abrupt and the blank always thin.

Retouched Microblade. (See *lamelle Dufour*)

Scaled Piece. The definition of Tixier (1963, pp. 146-149) is accepted. He defines a *pièce esquillée* as a generally rectangular or broken piece, sometimes of small size, with two extremities (rarely only one), usually exhibiting bifacial scaling caused by violent percussion. Those found in the Negev are of the rare type which shows bifacial scaling only on a single extremity.

BIBLIOGRAPHY

BAR-YOSEF, O., 1970. "The Epi-Paleolithic Cultures of Palestine." Ph.D. dissertation, The Hebrew University.

BORDES, F., 1961. *Typologie de paléolithique ancien et moyen.* Bordeaux: Mémoire 1, Publications de l'Institut de Préhistoire de l'Université de Bordeaux.

_____, 1967. "Considerations sur la typologie et les techniques dans le paléolithique." *Quartar* 18:25-55.

_____, 1970. "Observations typologiques et techniques sur le Périgordien supérieur de Corbiac (Dordogne)." *Bulletin de la Société Préhistorique Française* 67:105-113. CRSM.

BREZILLON, M., 1971. *La dénomination des objets de pierre taillée.* Paris: CNRS.

GARROD, D. A. E., and BATE, D. M. A., 1937. *The Stone Age of Mount Carmel* 1. Oxford: Clarendon Press.

de HEINZELIN, J., 1962. *Manuel de typologie des industries lithiques.* Bruxelles: Institut Royal des Sciences Naturelles de Belgique.

PRADEL, L., 1962. "Du burin busqué au burin nucléiforme: Formes de passage." *Bulletin de la Société Préhistorique Française* 59(9-10):684-92.

de SONNEVILLE-BORDES, D., and PERROT, J., 1954. "Lexique typologie du paléolithique supérieur: Outillage lithique—I, Grattoirs—II, Outils solutréens." *Bulletin de la Société Préhistorique Française* 51(7):327-35.

_____, and PERROT, J., 1955. "Lexique typologie du paléolithique supérieur: Outillage composite—III, Perçoirs." *Bulletin de la Société Préhistorique Française* 52(1-2):76-79.

_____, and PERROT, J., 1956*a*. "Lexique typologie du paléolithique supérieur: Outillage lithique—IV, Burins." *Bulletin de la Société Préhistorique Française* 53(7-8):408-12.

_____, and PERROT, J., 1956*b*. "Lexique typologie du paléolithique supérieur: Outillage lithique—V, Outillage à bord abattu—VI, Pièces tronquées—VII, Lames retouchées—VIII, Pièces variés—IX, Outillage Lamellaire, Pointe Azilienne." *Bulletin de la Société Préhistorique Française* 53(9):547-59.

TIXIER, J., 1963. *Typologie de l'epipaléolithique du Maghreb.* Mémoires du Centre de Recherches Anthropologiques, Préhistoriques et Ethnographiques. Paris: Arts et Métiers Graphiques.